Mark Helyar

Rising from the Dust
India's Hidden Voices

empty canvas
www.emptycanvas.co.uk

First published in the United Kingdom in 2008 by empty canvas
www.emptycanvas.co.uk

Content copyright © Mark Helyar 2008

Illustrations, images and maps copyright © Mark Helyar 2008

The moral right of the author has been asserted

All rights reserved
No part of this publication may be reproduced, stored in a retrieval system, or transmitted, in any form or by any means, electronic, mechanical, photocopying, recording or otherwise without the prior permission of the copyright holders

A CIP catalogue record of this book is available from the British Library.

ISBN 978-0-9559430-0-3

This book is sold subject to the condition that it shall not, by way of trade or otherwise, be lent, re-sold, hired out or otherwise circulated without the publisher's prior consent in any form of binding or cover other than that in which it is published and without a similar condition including this condition being imposed on the subsequent purchaser

Typeset in Palatino Linotype 10/12

Cover design by Minh Hue-Vashon

Printed and bound by Antony Rowe Ltd

The author would like to thank the following for permission to use copyright material: The Panos Institute, London, for use of material from the *Mountain Voices* project; Universal Music Publishing Group on behalf of Neil Hannon for use of *The Divine Comedy* song lyrics. If any copyright holders have been inadvertently overlooked, the author will be pleased to make the necessary arrangement at the first opportunity.

To Bhawani Bhai,
now passed into his next avtaar,
and all those big-hearted people whose
voices are rarely heard

When a great people rises from the dust… what power
is the resurrecting force of its resurgence?

Sri Aurobindo

Contents

	Preface	vii
	Acknowledgments	viii

The South

1	Ignorance is Bliss	11
2	Little Acts of Kindness	32
3	Festive Road	68
4	Freedom Road	98
5	Here Comes the Flood	120
6	Bad Ambassador	163
7	Logic Vs Emotion	184

The North

8	In Pursuit of Happiness	229
9	The Booklovers	238
10	Don't Look Down	256
11	Note to Self	275
12	Going Downhill Fast	289
13	The Wreck of the Beautiful	308
14	Charmed Life	332
15	The Certainty of Chance	347
16	Love What You Do	366
17	If...	377
18	There is a Light That Never Goes Out	386
19	Tonight We Fly	398
20	Regeneration	407

	Key Players	425
	Notes	427
	Glossary	439
	Further Reading	444

Preface

I never intended to write a book, just as I never had any great desire to travel to India. But I went and, somewhere in those six months, the book found me. This is the story of how it happened.

Some episodes may seem incredible, but everything I recount is based on real events. Though I've taken a degree of artistic licence with the stories, I've not consciously misrepresented any information. A few people's names have been changed to protect their identity. Some events and characters are composites of several incidents or individuals.

It is profoundly difficult to write about India without falling into cliché, stereotype and generalisation. At times, I'm guilty of all three. My intention is to offer an honest portrayal of my experiences and to place them in my understanding of their context. In so doing, I present difficult, unpalatable issues for debate.

The book is amply scattered with anecdotes and observations informed by personal experience, conversation and copious research. Every opinion could be counter-argued by a dozen others. That's India: a land where nothing and everything can be true, at the same time.

All the facts I've quoted have been verified as far as possible, including those that conflict with one another. These, along with all other sources of material, are attributed in the notes at the end of the book. Any omissions or errors are unintentional and will be corrected in future editions. Just as many of my observations could be preceded by "it appears that", many of the facts should be qualified by "about".

I've used italics on each occasion that words in Hindi, Sanskrit, Telugu or Garhwali first appear. Though I've aimed to be consistent in the transliteration, I encountered many variations in spelling. My general rule of thumb has been to lean towards simplicity rather than strict authenticity.

Acknowledgements

The generosity of the many people who have supported me over the last three years has been overwhelming.

Thanks for all the love and support from my family, especially for putting up with my evasive answers to the question, 'So, when *is* the book going to be finished?'; to my good friends Mark and Julie Thomas for introducing me to Lakshme Roja; and to Hazel Valentine, for daring me to dream.

I wish to express my deep gratitude to Barbara Large, my editor, for her unstinting encouragement, guidance and wisdom in supporting me throughout the entire process.

Then there are all my friends in India who have contributed to these stories. A tremendous thank you to Jennie Prabhakar, Esther Kovvada and her family, Subhakar Nekuri, Raju Meripo and all the girls and staff at Hebron Hostel; to Manihara and Bhakti Norton for welcoming me into the SKCV clan as a member of the family and to everyone else at SKCV, in particular, Sudhama, Krishna Prasad, Vijay and Dr and Mrs Shanker.

Thank you to all my friends at KHW: Jaywant Pratap Singh, Robert Simon, Dee-zane Pamei, Anubha Williams, Sujan Singh, Ramesh Prasad, Shanti and Sandeep Singh; to Dolly Francis, Ajay Issachar, Saira, Sandhya and all the teachers and pupils at Dehradun Public School; to Shailender David and all the staff at SASA Academy; and to Devraj and Saroj Singh, Sumit Solomon, Budi Singh Dogra, John Martin Sahajananda and the late Bhawani Bhai.

Thank you to Pete and Dot Wildman for giving me access to the library at Woodstock International School, Mussoorie; to Darab Nagarwalla for sharing his wonderful knowledge and archive material and to Agnes Huttenlocher for her Samvedna research in the Garhwal foothills.

Thank you to Minh Hue-Vashon for turning my photographic images into a fantastic cover design; to Geoff Fisher for his guidance through the final production stages; and to Katie Machell for her meticulous proof-reading.

I am indebted to everyone I cajoled into reading the manuscript at various stages of its development, especially Jamie Barry, Nater Singh and Krishan Khanna. Their constructive feedback and insight is much appreciated. Thank you also to everyone else who has supported me along the way, including Ruth and Peter Bentall, John Ponnusamy and Tricia Norton.

To all those friends, too numerous to mention, who persuaded me to embark on this project in the first place with the simple words, 'You write great emails; you should write a book' – thanks! I've spent the last three years discovering that the transition from one to the other is easier said than done. Despite a number of distractions and the occasional crisis of self-confidence, I've never considered giving up. The encouragement of those same friends has kept me going.

Finally, a huge thank you to Lakshme Roja. Were it not for her, I might never have travelled to India. This book would have found another voice.

India's States and Union Territories

1
Ignorance is Bliss

*Every moment stretches;
they call it Indian Time*

'Keep your head down, don't stop and follow me,' instructed Mark as he strode out ahead.

'Easy for you to say,' I muttered, watching with envy as his wheelie suitcase glided effortlessly along the grey tiled floor. It sounded like a good plan, but within a few metres I was struggling to keep up. Burdened by a hefty rucksack that grew weightier by the second, I was bent double, my nose almost scraping along the ground. My first taste of Indian soil was a shuffling mass of trouser legs, *sari* hems, *pyjama* bottoms, ankle chains, painted toenails, sandals, slippers and *chappals*.

It's not as if I'd pitched up on a whim. I'd planned fastidiously for months: devouring my local library's healthy stock of travel literature; avidly reading the *Lonely Planet, Footprint* and *Rough Guides* for information; gathering equipment, medication and toiletries from Millets, Blacks, Boots and Superdrug and scouring innumerable websites late into the night for travel tips, tricks and advice.

Anticipating an exit from Delhi Airport into a mass of clamouring arms desperate for a piece of me, I'd harboured fears of hungry hands waiting to wrench my rucksack from my back. Visions of thieving fingers trying to snatch my Velcro-sealed wallet from my pocket had haunted weeks of planning. But I was prepared. My rucksack featured a whistle cannily incorporated into one of its toggles and a weighty length of chain attached my wallet to the belt on my khaki combat trousers. Every compartment secreted emergency contact numbers and back-up copies of important documents.

My travelling companion, Mark Thomas, was Operational Director of CHILD's Trust, a UK-based charity that supported several children's development programmes throughout India. Although he and his wife, Julie, ran the trust voluntarily, he flew to India at least twice a year to visit the projects. When he asked if I wanted to join him on his next trip, I jumped at the opportunity.

I had a good reason. Her name, Lakshme Roja.

Lakshme lived at Hebron Hostel, a girls' home situated just outside Nidadavole, a small town in Andhra Pradesh, South India. I had sponsored her, through CHILD's Trust, for the past five years. Having corresponded with her every birthday and Christmas, I always looked forward to reading about the hostel, her friends, and her favourite studies at school.

Although we'd never met, Lakshme had become an integral part of my life. How could I refuse the chance to meet her? Yet I felt apprehensive.

'Are you OK?' Realising that I wasn't by his side, Mark glanced around.

'I know you said don't stop, but can we pause for *just* a moment?' I gasped. 'I need to re-group.' Turning awkwardly to look for a seat, my rucksack and I swung around as one unwieldy bulk, almost propelling a mother and her two young daughters into a cleaning trolley.

'Sorry!' I exclaimed, putting my palms together, *Namaste*-style, but somehow managing to tangle my fingers in the strap of my rucksack. 'Er, I'm sorry!'

Stepping backwards, I collided with a spectacled man in an open-necked cotton shirt. His withering glint of contempt froze my baggage and I to the spot. He marched off, briefcase in hand, trailing a scent of sweat and sandalwood in his wake.

'You are looking vee-rrrry heavy traveller!' observed the woman. 'India first time?'

I nodded sheepishly. The youngest child, bedecked in beads and frills, giggled. Her gum-chewing sister eyed me coolly.

'You will enjoy!' Tugging sharply on her daughters' arms, she scurried off.

Mark smiled. 'What have you got in there?' he asked as, bending my knees, I gingerly lowered my rucksack onto a seat.

'Well, there's the medical kit for starters,' I replied. 'Sterile needles, syringes, bandages, plasters, dressings, lotions, potions, pills...'

'...Enough to found a small hospital!' he teased.

'That's not all. Thanks to Dentanurse,' I added proudly, 'I have all the necessary tools to perform my own emergency fillings.'

'I'm impressed.'

'Then there's the pocket-size personal purifier that can clean enough water to keep a whole village hydrated for at least a year, rehydration sachets to combat potential dehydration, peanuts to replenish lost salt and muesli bars to replace lost sugar. I've got three bottles of antiseptic handwash strategically placed in each compartment and four packets of vacuum-packed toilet paper crammed into the remaining crevices.'

'Anyone would think you were visiting a third-world country!'

'What's more, I know exactly where it all is,' I said brandishing a meticulously itemised list. 'I've got six copies of this.'

Though I was armed with an assortment of tablets to combat every conceivable form of diarrhoea, ranging from mild to acute to explosive, I needn't have worried. Belted, braced and prepared for all eventualities, no one could have arrived in India more anally retentive than me.

'What about anti-malarial medication?'

'Ah.' I hesitated.

Mark looked worried.

'I don't have any.'

He looked even more worried.

'My GP's nurse said that the most common drug would make me nauseous every morning,' I explained. 'So I asked for an alternative. She suggested one that I could take weekly.'

'Mefloquine?'

'Something like that. Anyway, she said it had hallucinogenic side-effects. I didn't fancy that either.'

'So?'

'So I decided to get a second opinion. I consulted a private doctor.'

'And what did he say?'

'Not to bother with anything.'

'What!'

'Apart from common sense. "Use the local mosquito cream and cover up at dusk," he advised. Then he handed me a sheet of paper and a small box. "This describes the malarial symptoms. Take these four tablets if you show any sign of them. Then find a hospital. You'll be fine."'

'Hmm.' Mark looked dubious.

His concern was well-founded. We were only going to spend the first two days together. He then had business to conduct for CHILD's Trust in Delhi before returning to the UK. I was sailing closer to the wind. My flight was booked for six months later: 29 May 2005, the day my visa expired. I believe in value for money.

'Taxi! Taxi!'

'Auto rickshaw, yes?'

'Taxi, yes?'

'Good-good price!'

'Sirs...?'

Ignoring the touts, we aimed straight for the pre-paid taxi booth. Then, swiftly negotiating the throng of demanding eyes and outstretched hands outside the airport doors, we located our waiting taxi and jumped in. It may have been a different story had I been on my own but, having flown into Delhi on several occasions, Mark knew the score exactly.

To Do
- *Buy water*
- *Call Hebron to confirm arrival time*
- *Set watch alarm*

| *Hello* | *Namaste* | NA-MA-STAY |
| *Thankyou* | *Dhanyavad* | DAN-YA-WODD |

Two days later, I *was* on my own, or about to be. Having experienced an obligatorily hectic tour of Old and New Delhi's proud monuments to ancient religion and modern retail, Mark and I would soon be parting company. He was staying in the city for a few more days; I was travelling south to Andhra Pradesh. As I'm a lousy tourist, two days of sight-seeing was more than enough.

It felt like two months. Every moment stretched.

'They call it Indian time,' said Mark, as our white Ambassador Taxi rattled and honked towards the station, its shrill beep indistinguishable from all the other shrill beeps that exhausted the choking city air.

'Tell me about it!' I hadn't taken long to grasp that a lunchtime appointment might be honoured, if I was lucky, by late afternoon. This relaxed attitude sat quite comfortably alongside an over-zealous Indian pre-occupation with bureaucracy and paperwork; so laid-back in one way, so officious in another.

When we checked into Delhi YMCA on our first night, for example, Mark and I were required to produce countless forms, passport, visa and other documentation for verification. Had we dared to leave without written evidence of our stay, scribed, stamped and processed in triplicate, we'd have been in serious trouble.

'Docket, please!' the gruff doorman had requested as he held open the door with his left hand while thrusting forward his right palm demandingly.

'That was a canny way to get a tip,' I observed, once we had settled into the back of the taxi.

'You're right,' Mark replied. 'But how else will he make a living? Doormen often earn as little as 400 rupees a month. That's about a fiver. We're not the ones being exploited.'

I felt less ripped off.

As we paused at a set of traffic lights, a lanky youth tapped on my window. Beaming toothlessly, he held out a basket of red-skinned peanuts. I smiled back and shook my head. The lights turned green and he darted to the pavement, nimbly dodging the lurching mass of vehicles: cars, taxis, trucks, rickshaws, bicycles, buses and carts.

It struck me that an Indian road resembled a bowl of pasta. In the UK we drive like raw spaghetti: hard and straight. Arguably too fast, but generally in a linear direction. These Delhi streets were more like a tangled mass of cooked tagliatelli. Vehicles wove in and out, passing on both sides of the road, zigzagging backwards and forwards in the most complicated series of manoeuvres.

Only two rules of the road seemed to apply. One: when overtaking, honk your horn. Two: the vehicle in front has right of way. The only exception was the cow, goddess of the road. Drivers would rather hit each other than collide with the sacred beast wandering willy-nilly through the traffic, completely oblivious to the erratic clamour surrounding her.

'Are you looking forward to seeing Lakshme?' Mark asked as we narrowly avoided four people wobbling on a moped.

'Of course! And slightly apprehensive, if I'm honest.'

'Why?'

I thought for a moment. 'Lots of things. For a start, I'm not sure what to say to her... can I give her a hug... what's the protocol? And I don't speak the language!'

Mark smiled. 'Don't worry! Just behave respectfully and take your time,' he advised. 'Many of the staff speak *some* English. They'll help you.'

'That's good.'

'But be mindful of where you are.'

'What do you mean?'

'It's very rare for sponsors to visit their children,' said Mark. 'In fact, many charities discourage it.'

'Why?'

'It can set up unrealistic expectations for the child and their friends. It's important to treat them equally and not show favouritism. You're very privileged, you know.'

'Hmm.' The responsibility felt quite daunting. *How many sponsors would like to be in my shoes*, I wondered?

Our taxi suddenly swerved across two lanes of traffic. Tooting casually, the driver overtook a truck on the inside. I gripped the seat.

Mark laughed. 'Still sure you want to go by train?' he asked. 'You could have flown. It would have been much quicker.'

'I want to see India at ground level, not from 30,000 feet above it. There's no hurry. I've got six months!'

At which point I realised that, having crossed the central reservation, we were cruising up the other side of the road headlong towards an elephant.

'True! But, you're not going on the regular tourist trail, so you must look after yourself.'

'Exactly! No guided tours for me, thanks.' The taxi, shimmying back onto the correct side of the road, squeezed neatly in between an auto rickshaw and a bicycle. The elephant continued to plod obliviously away from us. I looked at Mark. 'I'll take care, don't worry.'

'Do you have any plans after you've visited Lakshme? I'm sure Jennie would love you to stay until at least Christmas.' Jennie was the Superintendent of Hebron Hostel.

'I'm hoping to spend a few weeks with the street kids project in Vijayawada. You remember me telling you about SKCV, the place run by Manihara, a friend of my family's?'

Mark nodded. 'And then?'

'Dump half the contents of my rucksack.'

'Seriously?'

'Seriously.'

'And?'

I shrugged. 'Who knows?'

Seeing Mark's expression, I knew I was on dodgy territory.

'I'm not going to do anything stupid,' I assured him.

'You've got your *Rough Guide to India*?'

'It's in the rucksack, next to the emergency malaria medication.'

'And your mobile?'

'In my pocket.' Mark had helped me to buy a SIM card and connect with Airtel, one of India's many phone networks, the previous day. This would prove invaluable for keeping in touch with my family and friends throughout my trip.

'Call if you need anything.'

'I will. Thanks.'

'And make sure…'

'Mark,' I interrupted, 'I may have been a bit overwhelmed when we arrived but I'm beginning to get the hang of things now. Don't worry!'

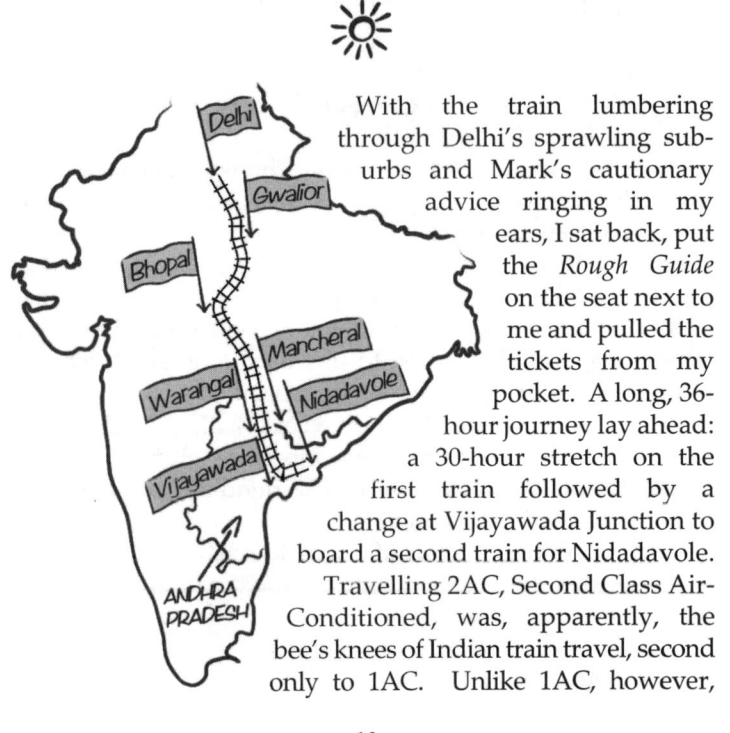

With the train lumbering through Delhi's sprawling suburbs and Mark's cautionary advice ringing in my ears, I sat back, put the *Rough Guide* on the seat next to me and pulled the tickets from my pocket. A long, 36-hour journey lay ahead: a 30-hour stretch on the first train followed by a change at Vijayawada Junction to board a second train for Nidadavole. Travelling 2AC, Second Class Air-Conditioned, was, apparently, the bee's knees of Indian train travel, second only to 1AC. Unlike 1AC, however, which contained four berths per sealed carriage and looked like a refrigeration unit from the exterior, 2AC had several cubicles. These comprised a pair of shiny blue bench seats above which two bunks were suspended. Four people could be accommodated per compartment, two upper and two lower:

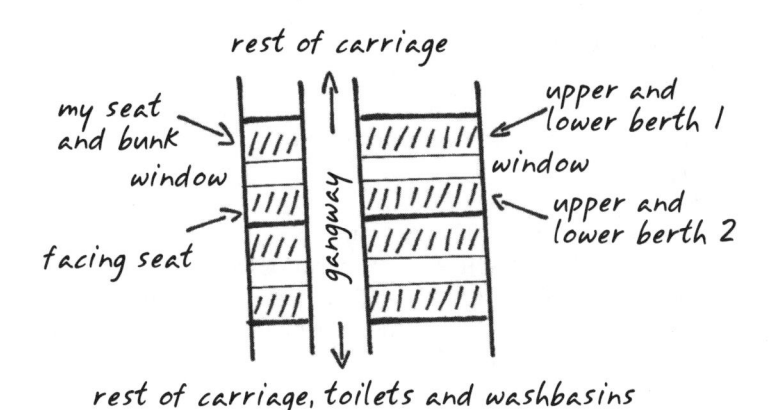

[Diagram: A hand-drawn plan of the 2AC compartment layout showing:
- *rest of carriage (top)*
- *my seat and bunk / window (upper left)*
- *facing seat (lower left)*
- *gangway (centre)*
- *upper and lower berth 1 / window (upper right)*
- *upper and lower berth 2 (middle right)*
- *rest of carriage, toilets and washbasins (bottom)]*

A curtain segregated each compartment from a corridor which ran through the carriage. Two additional berths were located on the other side of this passageway, the lower one of which was mine. It converted into a firm, but comfortable, bunk by folding down the backs of the two facing seats. The upper berth, accessed by climbing two metal rungs at the end, was unoccupied.

'Sir?'

A moustached young man in a light khaki uniform handed me a brown paper packet containing two crisp, white sheets, a pillow case and a face cloth. Its printed label read: "THIS LINEN HAS BEEN MACHINE-WASHED AND PACKED BY LEADING DRY CLEANERS AND LAUNDERERS OF DELHI."

Dropping a thick, grey blanket onto the seat beside me, he continued down the carriage. A tiny brown mouse peeked out from under the seat opposite and scampered along the floor after him.

No sooner had it disappeared than another moustached young man in a khaki uniform appeared, notebook in hand.
'You are making dinner order, sir?'
I wasn't expecting this. 'Er, what do you have?'
'Veg-*pilau*-and-*khichari*, sir.'
I hesitated, confused. 'OK. I'll have that, thank you.'
'Which, sir?'
'What you just said.'
'Veg pilau *or* khichari.'
'Ah, I see. What's ki-char-ree?'
'Rice and *dal*, sir,' he replied patiently.
'Vegetarian?'
'Yes, sir.'
'That sounds good. Thank you.'
Two hours later a glutinous mound of fragrant rice, lentil and vegetables was served, with a fork and a smile, in a disposable tin tray. I spent the rest of the evening picking fragments of cumin and cloves from between my teeth.

During my months of preparation, I knew that I'd miss one of my possessions more than any other: my piano. From the age of four through to leaving university and music college, I was one of those annoying kids who loved to practise. But, lacking the temperament and technical skill, I knew that I'd never reach the standard and dedication required of a classical concert pianist. Besides, I could never memorise the dots. That said, I exploited every other professional outlet, cabaret, accompanying, gigging, teaching and composing, to pursue my career. As far I was concerned, being a pianist perfectly complemented my work as a theatre director, the other professional string to my bow.

Though Tony Hawks may have done it with a refrigerator, travelling the length and breadth of the country with a piano on my back wasn't the kind of challenge that I sought. A guitar would have been the obvious choice but, despite many attempts, I'd never been able to progress beyond the chords of A and D. My fingers couldn't, or wouldn't, stretch over the frets.

I searched the Internet. Criteria: a small, light instrument on which I could pick out a tune with ease. Thanks to Google, three days later a reasonably-priced, petit mandolin, handmade from Romanian maple arrived on my doorstep. All I had to do was learn how to play the thing. Now, though, was not the time.

I propped the instrument against the wall at the end of my bunk, fearing it may get squashed by other passengers' luggage if I stowed it under the seat with my rucksack.

Drawing the faded blue-flocked curtain across my little side compartment, I felt a tremendous sense of adventure. I recalled my first camping expedition when, as a small boy, I swapped my bedroom for the back garden one night. Separated from the creepy crawlies by only a thin layer of canvas I had felt, nevertheless, cosy and safe. Now lying in my own little tent on wheels while this strange, new land rolled past in darkness, I experienced that same irrational sense of security. I couldn't look out, ergo, no one could see in. I was out of harm's way, doubly protected by a cosy blanket and freshly laundered sheets.

I put my headphones in my ears and plugged the other end of the cable into my mobile phone. Before leaving the UK, I had loaded a number of CDs onto its MP3 playlist, including the complete works of The Divine Comedy, one of my favourite bands. When asked once who his main influences were, lead singer Neil Hannon cited U2, Kurt Weill and Bach. Sharing his musical taste, I decided the band would provide the perfect soundtrack to my travels.

Over the next few hours I enjoyed a fitful sleep, disturbed first by a young Delhi couple in the next compartment tucking into a pungent meal extracted from various pre-prepared tiffin tins. Then again by a family of seven embarking at Gwalior just before midnight. Accompanied by an excessive amount of whining from their youngest child, they took forever to squeeze themselves and their luggage into their compartment before noisily swishing across the curtain. On each occasion, however, I was soon lulled back to sleep by the clatter and sway of the train and the mellifluous tones of Neil Hannon:

> *There's not enough lines on the stave*
> *to capture the music I crave*

As dawn broke, an intoxicating brew of coffee, toothpaste, fried nut cutlets and mothballs tantalised my nostrils. A steady stream of people had started to shuffle up and down the carriage, face flannels and tooth brushes in hand, to the small washbasins situated at either end. I kept my blue curtain drawn across, dozing, contemplating a further day and half another night on the same train. There was no rush.

I was fully awake, washed and dressed, however, by the time we pulled into Bhopal, site of the world's worst industrial disaster, just after six o'clock. I converted the bunk back into a seat, sat down and dug out my *Rough Guide*.

Reading about the event that had occurred close by, I was struck by the horrific scale of the tragedy. Late in the evening of 2nd December 1984 a toxic chemical explosion annihilated 1,600 people, leaving over 100,000 survivors to suffer with chronic health problems for the rest of their lives. A further 20,000 were to die in the ensuing weeks and months. Accompanied by a flask of sweet coffee courteously delivered to my seat, this was sobering information to digest so early in the morning.

The *Rough Guide* remained by my side throughout the day, periodically gleaned for information about my odyssey through India's heartland. It added little more to my knowledge, however, than the experience of viewing everything first-hand through the yellow-tinted carriage windows which, due to the air conditioning, were sealed shut and mottled with streaks of condensation between the glass panes. The passing landscape appeared shrouded in a sepia mist, comparable to watching a vintage movie reel of classic rail journeys. Nevertheless, Madhya Pradesh: "a vast land-locked expanse of scrub-covered hills." Yes, definitely. The next state, Maharashtra: "vast and rugged." It was difficult to disagree. *Everything* was vast.

To relieve the monotony I imagined how various places, based solely on their names, might be described in a travel brochure. Mancheral, for example: "the fusion of a northern English city and a southern Spanish beach resort. Enjoy a heady evening of flamenco and paella washed down with a refreshing pint of Worthingtons!" Warangal conjured up images of "a once-thriving mining town in the Australian outback, now inhabited by a lone pack of marauding dingoes. Visit if you dare!" Its name actually means "one stone" but it, too, had claim to better days as the booming Hindu capital of the Kakatiyan Empire in the twelfth and thirteenth centuries.

By the time we reached Warangal, the scrubby trees had yielded to elegant coconut palms that bountifully graced the horizon. The landscape, though predominantly flat, was distinguished by the occasional rocky outcrop bursting through the earth like the head and rump of a semi-submerged dinosaur; a huge dormant mound lurking with ground-stomping potential after millions of years of slumber. The smouldering glow of the setting sun enhanced the prehistoric ambience, silhouetting the palms against a blazing haze.

'Beautiful, sir?' I looked around. The question came from a middle-aged Indian who had just slid onto the seat opposite.

'Definitely a moment to savour.'

He peered at me intently. 'Meaning?'

Meaning? I thought. 'Ah... meaning. Beautiful. Yes?'

He nodded vacantly and continued to stare into my face. Two hoary eyebrows, arching above a pair of steel spectacles, exaggerated the magnitude of his probing eyes. Leaning in closer, his tilting face offered an arresting view up his tufted nasal cavities.

I swallowed. 'Er...'

'You are being married?'

'No.'

Pause.

'Why?'

'Because I, er, I...'

But he was not interested in my answer. His attention had shifted to the cell phone extracted from the top pocket of his drab grey shirt. He fiddled with a few buttons and then, pointing it at my face, twisted the angle one way, then another. Unsatisfied, he stretched across my body and, drawing the blue curtain, enclosed us both intimately in the corner.

I gulped.

Flash. A semi-approving nod. Another flash. Bingo.

I allowed all this to happen? Well, yes. What else to do? Maybe this was customary practice on Indian trains. I was a virgin passenger. What did I know?

'Your good name, please?'

'Mark.'

He tapped the information into the phone's keypad. 'Native place?'

'Er, England.'

Tap, tap.

'Your number.'

'Don't know.' True; I hadn't memorised it yet.

I decided to play him at his own game. 'What's your name?' I asked.

'Viraj.'

'Your job?'

'Seed seller.'

'From where?'

'What?' he barked.

'Live. Where. You?'

'Vijayawada. I. Home. Going.'

A momentary lull.

He yawned. 'You liking whisky?'

'Yes.'

'You want?'

'No, no, no...' Well, maybe, but I was unsure where this dialogue was leading. I had heard stories of guys offering spiked food and drink to tourists, then making off with their luggage once they were safely comatose. I'm sure this inoffensive grey man intended no harm, but I declined nevertheless. Besides, I had my own hip flask, a gift from my parents, stashed in my rucksack.

'My wife is not allowing it,' he whispered as if she were within earshot. He then sloped off to the other end of the carriage. I never saw him again.

This was the first of many non sequitur conversations that I was to experience throughout my travels. Terminating as abruptly as they began, their random themes, plucked from the ether, never failed to entertain.

> **To: Parents**
> 14-Dec-04 19:08
>
> Hi, hope you're both ok. I'm fine, on train in middle of india... somewhere - got signal though!! 10 hours to hebron. love to you both. Mx

When the train eventually pulled out of Warangal station, I was introduced to new neighbours. The two young men, each carrying a small satchel, were travelling light. They both nodded cheerily as they sat down in the opposite compartment.

'Hi,' said the slightly younger of the two. Dressed in jeans and a denim jacket, he had a very easy-going manner. 'Your name?'

Exchanging pleasantries I discovered that Mukesh and his jovial travelling companion, Dinkar - 'but my friends are calling me Bunty' - were partners in a construction company. They, too, were on the way to Vijayawada to negotiate a potential business deal.

'The market is looking very strong,' explained Dinkar. 'It is making good work for us.'

The fact that they were travelling Second Class AC was a clear indication of their success.

'Vijayawada was major trade and hub of industry since nineteenth century,' Mukesh informed me. 'It is known as gateway between north and south India.'

'Are you both from Andhra Pradesh?'

'Of course,' replied Mukesh proudly. 'It is a very good state. Generally we are calling it the rice bowl of India. Veerry veerry fertile land.'

'It is the largest state in South India,' added Dinkar, 'and having the most people.'

'Is that a good thing?'

'Actually, it's a fact.'

'Our rice is so, so tasty,' said Mukesh.

'I'm sure.'

'Yes, indeed.'

The train eased up, the conversation eased off, we smiled, looked down, looked up, looked out the window...

'Do you...'

'Are you liking our trains?' Mukesh and I broke the silence simultaneously.

'This is the first one I've been on, but the compartment is very comfortable.'

'Indian Railways is having at least nine different classes of train travel,' he said. 'It is the world's largest employer of people.'

'Really? How many?'

'Over one point six millions.'

'Yes and it is transporting twelve million passengers each and every day,' added Dinkar, keen not to be out-facted by his friend. 'Forty-two thousand miles of track.'

'Wow, that's a thing.'

'Yes, it is second biggest rail network on our planet.'

'Really?'

We continued to chat for a while until my brain, sated with rice and railways, was bulging. I politely suggested that I ought to rest before reaching Vijayawada. Scheduled to arrive at 23.10, the train was running at least an hour late.

That I didn't mind; my connection to Nidadavole Junction wasn't due until 3 am. I felt happier, safer, dozing on a delayed train than waiting on a platform in the middle of the night for several hours.

I picked up my notebook to check my TO DO list. A photograph fell out.

Smiling up at me was a young girl, aged about ten, seated on a blue wooden chair. Wisps of dark hair, trickling down the side of her face, framed a mid-brown complexion. Two softly-cushioned cheeks, slightly paler than her other features, highlighted the crescents under her deep, liquid eyes. She wore a pale yellow dress, slightly too big, puffed at the shoulders with a delicate floral pattern embroidered above her tiny waist. Two little green bows and a short length of ribbon dangled from the neckline. She looked dressed for a party.

With the thought that in less than 36 hours I would finally be meeting Lakshme, I drew the curtain, closed my eyes and nodded off.

'Sir, we are nearly before Vijayawada.' Mukesh was nudging me. I glanced at my watch: just gone 00.30.

Crouching down, I undid the combination padlock that attached my rucksack, via a cable, to a metal hoop under the seat. The moment the train stopped, three porters in maroon uniforms boarded the carriage.

'Carry, sir?' demanded the first, just as I had hoisted my rucksack over my shoulders and picked up the mandolin.

'No!' I shook my head.

'Help? Please.'

'I'm fine. Thank you.'

'Goodbye, Mark!' called Dinkar as he and Mukesh walked the other way down the platform. 'Happy journey!'

I was surprised by the station's liveliness for the time of night, more akin to Clapham Junction at rush hour. Unlike Clapham, however, there were sleeping bodies to climb over, tea chests and trunks to navigate, food vendors to negotiate and beggars to ignore. Well, there were some similarities.

I found a sign indicating a waiting room for first and second class passengers on platform one. Most information was displayed in Telugu, the state language, and English. On entry, I was immediately stopped by a shrewish woman in an ochre sari.

'Name!'

'Mark,' I declared, digging into my pocket for my ticket.

'No! Name!' she repeated, tapping a hefty black book on the table in front of her. Evidently I had to sign in. That done, I slumped into a blue plastic chair riveted to the wall and watched life pass by for two hours.

It was a tedious wait, but eventually my next train was announced:

'Train number 2738 Goutami Express to Kakinada Port will shortly be arriving at platform number five.'

Everything about Vijayawada Junction was oversized, especially the length of, and distance between, the platforms. Scaling the broad, busy staircase, I was swept along the footbridge by a swell of people cascading down the steps to platform two, surging up from platform three. Weak, drowning eyes stared up at me. Limbs stretched out from bundles of bones huddled on the steps.

I lost my bearings; all the signs in English had disappeared. I guessed I was near platform five but I wasn't certain. Panic set in.

'Five? Five?' I asked a man rushing towards me. I held up my hand, fingers splayed to emphasise the question.

He turned, pointed behind him – 'Straight, straight,' – and carried on. Trusting his direction, I found the staircase he was indicating. Before descending, I checked once more.

'Yes, yes, that is correct.'

'Thank you.'

'German?'

'English!'

'Very good, sir. Happy journey!'

Although it took nearly ten minutes to reach platform five, my haste was in vain; the train didn't arrive for a further twenty. A number of coaches chuntered past before mine made an appearance. Catching up with it, I found the chart of seat reservations pasted on the side of the carriage. Glancing down the list of names, I spotted one I recognised. Mine. Coach A1, Seat 0029.

I climbed on board.

'Sir, I am expecting you.' It was the TTE, Travelling Ticket Examiner. 'Come!'

He led the way down the narrow corridor of blue curtains to my bunk, the bed already prepared.

'I would wake you before Nidadavole?' he offered courteously.

'Wonderful. Dan-ya-wodd.'

'Sir?'

'Dan - Ya - Wodd,' I emphasised.

He looked at me quizzically. 'Sir?'

'Thank you.'

'Ah! You are most welcome, sir.'

I lay back, amazed. Not only was I greeted personally on a train in the middle of the night but also my name, spelt correctly, was printed and glued to the side of the carriage, along with those of all the other passengers. Where in the UK would that happen?

My love affair with Indian Rail was cemented. For the time being at least.

Exactly two hours later, the train staggered to a halt. Nidadavole Junction, five o'clock in the morning, thirty-six hours from Delhi. Though hot and frazzled, I had arrived in one piece.

As my luggage slumped wearily onto the platform, I was approached by a young man whose broad smile lit up both our faces. Here, I presumed, was my promised escort to Hebron Hostel.

'Mark?' he asked. 'Come, sir!' Effortlessly throwing my rucksack over his shoulder, he led me to the waiting Ambassador Taxi. Relieved of my burden, I felt a rush of anticipation course through my veins.

'What's your name?'

'Raju, sir.'

'Pleased to meet you, Raju. Your job?'

'I am working at Hebron.'

'Good man. How far is it to the hostel?' I enquired, looking forward to a good breakfast.

'Just two years,' Raju replied, his teeth glowing luminously in the dark.

He wasn't far wrong. The road out of Nidadavole was in a parlous state. Ruts and deep holes made the journey to Hebron Hostel, though only two kilometres, seem much further. The taxi swerved continually to avoid getting stuck or losing a wheel.

'Bumpy, bumpy!' laughed Raju.

'Ye-es,' I replied, grasping the front passenger seat to steady myself.

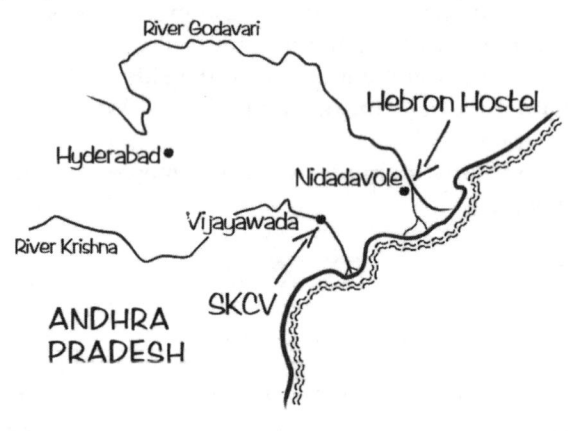

A canal ran parallel to the road, one of many in the region that formed part of an extensive network of waterways throughout the district of East Godavari.

'Canal built by Cotton,' said Raju. 'Very good man.'

Raju was referring to Sir Arthur Cotton, a British engineer, who served as a General in the First Burmese War. Claiming that "there is water enough in India for every conceivable purpose ten times over", he devoted much of his life to constructing a comprehensive network of irrigation and navigation canals. He brought water to millions of people who, to this day, worship him as a demi-god for his unstinting achievement in averting famine. Bronze statues erected in his honour are evident throughout the region.

Thanks to Cotton's endeavours, Hebron Hostel sits amid lush green paddy fields and coconut groves in a band of land, half a kilometre wide, located between the railway track and canal. Originally established as a missionary boarding hostel in Chettipeta in 1890 for poor girls with health or family problems, it relocated two kilometres down the road to its current site on the outskirts of Nidadavole in 1954. It is now home to nearly 300 disadvantaged "orphan" girls.

'When we arrive, breakfast!'

'Superb!' I replied, though I wasn't very hungry. Having been awake most of the night, I was desperate to catch up on some sleep.

The sun was beginning to rise as the taxi turned off the main road. A hundred metres down the track, we passed between two concrete gateposts.

My stomach fluttered; I had waited so long for this moment. A yellow banner, suspended between two coconut palms, flapped in the early morning breeze. Stencilled in bright orange letters:

| HEBRON HOSTEL WELCOMES MARK UNCLE FROM ENGLAND |

2
Little Acts of Kindness

*I had entered a world in which
equality simply did not exist*

I was bewitched. Bewildered. The girls possessed a gentle manner that I found both alluring *and* disconcerting. 'Sit, Uncle!'

'But I would like to...'

'No Uncle, *we* do'. I wasn't permitted to carry my own bags, wash my clothes or even collect my own water. I found it difficult to accept, but that was the culture. They couldn't help themselves and I couldn't help but feel uncomfortable by their willing servitude.

On my arrival, the hostel had been quiet, the girls asleep. When I reappeared, refreshed by a few hours' rest, it was mid-morning. Everywhere I walked, bare-footed children came running.

Immediately I became acutely aware of three non-negotiable facts: I was English, male and white; qualities that, back home, signified cultural baggage of a completely different kind.

'Good evening Uncle!' a girl called enthusiastically, the sun high in the sky.

'It's ten o'clock,' I corrected gently. 'You mean "Good morning"!'

'Uncle, yes. Good evening!'

'How are you I am fine?' greeted another.

The younger girls pushed and shoved to grasp my hand. They sat at my feet and expected... what?

Well, that was the other side of it. Such reverence flattered my white, male ego but the trade-off was that I would deliver something in return.

'Tell story, Uncle; sing song, Uncle; talk to us, Uncle,' they implored.

I played along. Some of the very youngest girls eyed me nervously. Wary of my presence, they hid behind each other as I drew near. Then, tentatively, their inquisitive heads re-emerged, shyly reciprocating my smile. When the bell rang to signify the end of break time, they skipped happily back to their classroom.

Having heard so much about her, I anticipated my first encounter with the Superintendent of Hebron Hostel with trepidation. By all accounts, Jennie Grace Prabhaker was a formidable character.

Hebron Hostel, on her appointment in 1994, had accommodated 130 girls. Over the following years, with financial support from within India and overseas, she had extensively developed the hostel's limited resources, building a school, kitchens and storeroom. By the time of my visit, construction work for a new dormitory block, Hosanna House, was nearing completion.

At the end of August 2004, Jennie was involved in a serious car accident.

'It's a miracle she's still alive,' her daughter, Esther, told me. 'Actually, many people doubted that she would survive.'

'Was she badly injured?'

'Mother fractured four limbs, including her hip. She spent several weeks in hospital.'

It was mid-morning. Esther and I were sitting in the large room at the front of the main bungalow. Being of a similar age, we had immediately clicked. Her approachable manner, aided by a perfect command of English, had put me at ease. Following her mother's accident, Esther had been granted six months' leave from her post as a science teacher in Kakinada, a city further up the coast. With her three young children, Jane Shirley, Joanni and Ritchie, she moved to Hebron to care for Jennie and to assist in the management of the hostel.

'When mother's car crashed, her life suddenly changed direction. She used to be like a butterfly. She flew around the compound, wrapping the needs of every girl in her wings. Now it is like meta.., how do you say...'

'Metamorphosis?'

'Yes. But backwards. She is in a cocoon.'

'What do you mean?'

'Her physical incapacity. So many daily routines, restrictions. Physiotherapy, doctor visits, medication. She can only eat small meals and talk for short times. Then she must take rest.'

'But she is making progress?' Running her fingers through her shoulder-length hair, Esther smiled.

'Slowly, slowly. Last week mother was unable to lift her left hand from the arm of the chair.' Her eyes sparkled. 'Today morning she could raise it two centimetres.'

'That's great.'

'Yes. Slowly mother is emerging from her cocoon.'

'And one day she'll fly!'

'Yes. That is what we are praying. You will meet her in a minute. Her physio has nearly finished.'

A toy car shot across the floor. Hot on its tail skidded a young boy in vroom-vrooming pursuit.

'Ritchie!' cried Esther.

'Sorry, Uncle!' he squeaked and tried to run away. Esther gently grabbed his arm.

'Ritchie, say hello properly. This is Mark Uncle from England.'

'Hello, Uncle!'

'Hi Ritchie,' I said, putting out my hand. 'How old are...?' But he was gone.

Esther laughed. 'He's six.'

'He's tall for his age.'

'And shy! But he'll get used to you. Actually, he will appreciate you being here.'

'He must find it odd being surrounded by so many girls?'

'You must feel the same!'

'I guess. It's not what I'm used to, for sure!'

One of the older girls entered carrying two glasses of a cloudy liquid on a tray. She offered one to me.

'Please, drink!' said Esther.

I took a sip. It was sweet, slightly warm. 'Coconut!'

'Yes. You like?'

'I do.' Despite looking like dishwater, it tasted good.

Spanning the entire length of the building, the brown-tiled room in which we were sitting functioned as a reception and eating area by day and a dormitory at night.

'Some of the girls like to sleep in here,' said Esther. 'The floor is very cool.'

It contained a number of large windows reaching from floor to ceiling filled, not with glass, but a diamond-patterned mesh. This maximised the much-needed circulation of air throughout the building. The windows also enabled Jennie, when seated in her wooden armchair, to see and hear what was happening across the compound. She and the rest of her family occupied two rooms at the back of the bungalow, her bed having been moved into her private day room for easy access.

When Jennie eventually appeared, pushed in her wheel chair by Sharon, the hostel matron, the likeness between mother and daughter was immediately apparent. Despite her obvious discomfort, her eyes radiated great warmth. She winced as she was lifted into her cushioned chair, taking a few moments to settle herself. Sharon then carefully lifted her ankles, placed her feet on a small wooden platform for support and sensitively adjusted Jennie's floral-patterned sari.

She looked up. 'Mark, you are most welcome at Hebron,' she said, embracing me with a glowing smile. 'We've not had a visitor from England for a while. Stay as long as you wish!'

'Thank you. I may well accept your offer!'

'You've had a long journey. I hope you will be comfortable here.'

'I'm being extremely well looked after.'

'You have had breakfast?'

'Yes, thank you. Raju is a great cook! Two girls brought a dish of potatoes, *chapatis* and coffee to my room shortly after my arrival.'

Jennie uttered a few words to Sharon in Telugu, who then helped to adjust her position in the chair slightly.

'You are in much pain?' I asked.

'By God's grace I am still here. That is what matters.'

'How is Lakshme Roja?' I asked.

'You've not seen her yet?' she exclaimed. 'Mark, I will send her to you when she returns from school.'

Later that afternoon I lay on my wooden-framed bed, shrouded in a mosquito net that hung from its beams. The compound was quiet, the air listless. I dozed.

Tap, tap. A tentative knock on the door startled me. Tap, tap, again, followed by a burst of nervous giggles.

I rubbed my eyes, taking a moment to surface. 'One sec!' I called, fumbling for a cotton shirt.

'Uncle?' called a voice from outside. 'Uncle?'

I walked through the curtained archway that led from the bedroom into a concrete-floored lounge covered with straw mats. A suite of antique furniture, two straight-backed armchairs and a lumpy sofa, lined the walls, affording a level of comfort to suggest that the British colonials rarely sat down.

'OK. Come in!'

Three twelve-year-olds in white blouses and pleated blue skirts scuttled into the room. There was no mistaking the slight, delicate-featured girl in the middle.

'Lakshme!'

'Yez, Uncle.'

Unsure how to greet a twelve year old Indian girl, I extended my hand. Somehow it seemed wrong. Awkward.

Before she had a chance to reciprocate, poor Lakshme found herself enveloped in a heartfelt, but modestly-executed, hug. She felt fragile and was shaking slightly, her plaited hair perfumed with a hint of jasmine.

'How are you?' I asked.

'Fine, Uncle. You?'

'Fine also.' Pause. 'How was school today?'

Silence. Lakshme shook her head.

'No, Uncle,' she said plaintively.

Observing her embarrassment, I realised she'd already exhausted the extent of her English.

I smiled at the other two girls.

'Er... friends?' I asked, pointing at them both.

'Yezz, Uncle. Hema,' the tallest of the three, and 'Sadhana,' the giggler.

'At school, same class?' I asked all three, hoping one of them might understand.

'Yes, Uncle. Class Six,' replied Hema.

Another ticklish pause, more fidgety giggles.

'Uncle. What izz?'

I followed the direction of Lakshme's pointing finger. My mandolin was leaning against a chair leg.

'Ah, mandolin!'

'Man-dor-leen?' The girls looked inquisitively at each other.

'Music! I'll show you.'

I picked up the instrument and perched on the corner of the chair.

Twang, twang. I strummed a couple of notes. The girls laughed.

'Song, Uncle?' asked Hema.

'Ah.' *What to play?* My repertoire was limited. *Make up something. They won't know.*

'As it's nearly Christmas, how about... Jingle Bells?' *I can busk that.*

'Yezz, Uncle!'

'English song.' As I struck the first note, I realised that I'd never played the mandolin in front of anyone before. Concentrating hard, I shakily plucked out some semblance of a tune.

This is painful. I wish I had my piano here. Embarrassed, I didn't look up for fear of seeing the girls' reaction. *Oh well.*

'...in a one horse open sleigh.' I eventually finished.

'Uncle, veerry beaut-ee-ful,' said Hema. Sandhana clapped enthusiastically.

'You try?' I offered Lakshme the mandolin.

'No, Uncle!' She shyly shook her head.

'Maybe another time?'

Observing Lakshme's small hands tremble nervously, I tried to imagine myself in her position. *I wonder what she makes of her strange, white "Uncle"? Am I what she expected? I wonder what she and her friends might say about me in private?*

A bell rang.

'Uncle, bye.'

That was it. My first meeting with Lakshme Roja.

'See you later, girls.'

Walking out the door, she turned her head and smiled coyly. I don't think she wanted the others to see.

That secret, shared moment made all the difference in the world. Five years ago, Lakshme was a young girl living in a distant land to whom I'd made a sponsorship commitment. Now we were a tangible part of each others' lives. Mark Thomas was right. I was privileged.

In the cool early evening, a group of girls gave me a tour of the compound. Clutching my fingers, they pointed out the names of various objects as we walked. They jostled me gently to and fro like a mob of mini football fans, each one vying for a few exclusive moments of my attention.

'Uncle!' cried a little girl in a blue-checked pinafore dress, pointing to one of the many palms growing in the grounds, its fruit hanging in clumps like oversized bunches of grapes. '*Kopra kaya.*'

'Ko - prah kie - yah,' I repeated slowly.

'Ah,' she nodded. 'Telugu meaning: coconut tree.' Like most of the girls, her ears were pierced with two delicate gold hoops. Others wore silver earrings, some had studs.

Another girl tugged my arm. '*Chandrudu*, Uncle!'

I followed her gaze. The moon was just rising above the school.

'Chan-dra-loo.'

'No, Uncle, charn-droo-*doo*. Doo. Doo.'

I tried again. 'Charn-droo-doo.'

'Yes, Uncle!' She leaned in, eyes widening sagaciously as if she had just imparted some great pearl of knowledge.

All the girls, including Lakshme, called me "Uncle", not Mark. Along with "Auntie", these were respectful titles that children commonly used for adults that they regarded as friends or part of the "family", though not specifically related.

The hostel comprised a number of buildings securely enclosed by a high concrete wall. Immediately inside the main gate stood Hermon School, attended by the younger girls. The ground floor housed the classrooms for Years One to Five. A flight of steps led up to the second floor.

'Uncle, rooms for sleeping. Young girls.'

Along the front of the classrooms ran a path opening onto a terraced area used for morning assembly and evening prayers. As with many of the buildings, the sand-coloured school was in need of a fresh coat of paint, particularly to conceal the grey residue from the previous year's rains that streaked the walls. A prolific creeper crawled across the building's facade, its straggling tentacles obscuring the sign:

HERMON SCHOOL ~ LOVE & SERVE IN UNITY

'Uncle, come! Look – flower!'

'Bush!'

'Butterfly!'

'Bird! Veeeerry beautiful.'

'Wait a moment, girls,' I said, reaching into my pocket for my notebook. I knew that I would never remember the words unless I wrote them down.

We had reached the playground by this point. Maintenance-wise, it fared no better than the front of the school; two of the swings lacked seats, the see-saw wouldn't budge and the rickety tree-house was unstable. Only the wide, metal slide was in reasonable condition.

The group crowded in, nudging to admire my scribbling.

'Uncle, writing. Super. Sooo-per,' commented one of the older girls, bringing her index and middle finger together to make an OK sign.

'I wish you had told my schoolteachers that!' I joked.

'Yes, Uncle,' she giggled, not understanding.

'*Cheyi*,' said a girl indicating my hand.

'*Mukku*,' suggested another, signalling her nose.

'*Tala*. Telugu meaning: head, Uncle.'

'Your head, Uncle: white!' laughed an older girl who had just joined us.

'*Juttu*,' piped up a little girl behind me, showing me her hair tied in two elaborate plaits fastened with blue ribbon.

'Joo-too lay-doo!' I responded, slapping my bald crown. 'No hair!'

The girls collapsed in laughter. 'Uncle funny!'

Concede. I was unable to do anything about my nationality and gender. Or the colour of my skin.

In England, a tan is frequently regarded as a sign of good health. Here, I observed that many women and men coated their faces with pale makeup to lighten their natural complexions. Everyday face products, including soap and moisturiser, contained skin whitener, making it impossible to discern the heredity of the ashen-toned models that advertised the latest televisions, cars and fashion accessories on the city billboards.

The reverential treatment I received made me uncomfortable. It rubbed, but I had to accept that I had entered a world in which equality simply did not exist. I tried, slowly chipping away, my wry smile occasionally betraying my bemusement at the girls' social graces. I made every effort to learn Telugu, to laugh at myself and lower my status. Slowly we relaxed and found a way of living together.

As for the skin colour? I guess the grass is always greener.

☼

A bell rang each morning at 6am to herald the new day. As the crow-rasping dawn chorus mingled with the mumbling babble of waking girls, I tried to turn over and continue sleeping. Rarely, though, did I ever manage to doze beyond seven o'clock.

Blearily pushing aside the mosquito net on my second morning, I stumbled out of bed, threw on a pair of shorts and T-shirt and opened the door. I flinched as a shaft of sunlight stabbed my yawning eyes. A narrow walkway led from my bedroom on the first floor to a parapet overlooking the main courtyard. Below, the girls were preparing for the day ahead, a mass of colour in their different uniforms: the youngest girls in bright pink blouses and green skirts, the high school girls in blue and white and the college students in assorted shades of Punjabi dress. The clatter of metal buckets accompanied the voices of the smallest children singing Telugu nursery rhymes as they washed their hands and faces.

The other side of the building commanded a clear view over the neighbouring paddy fields. A thin layer of mist hovered over the land through which the coconut palms poked; silhouetted lollipops on long, curved sticks. The stickiness of the ensuing day already clenched the morning air with its clammy fingers.

I heard whispers behind me. Two ten year olds were hanging out their washing.

'Rice?' I questioned, indicating the vast expanse of green beyond the wall.

They looked at each other quizzically and, shaking their heads, declared together: 'No, Uncle!'

I don't think they meant 'no, they're not paddy fields,' but 'no, we don't understand your question.' As soon as I turned, they broke into laughter.

A girl stopped me on the stairs. 'Hello, Uncle. My name you remember?'

'Er...'

'What about mine?' asked her friend.

'Ah, well...'

The girls' expectation that I could memorise nearly 300 names was absurd, especially as many were difficult to pronounce and extremely similar in sound. Every time they asked, I had a go - 'Aradhana, Sandhya, Sanjana, Anjana, Jitana, Jitisha, Jigisha, Digisha...' - then gave up.

'But we know *your* name, Uncle.'

That's not so difficult, is how I wanted to respond. *I'm the only man here. Mark's easy to remember, easy to say.* But I didn't, simply because most of them wouldn't have understood. Besides, several of the girls *did* have difficulty saying my name. Pronouncing "M" as *YEM*, Mark invariably sounded like York or Yack.

Actually, I wasn't the *only* male around. Raju, the personable guy who met me at the station, was responsible for a number of duties at the hostel. A superb cook, he cycled to the market almost every day to buy fruit and vegetables and undertook whatever other jobs required attention. Like many Indian men, his boyish face and infectious laugh belied his real age. Initially imagining him to be in his mid-twenties, I was amazed to discover later that he had two grown-up sons who also worked around the compound. Raju was good company, though it took him a few days to become familiar with my accent.

Every morning the Sixth to Eighth Class girls assembled outside Jennie's bungalow ready to process, crocodile-fashion, two kilometres along the canal road to the high school in Chettipeta.

'Good morning, Amma!' they called to Jennie before walking, many of them barefoot, down the driveway bordered by coconut palms and brightly-hued bougainvilleas.

'I do wish they would wear their chappals,' I once overheard Jennie comment wistfully.

The older Ninth and Tenth Class girls studied for their state School Certificate exams at the high school in Nidadavole. The eldest students attended a local college to obtain certificates in health work, nursing, information technology, teaching and tailoring. They always presented themselves beautifully in their Punjabi dress; pyjama, kurta and scarf made from light cotton silk. Had they not been burdened by such heavy schoolbags, I imagined that they would float off in the morning breeze like angels. I was often amazed by the excessive weight of books I saw strapped to the backs of young people as they walked to school, a common sight wherever I went in India.

By day, the black arching crows cawed to each other in uncannily human tones. Cries of 'Hello, hello, friend. How's that? Hello, friend,' competed with the rote-chanting rhymes that droned through the open classroom doors. Even during the night they cackled with rasping regularity, punctuated by the occasional comma of the chattering gecko.

More pervasively from dawn till dusk, the banging, hammering and shovel-on-concrete scrapings of the construction work pounded the air; the trains approaching Nidadavole Junction two kilometres down the track blasted their horns and, at regular intervals - 8am, 12.30pm, 2pm and 5pm - the siren from the neighbouring KRISHNA INDUSTRIAL CORPORATION instructed its employees when to work, break, work and finish for the day. The fertilizer factory also emitted a noxious smell which, depending on the direction of the wind, hovered over the hostel towards the end of the afternoon.

At twilight, too, the compound bustled with noise as the girls chitchatted in joyful chorus. Some prepared food while others washed their laundry, slapping wet clothes onto the concrete slabs with a sloppy thud. A bucket, lowered into the well by a grating chain, clanged against the wall before breaking the water's surface with an echoing splish.

At seven o'clock, a bell signalled dinner time. Girls emerged from doorways, metal plates in hand to join the impatient queue. Once laden with food, they stood, sat or perched wherever they could amid the rubble and sand. In a few weeks' time the smart quadrangle, enclosed by the new dormitory block and dining hall, would be completed. But, for the time being, the girls ate their meals on a building site.

Following dinner each evening, the older girls studied for a further couple of hours while the younger children assembled on the terrace outside Hermon School for a song and story before bed.

'Would you like to talk to them?' Esther asked me on my third evening. 'Maybe a short story?'

'But...'

'Preferably with a moral.'

Gulp. 'I tell you what,' I suggested, stalling for time. 'Why don't the girls sing something first?'

Without prompting, they burst into a rendition of

Trinkle trinkle lillel star
Ah I wandah war the are.
Up above nyah nyah nyah nah
Nyah Nyah die mond in de sky...

'Fantastic,' I smiled, not wishing to dampen their spirits. Esther gave me a knowing grin.

'How about a Telugu song?' I proposed, hoping they might sing themselves to sleep and forget about the request for a story. Launching into a delightful folk tune and dance, over 100 shrill, nasal tones filled the compound, compensating with enthusiasm for what they may have lacked in musicality.

But my plan didn't work.

'Now you, Uncle!' a pig-tailed girl called out when they had finished. 'Story.'

'But I don't speak Telugu,' I procrastinated.

'Don't worry. I'll translate.'

'Thanks, Esther.' Clearly I was not going to get away with it. Thankfully, the germ of an idea had just popped into my head.

'Here we go. There was once a young girl called Sumitra.' Pausing for Esther to translate, I bought myself a few moments to decide what to say next. 'She lived in a small village in South India with her mother and two younger brothers. They were a happy family, but very poor. They worked hard to grow their own food.

'Every day after school Sumitra ran as fast as she could to help her mother in the fields. One afternoon, as soon as the bell rang, she hurried across the paddy fields to find her mother.

'Suddenly, she heard a voice call out: "Help me, help me, please!" She listened to where the sound was coming from. There, under a tree, lay an old man.

'"What has happened?" asked Sumitra.

'"I fell and hurt my leg. I cannot move", replied the old man, "Please help me up again."

'Sumitra smiled and offered her hand to the old man. Slowly she pulled him up and helped him walk to the nearest path.

'"Thank you," said the old man. "You have been very kind. As a reward, I want you to do one thing. Before you go to sleep tonight, please make a wish."

'As if by magic, the old man disappeared. Sumitra rubbed her eyes. Maybe she'd been dreaming.

'But she didn't forget what the old man said. As she lay on her mat that night, she thought of all the things that she could wish for: a new dress, games and toys, a bigger house. But no, she wished for something else. And do you know what that was?

'Early the next morning Sumitra woke up and ran outside. By the front door sat a big pot, filled to the brim with rice. It was enough for her and the rest of her family to enjoy.

'From then on, she found a pot of rice by the front door every morning. Her family were never hungry again.'

I looked around. Deepali, one of the youngest girls, having closed her eyes, was leaning on her friend's shoulder. Esther continued to address the girls with a few more sentences in Telugu, probably wrapping up the tenuous moral message I had fabricated. They smiled and nodded appreciatively.

'What did you say?'

'I asked if they had understood the story.'

'I'm surprised that more of them haven't fallen asleep!'

'Mark!' Esther rebuked. 'They enjoyed it.'

'Uncle, uncle!' a small voice piped out, 'Man-do-leeen!' It was giggly Sandhana, Lakshme's friend. 'Chinkle Bells!'

Esther looked at me. 'I brought a small mandolin with me,' I explained.

'Oh?'

'But it's in my room.' I could see that several of the younger girls were very sleepy. As my room was on the other side of the compound, it would take me a few minutes to get the instrument. 'It might be better if I played another day.' That would also give me time to practise. 'Please tell the girls.'

'As you wish.'

'Yes, Uncle,' they responded as Esther explained. 'Goodnight, Uncle!'

Following a short prayer, Esther asked them all to stand up. Row by row they filed up the stairs to bed.

To Buy
- *Plum cake for girls*
- *Presents for Jennie, Esther, family + staff*
- *Soap*

I conducted a daily curry count. By day fourteen I had reached forty. My stomach applauded the diet, breakfast, lunch and dinner. That morning I'd enjoyed a boiled egg, chapati and chilli pickle. Previous breakfasts had included *dosas*, curried tomatoes, couscous and fresh fruit. Lunch, later that day, consisted of rice, as did most meals, beetroot curry, dal and omelette. Raju had recently discovered that I liked eggs, hence the abundance in *all* meals that day.

The Indian dietary league is split into two divisions; *veg* and *non-veg*. This I liked. Although the vegetarian is tolerated in much of the world, generally-speaking the flesh-eater prevails; the vegetarian is the exception, the one opting out of the norm. But in India, linguistically at least, the vegetarian rules; choose to be a carnivore if you wish but you are a *non-veg*, a negative eater.

This makes dining particularly straightforward; most hotels and restaurants display their veg or non-veg status above the door alongside their name. South India, especially, is a vegetarian's paradise.

I discovered that a *true* Indian veg does not eat eggs, though other dairy products are permissible. Raju, until he discovered otherwise, had assumed this to be the case with me.

The variety of dishes he cooked was incredible; forty meals and every one of them different. Potato curry, bitter gourd, pumpkin, bean... the list went on. Not to mention the *sambar, parathas,* dal, dosas, chapatis and pickles: mango, lime, chilli and coconut.

I had observed from my first day in India that most people ate with their fingers. Their *right* fingers. Now this may not be an issue for many westerners. But, as I am left-handed, *extremely* left-handed, it proved to be a monumental challenge for me. Yet, despite my inept right-hand-to-mouth coordination, I was determined to give it a go.

Filling one's mouth with a handful of rice and vegetables, in theory, doesn't sound difficult. But to do it cleanly, swiftly and in such a way that it neither offends nor puts everyone else off their food, is another matter. As at least one meal a day was served in my room, I was able to train in secret. On my first attempt, most of the food, which took over an hour to eat, ended up everywhere but in my mouth.

Instinctively I do everything with my left hand, a practice which, I believed, was unacceptable in India. The left hand was for the jobs where the right hand would rather not go. Thankfully, I soon discovered that left-handedness was less of a curse than I had anticipated. Most people tended to laugh it off derisively: 'Ho ho, so you're a leftie then?!'

'Yes,' I would confess ashamedly. Being left-handed, it seemed, was enough of an issue to be branded "leftie" but not so severe a social affliction as to warrant ostracism from polite company entirely. Nevertheless, it was still etiquette to eat with one's right hand.

Techniques varied not only from place to place but from person to person. I had studied carefully: in Delhi, on the train and now at Hebron. Some people closed together the four fingers of their right hand to make a kind of shovel with which to scoop up their rice and dal. Others mixed together a few items, rather like blending paint on a palate, to form a small glutinous ball. This they then picked up and pushed, with their thumb, along a channel, formed by their fingers, into their mouth. The technique was more difficult, but less messy. Regardless, it was considered bad practice to allow food to stray beyond the second knuckles.

Whether I used a fork or my fingers, I always finished last; eating seemed to be the only activity in India that was conducted with any sense of urgency.

After the main courses at Hebron, we usually ate fruit, invariably bananas. One evening, though, Raju produced a different desert.

'*Seviya*,' he said, placing the bowl in front of me. 'It's like *kheer*,' a milk pudding made with rice. This dish, though, consisted of fine vermicelli noodles floating in a rich sea of buttery milk garnished with sultanas and roast cashews.

The first mouthful, scorching hot, nearly burnt my tongue. Sampling it again after a moment or two, I detected a familiar flavour.

'You like, sir?' Raju asked.

'I do very much. But there's a fragrance I can't quite place.'

'Cardamon, sir.'

Of course.

Although I loved all the dishes that Raju prepared, I developed a firm favourite.

Sitting down to lunch with Esther one day, I was served a pot of unappetising thick, woody stems in a golden sauce. Two inches in length, they were dark green with tough, ribbed skins. *What to do with this?* I wondered.

Esther caught my bemused expression. 'I bet you've never had anything like these before?'

'Nope. What are they?'

'Drumsticks. You eat them like this.'

Picking up a piece between her thumb and forefinger, she put it in her mouth and then dragged it back through her teeth, sucking at the same time.

'You try.'

As my teeth scraped along the rough skin several sweet, pea-like seeds slipped out, tasting similar to asparagus.

'That's delicious,' I declared, the sauce dribbling down my chin. Intrigued to see what I had just swallowed, I split open another pod with my thumb. It oozed an opaque, creamy flesh containing a cluster of winged seeds.

'Why are they called drumsticks?' I enquired.

'Wait until we've finished. I'll show you.'

When Raju had cleared away the dishes, we went outside. Esther pointed to an elegant tree with delicate, fern-like leaves growing near to the kitchen. Dozens of fruit dangled from the branches, some reaching two feet in length.

Tapered at the end they looked...

'...just like drumsticks!'

'Exactly,' replied Esther. 'Now you see.'

'What's its real name?'

'*Munagakaya*. It grows throughout India but is particularly common in Andhra Pradesh.'

Needless to say, eggs, seviya and drumsticks featured prominently on the menu for the rest of my time at Hebron.

Recipe for Drumsticks (for 4 people)

Lightly scrape 2 drumsticks (2 feet long or 3 shorter ones) and cut into finger-length pieces.

Soak a lemon-sized piece of tamarind in enough water to cover it.

Chop 3 or 4 onions and 2 green chillies.

Fry onions and chillies in a pan in 2 tbsp oil until golden brown.

Add half tsp of turmeric, 1 tsp salt, 1 tbsp red chilli powder and 2 curry leaves.

Squeeze water from tamarind pulp into pan.

Add drumsticks and enough water to cover them.

Bring to boil, simmer until soft (about 10 mins).

Sprinkle with coriander leaves and serve with rice and coconut chutney.

Catching sight of my reflection in the dressing table mirror I thought I was developing a tan. On closer examination, it seemed that the deceptive glow was produced by several layers of ingrained dust.

A good bath would have helped. Some chance. I washed with hot water brought to me in a large tin container, heated on a fire fuelled by rice husks. I flushed the toilet with a plastic bucket and cleaned my teeth with boiled water.

The festive season, as I've always known it, couldn't have seemed further away. The sweltering heat on Christmas Eve felt especially strange. Christmas should be cold.

Only the Tenth Class and the college girls were staying for the holidays; they had to revise for their exams in early January. All the others were expecting to see their families. Although by early evening most of them had gone, at least four girls had tearfully received the news during the day that their parents, for a number of personal reasons, would not be coming to take them home.

An eerie hush tiptoed around the compound.

An almost inaudible sigh breathed close by. A short sob. Then another.

As I sat beside four year old Bina, my heart was wrenched from my body. Hunched, alone, on a pile of rubble, she was one of the few girls whose parents had not come to collect her.

'Don't cry,' I spluttered, although I knew she couldn't understand me. 'We'll make tomorrow special.'

Bina sniffed and offered the faintest glimmer of a smile.

A pale shadow fell across her face.

'Hello, Uncle!'

I turned. A girl had appeared behind us, her slight figure silhouetted against the moonlight.

'Lakshme!' I was astonished. 'You're still here?!'

'Parents...' Unable to find the words, she shrugged forlornly.

Her delicate gold earrings glinted with light reflected from the wall lamp. Lakshme was small for her age but as bright and intelligent as any twelve year old. Her understanding of English, though not as good as that of her friends, was recompensed by her willingness to please. For now, in her unassuming way, she just wanted to sit quietly.

In the west, orphans are generally regarded as children without parents. In India the term is used more broadly to include those whose parents, though still alive, are unable to care for their child. They are sometimes referred to as semi-orphans. Such was the situation for Lakshme Roja's family.

I missed my own family dearly. That Christmas Eve, though, my heart belonged to those girls. But what could I say when we only knew a smattering of words in each others' language?

I had an idea.

'One minute, I'll be back,' I signalled with my hands. I dashed up to my room, returning moments later with my mandolin.

'We sing this in England at Christmas,' I explained, 'although the tune comes from Austria.'

'Oss-tree-ah!' repeated Bina timidly.

'Uncle!' said Lakshme. 'Bina name meaning, musical instrument.'

Accompanied by the ticking cicadas, the wobbly strains of Silent Night twanged through the still evening air.

I was woken at 4.30am on Christmas Day by carollers from Chettipeta who, I was told later, had strolled the neighbourhood singing throughout the night.

I had just fallen back to sleep when the sounds of "O come all ye faithful" in Telugu breezed through the air. This time, I got up, threw on a T-shirt and shorts and went outside to witness the girls in full vocal flow.

'Happy Christmas, Uncle!' they shouted and waved. Christmas wishes were exchanged all round. I then returned to bed. It was only five-thirty.

After resurfacing for the second time, I spent the morning quietly chatting to Jennie, Esther and her family.

The Christmas lunch table bowed with bowls of special rice, chutneys, pickles and a rich variety of spicy vegetable dishes including, of course, drumsticks. Raju had excelled himself. As a treat for the girls, he cooked a special chicken recipe. We all ate from large, golden disposable plates.

'Raju!' called Jennie, once we were seated. 'You've forgotten Mark's fork and spoon!'

'No, I'm fine, thanks!' I said quickly, proceeding to eat the entire meal with the fingers of my *right* hand. Very little food ended up on the table or floor.

'Mark, I am impressed!' laughed Jennie. 'You have been practicing?'

'Well, you know, when in Rome…'

After lunch most of us walked down the road to the local church in Chettipeta.

'It was a curious service,' I explained to Jennie afterwards. She had spent the afternoon resting in her room.

'Why are you saying that?'

'Though it had started while we were still here eating, one of the villagers told me that it didn't really liven up until an hour later. By the time we arrived at two o'clock the service was in full swing.'

'That sounds normal!' she laughed.

Packed with Indian Christians from the surrounding villages, the white stone building had reverberated with celebration. Six of the Hebron girls had sung a Christmas Telugu hymn, a few others had danced to a schmaltzy American soundtrack of "Joy to the World" and the pastor delivered an hour-long sermon.

'Did you understand it?' asked Jennie.

'Not at all!'

On the way back to the hostel we stopped for a picnic in the grounds of a nearby derelict house; the overgrown garden and dilapidated building made a perfect location for hide and seek. The girls then taught me an energetic game that involved a lot of jumping in and out of a circle.

'I need a rest,' I gasped after a few minutes. 'It's too hot.'

'But it's Christmas Day, Uncle,' said Sailaja, one of the older college girls. 'It is customary to be playing games.'

'Where I come from, it's traditional to fall asleep on Christmas afternoon!'

Lakshme's dusky eyes widened in wonder as I handed her a small package.

'Happy Christmas, Lakshme!'

'Thanks, Uncle!'

With nimble fingers, she tore off the gold cellophane. Although I found presents for everyone else locally, I'd brought this particular gift for Lakshme from England.

She looked puzzled. 'Uncle?'

'Hold out your hand.'

I demonstrated. With the object resting in her palm, I turned its tiny handle. As the intricate pins on the rotating drum twanged the sprung metal comb, the melody of "My Favourite Things" tinkled hesitantly.

'Beautiful, Uncle!' she said sweetly.

'It's a music box. You can listen to it with your friends.'

Later that evening, I gave the gifts that I'd found in Nidadavole to Jennie and her family. Even in the smallest of towns it was possible to buy almost anything.

'Mark, you shouldn't be giving me a present,' she said graciously. Jennie pulled off the newspaper wrapping to reveal an oil painting of waves crashing dramatically onto a beach at sunrise.

'I thought it might brighten up the drab green walls.'

'Thank you! The colours are breathtaking.'

'Why don't you hang it where you can see it from your bed?'

'Raju!' she called. Despite her incapacity, Jennie never wasted time.

'*Haan ji!*' Within moments, he was hammering a nail into the wall.

'Are you feeling homesick, Mark? she asked.

I thought for a moment. 'No, not really. But I miss my family today. This is the first Christmas we've spent apart.'

'You are with your *Indian* family this year,' she smiled.

Just before bed I managed to receive a weak signal on my mobile. My parents were surrounded by mountains of wrapping paper, boxes and toys. I could hear my nephew and niece playing excitedly in the background.

'Mum, I have someone who'd like to talk to you.'

Beside me stood Lakshme clutching her music box. I handed her the phone.

'Hello, Auntie,' she said. 'Happy Christmas!'

'Lakshme!' my mother exclaimed. 'Happy Christmas to you too. You've made my day!'

And what a day! All the girls received a gift from the hostel; two boiled sweets and a banana. They were delighted.

Simple Coconut Chutney

Using a food processor, grind the flesh of one coconut and 2 or 3 green chillies into a fine paste.

Stir in the juice of half a lemon and enough plain yoghurt to make a creamy, smooth chutney.

Add salt to taste and serve.

The bell rang the next morning at 6am. As it was Sunday, I would have appreciated a lie-in. But for the Hebron girls, the first day of the week was not a day of rest. Sunday, holiday or otherwise, meant a three kilometre walk to church in Nidadavole.

'You are coming with us, Uncle?'
'Let me think about...'
'Good. We leave in thirty minutes.'

Everything I saw on our walk into Nidadavole was so unlike a typical English Boxing Day: women washed clothes in the canal, children pumped water from the well and piglets waddled in the gutter. Christmas was over. Life went on.

I stared at the cows wandering nonchalantly down the street. People stared at me, continually. It was extremely unnerving.

'Look! A white man.' I imagined them muttering. 'A *bald* white man. How odd!'

I had not seen another pale face since my arrival in Nidadavole and, judging by their gazes, neither had they. If ever, it seemed.

I noticed many intricate patterns, flowers, birds and more abstract designs, drawn in white on the pavements.

Manasi, one of the college girls who had stayed for Christmas, saw me looking.

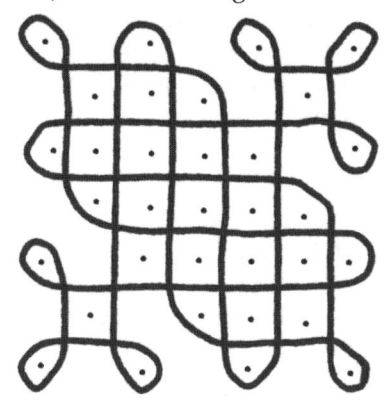

'*Muggulu,*' she said. 'That is Andhra Pradesh name. In other parts of South India name is *Kolam.*'

'Who draws them?'

'Mainly Hindu women and girls. It is making art. Girls learn from mothers, grandmothers and aunts. Then teach children.'

'They must take a long time to paint?'

'Actually, no. They are using dot pattern then painting design with rice flower. Decorating courtyards and prayer halls also. Festivals and weddings rice flour paste is using. And bright-bright colours!'

'What are they for?'

'Home making beautiful to visitors like "welcome mat". Very very auspicious guest is Lakshmi, goddess of wealth. Everybody wanting to make welcome for her!'

'It's OK to walk on them then?'

'Yes, yes. Christmas is finished.'

'But aren't these Hindu homes? They don't celebrate Christmas, do they?'

'Actually, we are loving to share all festivals!'

We arrived at the church, removed our shoes and filed in: men on chairs to the right, women on the floor to the left. I bit my tongue.

The service was similar to that of the previous day but magnified in every way: more people sang much louder for a longer period of time. Five hours in fact. Sadly, though, with the inclusion of two hefty sermons, it was no more comprehensible.

As proceedings drew to a close, the gentleman sitting next to me zipped up his weighty, leather-bound Telugu bible and smiled charismatically. 'Brother, welcome to our community,' he affirmed, pumping my hand vigorously. 'You are coming to my home for lunch.'

Question or a statement? Either way, I felt I had little choice. 'I am,' I replied ambiguously.

'I will send message to Jennie.'

'You know her?'

'Of course. Come!'

Leaving the girls to walk back to the hostel, I was ushered into his waiting car.

Mogul-inspired, Simeon Reddy's house was an audacious construction compared with other property in the vicinity. Situated on the other side of Nidadavole, it was fronted by a meticulously-kept ornamental garden and a wrought iron gate that silently glided open as the car pulled up. His two sons, both successful businessmen in their late twenties, had left home. Simeon now lived alone with Sonia, his wife, plus two boisterous German Shepherds, his driver, two servants and a gardener.

'It is giving them work and an income,' he said of his employees, as if he felt he had to justify their existence.

On the grand tour he proudly explained that he had designed the marble-floored property himself ten years ago.

'I devoted so much of time and effort in finding the right builder.'

'The ceilings are wonderfully high,' I remarked, unsure what else to say as we entered the fifth bedroom.

'Very necessary in this climate. I am showing you the balcony. It runs all the way around the second floor.'

Coming downstairs into the hallway, I was greeted by a slight woman hovering diffidently under an archway that led into the lounge.

'This is Sonia, my wife,' introduced Simeon. 'She's a very good cook.'

'I'm very pleased to meet you,' I said, nodding my head in respect. 'Thank you for your hospitality.'

'It is our pleasure.' She turned towards Simeon, her voice dropping. 'Have you seen the television?'

'Why?'

I followed them into the lounge.

A wide-screen satellite TV was broadcasting the CNN News. Reports were just coming in of an earthquake somewhere in Asia. It had caused an enormous tidal wave.

'My God!' exclaimed Simeon.

Later in the afternoon we heard that India had been hit. The word *tsunami* was used for the first time.

Thousands had already died.

For the rest of the day I was haunted by the painting I'd given Jennie the previous evening.

'Breathtaking,' I recalled her saying.

Ordinarily I'm not superstitious. But I did wonder.

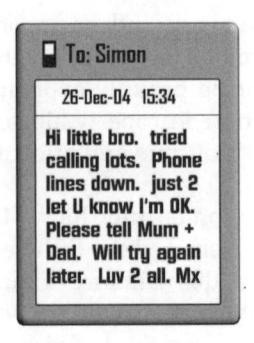

> **☐ To: Simon**
>
> 26-Dec-04 15:34
>
> **Hi little bro. tried calling lots. Phone lines down. just 2 let U know I'm OK. Please tell Mum + Dad. Will try again later. Luv 2 all. Mx**

The next morning, Raju cycled into Nidadavole to buy a copy of the *Deccan Chronicle*. I read that the death toll had reached at least 12,000 in Sri Lanka and was still rising. There was no information about the situation on the Indian coast, despite its proximity.

Later that day I received an impromptu invitation. Pinak, the son of a friend of Jennie's, was visiting the hostel. Home from university for the vacation, he had dropped by briefly to say hello.

'Actually, I must be leaving,' he said after a few minutes. 'I have Christmas gifts for the leper colony on the other side of town. I am promising to visit on behalf of my family.'

I stood to say goodbye.

'Perhaps you wish to come with me, Mark?'

I looked at him for a moment. My gut response was fear. Leprosy was a disease I knew little about.

'They would love to see you,' he encouraged, sensing my hesitation.

Go with it, urged a voice in my head.

'In that case, thank you.'

We stopped at the market en route to buy bananas, oranges and some sweets for the children. I had also thrown a couple of shirts into my bag that I no longer required.

'Is leprosy contagious?' I asked Pinak.

'Yes, but you should not be worrying!'

'I wasn't thinking of that. I just wanted to know more about it.'

'Actually, I'm not an expert,' said Pinak. 'I am understanding that it is a chronic disease that attacks the nervous system. It is affecting the hands, feet or face. Because it causes loss of sensation, sufferers may harm themselves without knowing it. Those injuries are then becoming infected.'

'Is it curable?'

'Yes, although it is leaving people deformed or crippled if untreated.'

'And still a major problem in India?' I asked.

'I think about four million people are having the disease.'

We drove off the main highway onto a narrower track. After about 100 metres we stopped next to a small stone church. A gaunt man in a white *dhoti* approached us. He and Pinak exchanged a few sentences in Telugu.

'This is Suresh, one of the project leaders,' explained Pinak. We shook hands.

'Please,' Suresh said, implying we should follow him.

People were emerging from their homes to greet us. The colony was a self-contained village of grass-roofed huts, separated by narrow, dusty lanes, each home consisting of one dark room. Small wood fires burned within stone rings on the dry mud outside some of the huts.

We handed the gifts to Suresh.

'He says "thank you".' Pinak translated. 'They will distribute them to the neediest families.'

A temple imbues a sense of holiness. A theatre buzzes with expectation. This isolated, self-contained habitation breathed a total lack of self-esteem, its stillness resonating more profoundly than if our arrival had been heralded by a brass band. Devoid of the hustle and bustle of other villages, the atmosphere strained, as if all the energy of its inhabitants was channelled towards clinging onto their remaining scraps of dignity.

This was the first time since coming to Nidavavole, though, that no one gazed at me inquisitively. *I* was the one staring as we walked around: an elderly man reaching out with a stump for an arm; an emaciated woman with watery, vacant eyes peering into the middle distance; a young girl with rotten teeth protruding from her raw gums.

'How many people live here?' I asked.

'About seventy men, women and children.'

As we passed one hut, a man beckoned me over, pointing to a hammock being rocked gently by his wife. Resting inside was a baby, naked and weak.

'How old is he?' He looked about six months.

'One year, three months,' Pinak translated. The man whispered a few words. 'His parents would be honoured if you could pray for him.'

I had never felt so humbled. I cannot remember what I said, but the gist was 'God, help them.'

'Tanx, sir.'

They seemed appreciative and I felt a fraud.

But fraudulence was a perennial burden. Who was I to be treated with such honour wherever I went? Talking to people; taking their photograph; shaking their hand; even smiling - it all elicited the same response:

'Thank you, sir, thank you.'

This was their country, their land. I didn't deserve such respect.

※

Jennie managed Hebron Hostel with an iron rod and a heart of gold. No attention to detail was overlooked. At least not before her car accident. But, due to her confinement for several months, certain areas of the compound had fallen into neglect. This was becoming an issue; the new dormitory block, Hosanna House, would be inaugurated on 26 January, less than a month away.

Esther, functioning as Jennie's eyes and ears around the hostel, suggested making an action plan to ensure that all the necessary tasks were completed in time.

'Would you help me draw one up?' she asked.

'No problem.' With my experience in project planning, I was happy to do what I could.

Papers in hand, Esther and I spent a whole afternoon walking around the compound, noting down all the jobs to be done: clearing and re-laying the stones on the front drive; cleaning and painting the rusty gates; designing a new entrance sign; decorating the front of the school; pruning the trees; making safe the swings and tree house in the playground; emptying the current rubbish pit and digging another for composting; the list was endless...

Action would begin the following day. And the workers? 'Don't worry, Mark,' said Jennie, 'leave that to me.'

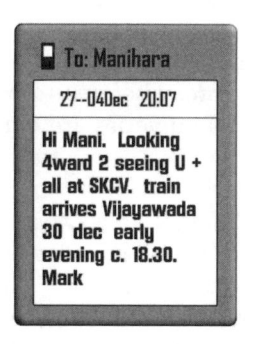

> **To: Manihara**
>
> 27--04Dec 20:07
>
> Hi Mani. Looking 4ward 2 seeing U + all at SKCV. train arrives Vijayawada 30 dec early evening c. 18.30. Mark

Despite rising at six o'clock the next morning, I found that Raju's sons and several friends had beaten me to it. They had already made considerable progress clearing the grounds. The smell of burning rubbish filled the air and the entire compound buzzed industriously. Though it was still early, the sun had cut through the morning haze and my cotton shirt clung to my back.

A tear-shaped garden plot, about the length of a badminton court, lay between Hermon School and the main building. Surrounded by a low wall and featuring a central fountain, it had become dry and overgrown with hibiscus plants. Although the hips made excellent jam, I proposed that, after picking the buds and sending them to the kitchen, we dug up the whole area to start again from scratch.

By ten o'clock the land, apart from the end adjacent to the bungalow, had been cleared. An abundance of bougainvillea, white, pink, yellow and purple, cascaded from the roof, over the supporting archway, into the garden.

'That *must* stay,' instructed Jennie.

I assumed that Esther would buy the plants over the next few weeks. Like mother, like daughter, however, she decided that there was no time like the present.

'We'll visit a nursery.'

'When?'

'Today. Now!'

Within the hour we were driving along a stretch of the national highway flanked on both sides by acres of young plants, shrubs and trees.

'This is incredible,' I commented, dazzled by the gigantic patchwork of colour spread before us. 'Where are we?'

'Kadiyapulanka. Its nurseries are famous throughout India.'

'They go on for ever!'

'Yes, they extend for about ten kilometres.'

Although the area contained over 600 nurseries, Esther knew exactly which one to head for. With every conceivable plant on show, we were spoilt for choice.

'Perhaps we should limit ourselves to a few varieties?' I suggested, concerned that maintenance should be kept to a minimum.

'Good idea, such as?'

'I don't know what you call them here!'

'One of the gardeners will tell us.' She called over a young man.

'What's this one?' I asked, indicating a plant that resembled what I know as Joseph's Coat.

'Croton,' replied the gardener.

'Right, we'll take eight of those. And that?' pointing to a different shrub with sharp, yellow leaves.

'Croton.'

'But the other…'

'Also croton, sir.'

'OK then, a dozen of those. They'll work well as borders. And this?'

'Croton.'

I looked at Esther. She shrugged. 'Obviously croton has many kinds!'

We proceeded to make the rest of our selection in this fashion, adding roses, jasmine and a bright red ball of fiery blooms, a "flaming sphere", to the display. I was beginning to visualise how the garden might look.

Later in the afternoon Esther arranged for a vehicle to transport the plants back. There was no room for us.

'We'll take the bus,' she declared.

As we were about to leave I spotted an attractive fir that looked like a Christmas tree. 'What's that one called?'

'Christmas tree.'

'OK. Throw it on the truck!'

I was dumbfounded. Standing with the girls outside the main building at dusk, I thought the sky was being ripped apart. With a tremendous crack a large object plummeted directly from above, whistling past my face like a bullet. It fell no further than eighteen inches from my nose.

One of the girls, Rama Lakshme, immediately slumped to the ground. Struck on the head, she was out cold.

A strangled wail perforated the air.

Tears started to flow uncontrollably.

Shoulders rose and fell in anguish.

"Death by coconut" is not uncommon in South India.

A few of the girls remained remarkably calm, in shock as much as anything. I ran inside to grab a towel and water. By the time I had returned, Esther was astride her scooter with Rama Lakshme sandwiched between her and Sharon, the hostel matron.

They sped off to the hospital in Nidadavole. There was no call-out emergency service.

I went to see Jennie. 'What should I do?'

She looked remarkably calm. 'Stay with the girls and pray,' she advised.

I've never seen people fall to their knees so quickly. Although I couldn't understand their low-pitched murmurs, the magnitude of their fervour astonished me.

They continued, heads bowed, bodies rocking, lips quivering.

After an hour or so, Jane Shirley, Esther's daughter, rushed in.

'Mother has just called from the hospital. Rama Lakshme is conscious! The doctors say is OK,' she reported excitedly. 'She is on a saline drip and will stay for two or three days observation.'

Heads raised, the colour slowly returned to the girls' cheeks and their quiet sobbing petered out. I even saw a few smiles.

Raju later split open the coconut. Curiously it was empty. The fruit would have been very much heavier had it contained milk. The outcome, very different.

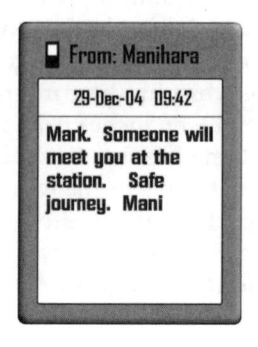

> **From: Manihara**
> 29-Dec-04 09:42
> Mark. Someone will meet you at the station. Safe journey. Mani

My final day was devoted to laying out the shrubs for Narendra, one of Rajus's sons, to plant. He had been assigned the role of chief gardener.

'I would like straight lines,' Jennie had requested. Consequently, I divided the garden into segments with orderly borders and bursts of colour in the centre of each. That was the theory.

'They will need to be planted and watered urgently,' I explained to Narendra. 'Every day it is getting hotter!'

'Yes, sir!'

During the course of the afternoon I was distracted by a family of sleek dark-faced, langur monkeys amusing themselves in the girls' playground, up and down the slide, in and out of the tree house. Behaving like mischievous children, one youngster even sat on the swing as an adult pushed it back and forth. Living on a diet of leaves, flowers and fruit, these creatures were regarded as pests, wreaking damage and havoc in trees and roofs. For me they were a novelty.

'Uncle, funny!' I recognised the giggles.

'School finished, Lakshme?'

'Yez, Uncle.'

She had been watching me watching the monkeys.

'Monkeys, England, no,' I tried to explain, pointing and shaking my head.

'Monkeys bad,' Lakshme replied. She pulled a face. 'Tomorrow leave?'

'Yes.'

'Leaving bad.'

'I know. One day, I come back.'

'Yez, Uncle.' She paused, looking at the yellow-leafed plant I was about to dig into the ground. 'Flower, beautiful.'

'Yes. Name, croton,' I said.

'I help you.'

Although we didn't talk much further, Lakshme spent the rest of the afternoon carrying plants back and forth, positioning them where I indicated and gently patting the dry soil after Narendra had dug them in. By the time the evening bell rang, the garden was shaped with lines of budding shrubs. Now all they required was water and careful nurture. The Hebron garden would soon be blooming.

***

After dinner, Jennie, Esther and I sat chatting in the front room. The sultry atmosphere had encouraged the mosquitoes out in force. Despite my thick coating of Odomos,

India's favourite repellent, they were diving hungrily at every piece of exposed flesh.

'Tomorrow you are going to Vijayawada?' asked Esther.

'That's right.'

'You're leaving already!' said Jennie, wistfully.

'I have plans to visit SKCV, a project for street kids.'

'How many children live there?'

'Over two hundred, I think, but I don't know much about it. I met Manihara for the first time last year when he came over to the UK for SKCV's twentieth anniversary celebrations. My mother has known him since he was a little boy, though. She lived next door to his family in Norwich and used to baby sit for him. His name was Matthew then.'

'And he set up the project?' asked Jennie.

'Yes. He told me that he ran away from home when he was a teenager and lived on the streets of Europe. He then had the opportunity to go to America where he worked in the movie industry. Eventually he travelled to India…'

'Hollywood to Bollywood!' Esther joked.

'Not quite! He was struck by the number of children living rough, particularly on the railway stations. He lived in Mumbai for a while in the early eighties and opened up his home, just a small room, to the young people there.

'Then he moved to Pune and rented a house for about twenty boys. That's where he met his wife, Bhakti. After a while the mayor of Vijayawada heard about SKCV and invited Manihara to relocate to Andhra Pradesh. Apparently there was no organisation in the entire coastal region helping street children.'

The night breeze delicately fingered the palm fronds like a light shower of rainfall, pitter-patter, interspersed by the occasional gust of wind.

'What will you do there?' asked Jennie.

'Not sure. They run a volunteer programme but, as I only intend to stay a few weeks, I think I'll wait till I arrive,' I replied. Mani was adamant that I visited when he discovered I was coming to India, even though he's not been in the best of health recently.'

'Oh?'

'He has had problems with his hip. He may need an operation.'

'Dear me.' Jennie's warm face creased into a frown.

'It's weird, really, because my only connections with India are here and SKCV. When I was planning my trip and checked the map, I was amazed to see how close they are.'

'It was meant to be!' laughed Esther.

'Who knows? But I'm here now and just about to achieve my next goal.'

'You promise to come back and see us?' asked Jennie, seriously. 'You must make this the last place you visit before leaving India.'

'I will do my best,' I replied, choosing my words carefully. I was learning not to make promises; people were inclined to take me at my word. But I had already decided, even if it meant travelling the length of the land, I would do everything I could to visit Hebron again before returning to the UK.

'If I do, I want to see you walking!'

Jennie's eyes danced. 'We'll see!'

3
Festive Road

An estimated 22,000 children live on the streets of Vijayawada

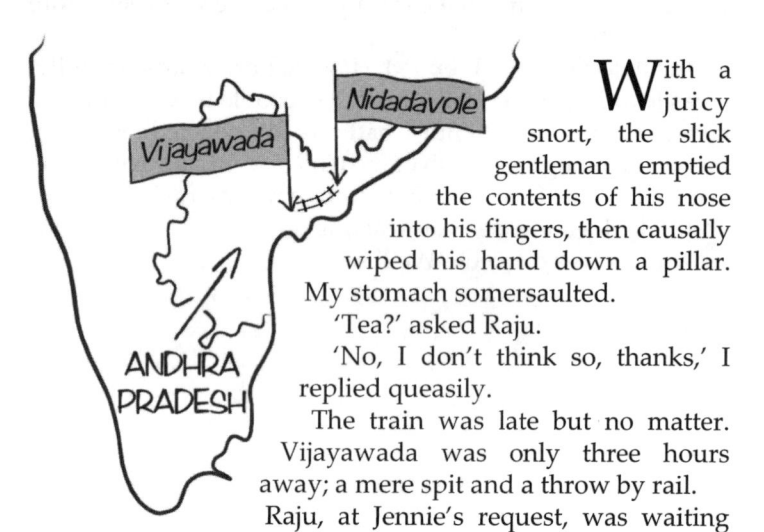

With a juicy snort, the slick gentleman emptied the contents of his nose into his fingers, then causally wiped his hand down a pillar. My stomach somersaulted.

'Tea?' asked Raju.

'No, I don't think so, thanks,' I replied queasily.

The train was late but no matter. Vijayawada was only three hours away; a mere spit and a throw by rail.

Raju, at Jennie's request, was waiting patiently with me on the platform in the mid-afternoon sun. Two frisky children, a cutesy girl and her younger brother, chased each other around our ankles until the boy tripped over and burst into tears. His mother rolled her eyes.

'Tomorrow evening New Year,' said Raju.
'Big parties?'
'For many. Firecrackers, music, dancing.'
'You'll dance?'
'Raju laughed. 'I sleep!'

Not me; an early night wasn't on my itinerary. Having experienced my first Indian Christmas at Hebron, I was looking forward to celebrating New Year, SKCV-style.

Shortly following a garbled announcement, the train rolled in. Raju and I parted company.

'Happy journey!' he said, releasing my hand from a firm shake.

'Thank you, Raju. Happy New Year!'

Although the Second Class compartment was crowded, I managed to find a seat. It was unnecessary to make an advance reservation with this class of travel, but Raju, again at Jennie's bidding, had cycled to the station earlier that morning to buy my ticket. The carriage, though more cramped than the air-conditioned sleeper in which I'd travelled before Christmas, was undoubtedly more entertaining. Included in the price was a non-stop rolling cabaret show: a continual parade of *pakoda*, cutlet, coffee and tea sellers, beggars, singers and dancers.

'IN-RAH-BAH, IN-RAH-BAH, TEEEEEEEEE-EEEEEE!' chanted a young man as he carried an urn of sweet, milky tea through the carriage.

'KOR-FEE, KOR-FEE!' cried his colleague.

'CUTLET, CHUTNEY, CUTLET, CHUTNEY!' drifted through the open doors of the next compartment.

Additional on-board distractions were provided courtesy of Babu, a portly inebriated chap seated opposite me. Reclining on the wooden-slatted bench, he managed to soak both the floor and my rucksack with an explosive bottle of mineral water.

'Sorry, sorry, sir. I am so-so sorry.'

A few minutes later his can of orange fizz jettisoned juice all down his white dhoti.

'They are very happy – hic – bubbles,' he giggled.

Babu was travelling with his brother-in-law. He narrated the tragic tale of his sister who had recently experienced problems with her knees.

'The doctor was administering the wrong medication. She expired a few days later,' he lamented. 'All the family are very grieving.'

'I'm sorry to hear that,' I said sympathetically.

'Actually that was last week,' he concluded with a twinkle in his eye. 'Tomorrow I am assisting my bereaved brother-in-law', the woefully embarrassed gentleman sitting beside him, 'in finding a new good wife!'

Exhausted by his anecdote, Babu was soon asleep.

I feigned forty winks some of the journey, partly to ignore a ragged waif who persistently poked and slapped my arm for several minutes. It developed into a battle of wills.

'Ji! Ji!' her voice bleated. Jab, jab, nagged her finger. *Go away*, I wished. But she wouldn't.

Conceding defeat, I opened my eyes. Her reward: one silver coin deposited in the palm of her grubby, needy hand.

※

The train deposited me safely in Vijayawada from where, the next afternoon, I travelled to Prema Vihar Village in one of SKCV's big yellow buses. Fuelled by the animated singing and joking of a dozen high-spirited lads, the vehicle rocked and rolled through the city's chaotic streets. As we entered the village gates, I saw boys working industriously everywhere: stringing coloured lights between bushes and trees, sweeping the grounds, tidying their rooms and preparing food. The air zinged with expectation.

Colloquially called "the village", Prema Vihar was, in effect, a community comprised almost exclusively of 150 boys and young men committed to putting life on the streets behind them. Situated on the banks of the River Krishna, its extensive grounds, containing accommodation for sleeping, eating, teaching, working and relaxation, provided a productive and safe environment away from the hassle and pressures of the city eight kilometres away.

'Come, I show you my garden,' urged little Bashir, bouncing with enthusiasm as he grabbed my hand. 'I'm growing carrots and gourds.'

A strong arm enveloped my shoulders: 'You must see the cowshed where I work,' insisted Chenti, an older lad.

'And our rooms!' said Sunil, embracing my waist.

Surrounded by an entourage of eager boys, I was being tugged in all directions.

'Whoah! There's plenty of time before midnight!'

'Brother, come!'

First stop, then, Chenti's cow shed. In front of an open-sided, corrugated-roofed barn ran a double row of troughs from which a number of large beasts and smaller calves were feeding. My nostrils swelled with the glorious whiff of dung as the ground squidged beneath my spattered sandals. I had often entertained the notion of becoming a farmer when I was a child. I suspect, though, that I was more in love with the idea than the reality. The brown sludge and smell reminded me why.

'I am waking at five for milking,' said Chenti. 'We drink buttermilk with most meals. Very good for body.'

'How many cows are there?'

Forty-eight, but more are coming.' He indicated a bulky creature who looked as if she could go into labour at any moment. 'You want milking?'

Looking bemusedly at her dangly teats, I was unsure where I'd begin. 'Perhaps another time.'

Chenti shook my hand. 'Five o'clock tomorrow morning,' he grinned.

'We'll see!' Aged about sixteen, the frame beneath his blue cotton vest was lean and sinewy, the grip of his hand, tough. I could imagine encountering him on the street and feeling intimidated. But the warm glint in his eye and his genial manner belied his physical appearance. In those early days, like many of the SKCV lads, I found Chenti inscrutable.

'My vegetables. Come!' It was Bashir grabbing my hand again, pulling me in the direction of his garden. All the boys were divided into groups and assigned duties such as cleaning, washing and food preparation. Each team was allocated a plot of land on which they cultivated a variety of fruit and vegetables: potatoes, gourds, chillies, spinach, tomatoes and *brinjal*. Some of these crops were eaten in the village, the rest were sold to earn money for the boys. This they managed and saved in their own accounts.

On the way to Bashir's plot, I was introduced to the ducks, rabbits and Anji, the resident monkey, cute from a distance but blessed with a mouthful of vicious incisors. We walked past a large building fronted by carved wooden doors.

'What's in there?' I asked.

'Prayer Hall. Every day we are praying.'

'Hindu Prayers?'

'Yes. We are also having Muslim and Christian boys here. And one Sikh, Vikram. He's my friend.'

Other lads joined us, taking turns to clasp my hand and fold their arms around my neck. Several of them displayed unflagging attention for an hour or so, then disappeared for others to take over, as if, working in shifts, they had assigned an unspoken rota to look after me.

The boys' gardens stretched between the main entrance gate and the school building, a distance of about four hundred metres. Several of them were working on their patches of land, weeding and turning the soil.

'Show me yours, then, Bashir,' I said as he dragged me off the path. 'What did you say you were growing?'

'Carrots,' he grinned proudly. With two of his top teeth missing, he spoke with a slight lisp.

'How old are you?'

He looked at his hands and held up eight fingers. His nails, I noticed, were remarkably clean.

'Hi, brother!' called a young lad who was breaking up the earth with a small metal implement. 'My name is Prakesh.' Then he giggled and pointed at another boy wearing his underpants over his trousers. A tatty piece of red cloth was draped around his neck.

'And I am Superman!' shouted Superman.

'What are you doing, Superman?'

'Digging ground for brinjal. Mmmm, tasty!' Putting his fingers to his lips, he flicked them away as a food connoisseur might praise a particularly delicious dish.

The boys' tour of the village, demonstrating a sense of pride that I found uplifting, continued in a similar vein to that of the Hebron girls a few weeks earlier. Despite having so little materially, they were determined to make the most of every opportunity. An aspect of Indian life was emerging that I had not anticipated.

Unlike the girls, the boys called me "brother", not "uncle", which I preferred. The name indicated an underlying fraternal regard for not just me, but each other.

Another lad wandered up beside me.

'Hello, brother. Would you like to see our rooms?' he asked in perfect English.

'I would love to. What's your name?

'Harish.'

'How long have you lived here, Harish?'

'Four years. It is my home.'

From then on, hardly an hour elapsed without Harish appearing, taking my hand and tagging along beside me. Always cheerful, he had the most enquiring of minds and loved to explain how things worked in the village.

'Mark, where are you from?' He asked.

'England.'

'Is that the same as France?'

'No. But they're near each other.'

He thought for a moment. 'Brother, what is the difference between England and France?'

'Well, Harish, they're two completely different countries.'

'Oh,' he said, laughing at himself. 'I though they were the same place!'

And why shouldn't they be as far as he was concerned? There was less difference between a Frenchman and me than between Harish and a ten-year-old from Delhi.

'Brother, eat!' Before I realised what he was doing, Bashir had re-appeared and popped a small, round object between my lips. Biting it, my mouth was filled with a number of sour pips.

'What was that?' I asked in surprise.

'Berry. Look!' He held out four gooseberry-like fruit in the palm of his hand. 'More?'

'No thanks. You eat,' I replied, slightly apprehensive about what I had just swallowed. 'It was delicious, though.'

He smiled. 'Bye, brother. I swim now,' he said, running towards the river.

In 1998 the River Krishna flooded and washed away the entire village. Within two years, Prema Vihar was rebuilt, including six flood-proof cottages, each with enough space to accommodate 25 boys.

In the weeks before Christmas, the lads had decorated these rooms with artwork worthy of Michelangelo. Hundreds of lovingly crafted newspaper chains hung from each ceiling, so numerous that, en masse, they resembled heavily detailed stonework. With ornate flowery frescoes adorning the walls, each dormitory looked more like a miniature Sistine Chapel than the sleeping quarters of boys from the street.

My reception at SKCV had been overwhelming. Unlike at Hebron, however, I was not the guest of honour. This distinction, thankfully, was reserved for five of the charity's English trustees who, having flown in from Hyderabad, arrived at the village shortly after nine o'clock.

Lavish hospitality is central to Indian culture, frequently demonstrated by exuberant welcome rituals, each guest honoured with a garland of marigolds. Finding such expressions of unmerited acclamation mildly embarrassing both to watch and receive, I was more than happy to merge into the background on this occasion. But not for long.

'Mark! Where've you been hiding?!' Two arms squeezed me in a bear hug; a bushy beard tickled my neck. 'Great to see you.' It was Manihara, founder of SKCV.

'You too, Mani. Actually, I've been here a few hours.'

'How are your parents?'

'They were fine last time I spoke to them. They send their best wishes.'

Propped up by a walking stick, Manihara looked well. Having met the trustees at the airport, he had arrived with them a few minutes earlier. Next to him stood a serenely-poised lady attired in a white cotton sari embroidered with delicate green leaves.

'This is Bhakti,' said Mani, introducing me to his wife.

'Namaste!' Bringing her palms together, she bowed her head graciously. 'I'm so pleased you have arrived safely. This is a festive night!'

'I'm looking forward to the celebrations!'

'Anand is about somewhere,' Bhakti said, looking around. 'Ah, over there,' she pointed to a lean twelve year old laughing with a group of other lads. Anandamoya was Bhakti and Mani's adopted son.

Though I had already discovered how much Indians enjoyed their festivities, I completely underestimated the extent to which the SKCV boys loved to party. As dusk fell, the lights hanging throughout the village flashed into life and music filled the air. Moving with energy and passion in a phenomenal programme of dance, the young men performed scenes from the movies as well as more traditional routines.

Choreographing the dances themselves, they had also designed and stitched several stylish changes of costumes. The audience erupted wildly when, dressed in plum-sequinned shirts and ivory pyjamas, the lads cut loose to a track from the blockbuster *Dil Chahta Hai*.

Close to midnight, the sultry atmosphere bulged with exploding firecrackers, pumping music and glistening bodies. Lord Krishna gazed on approvingly from his watery banks. He may even have had a little dance himself.

I felt a tug at my hand. Looking down, I spotted the whites of Harish's eyes gleaming up at me.

'Happy New Year, brother!' he shouted over the joyful commotion.

'And to you too, Harish!'

> **To:** Friends' Group 1
> **Subject:** Indian Adventures
>
> Dear all,
> Having promised to keep in touch, this is my first opportunity to find the technology to make it happen. I'm writing on 1 January but do not know when this might reach you, if ever.
> Thanks to all who've been asking after my safety. I was a few miles inland when the tsunami struck last week. It has been difficult to follow events despite being so close, but I am aware of the mass devastation. I'm not sure how I can help...
> ...Appropriate words do not come easily to describe the last month. My experiences have been many and varied; each day I wake not knowing what may happen from one moment to the next. Priorities have shifted entirely. There's a man walking down the street selling hot water. Tempting - not had any for five days.
> I wish you a very Happy New Year! Will try and write again soon.
> Mark

To call it an Internet Café might be over-generous, but I found a small shop near my lodgings that housed three serviceable computers in a cramped and sweaty back room. Maintaining a dialup connection for any length of time, however, was another matter.

Eventually, between a power cut, a computer crash and four losses of connection, I managed to make brief contact with the rest of the world. For the sum of ten rupees an hour, about eight pence, I couldn't complain.

I was staying in the medical quarter of Vijayawada at the home of Doctor Shanker, former mayor and an SKCV trustee.

It seemed that shops and public services in many cities were clustered around a particular retail theme. In Delhi, for example, I came across entire streets of stores trading in fabric, jewellery or, in one area, a whole row of shops selling Singer sewing machines. How they maintained a steady business was anyone's guess.

Vijayawada was no exception. Exploring the neighbourhood, I discovered that, around the corner from the Shanker's house, stood the SUPER SPECIALITY DENTAL CENTRE. Its colourful sign made the business of tooth extraction sound like a tantalising menu item. Numerous surgeries lined the same road, each specialising in alliterative ailments: the CHEST AND CHILD CLINIC, the LABORATORY FOR PAIN AND PARALYSIS and the DIARRHOEA AND DYSENTERY DISPENSARY.

The street also contained several chemists, a hotel, two bakers, and a few general stores. By the side of the road, various carts peddled fresh, deep-fried chillies and pakodas and women crouched with baskets of oranges and bananas.

On the corner of the main road stood the WINE SHOP, a seedy-looking establishment fronted by a metal grill through which men exchanged rupee notes for bottles wrapped in brown paper bags. It was possible to purchase most forms of alcohol from this outlet, cheap whisky and beer being the most popular, with one notable exception. The WINE SHOP didn't sell wine. Nor, it seemed, did any other wine shop throughout the land.

Dr and Mrs Shanker's spaciously gloomy house was located in a lane just off this street. It was a large concrete building surrounded by a tree-lined courtyard garden that prevented most of the sunlight from entering the ground floor windows. My bright and airy room, however, was situated on the first floor, accessed by an outside staircase. It was comfortable but functional. I had my own bathroom, containing a shower, but no hot water.

Because the SKCV village lay eight hot and dusty kilometres from the city centre, I soon got into the habit of picking up an auto rickshaw each morning from outside the house. It was the quickest form of transport that dodged the anarchic traffic. Negotiating the fare, however, was always a chore. As far as the drivers were concerned, rupees were tattooed across my forehead.

'SKCV Prema Vihar Village, please.'

A quizzical look...

' Near Bhavanipuram Durga. Temple. Yes?'

...invariably flicked to a look of recognition.

'How much?' I had got into the habit of confirming the fare before every trip.

'Eighty rupees.'

'Come on! I paid twenty-five yesterday.' I hadn't, but I knew that was closer to the going rate for locals. I was prepared to trade marginally on my skin colour.

'Sixty.'

'Thirty.'

'Fifty.'

I walked away.

'OK, sir, forty.'

'Thirty-five.'

A wobble of the head, interpreted as "yes".

'Let's go.'

Everyday the same. Occasionally I negotiated thirty rupees, sometimes, when the hassle and the heat were too much, I paid fifty.

The greatest challenge, though, came after dark when the noise from the street below my bedroom window raged relentlessly.

'**CHARLEE CHAI! CHARLEE CHAI!**' Touting street vendors; tooting autos; howling dogs; stick-tapping, whistle-blowing security guards - all cumulatively added to the aural cacophony of the night and my accruing sleep deficit.

'What do you think of our village then?'

It was the first time since my arrival that Manihara and I had found the opportunity to chat. What with the New Year celebrations and the trustees visiting from England, the last few days had rushed by.

'I'm astounded.'

He smiled assuredly. 'I thought you might be. The boys have really made it their own.'

Mani had just returned from a meeting at SKCV's offices in the city. Looking tired, he lowered himself into a wicker armchair with a grimace. He had not enjoyed good health in recent years and, due to avascular necrosis in both hip joints, endured continuous pain. One hip had been replaced and he awaited surgery on the other. As he was unable to drive, he relied on Vamsi, his driver, to get him from A to B.

Whenever Mani talked about the boys, however, the mouth beneath his greying beard relaxed and the stress visibly fell from his face.

We were sitting in the main lounge of the village, situated in a building that also contained two bedrooms, two bathrooms and a kitchen. Before moving to another property one kilometre away, this was Manihara and Bhakti's home. Two ceiling fans circulated a welcome flow of air around the spacious room comfortably furnished with a few armchairs and a lengthy sofa. A number of photographs hung on the wall. One in particular caught my eye, a broodingly handsome portrait of Amitabh Bachchan, India's most famous actor.

'Amitabh's a great supporter of SKCV,' Mani told me. 'He visited us a few years back and was very impressed.'

'I'm not surprised – I am too!' What amazed me most was the boys' self-discipline. Whenever a bell rang at frequent intervals throughout the day, the boys ran from all directions to assemble in six straight lines outside the dining hall. Usually no adult staff member was present. Roll call completed, they continued with their assigned tasks for the day, cleaning, sweeping, washing, without shirking or complaint.

'That's because they want to be here,' said Mani. 'Nothing compels them to stay. They're free to leave whenever they want.'

'And do they?'

'One or two maybe, usually because they miss their families. If they want to return home, we encourage them to do so.'

'How do they end up on the streets in the first place?' I enquired.

'They've often run away or been kicked out by their parents or step-parents,' Mani replied. 'Some kids are abused or get involved in family conflicts, but they're usually problems beyond their control.'

'Such as?'

'Their father might be unemployed or an alcoholic who vents his frustration on his children. When they reach the point where they've had enough, they run off. Some are abandoned or physically thrown out. Other kids leave of their own accord, often lured to the city by glamorous media images they see in magazines and the movies.'

'Do they think life's going to be better there than at home?' I asked.

'Yes,' replied Mani, 'or they just want the chance to go to school.'

'And they don't get that at home?'

'Not always. But neither do they find it on the streets. Their dreams are usually squashed out of them.'

'What's getting squashed?' Turning my head, I saw Sudhama, KP and Vijay enter the room on a wave of warm air. Sudhama, SKCV's General Manager was one of the first boys to live in the village many years ago. KP, Krisha Prasad, ran the night shelter and lived with his wife, Suvarna, and their two children in rooms at the top of Santosh Bhavan, SKCV's city base. Sudhama, too, was married. He and his wife, Pavani, shared one of the bedrooms in the building in which we were sitting.

Vijay, a tall young man with a confident smile, was slightly younger than the other two. He was Head of Handicrafts in the school.

'I was just talking to Mark about how the boys end up on the streets. These guys will tell you what it's like,' Mani said, turning back to me. 'They've all been there.'

'Excuse me a moment, Pitaji,' said Sudhama. I had noticed that everyone, including the older boys and staff, affectionately called Manihara and Bhakti *Pitaji* and *Mataji*, father and mother. 'I've taken the trustees to Doctor Shanker's house and he's giving them lunch. He'll send them back when he's finished with them.'

'They'll probably need a rest, then!' Mani joked.

I knew exactly what he meant. Though in his twilight years, Dr Shanker, my host, possessed the boundless energy of a lively toddler. Just five minutes in his company proved exhausting. Only that morning I had been party to a simultaneous four-way dialogue between his landline, cell phone and long-suffering wife. Multi-tasker extraordinaire, Dr Shanker was one of SKCV's most loyal champions.

'So what brought you to SKCV?' I asked KP as he settled into an armchair.

'Pitaji found me. I ran away from home and had been living in the station since a long time. That was over ten years ago.'

'KP now has a degree in sociology,' added Mani, 'and is studying for a masters in applied psychology.'

'Actually I am wanting to be more involved in counselling work,' said KP earnestly.

'Many of the boys who came to SKCV years ago now have professional qualifications,' said Mani. 'Some, like these three, work as teachers and managers for the organisation. We recognise and nurture individual talent. The boys are encouraged to pursue a wide range of interests and college or vocational training.'

'How about you, Sudhama?' I asked.

'My mother died when I was young. My stepmother kicked me out at age eight. I jumped on a train and ended up in Vijayawada.'

'It's very common for kids to travel between cities by train,' explained Mani. 'They climb onboard unnoticed and stay until they reach somewhere that appeals. Many come to Vijayawada because the station is so large.'

Hearing a sudden clunk overhead I looked up to see the ceiling fan falter.

'Current gone,' said Vijay standing up. 'I go and come.'

'Stay still!' exclaimed Mani. 'What's to do? It'll be back soon.'

Vijay nodded obediently and sat down again.

'How many kids live on the streets here?' I asked Mani.

'About twenty-two thousand…'

'What!'

'…eighty per cent of whom are boys. Over eleven million children live on the streets throughout India.'

'I can't believe it's that many. How do they manage to survive?'

'Oh, the boys manage, but it's tough. Life for girls, however, is even more precarious.'

'Why?'

'They're more vulnerable and harder to trace. Within hours of leaving home, for example, girls as young as eight are enticed into prostitution on the false promise that they could earn a good wage. Many are put on trains and sent to the bigger cities, never to be seen again. Often they die from AIDS-related problems.

'Children contribute to more than twenty per cent of India's GNP,' he continued. 'Street kids make up a considerable proportion of that figure.'

'How?'

'Ask the boys who've been there!'

I turned to Sudama and KP.

'Selling newspapers and flowers, rag picking,' started KP, 'cleaning…'

'Carrying bags, pick-pocketing,' interjected Sudhama. 'Like me.'

'Begging?'

'You've noticed, *nahi*?' laughed KP.

'They seem to be everywhere: outside the station, bus stops, bazaars. I've often seen kids hanging around in small gangs,' I said.

'Yes, you rarely see them on their own. Safety in numbers,' said Mani.

'Where do they get food?'

'Stealing from the street sellers or hunting for scraps in dustbins at the back of restaurants. Begging provides a few coins, but most people tend to ignore them.'

'And sleep?'

'On pavements, under bridges, wherever they can find, really. The station is a very popular place. It provides shelter and the opportunity for casual work: luggage carrying, that kind of thing.'

'Or, of course, there's SKCV!' said KP.

'That's quite a set-up you have there.' I had briefly visited Santosh Bhavan, SKCV's city base, the evening I arrived in Vijayawada.

'Yes, on three floors we are having administrative offices, vocational workshops and the night shelter.'

'Also the day centre for boys still living on the streets,' added Vijay.

'Santosh Bhavan was our first building,' said Mani. 'We constructed it on land donated by the Municipal Corporation. It can accommodate up to eighty boys a night. We also operate a separate residential centre, Bala Prema, for the girls. That sleeps up to sixty, with day care provision for many others.'

'The lads at Santosh Bhavan greeted me like a long-lost brother when I arrived, even though they'd never seen me before!'

'There you go,' Mani said, in a tone implying that he wasn't surprised.

'Two guys were particularly friendly but their eyes were unfocused. Wild, almost.'

'Possibly glue,' said KP. 'It's a problem.'

'They are sniffing it to escape,' said Sudhama.

'Of course, it is not working,' continued KP. 'It's a quick fix. So we are offering counselling and assistance to really help kids get off the streets. Sometimes they stay for a few days. Actually, they are wanting to get sorted but then they are returning to the streets.'

'Why?'

'Freedom. Pulling them back, isn't it?' said KP. 'It's addictive, like the glue.'

'That must be very demoralising.'

'Yes, but we do what we can,' said Mani. 'Even a small amount of medical support can help.'

'Is that why you have a hospital?'

'Yes, the health of many street kids is poor,' said Sudhama. 'They are spending so much time outside. You are seeing how dirty the streets are. The air pollution is not helping. This is making them very open to chronic diseases like TB, typhoid, malaria and scabies. I got sick with hepatitis and spent three months in the hospital.'

'What about AIDS and HIV?'

'Generally widespread also,' Sudhama replied. 'And venereal disease.'

'I understood that "free" government medical treatment is supposed to be available in all Indian cities,' I commented.

'Oh yes, like so many things,' replied Mani cynically. 'But the kids are invariably blocked by hostile staff. Some authorities would rather let them die anonymously in the gutter than help. Street kids have always been the invisible members of Indian society. You know, it was not until 1993 that the term "street child" really figured officially. Even today, apart from a poorly-administered "Scheme for Assistance to Street Children" implemented by central government...'

'...and abused by phoney NGOs...' interjected KP.

'there's no other federal support specifically for street children.' The air in the room was beginning to heat up.

'So they're not protected by law either?'

'Far from it. They live in total fear of exploitation by the judicial system. No one takes responsibility for them. No one acts as their voice within society. The kids easily find themselves caught in a vicious circle of arrest, containment and abuse. They run away, are found, locked up... and so the cycle continues.

'Legal representation doesn't exist,' Mani continued, 'and the few occasions when family members are contacted rarely have a positive outcome. Parents, because they are poor, don't want to know.' His face reddening, Mani was becoming quite impassioned. 'Older kids may eventually escape the clutches of the law, only to emerge as hardened criminals at the age of eighteen with total contempt for a society that has implicitly sanctioned such physical and mental abuse.'

Click. The ceiling fans whirred back into life.

'Actually the situation is improved since recent times, Pitaji,' Sudhama suggested calmly, keen, I sensed, to address the balance.

'Fair enough, you're right,' Mani replied. 'Some municipal corporations are now more considerate towards street children. Large numbers of locally-supported programmes exist throughout the country.'

'Like SKCV,' said KP.

'Exactly. But it has taken years of chipping away at the establishment. It's true, though, Government officials, the courts and other legal bureaucracies are much more inclined to listen than they used to be. You know, SKCV was recently designated an official training centre for sensitising the police.'

'How does that work?'

'Officers are invited to spend time with the children to help them appreciate their situation more fully.'

'So, instead of raising a stick, they offer advice?'

'That's the theory.'

At that moment the bell rang. Vijay looked at his watch. 'Lunchtime. Come, Mark! Let's eat with the boys.'

The large dining room reverberated with the hubbub of chattering tongues and clattering plates. Appetising aromas of lightly-roasted coriander, cumin and chilli wafted in from the kitchen at the side.

The boys took turns serving the food, walking around the tables with large pans of rice, dal and vegetables, plenty for everyone. Towards the end of the meal, a jug of warm buttermilk hovered over my plate. Poured onto the empty dishes, the milk was customarily swilled around then lifted to the lips to drink. I put out my hand.

'Mark, you like, no?' asked Harish, sitting between Vijay and me.

'I love it all apart from this stuff,' I replied. This was not quite true, for the flavour and texture of buffalo curd also made me squirm. It tasted like lumpy yoghurt with a tang of farmyard.

'Why?' asked Harish, a white ring staining his mouth. 'It's good for you.'

'I'll take your word for it!' I replied, unconvinced.

Vijay laughed at me.

'Tell me,' I asked him. 'How did you end up living on the streets?'

'I ran away from home.' He paused. 'My mother used to beat me.'

'Oh? How old were you?'

'Nine,' he replied, 'but the problems were lasting many years.'

Although Vijay seemed happy to talk, the noise in the dining hall made conversation difficult.

'Shall we go outside?' I suggested when we'd finished eating. 'I'll see you later, Harish.'

'Yes, brother,' he responded with a milky grin.

Vijay and I wandered down to the river edge and sat on the concrete jetty that stretched into the water. Taking my bandana from my pocket, I wrapped it around my head. The sun, beating intensely through the still afternoon air, danced on the light ripples lapping over the jetty steps.

Two lads crouched at the water's edge washing a bundle of shirts.

Vijay started his story again.

'I was born into a good family. I am the youngest of three sons.'

'How old are your brothers?' I asked.

'Raghava is four years older than me and Chinna, two. Our *varna* is Kshatriyas; we are kings!

'When we were small my father used to run a successful transport company and owned eight lorries. He was earning a good salary. We lived in a large house in Vijayawada with its own courtyard and entrance gate. We were very well-fed and cared for by our mother. She loved to grow flowers and vegetables in the front garden. Friends and relatives came to visit many times. I have happy memories of our house so full of people laughing and enjoying themselves.

'My father's company used to take him to other cities. After several days away, he would return home with small gifts for my brothers and me. Once he came back from Tirumala in the south of Andhra Pradesh with a brightly decorated box. "Look what I have!" he exclaimed. Inside was a feast of golden, sugary *laddu*.

'"Thanks, dad!" we cheered, our chins dripping with syrup.'

'Those sounded like good times,' I commented.

'They were,' Vijay replied. Then his eyes dropped to the ground. 'But when I was five years old, circumstances began to change. The business was in difficulty and my father had started to drink. His problems badly affected him. Slowly, slowly he spent everything. When he was drunk he changed so much.'

'How?' I asked.

'He used to come home at twelve or one o'clock and beat each of us in turn. Every night this happens. I am lying in bed frightened to death. But without drink he loved me so much. If anyone ever hurt me, he could not bear it and he'd go and beat them.

'Life got worse and gradually my father lost the entire business. He was taking so many loans that he needed money to pay off his debts. One night he came home looking sad.

'"Boys," he said, "I am having bad news. We must leave this house."

'My father had sold our family home at a huge loss. Although it was worth five *lakh*, he sold it for only twelve thousand rupees. He separated from my mother and left home. We had no money or anywhere to live.'

'How much is five lakh?' I asked.

'Five hundred thousand rupees,' Vijay replied.

'That's a huge loss,' I commented.

Vijay nodded.

'So what did you do then?'

'We moved to slum area of Vijayawada. We became very poor and rented a tiny, one-roomed house built from asbestos. There was only space for one bed, which we all slept on. Our friends and relatives disappeared. Nobody was coming to visit us anymore.'

'What about your mother?'

'Until that time she was a housewife. All burden of bringing up our family now fell on her. She had to get work. After some time she had a job in a hospital but was finding it difficult. When anyone scolds her, she comes home and is taking out her anger and frustration on me. Maybe because I was youngest and less strong. She ties me with a rope. She hits me and pours hot chilli powder in my eyes.

'"No, mum, no!" I scream in agony. I try to move my head away from her poking fingers. "Stop! You are blinding me."

Vijay paused for a moment, then inhaled deeply. 'Afterwards she cries and comes to hug me dearly. But I was paining so much. I couldn't open my eyes for many hours.

'"Please don't mind me," she used to say, "I am having a problem."'

'So she knew what she was doing?' I asked.

'Yes, yes, but she could not help herself.'

'How long did this go on for?'

Vijay's fingers, fiddling with the ground, gathered a handful of small stones. He threw them, one by one, into the river.

'My mother was treating me badly for two years. Children in the slum areas are often beaten. Neither my mother or father re-married, but it is quite common for one or both parents to be finding another partner and for children to be thrashed by their step-parents. It is different for each child. My brothers were also ill-treated. So was my cousin, Subbu. He was three months older than me. His stepmother was hitting him regularly.

'Up to the age of nine I suffered that life. But eventually I could bear abuse no longer. "Why don't we make plans to run away?" I suggested to Chinna and Subbu one morning.

'"I'm not sure," Subbu replied. He was nervous. "How will we survive?"

'"Vijay is right," said Chinna. "Life is bad here. How would it get any worse? We must leave." After many days we had persuaded Subbu to join us.'

'All three of you ran away?'

'Yes,' Vijay smiled, 'but we don't know how to take care of ourselves. One night we slept on the side of the road. That night only we lost all our clothes. Somebody took them. Morning we don't know what to do. We don't have anything!'

'Subbu was worried. He wanted to go back.

'But I said, "No. We've walked ten kilometres from one side of Vijayawada to the other. We can't be giving up."

'Chinna agreed. "We must go on," he said.

'From then on, though, while two of us slept at night the other kept watch. After a few hours we used to swap around. Staying awake was difficult, but we felt much safer.'

The two boys washing their clothes at the river's edge had worked up a good lather by rubbing a soap bar up and down each shirt. Rings of foaming bubbles floated on the water's surface. When full of soap, each shirt was rolled into a neat bundle and placed on the ground.

'One day a friendly guy approached us. "Come with me and I'll feed you," he promised. "I am in charge of many street children and beggars." We were uneasy because we knew nothing about him, but for two days he looked after us. Then he changed and started to treat us badly. "You must go out and beg," he orders.

'"No," I answer, "you said you would look after us." He beat us.'

'How did you feel?'

'Frightened, betrayed. So we escaped to a suburb of Vijayawada and travelled around for a while before returning to the city. Chinna suggested we try the station. '"We would be safe with other boys the same age as us," he said. And we were, for a while.

'One night, however, we are woken up by loud voices. It is the police. Their heavy boots trample down the platform, kicking our few belongings. "Stealing from passengers is an offence," they bellow. "You must be punished." When they reach us we are all wide awake.

'"What?" I cry. "We have not taken anything."

'"We are just sleeping," says Subbu.

'But they ignore us. Instead they produce long, heavy sticks. So scared, I curl up in a ball, but they strike me violently. On my legs. *Whack*. Across my back. *Smack*.

'"Stop! Please stop!" I hear Chinna pleading as a club is beating down hard on his arm. "What have I done?" The police did not listen to him, or to any of us.

'"Search us!" I beg. "See, we have nothing." Our faces are filthy with dirt and tears, but they only continue to beat us. We were only children but they beat us like criminals.

'After the police had gone, we sat sobbing, huddled with our arms around each other. We did not return to the station for a long time after that night. We were too scared.'

'Where did you go to after the station?' I asked.

'The pavements under building complexes were good places to sleep.'

'What about food?'

'Sometimes we found scraps in rubbish bins. We used to survive several days without eating, although we always tried to get water. Nobody came forward to talk or help. People ignored us. They thought we were lazy bums.

'But we made many friends. We especially enjoyed going to River Krishna...'

'This river?' I asked, indicating the water in front of us.

'Yes, it is running through all of Vijayawada. In the city it is full of rubbish and smells bad but we used to take bath there and play. We used to jump from the bridge into the water. That only made life enjoyable even though it was very dangerous.

'While we were sleeping near the river a bearded man comes to talk to us. "Would you like to go somewhere safe where you can have food and shelter?" He was wearing a cream-coloured kurta and white pyjamas. His voice was soft.

'Chinna, Subbu and I look at each other. We were desperate.

'"But guys," Chinna pulls us away, "remember what we were told when we were younger?"

'"What do you mean?"

'"Foreigners sometimes come here and take away people's eyes and kidneys to sell for cash."

I look at the man again. He seems sympathetic but he has white skin. "Yes, but they were just stories," I reply.

'"And they will steal our money."

'"We don't have any!" But Chinna had made me nervous.

'"We're fine, sir," says Subbu. "We can look after ourselves."

'"OK. If you're sure." He smiled and left us alone.'

The boys, having lathered up all their shirts, unrolled each bundle one at a time. Soggy slaps punctuated the air as they beat the cloth in the water.

'Then what happened?' I asked.

'After some time, we found jobs in a hotel, cleaning pots. We earned about fifteen rupees a day, enough to buy food, and soap to keep our clothes clean. We worked there for six months and then decided to move elsewhere.

'We got a job on a building site washing down the pillars and walls. It stops the concrete from drying too quickly and cracking. We worked hard from seven in the morning until eight o'clock at night. I was in the water all the time and caught a fever.

'When we first started on site, the boss had not told us the money we would earn. He took long, long time to give us wages. We thought we would receive 100 rupees a day but he is only giving us one rupee and fifty *paisas* each.

'"You treat us like rubbish!" Chinna shouts at him. My brother has always a strong temper. I was too weak from my illness to say anything.

'We went back to sleep at the station.'

'Weren't you scared of the police?' I asked.

Vijay wobbled his head. 'Very scared. But I was so, so cold. My brother used some of the money to buy medicine. Both he and Subbu gave me their shirts to wear.'

'Do you know what was wrong with you?'

'I was ill with malaria fever. Since two weeks I was very sick and feeling no better.

'"I am worried about your brother," I hear Subbu say to Chinna. "What shall we do?"

'Chinna is thinking then says "What about that white man who told us about the night shelter?"

'"Can we trust him?" my cousin asks.

'"I know about him," says an older boy, listening to their conversation. "His name is Pitaji. He is a good man."

Other people also told us about SKCV. That was name of the night shelter. It was only a few blocks from the station. Subbu and Chinna could carry me there. We saw the white man again and he helped to look after me.

'What was your first experience of SKCV like?' I asked.

'The people used to care for me so well. After only fifteen days my health had improved.

'"Now you are well, what would you like to do?" Pitaji asked all three of us.

'We told him our background. "I want to study," I said. Before running away from home I had attended a government school and studied up to Third Class. It was now 1993. We had been on the streets for two years and I missed the classroom a lot.

'"You may go to school in the SKCV village if you wish," offered Pitaji.

'"Thank you, sir!" I was thrilled.

'I worked under the shade of the trees with the other boys. It was so hot. I studied many subjects. I was desperate to learn as much as I could to make up for lost time. I particularly enjoyed helping the teachers design games to make the lessons more fun. After school we would swim in cool water of the River Krishna. It was much safer and cleaner than in the city.'

'Were you ever curious about your family?'

'When I was on the streets I had never been tempted to return home, even when I was very sick. But I often was thinking about my mother. Then one day, after we had been at SKCV for about a year, she appeared.'

'Completely unexpectedly?'

'Yes. My uncle had been helping her search for us.'

'What did she say?'

'She said that she'd come to take us home.'

'How did you react?'

'We are surprised and lost for words. "We don't want to go with you." I reply after a while. Subbu had already returned to his family.

'"If you don't come, I will kill myself," she then says.

'Chinna and I look at each other. "We are learning things here and like it," I say. Her threat upset me, but I was determined to stay. Memories of my eyes overflowing with chilli powder and tears haunted me. I could not go back.

'But I did not realise that my mother was serious about taking her own life. She suddenly runs towards the river. With a loud cry, she throws herself in, fully clothed. Just here, where we are sitting.'

'What did you do?'

'I yell so, so loud. '"Quick, someone save her!" Straight away two of the older boys are diving in.

'They pull my mother from the water, kicking and screaming. "Leave me alone!" she shrieks, "I want to die."

'Standing on the river bank dripping wet, she is shaking with anger and shame. Her dark crimson sari is clinging to her frail body. It is a pitiful sight.

'Gradually she calms down. "Please come with me," she begs for a final time.

'"If your sons want to come, they will choose," says one of the boys who had rescued her. She is silent.

'Eventually my mother went away and left us alone. After six months Chinna returned to live with her. I remained.'

'What was it like seeing her again after all that time?' I asked.

'It was bringing thoughts of so much happiness, the good times when I was small. I missed her so much after she had gone. Soon I became so desperate to see her that I ran away. I stayed for two days. I was too scared to return to SKCV so I slept on the streets again. After one week Pitaji saw me.'

'Oh?'

'I felt so embarrassed. But he says: "Vijay, there's no problem. You may come back." So I returned to SKCV. But the picture of my mother and brothers remained in my mind.'

The boys, laughing and singing in their own world, were now rinsing their shirts. Plunging them, one at a time, into the river, they dragged each shirt through the water and then pummelled it vigorously to remove all the soap.

'Did you settle easily back at SKCV?'

'No. After some time, I ran away to my family again!'

'"Why are you here?" my mother asked.

'"Pitaji has given me permission to see you," I lied.

'I visited them three days. Then I became scared my mother would beat me so I left. This was the second time I had run away from SKCV so I was really afraid.'

'What did you do?'

'I hid. But after three days Pitaji finds me. Once more he says: "You know you are welcome to come back."

'I felt torn between my family and SKCV. I didn't know what to do.'

'How old were you by then?'

'Thirteen. I loved my family but feared my mother. SKCV used to give me everything I couldn't receive at home. I had become used to life in the village and had made many friends.

'I decided to return to SKCV. Sometimes, though, my family called by. "It is good to see you," they used to say and that made me happy. On some Sundays I was given permission to visit them.'

'Did you go back to school?'

'Oh, yes! I loved studying,' Vijay laughed. 'In 1998, our tenth maths class took public exam for the first time. No one had been entered before so we didn't know what to do. We wrote our answers on the multiple choice question paper not in the answer book. We all failed! But I retook the exam the following year and passed.

'Then I attended college on the other side of Vijayawada where I got free admission. I studied science and was competent in all the subjects - physics, biology, geology - except chemistry. That I found hard. The teacher was unkind to me. Whenever I am making mistake he forces me to stand on a bench and gives me a big slap in front of all my classmates.

'"You are stupid," he mocks. I was seventeen. Getting beaten in front of the girls made me so mad.'

'I'm not surprised!' I said.

'So I stopped my studies. For fifteen days I used to leave SKCV in the morning and pretend to go to college. But I just stay on the streets. Eventually the principal discovers what I am doing. He complained to Pitaji and I was sent home for one month as a punishment.'

'Then what?'

'After four weeks I returned to my studies and life improved. But not for long. I became very sick; for three months I lay in bed. I became so frustrated and behind with my work that I wanted to quit. I was six months into the course. Pitaji was very understanding and said, "If you wish to stop, you may. And if you wish to learn something else, that is alright."'

'How did that feel?'

'It felt good knowing that Pitaji valued me. It was a great encouragement. So when I was well again, I decided to help in the classroom and the night shelter at SKCV. Slowly, slowly I was learning how to teach and support the other children. I enjoyed sharing my experiences and knowledge with those who had similar stories to mine.

'After two years Pitaji asks me, "Would you like to join The Future Group?"'

'What's that?' I asked.

'It is twelve of the older boys and young men who are helping to run the village democratically. They are deciding its rules and codes of conduct. They support younger children who are in same predicament as they were several years ago. As Pitaji and Mataji know they cannot be around forever, they believe it is very important to train future leaders.'

'That must have been a great honour?'

'Yes. The way the system works is that all other members are asked first. There has to be one hundred per cent agreement before someone may join. Everyone knew me well so I receive a unanimous "Yes!" That makes me very pleased and in 2002 I became a future group member.

'I returned to my studies and started a commerce degree. This was possible, despite the break in my education, because I had achieved over sixty five per cent in my tenth grade exams. I found it hard work. I failed two subjects at the end of first year.'

'But you persevered?' I asked.

'Yes. Morning time I used to go to college. I helped in the SKCV school in the afternoon and worked in the village in the evening. Eventually I completed my studies and graduated with a degree in commerce.'

'Congratulations!'

'Thanks. I felt so proud. At one stage in my life, I was not thinking I would complete Tenth Class.'

'What about your family?' I asked.

A broad grin spread across Vijay's face. 'After many years my father went back to my mother. They are living together again. He is drinking no more but he has TB and cancer. Chinna is caring for him and paying his medical costs. Because he went back home to look after my mother, my brother was unable to complete his education. Instead, he worked hard to earn money for the family and is now an auto rickshaw driver. He is making five hundred rupees a day. He pays three hundred for hire of vehicle and keeps two hundred rupees as wages.

'My eldest brother, Raghava, is living in a separate house with his wife and baby.

'I see my mother every couple of months. Not enough, though. Now she is nice to everybody and loves me so much. She is happy because, although I ran away, I have received an education and did something with my life. I am now Head of Handicrafts at the school and do general administration duties. I am arranging exhibitions and filing entries for the Tenth Class exams.'

'Your parents must be proud of you.'

'I think so. I could have spoiled my life but I didn't. I still am having problems with my sight, though. If I am not wearing my spectacles, my eyes are paining and I get bad, bad headaches. Then I have to take medicine.'

'Do you see your brothers?'

'Yes, I see them often and we are very close. Sometimes they call me on my cell phone and we go to watch a movie.'

'How do you feel when you see other people living on the streets?'

'I try to bring my experiences to them. If I meet children sleeping outside, I stop to have a chat. No pressure. Before I am leaving them, though, I talk about SKCV and suggest they visit the night shelter. But it is just a friendly invitation.

'I do not require a degree to work at SKCV but my academic achievement is giving me a strong feeling of self-worth. I can never give as much as Mataji and Pitaji have done. They are such a wonderful mother and father to us all.' Removing his glasses, Vijay rubbed his left eye and smiled. 'But I do my best. I am receiving so many opportunities because of them.'

The two lads, having wrung out all the water from their shirts, spread them out on the concrete jetty to dry in the sun. Then, scampering bare foot over the hot earth, they raced each other back to their dormitories.

4
Freedom Road

To Buy
- Toothpaste
- Razor blades
- Notebook
- Red wine

'What you doing tonight?' asked Pavan, the art teacher at SKCV's school. He and I had struck up a good friendship; his easy-going nature made him excellent company.

'No plans,' I replied. 'Why?'
'We're going to cinema. Want to come, no?'
'What's the movie?'
'*Shankar Dada MBBS*,' said Pavan proudly.
'I'd love to. Is it any good?'
'Any good?'
Oops.
'It is *best* movie ever. I am seeing it six times. It stars Chiranjeevi, isn't it?'
'Wow, Chirnanjeevi, really?'
'Yes!'
'Who's he?'
'Only the best funny actor in Andhra Pradesh.' Pavan then explained that the movie would last nearly three hours in Telugu, no subtitles. Seeing the enthusiasm wane from my face, he added, 'Don't worry, Mark, I am translating for you.'

Later that evening half a dozen of us walked, hand in hand, down the main road to the cinema. Outside the huge, ugly concrete building, Indian municipal architecture at its best, groups of people stood snacking at the various pakoda, bhaji and chai stalls. The smell of wood smoke, sweat and spices blended gloriously with the night air. We joined the ticket queue.

'How much is it?' I asked.

'Sitting downstairs for five rupees or best seats in balcony for fifteen.'

'Let's go upstairs, shall we? I'll pay.' Pavan's face lit up. Although only pennies, that was a big deal for him.

'Are you going to the cinema much in the UK?' he asked.

'I like to,' I replied, 'but it's very expensive.'

'How many?'

His jaw hit the ground when I told him.

'In India, movies are very popular. We have over fifty cinemas in Vijayawada.'

The auditorium downstairs was packed with over 500 people but the balcony was less busy. We had no problem finding seats. I was amazed at the audience; parents, children, grandparents, couples and teenagers – a wide mix rarely seen in the UK.

Once the lights had dimmed we were treated to an excess of commercials for fast cars and skin-whitening products. The main feature eventually began amid cheers and clapping. The audience participation, however, didn't end at the opening titles; throughout the movie people shouted encouragement at the heroes, booed the villains, laughed uproariously at the comedians and sang raucously along with the production numbers. With six statutory songs, action, comedy, love interest and scenes of gratuitous violence, *Shankar Dada MBBS* was the archetypal Indian movie. For nearly three hours Pavan's warm breath tickled my ear as he whispered a translation of the dialogue.

'This movie wouldn't have been granted a family certificate by the censors in the UK,' I commented to him afterwards.

'Why?'

'It was very bloodthirsty in places.'

'Obviously this is India,' he replied. 'Families visit cinema together. We are having something of everything for keeping each person entertained.'

'But one moment Mr Shankar Dada was laughing and joking and the next he was smashing a broken bottle in a kid's face. That's hardly entertaining,' I pointed out.

'He was not meaning it, yes?'

There was little point in arguing. For such a clean living, predominantly violence-free society it was only natural that brutality seeped out somewhere; better in the movies than in reality.

I gradually became more adventurous in the eating establishments that I frequented outside the village. An extended family of Indian micro-organisms, happily adopted by my stomach, were encouraging me to live more dangerously.

One evening I ventured alone into a hotel bar in the centre of Vijayawada, about twenty minute's walk from my lodgings. I was attracted by the neon sign advertising

TASTY VEG CUISINE

I pushed open the below-street level door into a disappointing utilitarian establishment and sat down at the only vacant table. A few heads turned as the metal chair legs scraped across the stone tiled floor.

'May I see the menu, please?' I asked the elderly waiter who ambled over from the bar lined with many varieties of whisky.

'Sorry sir, no food.'

'But the sign...' I observed hungrily.

'Beer?'

Given his disinterested expression, it was clear that creating a fuss would get me nowhere. 'OK. Thank you,' I conceded not entirely reluctantly.

A few moments later, he re-appeared with a bottle of Kingfisher *and* a small silver dish of raw vegetables. I had misjudged the poor man.

'Complimentary snack, sir. Please be enjoying.'

I stared at the dainty slices of carrot, cucumber and onion. Strong stomach or not, what to do? Raw vegetables broke all the rules.

The stale air, choked by cheap cigarette smoke, rumbled unnervingly with the deep murmur of male voices. Women were conspicuous by their absence. The clientele comprised entirely of men from all walks of life: business, students, older gentlemen huddled in little groups, playing cards and knocking back shots of whisky. One young guy stole a glance over his shoulder to gaze bemusedly at my deliberations over the plate of raw vegetables. Turning back to his friends, his mutters were received with guffaws of laughter and further stares.

Given the culture, this all-male environment was disconcerting but not unexpected. How might they have reacted had I been accompanied by a female friend, assuming she'd been allowed entry in the first place?

The toilet facilities offered a clue: one small closet containing a single urinal. If that didn't communicate male exclusivity, what did? This, after all, was Vijayawada, a sizeable, but parochial, South Indian city in the heart of Andhra Pradesh.

Women + bar = zero.

Throwing caution to the wind I gulped down the raw vegetables and hoped to see another day.

I fell into a routine in the week after New Year, spending time in the mornings with those lads who, for a number of reasons, were not attending school. A few chose not to go. Others, having experienced some sort of trauma, preferred to be alone.

Taking on board a previous conversation with Bhakti, Mani's wife, I kept my presence as low key as possible.

'Some volunteers feel they are having to achieve much,' she told me in her assuredly calm way. 'Straight away they are wanting to teach English and be busy-busy. The boys find that difficult.'

'I'm not really a volunteer - I'm not here long enough!'

'I know, Mark. Actually you're more part of the family. It is the same, though. Just get to know the boys. Spend time with them. That's what they are really wanting.'

Bhakti means "devotion" in Sanskrit. Her placid composure served as a great foil to Manihara's down-to-earth English temperament. Though he'd lived in India for over 25 years, certain matters still provoked a sharp lash of his tongue; inefficiency and time-wasting to name but two. Whenever he bawled, 'Hel-lo-o. I want it done yesterday!' Bhakti would remain unflustered, regardless of whatever it was that needed doing.

On the matter of the boys, she was right. Many of them, bereft of a family, had received little love or consideration on the streets. Having become accustomed to their intense demands for attention, I found that spending time in their company was a pleasure. Given their frequent displays of affection, I often had to remind myself that they came from a background where survival of the fittest was paramount.

As I sat on a wicker chair outside the main building, a couple of lads would often join me for a chat. Although my Telugu had improved *slightly* since Hebron, our mutual understanding was minimal. Through the exchange of numbers and words, they learnt some English and I added to my small stock of Telugu phrases. Two of the boys, Naresh and Surya, who were initially extremely shy and withdrawn, enjoyed writing their names in the small notebook that I always carried with me. I suspect, though, that their patience was tested to the limit, trying to teach me to count.

'Okatee, rendoo, morjew.'

'No, no, no, Mark. Moor-*doo*!' said Surya.

'One, two, three. That's what I said,' I replied. 'Morjew.'

'Moor-*doo*, doo, doo!'

'Free, free, free!' bleated Naresh.

'No. Three. Tongue between your teeth. Th th th.'
And so it continued.

Eventually numbers one to ten were successfully traded in Telugu and English but Naresh and Surya fared much better in the deal. Telugu is not an especially difficult language; its challenge lies in too many similar-sounding words spoken at great speed. I could never quite get my brain around the profusion of *bhagas, bhagus, nalas, nalus, nanus, nanas, navas* and *naras,* employed in any number of combinations.

Naresh, like many of the boys, loved to thumb-wrestle. His hands were wickedly strong for an eleven year old. I soon became quite adept at the game but returned to my lodgings most evenings with sore fingers.

Late each afternoon, on completion of their daily chores, the boys would fling off their clothes, race along the concrete jetty and dive into the River Krishna. Loving the water, they displayed no fear whatsoever.

'Brother, you swimming?'

'I'm not sure.'

'Brother, it's good!'

'Maybe tomorrow?'

Although I harbour a latent fear of water, the boys' persistence eventually wore me down. Before long I was being dive-bombed and underwater rugby-tackled. Swallowing great gulps of the river I laughed, gasped and pretended to enjoy myself.

Drying ourselves in the setting sun one evening, I noticed that several of the older lads wore a length of cord around their abdomens.

'Does this have any purpose?' I asked Vinod, one of the swimmers who had particularly delighted in ducking me in the river.

'Yes, brother, it is Brahman thread. It used to be a sacred thing.' Seeing I needed more information, he added: 'When

Hindu boys are old enough they are coming into their varna at special ceremony.'

'Varna?'

'Meaning "colour". I explain. It is saying in Vedas that humans were created from different body parts of divine Purusha. He was sacrificed by the other gods.'

Vinod started to draw the shape of a human in the dust. 'Brahmins are coming from Purusha's head, Kshatriyas from his arms, Vaishyas from his thighs and Sudras from his feet.'

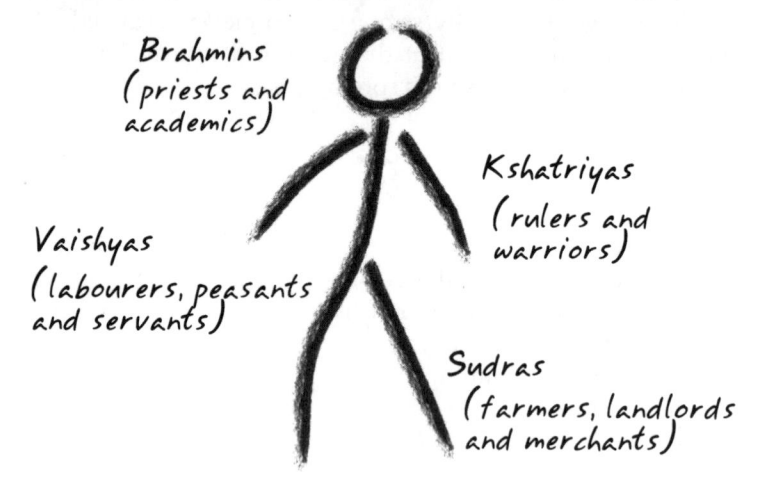

Brahmins (priests and academics)

Kshatriyas (rulers and warriors)

Vaishyas (labourers, peasants and servants)

Sudras (farmers, landlords and merchants)

'We are calling this varna system. Members of top three varnas are "twice born". Many are wearing sacred thread around waist as symbol of age coming.'

'You said the thread *used* to be a sacred thing?'

'Yes, brother. Now we are using it to keep our trousers up!' Thumping the ground, he threw his head back with laughter.

'Brother, what's funny?' asked Sanjeev, one of Vinod's friend, who had just joined us. He was holding something in his hand.

'Please, take!' I held out my palm into which he dropped several raw peanuts.

'Thanks.' The nuts were tough, but sweet. 'Vinod was just telling me about varna. It sounds like the caste system to me.'

Sanjeev sat down. 'Some people calling it caste. But word is misleading, yes?'

'How?'

'Generally in time of Vedas, people were born into four varnas. That is basis of social order since old-old times. Nowadays structure is still there, but it is *jatis*, or sub-groups you could be saying, that is important.'

'I'm confused.'

'That is because varna and jati are same-same, but different! Varna is the hier... you are saying?'

'Hierarchy?'

'Yes the hierarchy in society. And they are dividing into jatis.'

'Every Hindu is belonging to a jati, or community, in India,' said Vinod.

'How many are there?'

'Thousands!'

'Actually at least three thousand.' qualified Sanjeev. 'Jati is meaning "birth". It is social group people are born in. Some jatis are small, others are very big, many, many people.'

'Each jati is linking to a profession. I am knowing a man's jati by his name,' said Vinod. 'You are hearing *Dhobi*? That means washerman.'

'Every jati is making its own rules about jobs, marriage, where to live, relations with other jatis, isn't it?'

'So although the traditional hierarchy still exists,' I asked, 'the original four varna groups are now divided into hundreds of sub-groups?'

'Yes, generally that is correct,' confirmed Sanjeev. 'If you are a Brahmin, you are not having to be a priest. Many Brahmins are chefs and owning restaurants.'

'Why?'

'Because strict Brahmins are only eating food cooked by another Brahmin.'

'How complicated!'

'Wait, brother! I am complicating you more,' grinned Sanjeev. 'Every person is being born into a jati. What I am doing in previous life is making that happen. But not every jati is in the varna system.'

'Because?'

'Actually nearly one quarter of people in India are outside the varna system. Below the Sudras are people having no varna. Their jobs are cleaning streets, burning rubbish, cremating the dead, isn't it?'

'Some are calling name Untouchables,' said Vinod. 'That is insult. Official name is Scheduled Caste.'

'Yes, then there is final group,' said Sanjeev. 'They are calling name *Hijras*. They are singing and dancing at marriage ceremonies. People are hating *and* respecting them.'

'Why?'

'Hijra blessing is very very auspicious,' he said mysteriously.

'It is meaning birth of a son,' said Vinod, looking serious. 'A curse is meaning bad luck.'

With a shriek, he leapt on Sanjeev and put his hands around his friend's neck. The two rolled around in the dust, laughing hysterically.

There's nothing like a last minute invitation to a Hindu marriage. Although I was still dressed in the scruffy T-shirt and shorts that I'd worn all day, Sudhama, SKCV's General Manager, insisted that I accompanied him to his cousin's nuptials one evening.

'It will be something for adding to your list of Indian experiences,' he suggested.

'But my clothes? I am under-dressed.'

'Don't worry, it's not your marriage. Nobody will mind.'

He was right. Not a single person was remotely interested in my attire; I was dressed no more casually than many other men. What made me stand out, as usual, was the colour of my skin. But, by then, I had become used to all the staring.

We arrived at Madhu Kalyanamabapam, Vijayawada's civic wedding hall, at about six o'clock. Near the entrance a small threshing machine-like contraption blew out jasmine petals as people walked by. Two young boys were having great fun feeding it with handfuls of white flowers to shower unsuspecting guests with the sweetly-scented natural confetti.

The wedding hall was an enormous purpose-built civic centre designed specifically for marriages, comfortably accommodating well over a thousand people. Two ornate thrones were positioned beneath a showy floral canopy, ready for occupancy by the bride and groom later in the ceremony. Orange and yellow marigold heads were strewn extravagantly across the platform.

Guests milled around, chatting politely, while young children played hide-and-seek between Uncle's legs and the folds of Auntie's sari. The women were dressed in reds, ochres and shimmering greens. The men were more soberly attired, some sporting suit and tie, others in polo shirts and chinos. There was no sense of urgency. The wedding would happen sometime that evening, but no one really knew for sure.

Towards the back of the hall was another open doorway, near to which the function band performed. I use "perform" in the loosest possible sense. Eight men in shabby red uniforms and pointy hats held musical instruments under their arms and to their lips: drums, whistles, trumpets and clarinets. One elderly fellow dusted his fingers up and down the plastic ivories of a Casio keyboard.

The entire ensemble was rigged up to a mobile sound system consisting of two small speakers precariously balanced on a wobbly shopping trolley. With the volume pumped up disturbingly loud, each member trumped, banged or blew with great abandon, completely oblivious to the equally discordant efforts of his colleagues. The shopping trolley quaked sympathetically and the vastly inadequate speakers throbbed with the most excruciating din imaginable. It was torture.

Just at the point when I thought my brain would implode, Sudhama suggested that we should climb up two floors to the hall where food was being served. Two *miles* up would not have been far enough away from the cacophony below. Even from a distance, it made my efforts on the mandolin appear virtuosic in comparison.

Six narrow, fifty metre-long tables ran the length of the cavernous dining hall, each with chairs positioned neatly down only one side. Every table was covered with newspaper on top of which a long roll of silver disposable tablecloth had been unfurled.

At the far end of the hall, buckets of sambar and dal, pans of rice and plates of *papads*, chapatis and pickles were waiting to be distributed to the hundreds of hungry guests.

Clearly understanding the etiquette, everyone else knew what to expect. Sudhama must have caught the perplexed look in my eye.

'Just watch me and copy,' he advised reassuringly.

So I followed carefully as he picked up his glass of water, poured the contents onto the disposable, dustbin-lid-sized plate, swilled it around and tipped it, with a quick flick of his wrist, onto the floor on the other side of the table. When he had finished, I reverently conducted the same ritual. Pleased with my accomplishment, I sat back and enquired:

'What was the religious significance of that?'

'None,' replied Sudhama. 'It was for washing dirt off the plate before we are eating.'

I then realised why the seats were arranged only down one side. A series of waiters paraded up and down the aisles between the tables dolloping spoonfuls of vegetable dishes onto our plates. It was a culinary conveyer belt. With no cutlery in sight, I tucked into the veg treats. Mixing the sambar and rice with my fingers, I stirred in a pickle or two and scooped the gooey mixture into my mouth. The days of private practice at Hebron ensured that I didn't make a public fool of myself.

I may have cracked the style of Indian eating but keeping up with the pace was another matter.

'Mark, watch out! You must finish!'

Although it felt as if we'd only been eating for a couple of minutes I looked up to see a great wave of disposable tablecloth rolling towards me, gathering up the banquet detritus in its path.

'What's the hurry?'

'More people.'

At the end of the table, some fifty metres in the distance, another cloth was being unfurled as further guests surged into the hall. We were the first of many sittings.

It seemed unusual that we were enjoying the reception before the bride had even arrived, let alone wed. But Sudhama explained that this was purely practical given the sheer number of guests.

After further chit chat and an introduction to the groom, his cousin Das, Sudhama suggested that we leave.

'But we've not seen the wedding yet,' I pointed out rather obviously. I was also secretly hoping that a troupe of Hijras might appear to entertain the guests.

'Oh that won't be happening for hours, possibly very early tomorrow morning.'

'At the auspicious time,' I added knowledgeably. I had learnt that it's common practice for the bride and groom to consult an astrologer to read their charts and specify the pre-determined date and time for their marriage.

So my first participation in a Hindu wedding did not actually include the most important part: the ceremony itself. But I was not too disappointed. I had enjoyed a free dinner and clocked up another experience. Plenty more wedding opportunities lay ahead.

So we left with no sight of the bride. For all I know, the other guests may still be waiting.

The SKCV boys loved to dance. When they discovered that I did it professionally, I was asked to direct the dance programme for a special event, Manihara's birthday.

'I work in the theatre, not dance. It's a different discipline.'

'Yes, but production is same.'

'Hmm.' Apprehensively I agreed. Drawing on my knowledge and experience I gently dropped ideas into the mix, supporting them where I could.

I have never seen a group of dancers learn so speedily. The boys committed all their time and energy into picking up the steps that Nani, the choreographer, put together. He was an incredibly quick thinker, working on his feet to create each dance section by section until every routine was completed.

In soaring mid-day temperatures, the boys toiled like Trojans, swigging copious amounts of water from metal jugs to remain hydrated. They also knew how to rest, collapsing, after lunch, into a huge heap on the floor, embracing, holding hands, using each other as mattresses and pillows. Despite the heat, this was a natural way to relax. The pile of entwined bodies, as endearing as it was enigmatic, was totally alien to my own culture.

Imagine asking a dozen teenage boys in the UK to sit on the floor in a large room. Apart from creating a fuss about not having a chair, I guarantee they would spread themselves as far apart from one another as possible, each young man surrounding himself with an impenetrable bubble, proclaiming: "KEEP OUT OR DIE!"

But India, being so crowded, was a nation of people accustomed to living in close proximity with one another. They did not inhabit the defensive cocoon that we call personal space. Rules of non-engagement did not apply.

The three-hour long dance programme went down a storm. As it started, Nani thrust a microphone into my hand.

'Mark, please also be compering for us,' he asked.

'But I…'

No time to protest. With my scant command of Telugu stretched to its limits, I repeated *'Shankar Dada MBBS'* over and over to woops of delight from the audience.

Hooray for Tollywood!

Then, one day, it happened.

The day complacency picked me up, chomped on my naivety and spat me into the gutter.

The day the world spun.

I was on my way to buy breakfast at a café in the centre of town, when...

'Hey! What the...?!'

With the ferocity of wild monkeys, four scrawny creatures leapt through the air. Tugging determinedly at the canvas bag strapped across my shoulder, they knew exactly what they wanted. Fistfuls of grubby fingers flayed out, their sharp nails drawing blood as they ripped into my right arm like razors. They had seen what was in my hand.

'Chocolates. GIVE!'

Released from my grip by a vicious pinch, the handful of cellophane-coated sweets, the chocolates, scattered onto the pavement. Swooping to the ground, my assailants fell into a frenzied scrabble for their prize: half a dozen jewels glistening in the dust. Two scavenging paws grabbed a sweet simultaneously, wrestling with the slick emerald wrapping as if it contained the last pleasure on earth.

They'd seemed friendly enough a few moments earlier: a gang of scruffy, but happy, seven-year-old boys.

Seven-year-old boys.

Bare-foot and naked to the waist, each kid wore a grubby pair of grey trousers, ripped at the knees. As they'd played contentedly by the roadside, the sight of my hand reaching into the bag must have triggered a sixth sense. Eyes widening, noses twitching, they'd seized their chance the instant I stopped to offered them a sweet.

Maybe I was being foolish, I don't know. I had heard somewhere that carrying a handful of "chocolates" in lieu of coins was a good idea. I'm not so sure.

'Auto, sir?'

A yellow auto rickshaw crawled up beside me.

'No thanks.'

'Sir, yes!'

'I don't want. No!'

'No?'

'NO!!'

The driver wobbled his head then scooted off, spewing a puff of exhaust fumes in my face.

Leaving the boys to squabble on the pavement, I continued walking. After a safe distance, I paused, pulled my handkerchief from my trouser pocket and wiped the blood from the patch of skin gouged out of my arm. I spat on my fingers, rubbed the saliva into the wound, winced, and wrapped the handkerchief tight around the cut.

Quickening my pace, I sidestepped the limbless lad twitching prostrate in the dirt, his claw of disfigured fingers rattling a battered can. I stared straight through the mumbling old man, trundling his wilting wife in a makeshift cart. Dodging between a truck and a cow, I blinked at the mother repairing her dilapidated shelter on the traffic island, a rag-bundled baby hitched to her waist.

Back on the pavement, my foot skidded in a puddle. A shot of stale urine stung my nostrils. I gagged. Buses honked, street-sellers hollered, children wailed. I crossed the river, a filmy brew of floating debris, distracted momentarily by the four bookstands that stood on the corner, stacked high with volumes of medical, ethical and technical texts.

The sun's rays, bouncing off the concrete, seared my gaze. Squinting, I fumbled in my bag for my shades. In the stark, suffocating daylight, normality had resumed.

After four weeks, *all this* had become normal. Even my raw encounter with the street kids felt unexpectedly typical.

Yet something had happened to me. Lakshme and the girls at Hebron had charmed my soul; the SKCV boys had captivated my spirit. This raw street encounter caught me off-guard. I was relaxed. I really thought I knew what I was doing.

When I say the world spun, or more precisely *my* world, I mean exactly that. Yes, I physically reeled. In terms of the bigger picture, though, the episode represented one of life's seminal moments; past, present and future converging in one juncture in time.

Vijayawada was a far cry from home, Basingstoke, politely savaged by critics as the epitome of provincial boringness. The same could hardly be said about this place.

'I've been to India.'

'Oh? What did you think of it?'

'Quite pleasant, I suppose.'

I don't think so. India does things to people. Like me, just then.

It was not the boys' violence that perturbed me as much as my own naivety; I should have known better. The humiliation pained more than the torn flesh.

Had I quit my job, sold my house and travelled 5,000 miles from home for this? Gutted, shamed, all for the sake of a few miserable boiled sweets?

The *Shree Laksmi Vilas Modern Café* is situated in the main garment quarter of Vijayawada. Despite the street's usual busyness, the place was fairly empty. I found a quiet table in the shadows and gave my order, masala dosa and coffee, to the waiter.

There was a smell. I sniffed. A sharp tang: the urine-stenched puddle. My foot was still damp. *The smell* was me.

Preoccupied, I didn't notice a slight, middle-aged man approach my table.

'May I?' he asked softly, pulling back a chair.

'Please,' I replied distractedly.

He looked at me. 'You are European?'

I reluctantly returned his gaze. 'English,' I replied. Although he clearly meant no harm, I felt peeved that, of all the *empty* tables in the restaurant, he should sit at mine.

'I have been to England many times. I studied at Oxford.'

'It has many beautiful buildings,' I commented blandly. Oxford seemed so remote.

'You know it?'

'It's not far from my home.'

I shifted awkwardly in my chair, conscious of *the smell*.

The waiter returned. The man ordered chai. No food.
'You OK?' he asked.

I tried wrapped my feet around the chair leg to hide *the smell*.

'Yes. Fine. Thanks.'

I sipped my coffee, hot and sweet.

'Sure?' He noticed the stained handkerchief wrapped around my arm.

'Yes.'

His brow furrowed: *I don't believe you*.

I fidgeted. 'Just a little adventure on the street, that's all.'

'Oh?'

'I was being dumb. Stupid.'

His expression invited me to continue.

'OK. I offered some sweets to a few boys and they got a bit, well, excited.'

'They attacked you?'

'No, I wouldn't put it as strongly as that,' my pride responded.

'But?'

'I thought I was doing the right thing. I have a friend who runs a project for street kids…'

'Where?'

'Heard of SKCV?'

'Manihara's place!'

'You know him?'

'Not personally. But his reputation is good.'

'It's a great project. Naively I assumed that all kids living on the streets were like the lads at SKCV. But this lot were wild. Like monkeys.'

'Is that the only reason you're here? We see few Europeans in Vijayawada.'

There was something about this man seated opposite me, his head tilted attentively, that coaxed me to talk. I soon found myself entrusting him with information that I'd not even told my friends back home.

'There's not a straightforward answer to that question.'

He looked at his watch. 'I have a few minutes until my appointment.'

'What do you do?'

'I'm a philosophy professor at Hyderabad University.'

It was my turn to look puzzled.

'Vijayawada is my home town,' he said. 'My appointment is for the dentist.'

'Aren't there any good dentists in Hyderabad?'

'Of course! But he is a *very* good dentist.' He laughed. 'And an excellent friend.' He took a sip of chai. 'Anyway, you were telling me why you're here.'

'I have to back-track slightly.'

'Fine.'

'At the beginning of last year I took a sabbatical.'

'To do what?'

'I travelled to Australia and New Zealand. My youngest brother and his wife live in Sydney. Apart from anything else, it was a good opportunity to see them.'

'And what is your job?'

'At the time I was artistic director of a touring theatre company.'

'A good job?'

'Yes. I loved it.'

The water placed a dosa and two metal dishes of sambar and coconut chutney in front of me.'

'Thanks.' I nodded.

'Welcome, sir.'

'Towards the end of the trip,' I continued, 'I spent some time trekking on New Zealand's South Island. One late afternoon I was standing on the shores of Lake Marian, Fjordland, surrounded by the most incredible mountains and scenery. Suddenly I was reminded of some words that Danny Kaye once said.'

'Danny Kaye?'

'The American movie actor. He said: "life is a great big canvas and we should throw all the paint we can at it."'

'I like that!'

'Indeed. But then I had another, more morbid, thought: *If I was to make an early exit from this world, what would be my biggest regret?*'

'And?'

'I surprised myself with the answer. It was nothing about being a famous theatre director, earning a high salary, getting married, that kind of thing. It was much simpler: *I've not seen enough of the world.* It had to be done.'

'So, you went back and...'

'... resigned!'

'My!' he responded, raising his eyebrows.

I broke off a piece of dosa and dipped it in the sweet and sour sambar. 'Actually, it wasn't as straightforward as that. It took twelve months before I gave notice to the board. I needed time to put my plans in place.'

'Did you *have* to leave? It sounds like an enviable job.'

'If only the reality was like that. Don't get me wrong, I loved it, especially the people I worked with. But my time was increasingly dominated by policies, strategies and funding. Too much management stuff. I was in danger of losing sight of why I wanted to work in the theatre in the first place. Where had the creativity gone?'

'I see.'

'Although I enjoyed the business side of the job, it was time to take stock. On the horizon loomed more of the same. I wanted to leave while I still enjoyed it.'

'Brave decision.'

'Or crazy!'

He laughed.

'When I returned from my sabbatical I threw myself into the company one hundred per cent.'

'Though secretly you knew you'd be leaving?'

'Exactly.'

'Wasn't that difficult?'

'You bet. But I adopted Danny Kaye's statement as my motivation. In order to throw the paint, though, I needed an empty canvas. Sweep away life's clutter... what to keep, what to bin? The junk was not only in my loft.

'I had already begun working with an inspirational woman called Hazel on a professional mentoring programme. We met regularly to talk through all the tangled issues. Looking back, it all seems remarkably straightforward. But it really wasn't. The process was complex. Risky. Painful.'

'I'm sure.'

'Which piece of the jigsaw to unlock first: the house; the job; who to tell; what to say; when to say it…'

'Did you care how people might respond?' he asked.

'Of course! I cared too much,' I replied. 'But I did it. Twelve months later: house sold, job quit, clutter removed.'

'So why India?'

'I had to start somewhere! To be honest, I've never really had any great desire to come here. But the opportunity arose and I jumped at it.' I told him about CHILD's Trust, Hebron Hostel and Lakshme.

'She was number one on the list, SKCV number two.'

'Is there a number three?'

'Trekking in the Himalayas. I might have to wait for that.'

'I think you'll have time. You've embarked on quite an adventure. Keep going!' He glanced at his watch. 'I must leave. My appointment is in a few minutes.' We stood to shake hands. He sniffed. 'Can you smell something?

I look around. 'Fear? Excitement?'

He smiled. 'Goodbye. I hope you achieve all your plans.'

I sat down.

Plans. Itineraries. Lists. Aaagh, those wretched imperatives that drove my life forward. Daily agendas that, once scrawled on a scrap of paper, tied me to a catalogue of duty. Oh, the elation of ticking off "book train ticket" marred by the misery of realising I had forgotten to "buy more soap".

I yearned to wake up one morning without a TO DO list. The prospect of such freedom was exhilarating.

But it was more than that. The lists represented the western baggage that I carried: the artificial boxes and categories in which we all like to put "kinds" of people, jobs, expectations. I wanted to break free from those shackles, push beyond the boundary of my comfort zone.

On reflection, I found the events of that morning oddly invigorating. First, the incident with the street kids. Then the conversation with... I didn't even know his name.

Having lived within the relative security of people that I knew and trusted for six weeks, I felt energised. With two of my three objectives achieved, I now itched to venture out on my own.

I had needed a trigger. That was it: the moment on the street when I thought I was safe. In reality, though, I was at my most vulnerable. In pursuit of adventure, somehow I had given permission for things to happen. Those seven-year-old boys had not only propelled me beyond my comfort zone, they had *shattered* it. It was the worst thing that could have happened. And the best.

Something else, something inexplicable, was now starting to pull me through India. Maybe it had begun before I'd even arrived; the mysterious magnet that had drawn me there in the first place. I was being taken on a journey over which I had no control. Yet I had invited it.

None of this, of course, I knew then.

'Actually, I think it's time to move on,' is how the conversation with Mani unfolded as we sat chatting in his lounge the following evening.

'It is?'

'Yes. I'd really like somewhere to relax for a few days.'

'Have you considered Mamallapuram?

'Mamallala... Mallama... where?'

'Mamallapuram. On the east coast of Tamil Nadu. Famous throughout India for its stone carvings. You'll love it.'

Self-analysis aside, the events of the last few weeks were beginning to catch up with me. Having madly dashed around in the months prior to leaving the UK, then throwing myself completely into life at Hebron and SKCV, I was exhausted. Mani's proposed remedy, a few days chilling in Mammaland, sounded appealing.

'It's also called Mahabalipuram.'

'Maha... So how do I get to this place?' I asked Mani.
'Overnight train to Chennai, then an hour's taxi ride.'
I hesitated. 'Wasn't that area of coastline severely affected by the tsunami?'
'Yes, but I remember reading... Vamsi!' he interrupted himself, 'Where's yesterday's paper?'

Vamsi, a slim young man in his early twenties, was Mani's driver. He had grown up at SKCV and now carried the responsibility of escorting him around the city.

A few moments later, Vamsi re-appeared with the *Deccan Chronicle*.

'Ah, here it is.' Flicking through the paper, Mani found the page he was looking for.

'"Tourists encouraged back to coastal resort,"' he read aloud. The article continued to explain that, due to the tsunami, hotels and shops were losing business because tourists were staying away in droves. '"The estimated damage incurred by the Tamil Nadu Tourist Department is around five *crore*."'

'What's a crore?'
'Ten million.'
'So, fifty million rupees, that's...' I did a quick mental calculation, 'just over six hundred thousand pounds.'
'You got it.'
'I'm not sure,' I said apprehensively. 'It's only a month since the tsunami.' The thought of taking a holiday on the coast felt insensitive.

'You don't have to stay,' Mani suggested, 'but it sounds as if the locals could do with the trade. Life has to go on. They rely on the season's income for the rest of the year.'

Though it was a perverse justification, I managed to convinced myself that, by lying on a beach, I would be putting rice on someone's plate. A pang of unease, though, nestled up close to the unopened package of post-colonial guilt tucked away at the bottom of my western baggage.

Nor did it feature on my TO DO list.

Go with the flow, whispered a small voice.

'What's the worst that can happen?' asked Mani.

5
Here Comes the Flood

*I threw down my tools, scooped up
my children and ran for my life*

'It is the LAW!' blustered the Travelling Ticket Examiner, his eyes popping out on stalks.
'What law?'
'The Indian Rail Law. You are breaking it.'
'How?'
'You are arriving late.'
'But I was here!'
'Who knows?' he shrugged his shoulders.
'Who knows? *I* know. My friends know. I have a reservation. Look!' I waved my ticket under his nose. 'You've given my seat to someone else.'
He didn't deny it. 'If you are wishing to complain, visit the information counter.'
'Then I'll miss the train.'
'That is not my problem,' he smiled, wobbling his head contemptuously.
'But what…'
The TTE slunk away.

Compounded by the knock-on effect of several delayed trains, the waiting hall at Vijayawada Station was heaving with passengers.
'It has been busy-busy weekend for weddings,' explained Vamsi. 'Friends and relatives are home going.' Both he and

Pavan had insisted on accompanying me to ensure that I boarded the correct train.

'You really don't have to.'

'Yes, brother! You are family.'

Eventually the monitor flickered to announce my train's arrival, the 21.55 to Chennai, Tamil Nadu, now running 90 minutes behind schedule. Picking up my luggage, Pavan and Vamsi helped me to carry everything to platform seven. The train pulled in just as we reached the bottom of the steps.

'Which carriage?' asked Pavan.

'A1, Second Class AC.'

Unlike in the UK, it is not possible to buy a standard class ticket and sit anywhere; all long-distance journeys require a reservation. As Indian Railways has at least eight classes of travel, the booking procedure is a complex affair. It requires the completion of a detailed form and extensive queuing at the station several days in advance of travel. Though, in theory, there are rules of travel and special quotas for tourists, in practice, much is left to the whim of the Travelling Ticket Examiner.

Once a train is fully booked, a number of seats are sold as "RAC", Reserved Against Cancellation, for each class of travel. After all these have been allocated, "waitlisted" tickets are sold. When "reserved" passengers cancel their reservation, RAC ticket-holders are promoted to "confirmed" status and waitlisted passengers upgraded to RAC. The only compartment that doesn't require an advanced booking is Unreserved Second Class. You'd be more comfortable on the roof.

The booking system is complicated, bureaucratic and time-consuming. It does, however, work. Usually.

We located the second class AC compartment fifty metres down the platform and climbed aboard. I checked my reservation: A1/0029/ CONFIRMED.

A gentleman was occupying my seat.

'Excuse me, sir,' I said, showing him my ticket, 'I believe this is my reservation.'

'Yes, sorry, sorry. The TTE exchanged it so my good wife could sleep on a lower bunk. She is disabled.' He indicated her callipered right leg. 'Could you be taking her seat instead?'

'No problem. Which berth is it?'

He showed me the ticket. A1/0029 had been crossed out and A1/0040 written in pen.

With Pavan and Vamsi in tow, I squeezed past the other passengers to seat number 40 but it, too, was occupied.

'Is this yours?' I asked a middle-aged couple sitting opposite each other.

'Yes. We have a confirmed reservation from the TTE.'

'There must be some confusion. Another gentleman has this reservation which he exchanged with me.'

'Talk to the TTE, then,' the man snapped.

'But…'

Flicking his hand contemptuously, he looked away.

I looked down the carriage for available seats but every place was taken.

'Wait here,' I said to Pavan, jumping onto the platform in search of the ticket examiner.

Before departure, the TTE is often found, dressed in a black jacket and white trousers, surrounded by disgruntled passengers. The only way to grab his attention is to push through the mob and thrust your ticket under his nose. This is not considered rude; it's the way business is done.

'Problem,' I said, showing him my reservation details.

He seized my ticket, cast his eye down the chart on his clipboard then dismissively handed it back.

'Next train,' he bleated.

'This ticket is for *this* train.'

'Reservation void.'

'What?' The *next* train is tomorrow!'

But he had moved onto deal with another passenger's complaint.

'Quick,' I said to Vamsi, afraid the train would leave without me. 'Let's see if there are any empty seats further down.'

We signalled for Pavan to jump off and follow us. I climbed into the third class AC compartment. Completely full. So was the next.

Along the platform we found the sleeper class compartments.

'Try here,' suggested Vamsi. But it was useless; not a spare seat in sight. 'I think you should come back with us tonight. Tomorrow we re-book your ticket.'

'But I have a ticket – for *this* train!'

'The ticket collector is allocating it to someone else. You shouldn't be travelling on a train without valid reservation. You could be in trouble, no?'

'Even if I have the right ticket? It'll take two or three days to book another train.' As much as I loved SKCV, my sights were now set on the beach at Mamallapuram. Besides, there was a moral battle to fight.

Vamsi looked at me and smiled. 'I'll call Sudhama to see if he can suggest anything.'

As we stood in the gangway, other people were overhearing our conversation.

'You are having difficulty?' asked a studious-looking man in a green chequered shirt.

'You could say that. The TTE has given my ticket to someone else.'

'Why?'

I shrugged. 'Because he can?'

'That's not right.'

'Show me your ticket,' interjected another guy looking over my shoulder. 'It's very clear you have a reservation, yes?' he said after scrutinising it for a few moments.

'Are you sure it is valid?' suggested another. Within a short space of time, several men had joined in the discussion, unanimously agreeing that I had been wronged.

I wondered whether Vamsi had managed to contact Sudhama. The scheduled length of the stop at Vijayawada Junction was fifteen minutes. As we'd already waited for thirty-five, I was beginning to panic.

'Wait here with my rucksack,' I ordered Pavan. 'I'm going to find Vamsi.' I jumped off the train and dashed down the busy platform, hastily dodging in and out of everything in my path. Vamsi was not in sight.

The train lurched. Very slowly, it started to move. Time froze, though, just long enough for me to take stock of the situation. On the platform stood I, sweating, swearing, staring at the train on which I should be standing. On the train stood Pavan, dutifully guarding my rucksack, gazing open-mouthed at the platform on which he should standing. The second class carriage rolled past. We clocked each other. He raised his hands, shoulders, eyebrows: 'What to do?'

Grateful for the lumbering train's reluctance to gather speed, I leapt on board through the open door. Darting around the corner into the second-class compartment, I just caught Pavan dashing out the other end. Scrambling over cases, crates and children, I stumbled towards him.

'Pavan!' I yelled. He didn't hear me, but the rest of the compartment did. Conversations stopped as heads turned sharply in my direction.

'PAVAN!' I bellowed even louder. This time my voice reached him and he looked round. 'Drop my rucksack and GET OFF THE TRAIN!!'

I continued to charge past the mass of intrigued expressions: who was this puce-faced Britisher causing such a commotion? I reached the far end of the carriage just in time to see Pavan land on the platform. He turned and grinned. Running up behind him was Vamsi.

'Safe journey!' they cried, both waving.

Inhaling deeply, I walked back into the compartment to rousing cheers and applause.

Once the fuss had subsided, men crowded around to find out what was happening.

'This good man has received a great injustice, isn't it?' explained Arun, the guy in the chequered shirt I'd met earlier.

'Explain what is happening,' requested a well-groomed middle-aged gentleman.

I narrated the events leading up to that moment.

He nodded sagely. 'There is nothing to be doing.'

'What do you mean?'

'Obviously the TTE is taking a bribe. The other people arriving before you wanted a reservation.'

'But I had paid for it.' My blood was being to boil again. 'I have the ticket reservation in writing.'

He looked at me. 'Not any more.'

I realised I was screwed. Arun pulled me aside.

'Look. Wait till the next station and talk to him again. Maybe he will adjust a little.'

'What do you mean?'

'Perhaps he will bend the rules, with a little help...'

'Are you suggesting I should offer him money to withdraw the bribe?'

'He might choose to be a little flexible if...'

'Forget it! I'm not going to play games.' I interrupted again, although, I admit, I was desperate for some kind of revenge. I was incensed and, given the consensus of the carriage, quite rightly so.

I apologised to Arun for snapping. He smiled. The entourage of supporters gradually returned to their seats, muttering in small groups about my predicament.

Time to consider the immediate problem. The whole night lay before me with nowhere to sit, let alone sleep. Standing awkwardly in the gangway, I was painfully aware that my rucksack and I were causing an obstruction as people tried to squeeze past.

After thirty tedious minutes, the train slowed down.

'Are we coming into a station?'

'Yes, Tenali Junction.'

'Right!'

As soon as it stopped, I jumped off and walked quickly along the platform to find the collector. Realising that any attempt to retrieve my seat, through bribery or otherwise, was futile, I had formulated a plan. I would appeal to his better nature and request, nicely, if he could accommodate me somewhere, anywhere, on the train for the night. Accusing him of corruption, tempting though it was, would have been tantamount to asking him to throw me off the train. Any number of police colleagues could have been hiding around the corner, all too willing to bang me up for the night for travelling without a valid ticket. I had heard too many scary stories.

'Excuse me, sir,' I said, producing my ticket.

He recognised me. 'I dealt with you earlier.'

'You didn't *deal* with me, actually,' I responded patiently.

He turned to another passenger.

'Are there any available seats?' I persisted, moving back into his line of vision. 'Please! I am a guest in your country.'

It was then that he bawled at me about breaking the law – *the law?!* –, introducing the preposterous argument that, because I was late boarding the train at Vijayawada, he was within his rights to allocate my ticket to someone else.

Rage welled up from my toes to my stomach. My blood pumped, my chest pounded. With my tolerance stretched to its limit, I desperately wanted to kick up a mighty furore. Had I been in the UK, I might have done.

But, standing there on that cheerless platform in the dead of night, repelled by the TTE's stale whisky-breath, I had to admit defeat. Although I had been wronged, there was nothing to do but walk away and leave him to his clipboard and his karma.

AAAAAAAAAAGHHhh!

I felt deflated, jilted. My love affair with Indian Railways was on the rocks.

Climbing aboard, I was greeted by Arun. 'Listen boss!' he said, 'I am talking to my friends. We are clearing all our bags and cases. You sleep on the floor between the bunks, isn't it? Not so nicely comfortable, but better than nothing.'

'Are you sure?'

'Of course. You are our guest.'

How could I refuse? My only other option was to stand in the corridor next to the toilet all night.

As Arun's friends scattered sheets of the Deccan Chronicle on the floor, I pushed the bottom half of my rucksack under the seat and used the top to make a pillow. Pulling out my multi-purpose blue sarong, I stretched it over the newspaper. Bought in Australia, it travels everywhere with me.

Discovering that the rucksack-cum-pillow was too lumpy, I found a couple of shirts and rolled them into a sausage.

That's how I endured the night. "Endured", not slept. No, the juddering, bone-rattling wheels beneath the unyielding floor; the rib-jabbing baggage protruding from under the seats; the urine-stained sandals deposited near my face; the freezing fan overhead; the continual flicking on and off of the light switch; the fear of mice on a night raid; the inability to extend my legs; the pins and needles and cramp... all conspired to ensure that I *endured* the night. Only just.

One person slept soundly in our compartment who had not been party to our arrangements; an elephantine, sari-clad matron in possession of ten lethal fingernails. At one point I dozed off, suddenly waking to find a handful of menacing daggers dangling millimetres from my face. Lying motionless, I dared not move for fear of losing an eye.

Only one saving grace made those eight, long hours tolerable: the collection of The Divine Comedy albums loaded onto my mobile phone. Feeling as if I'd been dragged through Dante's Inferno backwards, I journeyed towards my paradisal retreat with a familiar friend.

Poetry in motion.

Mamallapuram was an idiosyncratic coastal resort, Antipodean in some ways, yet undeniably Indian. White cresty waves crashed onto a lengthy bay of golden sand, reminiscent of the North Beaches above Sydney. Unlike Oz, however, cows and goats mooched the dusty streets, listlessly oblivious to events of the last month.

A hundred yards from the shore lay a handful of hotels and restaurants resting in a sea of debris, the remains of battered palms, smashed up fishing boats, ripped nets and rubble. Tangled strands of seaweed, bottles, canisters and shards of driftwood scattered the sand, poked around by stray dogs and scavenging crows.

I checked into Wild Roses, a rambling establishment of eight ensuite bedrooms surrounding a leafy courtyard.

'Please follow, sir,' welcomed Madhu, the manager, pulling a key from his pocket. 'I hope you will be happy here.'

My room, reached by its own little staircase, featured a bijou balcony from which I could almost view the sea if I leant right over, stuck out my head and squinted.

'It's great.' My response seemed to please him; his gaunt frame swelled with pride. 'Business slow?' I asked.

'Yes. Few tourists coming since tsunami.'

Having already seen evidence of the physical devastation, I quizzed him about the personal impact on the community.

'Three local people expired by the waves,' he said plaintively. 'Generally about seventy fishermen and eighty traders were losing their business.'

'That must have affected the whole town?'

'Many people, yes, but not all. Over seven hundred, particularly their families. The hotel is making a collection.' He looked at me directly. 'You will contribute?'

His mild temerity caught me off-guard, but I didn't wish to appear insensitive. Neither, though, did I want to patronise him with a knee-jerk response by offering a few notes from my wallet.

'I will give it some thought,' I replied judiciously. And I would.

In the meantime, I had a night's sleep on which to catch up.

Jennie, Superintendent of Hebron Hostel

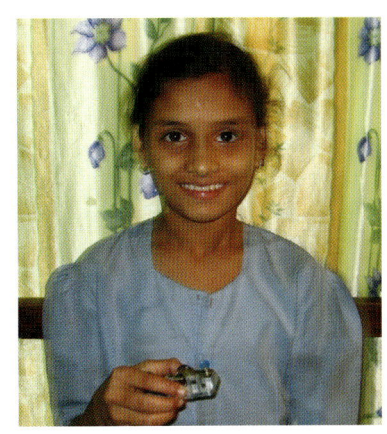

Lakshme with her musical box

younger Hebron Hostel girls in the playground

Christmas Day picnic

making mud cakes

Vijay

Santosh Bhavan, SKCV's city base

SKCV boys

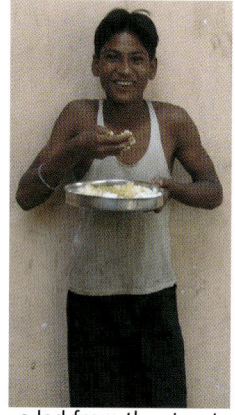

a lad from the street is given lunch

swimming in the River Krishna

reporting for duty at the SKCV village

Arjuna's Penance, Mamallapuram

working on the backwaters of Kerala

the shadow of Adam's Peak, Sri Lanka, cast onto the mist at dawn

Varkala, Kerala

kumkum stall in Mysore

Meenakshi-Sundareshwarar Temple, Madurai

tea plantation above Munnar in the Western Ghats

sunrise at the Taj Mahal

Exploring the town in bite-size chunks - I'm not a good sightseer - I soon discovered why Mamallapuram is famous throughout India. Once a thriving port of the Pallavan dynasty, it boasts a magnificent array of monuments and sculptures constructed between the seventh and ninth centuries, earning it UNESCO World Heritage Site recognition in 1995.

The ornate five-storeyed Shore Temple, sixty foot high, holds a commanding position over the Bay of Bengal, originally one of seven temples. The other six, reputedly, are submerged beneath the sea. Further inland, sixteen manmade caves and nine Ratha Temples scatter the area. Impressively carved from single pieces of rock, the latter are so-called because they resemble *rathas,* chariots. Five of them are named after the Pandava Brothers of the Mahabharata. Most imposing, however, are the two exquisite bas-reliefs sculpted into the granite hillside, Krishan Mandapa, and the 96 foot long Arjuna's Penance. The latter also depicts, according to legend, a scene from the Mahabharata.

As I ambled up and down the narrow lanes, I could hear the rhythmic chatter of chisels on stone ricocheting between workshop and shop front. Crouching intensively, men and boys chipped away with precision at solid lumps of stone, breathing life into their inanimate creations: elephants, cobras and flute-playing Krishnas.

A few other tourists and travellers strolled the streets, mainly pony-tailed Dutch and German couples, sober expressions pragmatically etched into their faces to deflect the persistent street sellers. I sympathised with them, feeling sorely tempted to retreat into shutdown mode myself at times. Though I started each day with a positive attitude, my patience was invariably worn thin by mid-afternoon. Clothes and souvenirs that appeared quite attractive at nine lost their allure by four. The pestering was relentless.

'Tell me somewhere you are not wishing to go and I am taking you,' beeped the rickshaw driver as I crossed the road.

'I have beautiful, over-priced silk rugs upstairs. Come, drink tea and I am persuading you to purchase one,' coaxed the smooth-talking Kashmiri businessman.

'Buy my nicely things!' urged the bangle-clanging saleswoman from her shop doorway. 'Making good present for wife!'

'I don't have one.'

'Maybe later, sir?'

I wouldn't lie. I refused to agree 'Yes, OK, maybe later,' knowing full well that I had no intention of ever entering her shabby emporium. I suggested, politely, that 'I *might*,' but soon learnt that equivocation was also pointless. A direct approach was required: 'I will *never* come back nor will I *ever* buy anything from your shop. Besides, I don't have a wife.'

'Very good, sir. Tomorrow then?'

Even plain-speaking was wasted breath.

Many hotel managers in India, particularly those catering for the foreign, rather than domestic, guest do not maintain the professional distance that we expect in the west. Regarding themselves as a "friend", they grant introductions to various colleagues as part of their personal service. They are, of course, consummate business people; the prospect of some healthy commission undoubtedly figures in their reckoning.

I was not entirely surprised, therefore, when Madhu escorted me over the road late on my second morning to meet Navaj, a pint-sized tailor with a fine sweep of wavy hair. I didn't protest; I fancied some new shirts and Navaj seemed a personable guy.

Unprompted, he started to tell me what happened the hour the tsunami struck.

'I was stitching in my shop near the shore when it all fell eerily silent,' he explained. 'I glanced up and saw the sea retreat a distance of four kilometres. It revealed an emerald plateau, so bright and lush. I saw fish flapping in the weeds.' The poetic tenor of his description took me by surprise.

'And then four temples appeared,' he added mysteriously, 'not seen above sea level for hundreds of years.' Panic crept into his voice. 'Suddenly a great wall of water rose up, sixty feet high, rushing towards the beach very-very forceful. There was no time for making decisions. I threw down my tools, scooped up my children and ran for my life. I left behind my silk, my business... my livelihood.'

'Did you lose everything?'

'My shop was washed away,' he continued. 'Next day I returned. A few remnants of silk but nothing else. My sewing machine, materials, tools - all gone.'

After talking to other villagers, the reality sounded more prosaic but incredible nevertheless: the sea pulled back half a kilometre and the three giant waves, when they hit, swelled up to five metres high. I wondered if the mysterious temples had been no more than a cluster of exposed rocks.

A month later, Navaj told me that he was renting the small unit in which we sat to rebuild his business. 'I am now thinking of December twenty-six as my birthday,' he said poignantly. 'It was beginning of my second life.'

'Everything you owned was destroyed, though.'

'Yes, but my family are still alive. For that I am so-so grateful to God.' He paused. 'Look!'

Pulling off his chappals, he showed me the blister scars on the soles of his feet, scorched and torn as he had leapt over the jagged rocks to escape the waves.

'Are they still sore?'

'No longer. Now they are just reminder.'

I asked Navaj to make me a shirt. As he cut a piece of jade silk from one of his rescued saris, the fine, translucent cloth reflected a dancing green light onto the white concrete wall.

'Have you received any relief aid from the government?'

'Nothing.' He wrapped his tape measure around my waist. 'The fishermen were offered a one-off payment of four thousand rupees compensation and a few basic provisions. Rice and clothes. That was all. No one else has a single rupee.'

This was at odds with the newspaper reports I had read. 'I thought the fishermen had received substantial government aid to help rebuild their businesses and mend their boats and nets?'

'Maybe other places. Not here.'

It seemed that only short-term relief, a sticking plaster, had been administered.

Walking along the beach later, I was approached by a young woman.

'Tsunami, tsunami!' she pleaded, clutching a small, chubby-ankled child. 'Give money, buy rice family.'

Moments later another mother stopped me. 'You help. My baby needing food. I nothing,' she implored, cradling a filthy bundle of cloth in her arms.

Though her persuasive language presented a compelling case, I hesitated. Genuinely not carrying any money with me, all I could do was show her my empty pockets, accompanied by a hollow 'Sorry'.

She looked at me accusingly. I felt bad, but I wasn't sure why. Was it because I had nothing to give or was it because, deep down inside – dare I admit it – part of me didn't believe her?

Appeals of this nature started to occur all too frequently, serving to feed my discomfort further. Wails of "Tsunami, Tsunami", snatched from the mouths of desperate women, were carried by the afternoon breeze into the uncomfortable ears of other bewildered tourists. I watched to see how they would react. Some blindly walked past, others handed out a few pitiful coins. One or two stopped to listen.

By the end of the afternoon, I was wrung out by the women's persistence. I could have saved myself the emotional energy by ignoring them, or by not walking along the beach. At some level, though, I felt obliged to engage with the situation. I was responsible, after all, for my decision to go to Mamallapuram. I might not have anticipated the specifics, but I knew what I was letting myself in for.

Yet something wasn't right.

It came down to this: was I witnessing the genuine outcome of an immense human tragedy or a carefully manipulated charade? Had the tough, daily existence of these women really been compounded by natural calamity or would life have been like this anyway?

This was no reason to treat them with any less humanity but my sense of curiosity was sufficiently provoked. Back at the hotel I chatted to Madhu. He counselled me not to be fooled.

'They are not needing money; they make up stories, this and all. Some even borrow babies.'

'What! You're joking?'

'No,' he shook his head. 'But tomorrow I show you who only needs help,' he added, compounding my confusion.

I went to bed, my head spinning. India being India, the reality of the tsunami impact was hard to gauge and the truth impossible to discern. Fact and fiction were tightly woven together in a tangled web of distorted rhetoric.

While chatting with Navaj the next day, a large shadow fell across his shop. A rugged Goliath of a man filled the doorframe, silhouetted in the mid-afternoon light.

Navaj bounced up from his stool. 'Navendra-ji, come in!'

I stood up and offered Navendra my hand. He gripped it earnestly.

'Navendra is a fisherman,' said Navaj.

'Ah.'

'*Was*. No working now,' he joked dryly, his doleful expression undermining his mighty physique.

'Have you received any compensation?'

'Yes, little-little, not much to do any...'

'It is as I said yesterday,' interrupted Navaj. 'Small aid is getting through. Big issue lies with the government and agency distribution.'

'There seems to be no shortage of funds nationally, or from overseas,' I commented.

'Yes, but not areas where so much needed. Like Navendra and his family.'

I understood. Mamallapuram was a relatively small town with, arguably, less significant aid requirements than elsewhere. Yet the personal need was equally intense, even if the scale of community disaster fell below that of other Asian regions.

'Four thousand rupees very small. I am needing more than one hundred thousands rupees to replace nets. Then my boat.' As Navendra spoke, I calculated that to be about £1,200. He then handed me a scrap of paper on which he had written his email address. 'Please write me when you return in England,' he asked sombrely. What he expected, I wasn't sure. What could I do?

Another face appeared in the doorway.

'Madhu, good afternoon. Tea?' asked Navaj. The time was approaching four o'clock.

'No thanks.' He looked at me. 'Sir, there is someone to meet – a very good woman. I remember our conversation last night. Come!'

I turned to Navaj. He shrugged.

'See you later.'

Around the corner stood a dilapidated, two storeyed building. Two boys were playing marbles. One looked up cheekily. 'Hi,' he grinned.

'Hello. What's your name?' I asked.

'Jishnu, sir.'

Faded images of flowers and birds decorated a sun-worn sign written in Hindi and English:

THE SMALL BLOSSOM HOME FOR ORPHANED CHILDREN

'Mark, this way!' beckoned Madhu.

I waved to Jishnu.

Creaking open the gate, Madhu led me down a dingy alleyway into an airless room. Apart from a few wrinkled books scattered around a threadbare mat, and a rickety, wooden table and two plastic chairs, the place was featureless and bare.

In contrast to the bleak interior, our entrance was warmly received by Ishita, the orphanage's amply-figured manager.

'Welcome,' she beamed. 'Please sit.'

'This is Mark,' introduced Madhu, 'from England.' Hovering for a moment, he caught Ishita's eye then left.

'Are you not staying?' I called after him.

'No, I have work.' His voice trailed around the corner.

'So, Marks, what is bringing you to India?' Ishita asked with a well-spoken, clipped accent. The gate squeaked shut. I fidgeted, unsure why I was there.

'Well, first of all...' She listened attentively as I explained briefly about my time at Hebron and SKCV. As I concluded, she clasped her hands together and smiled.

'Like me, you are interested in helping young people, yes?' she commented. 'That's good.'

'Tell me something about your work here,' I responded, guessing that was where our conversation was leading. 'How did the tsunami affect you?'

'I had just celebrated Christmas with the children. We had such good day. Then next morning. Tragedy.' With her hair pulled back tightly into a bun, a silver cross dangled from each ear. Ishita leant forward intensely as she continued.

'The waves washed down the street and into the orphanage where the children were playing. I gathered up the smallest ones in my arms and ran to safety.'

'How many children were there?'

'Twenty...'

'...and they were all OK?'

'Physically they were fine, but distraught. When I returned several hours later, I discovered that thieves had broken in and taken all we owned.'

'What the tsunami didn't destroy, other people stole?' I asked incredulously.

'Yes, many houses were raided by looters. We were not the only ones.'

My mouth fell open. Where was the justice? These people were impoverished *before* their lives were devastated by the tsunami. And *then* opportunistic crooks dashed in to exploit the situation further.

'Human nature can stoop very low,' Ishita lamented. 'Now we are having nothing.'

The sound of children's laughter breezed in from outside.
'Hasan!'

In scampered a lanky nine year old smartly dressed in a blue shirt and shorts. 'Go and get tea,' she ordered, handing him a ten rupee note pulled from her purse.

'Haan ji.' He turned to go.

'And Hasan,' she added sharply, 'say hello to our guest, Mr Marks. He is here to help us.'

'My name is Mark actually; there is no "s".'

'That is what I said.'

Despite the twinkle in her eye, I felt put in my place. I decided not to take issue with her reference to my "help".

Hasan smiled nervously, 'Hello, Uncle-ji,' and ran out of the room.

'How long has the orphanage been here?'

'I established it five years ago. Before that, I had a well-paid job as a teacher but I gave up my post to start the orphanage. I sold most of my belongings so that I could provide for the children.'

'That's a radical thing to have done,' I suggested.

'Yes. I am forty-two. I should be married! Instead, my family have disowned me.'

'That must make you very sad?'

'Oof, they think I should be a successful businesswoman. But I am totally committed to the children. They make me happy. Their joy is my joy.'

Hasan returned with two metal beakers of hot tea which we drank as we chatted.

Outside, I heard more young voices chattering cheerily. Ishita's willingness to give up everything for the sake of their wellbeing was impressive. Intelligent and well-educated, she could have pursued a highly successful and lucrative career.

'I have chosen a life of sacrifice,' she said simply.

'Have you received any tsunami funding from the government?' I asked.

'No. Actually I am Catholic and therefore of high class. The government is not acknowledging my request for help. I am too rich, they say.' I detected a slight bitterness in her tone. Her straight lips melted into a weak smile. 'So I do the best for the children I can.'

I scanned the room. A chart outlining Ishita's long-term aims for the orphanage hung on the drab concrete wall. The aspirations were educational and moral, Catholic-influenced. A sentence in bold capitals reiterated the maxim featured on the sign outside:

NO ONE HAS THE RIGHT TO BE HAPPY ALONE

'Marks, come!' she suddenly announced. 'Let's go to meet the children. They are mostly returned from school.' She gathered up her tightly-wrapped yellow sari and I followed her outside.

Leading from the alleyway to the flat roof was a short flight of concrete steps on which some of the children sat.

'Boys and girls, this is Mr Marks. He is here to help us. Say hello.'

Again I bit my tongue.

'Good afternoon Uncle,' they greeted me with one voice.

Half a dozen pairs of hopeful eyes stared up at me.

'What are your names?' I asked.

'Tarun, sir,' said one boy with a toothy grin. 'Where is hair?'

Rubbing my shaven head, I pretended to take offence. Then laughed.

'Tarun is our clown,' said Ishita. 'He can be entertaining at times but sometimes goes too far. I apologise.'

'No worries.'

One by one the children introduced themselves and we chatted. Some of them spoke English quite well and Ishita translated for the rest.

'They appear happy enough,' I commented.

'Yes, they are, but underneath they are still very traumatised. Although this used to be their home, they cannot stay here at the moment. They find it too upsetting. I have had to rent a small house in another village further inland so they feel they can sleep safely at night.'

'Because of the tsunami?'

'Yes, this building has many many unhappy memories for them. I meet those that attend school locally and then transport them to the other village in the evening. That is where all the other children are at the moment. We have used that building since two weeks.'

'Where do you get the money to pay rent for two properties?' I asked.

'It is a problem. But the Lord will provide.' I sensed that she wanted to change the subject.

'You must come and visit all the boys and girls. I would meet you here at four o'clock tomorrow and we go.'

Hesitating, I looked at the children.

'Please come and play,' Tarun smiled cheekily at me. 'You good man. You help.'

'OK. I will come to meet you.' That much I promised, unsure of what else I could, or should, do.

'Goodbye Marks, see you tomorrow.' She grasped my hand and shook it briskly.

'Nice to meet you.' I opened the gate and walked out. 'Thanks for the tea!'

―――

The next afternoon, when I arrived at the orphanage just before four o'clock, two middle-aged women in Punjabi dress were chatting to the children. They introduced themselves as Beatrice and Helen: 'We're from Belgium.'

'Are you here on holiday?' I asked.

'No, we've been involved with relief work elsewhere in Tamil Nadu,' replied Beatrice, 'and have come here for a short break before returning home. We met Ishita the other day and she invited us to come and meet the children.'

They both seemed at ease with the children. One of the young girls sat on Helen's knee, playing with the wooden beads around her neck.

'I am so so sorry.' The gate squeaked open and Ishita bustled in. 'I have had some paperwork to deal with at the bank. It took longer than I thought.' Her calm, self-assuredness was slightly ruffled.

'How are you, Marks?' she asked. 'Have you met my friends from Belgium?'

'I'm fine, thanks. Yes, we were just talking about the work they've been doing.'

Checking that the children were all present, she gabbled something in Hindi to Hasan who promptly disappeared.

I turned to the two Belgium women. 'Tell me, Beatrice and Helen, have you been approached by women on the beach asking for money for their families?'

'Yes,' replied Helen, 'and we…'

'Don't be bothered by them,' Ishita interrupted crisply. 'They are not needing help. Besides, they are liars; they cannot be trusted.'

Helen and Beatrice stole a glance at each other. 'We gave them a few rupees,' Helen said sheepishly. 'They seemed so desperate.'

Ishita remained quiet for a moment. And then, 'Come, let's go! The car is here,' she announced.

A taxi had just pulled up outside with Hasan sitting proudly in the front.

I looked around: four adults, six children, one car.

'Don't worry Marks, we'll all squeeze in. You go in the back with Beatrice, Helen and two of the boys. The rest will come in the front with me.'

Like dolls packed into a toy box, all the children knew their assigned places – they'd clearly done it before – and everyone easily fitted in.

We took the main road heading inland from Mamallapuram. After a couple of kilometres, the taxi turned off onto a smaller track.

We stopped. A barrier, manned by a weasly-looking official in a peaked cap, blocked the road. He uttered a few words to the taxi driver who, shrugging nonchalantly, turned to Ishita. She sighed, climbed out and pulled the official to one side. The dialogue started quietly but, rising in volume, pace and pitch, soon developed into a vehement exchange of choice Hindi phrases, abruptly terminated by a final sharp word from Ishita.

She opened the door and climbed back into the front seat again, squeezing her generous frame between two of the girls.

'There is a problem?' I asked.

'No problem.' She nodded curtly at the official who raised the barrier. We drove on.

'What was all that about?' I quizzed her further.

'This is a toll road and every non-resident vehicle is required to pay a fee. I told him that I am living here, so why should I give you money? He argued with me.'

'Yes, we heard!'

'I said I knew his boss. That shut him up and he let us through.' She smiled. 'This is India!'

A few minutes later we pulled up outside a two-storey house surrounded by a well-kept garden. A few boys were kicking a ball around and three girls perched on the wall laughing. As soon as we got out of the taxi they stopped playing and ran towards us.

'Good evening, Uncle.' Two or three lads grabbed my arm and pulled me into the house. There were more children playing inside. A few were watching a small TV in the corner.

Tarun, the impish clown whom I met yesterday, ran over and tugged at my hand. 'Come,' he said, 'I am showing you our nice house.'

The building, though sparsely furnished, was clean, spacious and well-maintained. A large room at the front led into a dining area, behind which a well-equipped kitchen and a couple of smaller rooms for sleeping were located. The outside staircase rose to a second floor occupied by other tenants.

Other children tagged onto the guided tour, clearly very pleased that we had come. The production of my digital camera was met with squeals of delight, particularly when they saw themselves on the screen.

'May I take?' asked Tarun.

'Of course, but you must hold the camera steady.'

As he snapped away the other children posed, crowding around and giggling at their images after each shot.

'Children!' a sharp voice called in Hindi. Tarun handed me the camera and ran inside. I followed, interested to see why they had been summoned.

The children had assembled in three straight lines on the clean tiled floor. Ishita was walking up and down the rows handing out small packets of biscuits. As they tore open the wrappers and ate hungrily, I secretly hoped that this was not their main meal.

'Snacks,' barked Ishita as if she could read my mind.

She then disappeared into the kitchen and the children watched television. Beatrice, Helen and I chatted.

'Ishita has the children very well organised,' I observed.

'They seem to respect her, though,' replied Helen.

'The last few weeks have been extremely hard for them,' added Beatrice, 'but they appear content.'

After some time Ishita returned. 'Dinner is ready. Come!'

This was unexpected. While we'd been talking, Ishita had prepared a meal. Various dishes were laid out on a table in the next room. 'This is a special chicken dish made with local spices,' she announced, pointing to an ornate silver bowl. 'Take!'

Though I dreaded this kind of situation, the platter of roasted wings made me squirm less than the prospect of causing offence by refusing to eat them.

'This looks very good but,' I started off tentatively, 'I have to tell you that... I'm a vegetarian.'

'No matter,' she responded lightly, although I sensed she was embarrassed. 'You should have said.'

I would, had I known you were cooking a meal, I thought to myself.

'But there are many vegetables as well,' she added, 'and dal. But it's nothing special.'

'Rice and vegetables are great,' I smiled at her genuinely. Thankfully, Helen and Beatrice tucked into the chicken wings appreciatively.

Despite Ishita's protestations that 'they're only boring old potatoes and carrots,' the meal was beautifully prepared.

'The children seem very happy here,' I observed.

'We are fortunate. The house is belonging to a friend who offered it when he discovered the children needed somewhere to stay.'

'It's so much better here than the cramped building you have in the centre of the village.'

'Yes, you're right. The children feel safe. The sea cannot reach them here,' Ishita replied. 'Oof, the tsunami has had a bad psychological effect. They still remember playing on the beach when it happened and seeing the waves rushing towards them. Now they are having nightmares. They refuse to go there.'

'Could you not move here permanently?' asked Beatrice.

'Ideally, yes, but the money is a problem. At the moment I am renting two buildings. The man who owns this is a friend, but I am paying a nominal amount for temporary residence. Moving would be so-so expensive. It is a nice-nice house, but too big for our needs.'

'What do you plan to do?' asked Helen.

'There is some land nearby. I wish to buy that and then build a proper home for the children.'

It seemed an impractically expensive option to me: 'Would that not be more costly?'

'Yes, at the beginning but once the initial outlay is covered, it would be ours.'

From a business perspective it made sense.

'First of all, though, I must replace those things the children have lost in the tsunami. The priority is new school bags, books and shoes. The children have nothing.'

'You seem to have it all worked out.'

'I am a business woman; I know the right way to do things. I am wanting the best for these children. I am their mother and father. Their joy is my joy,' she said, repeating a phrase I'd heard the previous day. 'Marks, you are helping us?'

'I, er...'

I was distracted by a sound behind me. Turning, I saw a pair of watery brown eyes staring up at me from the doorway. It was Rajdeep, the youngest of the boys. Aged four, he didn't speak. I smiled. His upper lip trembled nervously.

'Perhaps you would like to take him outside to play with the other boys?' suggested Ishita, 'It will be dark soon.'

As I stepped into the garden, a football bounced towards me.

'Oi! On me 'ed mate!' yelled Tarun, attempting a mock English accent as I kicked it back to him. Our laughter encouraged further antics.

'Where did you learn that?' I asked intrigued. It certainly wasn't from me!

'English men at beach,' he replied, throwing himself into a double somersault.

When it was time for Beatrice, Helen and I to leave, some of the children were visibly upset. 'Come please tomorrow,' Hasan implored, fighting back a tear.

'I'm not sure that's possible,' I replied. This was one occasion when I definitely didn't want to make false promises.

'Please, think about what you can do.' Ishita directed her words at all three of us.

As the taxi pulled away, I turned and waved. The children stood on the front step shouting, jumping up and down.

'See you tomorrow, Uncle,' they called. Ishita smiled, her hand resting on Hasan's shoulder.

I was silent.

Returning to the hotel I threw myself on the bed, physically and emotionally spent. The children troubled my conscience. But what to do?

The muggy night air suffocated my thoughts. Moths flitted tediously around the bare light bulb and the high-pitched drone of a mosquito whined in and out of earshot. I ached to smudge its bloody body against the wall. Instead, I lay motionless, stupefied.

My mind danced, though. A tangled tango, twisting through recent affairs, dallying with the honest deceptions, cavorting with the fabricated truths. Cries of "Tsunami, tsunami" sucked me into a befuddled sea of fact and fantasy, pulling me out of my depth...

I woke with a start. The mosquito, still whinging menacingly, hauled me from my inertia.

Bam. Got it.

Senses invigorated, I recollected a telephone conversation with Mark Thomas shortly after the tsunami. His trustees had allocated funds for relief aid; perhaps I could inform him if I identified any projects that required support?

I called him on my mobile. As the line was poor I came straight to the point.

'I've met a woman who runs an orphanage. The children are OK but they lost almost everything.' I briefly brought Mark up to speed.

'Do you believe this is a genuine project?'

'I have one or two reservations, but they are more about the whole post-tsunami culture than the orphanage in particular.'

We agreed that I would ask Ishita for some figures, Mark would discuss the situation with his trustees and we would communicate the following day.

9.25pm. Time for a beer.

Early the next morning I strolled down to the sea. I had discovered a path at the back of the hotel which led, via a patch of scrubby wasteland, directly to the beach. More importantly, it avoided the grasping souvenir sellers.

The strong current generated some mighty waves, perfect for a spot of body surfing. But as I ducked and dived with the sandy spray stinging my back, it felt odd, if not slightly obscene, playing in the same water that had caused so much devastation only a month earlier. Was it so very wrong?

The women who had hassled me earlier in the week perused the shoreline, scrutinizing the frivolous activity of the holidaymakers. I stayed in the water until they'd gone.

After two frustrating hours in the internet cafe, during which time I managed to send only one email, I wandered around the corner to see Ishita. On the way I called in to see how my shirt order was progressing.

'Hello Mark!' Navaj greeted me good-humouredly. 'Sit, drink chai!' He swept a pile of fabric from the bench. 'Your shirts are ready tomorrow.'

'That's what you said yesterday,' I jested.

'I know. Sorry. Work is hard at the moment.'

I suspect he meant motivation was hard but I didn't take issue.

Navendra laughed. He sat in the corner, his broad, muscular frame filling much of the poky, cluttered room. The ensuing lively banter about nothing-in-particular diverted our attention away from other matters for a few minutes. Inevitably, the conversation turned to the tsunami and an update on the aid situation.

'The fishing community is making a public meeting soon for talking about the future,' said Navendra. 'We are having no boats, nets or money. Even if we did, there are no fish.'

'No fish! What do you mean?'

'The tsunami destroyed them. It would be months till stocks are replaced.'

'Of course,' an obvious fact which I hadn't considered until then. 'And in the meantime…?'

Well, that *was* obvious: sit and while away the hours in the tailor's shop because Navaj had no work either.

'Where are tourists for stitching clothes?' he asked rhetorically. 'Mamallapuram is usually so busy. This year - nothing.'

'You know, Navaj,' I said after a moment, 'I reckon I could do with some pyjamas to go with the other things you're making.'

He took my leg measurements, smiling appreciatively. 'They are ready tomorrow.'

'With the shirts?'

'With the shirts.'

Leaving them to drink more chai, I walked round the corner to the orphanage.

Ishita was sitting in her office and beckoned me in. Compared to the previous two days, she was remarkably subdued.

'Are you OK?' I enquired.

'Actually I am paining, Marks,' she confessed. A common expression for "not feeling well", paining rarely referred to anything more serious than a headache or, as in Ishita's case, a cold.

'I have had it for several days.'

'Perhaps you should buy some medicine?'

'Oof. How can I, Marks? I have no money. Not for myself. Anyway, let's talk about the children.'

Steering the conversation towards budgets, I asked her to itemise all the immediate expenditure required to replace the children's items lost in the tsunami as well as a projection of running costs for the next month. This she did:

Replacement Costs

Toys and games	4,000 rs
Clothes	8,750 rs
School bags	2,000 rs
Cassette player	4,000 rs
Total	18,750 rupees (c. £235)

One Month's Running Costs

Food	11,400 rs
Utilities (electric, water, night watchman etc)	11,000 rs
School fees	4,150 rs
Total (to feed, house and educate 20 children per month)	26,550 rupees (c. £330)

'Thank you for this, Ishita,' I said when she had written down everything.

'Does this mean you will help?'

'It means I will give it some thought,' I replied, deciding not to say anything about my conversation with Mark at that stage.

'When am I seeing you again?'

'How about tomorrow for breakfast?' I proposed, knowing that I should have spoken to Mark again by then. 'I'll meet you in the hotel restaurant at nine o'clock.'

'Not today afternoon then?' she asked hopefully. 'The children will be here at four o'clock as usual.'

'I doubt it, but I might drop by if I'm passing. Besides, I'm sure you've plenty to do without being bothered by me.'

'Four o'clock, then. Goodbye Marks.'

Leaving Ishita to her paining, I set off for a swim. I decided not to return to the orphanage later.

As I walked through the shady hotel courtyard that evening, Madhu appeared furtively from behind a palm tree.

'Good evening, sir.'

'Oh, Madhu! You startled me!'

'Sorry, sir.'

'No worries. How are you?'

'Fine, thank you, sir.' A slight pause. His thin moustache twitched. 'Sir, are you helping the orphanage?'

Although he appeared genuinely concerned, as on the day I arrived, I was mildly irritated by his presumption. Nor did I recollect telling him that supporting the orphanage may be a possibility.

'Madhu,' I chose my words carefully, 'I have met the children and they are clearly in need. I am considering the best thing to do.' *Very diplomatic, very English*, I thought.

'I understand, sir. And the hotel's own collection for the tsunami victims?'

'I'll talk to you about that later,' I replied, edging to get away.

'Very good, sir.'

I turned to go.

'Washing, sir?'

'Maybe,' I said, not wanting to seem entirely dismissive. 'I'll send some down later,' and dashed up the steps to my room.

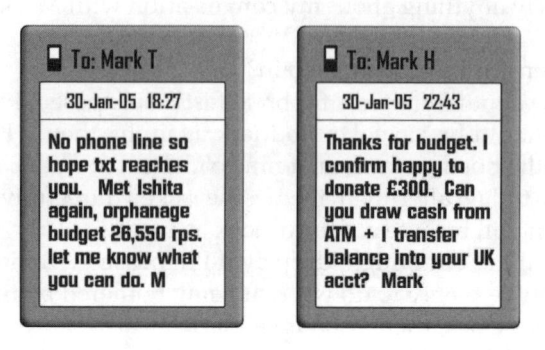

> **To: Mark T**
> 30-Jan-05 18:27
>
> No phone line so hope txt reaches you. Met Ishita again, orphanage budget 26,550 rps. let me know what you can do. M

> **To: Mark H**
> 30-Jan-05 22:43
>
> Thanks for budget. I confirm happy to donate £300. Can you draw cash from ATM + I transfer balance into your UK acct? Mark

I woke early the next day and ambled down to the Shore Temple before breakfast. Gazing at the magnificent stone structure, its clandestine crevices penetrated by the rising sun, I tried to imagine what the beach would have been like on the morning of the tsunami. Suppose Navaj was right: several more temples *did* appear, revealed briefly by the receding sea? A once-thriving civilisation – individuals, families, communities – drowned for a *second time* in the raging waves. As if once wasn't bad enough.

As I wandered back through the peaceful streets, traders were opening their stores; a soul-destroying routine to undertake every morning: arranging displays of carvings, clothes, curios, pictures and postcards outside their shops, all to be taken inside again in the evening. And in the interim: chat, chai, some browsing, a few sales, but little profit.

An elderly lady was spreading out her bags of saris, silks and shirts on the pavement opposite the hotel. I had noticed that she crouched there every morning, usually deep in conversation with passers-by. Today she was on her own. I cast a quick glance at her wares. She caught my eye and signalled me over.

'Hello sir. You like?

'You have nice things.'
'Name sir?'
'Mark.'
'Mok.'
Better than Marks, I smiled inwardly. 'You?'
'Bhuaji. Something you buy? Bring good luck.'
I grinned. 'Maybe later.'
Bhuaji nodded agreeably. She had a warm, weathered face and, to my surprise, accepted my answer without issue. Shrouded in a royal blue sari she clasped my hand, her glass bracelets jangling as she raised her arm. 'I see you. You live in hotel over street,' she whispered, indicating *Wild Roses* with her eyes.

Someone else tracking my moves! But I wasn't too bothered in her case; I liked Bhuaji and promised myself that I would buy something from her before leaving Mamallapuram.

It was just a few minutes after nine when I climbed the stairs to the small terraced area at the front of the hotel. Ishita, looking tired, was waiting.

We sat at a small table in the shade; even by that hour the sun was beating down intensely.

'Are you feeling any better?' I enquired.
'So, so,' she replied, dismissive of her cold, 'but it is no matter.'

Prakash, the dowdy middle-aged waiter, shuffled over to take our order.

'What would you like, Ishita?'
'Actually I'll just have tea.'
'You ought to eat something.' I sounded like my mother.
'Toast and honey then.'
'Sir?' Prakash drawled.
'Banana porridge and coffee, please. Strong,' I added.

We chatted about the children. Ishita confided her concerns about the finances.

'I have only enough money to feed them for a few more days. The rest is needed for rent.' Exhaling deeply, she seemed to bare the weight of the world on her shoulders that morning. 'I am so worried. I did not sleep last night. Generally I have not slept well since the tsunami. Always my mind is thinking what is best to do for the children.'

It was time to alleviate her misery. 'Ishita, I am in touch with a charity in England,' I said, looking directly at her. 'The trustees have agreed to donate twenty-five thousand rupees to cover the cost of the tsunami loss. That will allow a bit extra for other necessary items.'

A pause.

With her gaze focused on the table, Ishita's reaction was strange. Her face displayed no look of pleasure. All that I heard were the words 'as an initial payment...' muttered under her breath.

Contrary to my expectation, it was a strange response. Perhaps that was her manner, but what did she mean by 'an initial payment'?

'It will take a while to get you the mon...'

'How soon?' she interrupted brusquely.

'Well, give me a day or two. Why?'

'I am going to Chennai on Tuesday,' she softened. 'I am wishing to buy the children's provisions then. The city is cheaper than here.'

'I guess that makes sense. Leave it with me. Oh, and please, Ishita, I would like this to remain confidential.' I didn't want people to think I was wandering around Mamallapuram with an abundance of resources at my disposal. Ishita nodded.

Batteries recharged, she babbled on unremittingly about how happy the children would be: 'You must come and see them once they have their new clothes and bags. You know, their joy is my joy.'

'Yes, I know. You've told me.' *Many times.* My ears were beginning to ache.

What with Ishita's incessant prattling and Prakash's reluctant waitering, it was past mid-day before I eventually pushed back my chair to leave.

'Marks, when can I meet you next?' she demanded shrilly.

'Ishita, I've just spent three hours with you. I would really appreciate some time to myself now.'

'How about lunch? Or perhaps we could meet for dinner?'

'Goodbye Ishita.' I offered her my hand to emphasise the finality of my statement: 'I'll come and find you when I have the money.' She shook it limply.

I trod cautiously through the courtyard, wary of Madhu lurking among the palms, and headed towards the beach. Thankfully he was not about.

In the middle of the afternoon I returned to my room, took my mandolin from its case and, sitting cross-legged on the bed, started to fiddle. Having mastered *Santa Lucia*, I was feeling rather pleased with myself. A sharp rap on the door jolted me from my concentration.

'Ishita!' How did she know where my room was?

'Hello, Marks.'

'Yes.'

'What have you been doing?' she asked amiably, clearly wanting to chat.

I was in no mood, however, to account for my movements since our last conversation. 'Just enjoying some time to myself,' I replied with just enough charm so as not to sound completely rude. 'You?'

I suspected she was angling to be invited in, but I refused to oblige. I had been in India long enough to appreciate that certain codes of behaviour prevailed throughout all stratas of society; entertaining a single female in my bedroom, whatever the motive, would have been asking for trouble. Besides, I was beginning to find her bothersome; charity and children aside, her idle blathering was testing my good nature.

'I've been shopping...'

I suppressed a yawn.

'...buying vegetables for the children's tea.'

'Ah. That's nice.'

Lingering on the doorstep, she continued to witter on about sundry matters of little consequence for several minutes. I leant against the doorframe, wishing neither to appear discourteous nor to give any indication that I was happy listening to her until sunset.

'I wish I could do more for the children,' she lamented. 'They have so little. Their joy is...'

'I think perhaps you are doing as much as you are able,' I interrupted.

Ishita nodded. 'Yes, Marks.'

She then turned, surreptitiously scanning the courtyard with her gaze. When she looked back, a veil of conspiracy cloaked her expression. She tilted her head towards me.

'Marks, please do not tell Madhu, or anyone in the hotel, about your donation,' she hissed, her voice dropping to a whisper.

As if I would. 'Why are you asking...'

'I am not wanting the hotel to have any commission. It's *all* for the children.'

Interesting. Although I had already given her my own reasons for confidentiality, I was surprised by Ishita's insistence. Why was it in her interests to keep the donation a secret?

'Absolutely,' I replied assuredly, despite my bewilderment.

'I'm glad we understand each other.'

Then a strange thing happened: an unexpected wave of pity coursed through my body. I suddenly saw in Ishita a person who had tirelessly devoted her life to the wellbeing of the children in her care. To the neglect of her own personal concerns, she had acted as a shield in the direst of circumstances.

Before me stood a selfless, but very needy, woman.

That's where I knew my boundaries. Ishita's strength of character was admirable, dare I say, appealing. It merited an enormous hug of appreciation. From someone. But not me.

I wanted to run a mile. Although arranging the money had nudged me into uncharted territory, it was a deed I was happy to do. Servicing the personal needs of this obsessive woman would launch me dangerously into orbit, a journey that I was not prepared to make.

'If you don't mind, I have some things to do,' I said vaguely.

'Yes?'

'Well, er... I have to send some emails.'

'Very well.' Ishita seemed disappointed, unfulfilled, as she turned to leave. 'Goodbye, Marks.'

As she padded down the little staircase, my sympathy, like the long shadow of her sari in the late-afternoon sun, trailed a healthy distance behind her.

That evening Madhu spied me by the hotel gate.

'Hello, sir!' He scuttled over. 'Are you having a good day?'

'Yes, very pleasant,' I responded noncommittally.

'It is good you are helping the orphanage.'

I threw him a quizzical glance.

'By how much, sir?' he added.

I saw red. Gulping a huge lungful of muggy air, I counted to ten.

Then: 'Madhu. Please listen.' I said deliberately. 'I have not told anyone that I am helping the orphanage. Should I ever choose to do so, the matter is entirely between Ishita and myself.'

'Very good sir.'

'You do understand?'

'Sir.'

'Enough said.' I took a couple of steps and then, on a gut feeling: 'And Madhu...'

'Yes, sir?'

'In future, please do not give my room number to anyone.'

'Yes, sir.' He looked crestfallen. 'Sorry, sir.'

My hunch was correct. I smiled. 'Have a good evening, Madhu.'

'And you, sir. Please do not forget the hotel tsunami collection.'

Don't push me.

I was puzzled: why, when she had specifically asked *me* not to tell anyone, did Ishita blab to Madhu about the money?

'Agh!' I banged my fist against the cash machine in frustration. My card, which had worked perfectly well in Vijayawada, had just been declined by the Central Bank of India ATM. I was unable to access any cash. Another wasted morning.

Reluctant to use the official money changers in town because of their exploitative commission charges, I returned to the hotel. Pacing along the road, I consciously *and* completely blanked the shop traders. I really was not in the mood.

'Sir, you are not looking happy.'

That's because I'm not.

'Sir, making yourself happy. Come, buy a luxurious silk carpet! There is so, so much of happiness in…'

I'm not listening.

I explained my predicament to Madhu, allowing him to assume that I needed the money to pay my room bill.

'There is an ATM in next village five kilometres away. I arrange taxi?'

'Thanks Madhu, perhaps I'll go tomorrow.'

I felt disgruntled. Was I being selfish? I had come to Mamallapuram to relax but all my energy and time had been absorbed by Ishita. Perhaps I shouldn't be so begrudging.

But this place was maddening. Even the relatively simple task of withdrawing money was becoming a whole day's activity. The more wound up I got, the more exasperated I became with myself, Ishita, Madhu, the beach women, the shopkeepers, India…

Mark, stop! Deep breath.

A pot of ginger tea.

Regain perspective.

Later in the afternoon I went to see Navaj.

'Mark, good to see you!' he exclaimed. 'Your shirts and pyjamas are ready.'

At least something was working out. Enthusiastically I tried on each of them.

'You've done a great job. Thanks.' The light cotton was just what I needed, particularly as the temperature was rising on a daily basis.

'I'm pleased you are liking them.'

'At last I can give away some of my heavier T-shirts. Perhaps some of the older boys in the orphanage might like them?'

Then he did it. Navaj lobbed a colossal boulder into the conversation.

'You know, Mark, Ishita is not owning a *real* orphanage.'

'Oh, you mean it's just pretend,' I responded flippantly.

'No, I am meaning it's a business.'

Silence.

'Say again?'

'Oh yes,' he verified matter-of-factly, 'it's very common in these parts.'

'WHAT??!!'

'Business people like her are renting children from poor families to pretend as orphans. They are taking sizeable donations and subsidies. Small-small part goes to parents and is paying for room rent and food. Most is going straight for business.'

'You're serious?'

'Haan ji. Ishita is part of much large network working from Chennai.'

Utterly flummoxed, I put him to the test.

'How long has she lived in Mamallapuram?'

'Since two years.'

'She told me five.'

Navaj didn't respond but looked me straight in the eye.

I couldn't believe what he was saying. Despite my reservations about her personally, I had totally trusted Ishita's integrity as far as the children were concerned.

I felt sick, confused, completely ensnared by the web of lies and deceit. The tiny room suddenly seemed even more claustrophobic. I wanted to get out... but I had too many questions.

'How do you know so much about her?'

'I'm a part-time police officer.'

'NO?!'

He got me again. 'You're a small-time tailor who lost everything in...'

'Yes,' he interjected. 'I am also employed by the police. Look, here's my ID.' He took his wallet from his back trouser pocket and produced a laminated badge.

Sure enough, it displayed his photograph and some official-looking stamps. He smiled, reading my scepticism.

'I shouldn't, but I show you something more.' He was on a mission to prove his own probity. The plot was becoming more ridiculous by the minute. *You can stop filming now*, I thought. But there were no hidden cameras.

He removed a pile of fabric from a large wooden chest in the corner and opened the lid. Hunting around for a moment, he pulled out an envelope containing a letter from an organisation in Chennai. Intending to build a home for street children, it was seeking funds. Across the top, inscribed in flowery blue letters, were the words:

No one has the right to be happy alone

The same words on the wall outside Ishita's orphanage. The letter was signed K. Bhatt.

'Who is this man?' I asked.

'A clever-clever character,' replied Navaj, 'Ishita's boyfriend.'

Right, that's it. I was about to explode.

'Excuse me, Navaj, I must go outside for air.'

'I understand.' He handed me the letter. 'Take. Photocopy it. Return it tomorrow but do not tell anyone what I am showing you. If you are not believing me, talk to others. Listen to what they say.'

I headed straight to the nearest bar.

'Cold beer!' I demanded before the waiter had a chance to open his mouth. 'Please!'

He nodded. 'You are looking hot, sir!'

Hot?! I was flaming. I could have set the town alight with rage. I wanted to blast what I knew from the rooftops. I wanted to track down Ishita and...

...well, those thoughts are best kept to myself. But the children – Hasan, Tarun the clown, little Rajdeep – did they know? Were they willing participants? No, they couldn't possibly be. That I didn't want to believe.

With my blood cooled by a few gulps of beer, I reflected on the last few days. A pattern began to emerge from the thread of events.

Ishita and Madhu were undoubtedly in cahoots. Surely? It certainly would explain why Madhu, in his rather unsubtle way, kept pestering me to give money to the orphanage; he wanted his commission. It was he, after all, who had introduced us in the first place.

I'd specifically asked Ishita to keep the decision confidential. She'd then instructed me to do likewise. Was that because she didn't want Madhu to receive any commission? "It's *all* for the children." Was the woman being doubly devious, playing a game with both of us?

Strands of other conversations wove through my mind. I recollected the inconsistencies in Ishita's account of the morning the tsunami struck. Initially, she told me that the children were playing inside the orphanage. Their first experience of the tsunami was of water flooding down the street and into the hallway. A few days later, she'd said that they were all standing *on the beach* and witnessed the waves racing towards them over the sand. That's why the children were now so fearful of returning there.

Both versions couldn't be correct. Neither could the truth lie somewhere in between. There was a distance of about two hundred metres between the shoreline and the orphanage, from where it was impossible to see the sea; a line of hotels stood in the way. Another possibility entered my head: perhaps *both* stories were entirely fictional.

Ishita was always very specific about the times I should visit the orphanage. This would make sense if she rented the children from another village. Maybe she engineered Madhu to bring along unsuspecting tourists such as myself, Beatrice and Helen at pre-arranged times? I wondered if they knew? Perhaps I should find out where they were staying in order to warn...

'Hello, sir. Another heavy day!'

Interrupting my train of thought, Chandra, the manager had wandered over.

'You could say that.'

'The weather is changing. Tomorrow, rain maybe.'

'You think so?'

I had sat in this particular bar a few times and found Chandra easygoing.

More small talk. Then I seized the moment. 'What can you tell me about the orphanages in this area?'

'Why are you wanting to know?' He raised his eyebrows suspiciously. Was he party to the conspiracy as well?

'No reason, really,' I responded casually, backtracking. 'It's just that there seem to be quite a few. Surely there aren't that number of orphans in Mamallapuram?'

'No, you're right,' he said calmly. 'Basically only few are proper homes.'

'Really?'

'The one up the road is real,' he said unprompted. 'But most exist for making money. That is their decision.'

I decided to push it further. 'What about the Small Blossom Home for Orphaned Children?'

He looked blank.

'It's a few streets away. Run by a woman called Ishita.'

'Ah... yes.' His hesitation spoke volumes. 'That lady not long in Mamallapuram so I am not knowing many things.'

'That's interesting.'

'As I am saying, just few are real,' he said pointedly, 'if you are understanding me.'

Navaj could have been telling the truth after all.

On the way back to the hotel I stopped by another bar for a nightcap, pursued the same line of questioning and received a similar response. No one, it appeared, was prepared to declare Ishita an unmitigated scoundrel but there was little doubt that her dubious reputation was shrouded in mystery. To my astonishment, neither Navaj, Chandra, nor anyone, had intimated that what Ishita did was actually *wrong*. That was simply how some people earned an income. Live and let live.

What next? Confront Ishita, play her at her own game...?

Enough for one night. Sleep, let my anger subside and formulate a plan in the morning. I didn't want to do anything rash that I would subsequently regret. I dozed off, dreaming blissfully of the ATM that refused my card.

Chandra was right. The morning sky was overcast. Perhaps it was time to head for the mountains.

Although I had slept well, my subconscious had been unravelling the issues. Feeling remarkably level-headed, though still livid, I woke up realising there was little I could do. In the cold light of day, my instinct told me to pack my bags and quietly remove myself from the situation: *don't mess with a culture to which I don't belong, let alone comprehend.*

Since arriving in India, I had learnt two things. One: people didn't appreciate having their integrity questioned. Two: power lay in the hands of a manipulative minority who were always eager to turn every situation to their advantage. Although I was convinced that Ishita was acting fraudulently, I had no hard evidence to prove it. If I started to rock the boat, I could easily become the one swimming for my life, not her. I was not even sure what role Navaj, the undercover tailor, played in this. Where were his investigations leading? Was he anticipating a nice little payout to keep his mouth shut? If so, why tell me?

It was definitely time to slip away. After consulting my *Rough Guide*, I decided to retreat inland to the hill station of Kodaikanal in the Western Ghat mountains. The cooler air might clear my mind.

Though Mammallapuram was not situated on the railway line, it contained a small booking office from which I was able to secure a reservation for later that evening.

I decided to wait until the eleventh hour before informing Madhu of my intentions. Convinced he was in league with Ishita, I wanted to avoid any repercussions. I was prepared to pay for another night should my short notice become an issue.

'You were staying until end of week, sir?' Madhu commented later that afternoon when I told him I would be leaving shortly.

'Well originally, yes,' I replied, keeping the conversation as low-key as possible, 'but the weather seems to be changing and I'd like to get going again.'

'Shall I order taxi, sir?'

'Yes please, that would be good. My train leaves Chennai Egmore Station at eight this evening. About six o'clock will do.'

'Fine. And sir?' He looked at me.

'Yes Madhu?' Our eyes met. Then he averted his gaze. I sensed that we were caught in one of those classic moments: he knew that I knew that he knew that... and so we both said... nothing. No questions about the orphanage, no request for the hotel tsunami fund, no issue about checking out so late in the day.

'I'll send boy for bag carry when taxi is coming.'

I just had time to cross the road and say goodbye to Navaj. To my surprise, his shutters were down and locked.

'Where is Navaj?' I asked a neighbour.

'Chennai on urgent business. He is returning in the morning.'

In my hand I held the letter that I'd photocopied earlier in town. I bent down to slide it under the door.

As I stood, Ishita appeared. Her timing, spot on.

'I hear you're going, Marks?' She said curtly.

News travels fast. 'Madhu told you?'

Not a flicker of a response.

'Yes it's true,' I continued, 'and I'm sorry to say there's no money for you.'

'As you wish.'

What?

Her reply, devoid of emotion, caught me completely off guard. I was stunned.

'Are you not disappointed that your children – "their joy is my joy" – won't be receiving the funds for their clothes and books?'

'It is your decision, your will. I cannot do anything.'

Something snapped. Ishita's cool, unbending indifference had hit a nerve. I found myself shaking, seething with rage. I so desperately wanted her to be indignant, not for herself, but for the children I'd let down, disappointed.

'Shout at me! Call me names! Strike me! – a rich, white man who breaks his promises. I've shattered the dreams of all your children. Aren't you mad? Come on, Ishita!'

But she said nothing.

Instead it was me bawling in the street, hurling a piece of my incensed mind at her dispassionate, empty eyes. Though I remained in complete control of my tongue I couldn't let her get away with this. Not now. I had intended to walk away, refrain from interfering, but she had sought me out.

'You don't run an orphanage,' I goaded her, determined to provoke a reaction. 'You're a business woman. You exploit children, tourists and the genuine victims of the tsunami. All for your own pocket. You're sick!'

Everything I had experienced so far on my trip had been sullied by the events of the last few days. Was it all the direct result of the tsunami, or was life always like this? I felt dirty, used. Confused. Could I trust no one? Resentment rumbled in the pit of my stomach.

I was struck by an even more uncomfortable thought. How many other orphanages and children's projects similar to Ishita's were scattered throughout India? Were other people, like me, taken in by their scams? How would people in the UK feel if they discovered that their well-intentioned support was being misappropriated? Perhaps it might be best not to tell anyone about this.

Then I pictured the girls at Hebron, the boys at SKCV, confident, happy and secure. I wouldn't allow Ishita, nor anyone, to snatch away those experiences or undermine the good work of the majority of projects such as these. There was no questioning their integrity. No, it was important for people to know the context.

By now an audience had gathered around us.

'Do you know about this woman?' I asked.

But my question was lost in a sea of bemused expressions; a conspiracy of silence. I turned back to Ishita, still desperate for a response but she, too, remained speechless.

I wanted to spit contempt onto her loathsome, self-righteous face.

Suddenly, I, too, was struck dumb, burdened with the same pity that I'd experienced the other day. Was I being too swift to condemn? *Could she..? No... Perhaps... Perhaps she actually believes she's doing the right thing?*

I didn't understand. My capacity to think numbed, I was mentally and emotionally exhausted. It really was time to go. Turning my back on Ishita, I walked towards the waiting taxi.

As I shut the door, Bhuaji scurried across the road. Gentle Bhuaji; was she the only person with any sincerity in this town?

'Sir, sir, wait!' She clutched a large swathe of orange silk embroidered with dancing dolphins. 'This is for you.'

'Thank you so much, Bhuaji. It's lovely.' She thrust it into my hand and looked up, smiling expectantly. I glanced down; her crumpled palm was outstretched.

'Sir?'

'Yes, of course.' I reached into my pocket, withdrew three hundred rupees and pressed the notes into her hand.

'Thank you sir. You bring me good luck.'

As the taxi pulled away, I resisted the temptation to look back.

6
Bad Ambassador

The soundtrack to my adventures was now playing in someone else's ears

What about **my** good luck, Bhuaji? Enough for one day. Drained, my brain and heart ached. *No time for wallowing, though. Be positive:*

- *The train has left on time*
- *I'm heading for the mountains*
- *I don't ever have to see Ishita again*

Hoorah for small blessings. All I needed was a speedy journey to Kodaikanal.

I started to prepare my bed, a lower 2AC side berth, for the night. This involved the simple action of unlocking two metal catches in the top corners of the facing seats, then lowering them forward to meet in the middle. The blue curtain pulled across the upper bunk indicated that its occupant had already retired.

At precisely the moment that I released the catch on the first seat, the train suddenly lurched. The weighty seat lunged forward - *CRACK!!* - plunging the full force of its solid metal ridge into my skull.

I froze.

No pain, no stars, nothing.

I waited for my body's response to catch up with the impact. Nothing.

Surely something should happen: I'd been hit hard. Am I about to pass out... throw up... die... have I been knocked into my next life... is this Ishita taking karmic revenge...?

Letting the seat drop fully into place, I raised my hand to my forehead. It was wet, warm and tender. My fingers glistened crimson.

That's when the pain hit. Not where I had been struck, though, but a heavy, dull throb at the base of my neck. I fell into the seat behind me, shaking. *What to do?* The train, for once, was ploughing through the countryside at speed. *We're in the middle of nowhere... Where will the paramedics land their helicopter... Who will explain to my family what's happened... What...?*

Deep breath, cold water, stop the swelling. I stood up, staggered to the end of the carriage, pushed open the door and fell towards the washbasin and mirror in the corridor. The acrid tang of toilet-air socked me square in the nose.

'Hey! 'Scuse me!' A gruff, American accent slurred in my right ear. I turned. A red-eyed, silver-haired man lay sprawled across the porter's table-cum-bed. 'Say, wazza deal with these trains?'

'What do you mean?'

'I've not done one before and I'm dis-ori-en-ta-ted. I've been visiting friends in Chennai. Yesterday was my last day. They threw me a leaving bash and I spent the whole night drinking whisky... oh my, too much whisky... I've been asleep most of today.' He shook his big, dopey head like a puppy. 'I was still drunk when my friends put me on the train. I've just woken up and, man, I have the mother of all hangovers. What I'm saying is: D'ya have any water, please?'

Now's not a good time. Can't you see the bloody hole in my head?

'Sure. No worries,' I replied.

I stumbled back to my seat to retrieve my plastic bottle.

'Here,' I said, returning and handing it to him. 'Take this. I have another.'

'You're an angel,' he replied, guzzling it down in one.

'I'm sure someone will come down the train selling water soon, so you should be OK.' I could feel a trickling sensation down my arm. 'If you don't mind, I just need to, er...' I indicated my head.

'Hey, what happened to you?' He exclaimed.

Thanks for noticing.

'Had a fight with my bed.'

I pulled my handkerchief from my pocket and stuck it under the tap. Wincing, I pressed the soggy cloth against my forehead. I held it there for a few seconds then braved a glance in the mirror. A healthy bruise was developing nicely above my right eye, split in half by a three centimetre, leaking gash. It was difficult to determine its depth as the edges were smudged with blood. Reluctant to peel back the skin in case the jolting train caused my prying fingers to exacerbate the injury, I pressed the handkerchief to my forehead once more.

I felt a hand rest gently on my shoulder. I turned to see a petite woman in an aqua cotton blouse holding out a sticking plaster and an antiseptic wipe sachet. 'Here,' she said calmly. 'Perhaps this may help?' Her soft voice had a German lilt.

'Thanks, that's very kind.'

'I saw what happened.' Her voice was soothing. 'Are you OK?'

'A bit sore, but I'll live!'

'Is your tetanus up to date?'

'I think so. Had all my shots before leaving the UK.'

'I could do with something right now,' murmured my American friend. Wearing a scruffy "I love Bangkok" T-shirt he didn't look the picture of health himself. His face, though, framed with a neat reddish brown beard flecked with grey, suggested that, ordinarily, he was a man who took care of himself. I guessed that he was in his late fifties and well-travelled, Indian trains aside. 'My name's Frank, by the way.'

'Mark.'

'Pia.' She turned to me. 'Where are you from?'

'UK, a town called Basing...'

'Cold drinks! Soda!' interrupted a uniformed young man walked past carrying a large green bucket laden with bottles.

'Water? asked Frank.

'Yes, sir.'

'I'll take two. Are you from Germany, Pia?' he questioned, impatiently ripping off the bottle's plastic seal and lid.

Flicking her short bob, a few strands of auburn hair bounced from her fringe. 'Holland,' she retorted.

'Oops,' choked Frank, water dribbling into his beard.

I smiled, pleased the faux pas was his.

'What are you doing here, Mark?' Pia asked.

'Escaping,' I replied, rinsing my handkerchief under the tap.

'Sounds intriguing.'

I told them both about Ishita, her fake orphanage and Navaj, the undercover tailor.

'Wow, that'd make a great story,' said Frank when I'd finished. 'What did you say the name of the place was?'

'Mamallapuram.'

It transpired that Frank was a semi-retired journalist, now working freelance for a news syndicate. He lived, when not travelling, on Beaver Island, Lake Michigan.

'Yes, and it's *my* story. So keep your hands off!' I teased, checking my injuries in the mirror. Though the bleeding had stopped, a yellow, hardboiled egg now protruded handsomely from my forehead.

'So Ishita said nothing at all?' asked Pia.

'Nope. That was the problem,' I responded to her reflection in the glass. 'She neither defended nor denied her actions.'

'That must have been so frustrating.'

'I just wanted *some* kind of reaction. Anything. I don't get it. There was I, publicly accusing her of exploitation and extortion. Yet my words flew right over her head.' I peeled the back from the plaster and stretched it across the wound. 'But, you know, there's still a small part of me that gives her the benefit of the doubt.'

'How could you?' questioned Frank. 'Sounds like she was as guilty as hell. The fact that she didn't say anything speaks volumes.' He shook his head incredulously. 'As for that tailor. Undercover cop my...'

The train suddenly lurched, the toilet door clanged opened and a stench filled the corridor. I slammed it shut, securing its metal hook in place.

'I wouldn't ever want you on a jury if I was in trouble,' Pia said to Frank testily. 'The difficulty is, you really don't know in a country like this. You just do what you can.'

'What do you mean?' asked Frank.

'We've also been involved in some tsunami relief work over the last few weeks.'

'We?'

'Ah, sorry, my partner, Karl, is resting. He's not been feeling too well. Tummy,' she said, rubbing her own. 'I told him not to eat the salad!'

'What were you doing?' I asked.

'Helping to distribute provisions to people in a few villages south of Chennai. Rice, oil, blankets, clothes. Stuff like that.'

'That's very admirable,' said Frank. 'How did you get involved in that?'

'We were travelling around South India at the end of December. When the news broke, we felt we had to do something. So we took the train to Chennai and volunteered with a Red Cross team.'

'I'm not sure I could've done that. Wasn't it traumatic?'

'Didn't really think about it. We just got on with what needed doing.' Pia paused for a moment. 'Well, to be honest, at times it was tough. Horrible. The evenings were the worst. We used to move between the rows of temporary rehabilitation tents, talking, listening to people's stories. I spoke to a mother whose nine-year-old son was playing cricket on the beach with his friends. They were among the first to be washed away.

'Day after day, up and down the beach, mothers and fathers sat on the sand. They seemed shell-shocked. Rocking back and forth, repeating the names of their lost sons and daughters. I asked an Indian relief worker what they were saying. "My daughter," she repeated, "I'm waiting for you. Please come soon."

'A boy showed me a few sticks poking out of the sand. Rags of coloured cloth were draped over them. That's where his house used to...' her voice trailed off.

'Are you OK, Pia?'

A tall, pasty-looking guy had just appeared behind Pia. He wrapped his arm around her slim waist.

'Yes, yes. I'm fine. Frank, Mark, this is Karl.'

'How are you feeling?' I asked.

Karl looked at Pia. 'I told them about your stomach,' she said.

'Much better thanks,' he smiled weakly. 'I just needed some rest. What were you talking about?'

'Just comparing tsunami stories,' Pia answered.

Frank coughed nervously.

'Mark's been having fun,' she said.

'Oh, yes?'

'I'll tell you about it later,' she said, pulling Karl's arm around her more tightly.

'Could I ask you to be careful what you say?' I asked Pia.

'What do you mean?'

'I don't want people to be deterred from supporting work like this. Not the tsunami necessarily, I'm talking about the ongoing projects, children's homes, orphanages, that kind of thing. People are often sceptical about donating to charitable work overseas. They want to know, quite rightly, how much money directly goes to those in need and how much gets absorbed in admin costs. I'm not sure, though, that they appreciate how much time and effort is required to identify the bona fide projects. Sifting. Questioning. Investigation. I don't want them to think that every other orphanage is a scam. When people give in good faith...'

'Come on, Mark,' interjected Frank. 'It's obvious who the scoundrels are. You don't think people are dumb enough to be taken in by people like Ishita?'

'I nearly was.'

'Ah. Sorry.' He looked embarrassed. 'Point taken. I guess I may have been too.' He shuffled awkwardly.

'Mark's right,' said Karl. 'It's not always clear which projects are genuine. If it makes you feel any better, we heard some horrific stories too. In one place, villagers actually pulled down their own houses to get aid. They weren't even touched by the waves! Even government officials were taking backhanders to divert trucks of food from the communities of Dalit survivors to the higher-caste fishermen.'

'Dalit?' questioned Frank.

'Scheduled caste. Untouchables.'

'There are many families in Mamallapuram affected by the tsunami who are still in desperate need,' I said. 'I suspect the aid may never reach them.'

'I agree,' said Karl. 'There'll always be a minority who manipulate the situation to their own ends, whether it's the media, government or individuals.'

'Exactly, but they shouldn't be allowed to frustrate the goodwill and generosity of everyone else. Neither should they get away with tarring the genuine projects with the same, grubby brush. There's so much good work going on.'

'So what's the answer?' asked Frank.

'I haven't a clue,' I replied. 'All I can do is tell people what I saw and hope that others may intervene. There's no more I can do personally to prevent Ishita, and others like her, from continuing their unethical practices.'

'Sounds like a cop out.'

'Have you any better suggestions, Frank?' asked Pia.

He looked sheepish. 'Carry on the conversation in the morning?'

'Not me. I'm getting off at Kodaikanal Road. Where are you heading?' I asked.

'Madurai,' said Karl.

'Me too!' exclaimed Frank.

'Great!' I heard Pia mutter as she pulled open the carriage door.

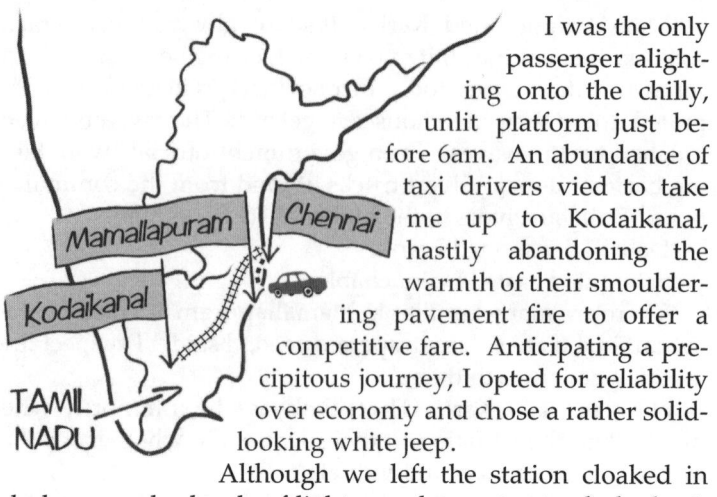

I was the only passenger alighting onto the chilly, unlit platform just before 6am. An abundance of taxi drivers vied to take me up to Kodaikanal, hastily abandoning the warmth of their smouldering pavement fire to offer a competitive fare. Anticipating a precipitous journey, I opted for reliability over economy and chose a rather solid-looking white jeep.

Although we left the station cloaked in darkness, pale shards of light soon began to streak the horizon as we slowly climbed above the valley floor.

I love early morning in rural India. As the day unfolds, villagers leisurely go about their business in an atmosphere of relative calm. Men chat and defecate by the roadside. Women amble through the fields carrying water pots, babies and huge bundles of wood on their heads. Wily, tan-coloured dogs sniff around scraps of food and each others' bottoms.

Kodaikanal, at an altitude of over 2000 metres, is a superb base for trekking the Western Ghats, India's second highest mountain range. At the height of summer, it is a popular retreat from the heat of the plains. The town swarms with flush Indians and students taking up temporary residence in the numerous Raj-era bungalows that colonised the area in the mid-nineteenth century.

The Hotel Yagappa, at first sight, appeared idyllically located on the side of the mountain. Verdantly lush bushes clutched the hillside, small birds twittered merrily and a thin wisp of mist bearded the treetops.

'Ah, how glorious,' I mused as the taxi rolled in.

'Aaaaggghh, how fffffreezing,' I moaned as I shivered in my room a few minutes later. In summer the hotel may have been delightful. In February, however, I would have been cosier kipping down next to a bag of frozen peas in Sainsburys. Having spent the previous six weeks in the sun, I noticed the biting air even more, especially as it pierced the wound on my forehead like a keen blade.

Blessed with a faulty internal thermostat, I easily feel the extremes of heat and cold. Moreover, when I'm chilly, everything else in the world assumes a mantle of bleakness. The Monet-esque mist, which hung so alluringly moments earlier, had shed its charm. No longer shrouding the landscape in mystery and magic, it had morphed into a numbing mass that irritatingly obscured the other side of the valley from view.

I spent the afternoon exploring the town in hot pursuit of a thermal fleece, woolly gloves and a pair of thick socks. When the sun did appear, I should add, the temperature rose considerably and the air became pleasantly warm. As darkness fell, though, so did my spirits.

Don't get me wrong, I loved the Hotel Yagappa. It was the archetypal rustic mountain haunt. Rural charm exuded from every crack, but icy water dripped from the bathroom tap and the bed was damp.

The wonderfully named manager, Fatamuti, was a little round ball of soap-scented hairy pudginess. A man of few words, he conducted his daily duties with an air of reluctant enthusiasm.

'May I order some coffee, please?' I would request.

'Ffmm,' he would snuffle through his beard.

Why he chose to run this particular hotel in the mountains eluded me. I'm sure he would have been far happier managing a retirement home for wealthy Brahmins by the sea.

It didn't take me long, though, to discover the one thing that sent Fatamuti into convulsions of pleasure: the hotel's liberal stash of beer. Although he consumed none himself, he certainly ensured that his guests, there were three of us, were never left wanting. It was good beer, too, served in a snug bar scantily furnished with wicker furniture and whitewashed walls decorated with ancient warrior swords.

Fatamuti's most endearing feature, however, was his extraordinary manner of breathing. Somewhere in his family history an ancestor must have enjoyed conjugal relations with a pressure cooker. For whenever he exhaled, a plosive "pssssshh" shot from his lips. I wouldn't have been surprised had a jet of steam spurted from the top of his head to complete the effect.

Watching him open a beer was worth the 200 rupees nightly rate alone. Flipping open its top, he and the bottle conversed in a secret language known only to themselves.

'Pssssshh!' Fatamuti exclaimed, expiring heavily.

'Psssskk!' the escaping gas replied.

Of course, the other guests and I had to keep ordering beer to sustain the flow of entertainment.

I tossed and turned, shivered and shook, but couldn't sleep. Pulling the blanket over my head or curling into a ball brought neither warmth nor suppressed the urge to urinate.

Eventually defeated by my bladder, I rolled out of bed and skated across the freezing tiled floor to the bathroom. I flicked the light switch. The power was off. With chattering teeth, I peed then washed my fingers in the icy water. At least the bed would seem warmer when I climbed back in.

Wrong.

Completely wide-awake by this point, I decided to listen to some music. Finding my maglite, I unzipped the pocket where I usually kept my mobile phone.

It wasn't there.

Had I put it somewhere else? Within a few minutes, the entire contents of my rucksack were scattered across the floor. As I frantically searched through my belongings, I was suddenly hit by one vague recollection and two stark realisations.

The recollection: I had used the phone as an alarm clock to ensure that I wouldn't miss my stop at Kodaikanal Road. Once awake, I had placed it on the bunk while tying up my boots.

Realisation number one: It was still there. That, however, wasn't the issue; I could buy another mobile. But my music?

Realisation number two: The soundtrack to my adventures was now playing in someone else's ears.

With the sun shining gloriously, I took my lunch and the *Bhagavad Gita*, which features on many travellers' reading lists, to the park. The wooded enclosure, an ambrosial affair situated near the lake, was graced with sweet-scented flowers, shrubs, birds, grass and, so I naively hoped, a shady tree under which I could relax, read and munch on my spicy masala bun. All the ingredients for a perfect, lazy Sunday afternoon.

But it wasn't to be. As soon as I had reclined under a lofty cedar, a group of male students ran over. Showering me with questions, they pursued, to the letter, a routine to which I had become rigorously accustomed over the preceding weeks:

QUESTION 1:	What is your good name, sir?
ANSWER 1:	Mark.
QUESTION 2:	What is your native country?
ANSWER 2:	England.
RESPONSE:	Ah, England. Veerrry good, sir. David Beckham!
FOLLOW-UP RESPONSE:	Yes, David Beckham. Ha, ha, ha!! (hearty guffaws)
QUESTION 3:	Where is your wife?
ANSWER 3:	I'm not married.
SUPPLEMENTARY QUESTION 3A:	Why not?
SUPPLEMENTARY ANSWER 3A:	Because I'm not.
QUESTION 4:	How old are you?
ANSWER 4:	Thirty-eight.
SUPPLEMENTARY QUESTION 4A:	Then why don't you have a wife?
SUPPLEMENTARY ANSWER 4A:	I enjoy being single.
SUPPLEMENTARY RESPONSE 4B AND QUESTION 5:	Ah sir, ha, ha, ha, veeerrry good! So what is your profession?

And so on. Occasionally, to make life simple, I invented a wife.

'Ah, sir, very nice! Where is she?'

'Er... shopping.'

I frequently had to fabricate a love of cricket, which was fine until I was asked to name my favourite player. Then I was stumped.

Back to this particular group of boys.

'Please, sir, taking group photo?' asked one beaming lad.

'OK, just one,' I replied, waving my hand to indicate that they should stand in a tight group.

'No, no with *you*!' he exclaimed.

So, posing in the centre with the other boys eagerly bunching around, I grinned inanely as the camera snapped.

'Thank you, sir, thank you!' the boys repeated, taking it in turns to shake my hand. Off they scampered.

Optimistically, I settled down once more with my book. Within two minutes, I was besieged by a gang of younger, noisier boys from the town. Like bullets from a machine gun their questions rang through the air, the boys barely allowing me the chance to answer one question before firing another. Twisting me back and forth, bang-bang-bang-bang-bang, their shrill inquisition battered on relentlessly.

A boy thrust the earphones of his Walkman in my face.

'Please, Uncle, listen! You will like.'

What joy, ding-ding strains to underscore the scene. I listened obligingly for a minute or two, nodding my head sympathetically to the bhangra beat blasting between my eardrums.

We then all shook hands, lots of hands, and exchanged hugs.

'Are you liking our town, Uncle?'

'It's the most beautiful place in India,' I declared charmingly through gritted teeth.

Well-satisfied with my response, they sped off merrily, taking the Walkman with them, thankfully.

Noise. Hmmm. What was it about Indians and noise? Continually, everywhere, morning, noon and night. Adults and children alike. Why, for example, did they talk so loudly, repeating the same words, phrases, questions over and over? Did no one ever *listen*?

Music was pumped into the streets from homes, halls, stores, temples, churches, hotels, buses... like the din, the list went on and on. Seldom played through a proper, balanced system, the racket sounded brash, tinny, distorted and **LOUD**. The style of music was rarely an issue for me, but the quality and volume seriously began to get on my nerves. Even in some of the remote mountain villages surrounding Kodaikanal, mud houses pumped out torturous levels of Indo pop.

Repositioned under the shady cedar, I settled back to my book and masala bun. Out of the corner of my eye, I detected a diminutive middle-aged man hovering about ten feet away. With my focus fixed firmly on the page, I sensed him edge in closer, lean over my right shoulder and try to see what I was reading. Feeling his breath on the back of my neck, I could no longer concentrate, nor did I have any inclination to start a conversation. I wanted peace.

After a few more awkward minutes he drifted off, his exit as enigmatic as his appearance.

Immediately, three more students, a few years older than the first group, strolled over to meet me. *Was I the guest celebrity in town?* I was beginning to wonder.

'Would you like a photograph?' I enquired, cutting to the chase on their behalf.

'Yes, sir! Yes, please!'

Snap, snap.

'Thank you, sir,' they responded, sitting down cross-legged on the grass, interpreting my offer of a photograph as an invitation to join my picnic.

'Sir, please sit!' the most garrulous of the three commanded. He was wearing a loud, red and green Hawaii-type shirt patterned with parrots and palm trees.

Enquiring politely after their background, I discovered that they were university students from Madurai visiting Kodaikanal for the weekend.

'What are your names?' I asked.

'Ramesh, sir,' replied parrot-boy, 'and this is Vikrant.' A curly-haired young man nodded, his left arm wrapped around Ramesh's shoulders.

'And I am John,' said a wiry lad sporting the downy growth of a first moustache. He was slightly shorter than his two friends.

'John?' He must have sensed the surprise in my voice.

'Yes, my family is Christian. What are you reading, sir?'

I showed him the book cover.

'*Bhagavad Gita*, ah?! Very good book. Are you understanding it?'

'I've not had a chance to read it yet.'

'It is from the Mahabharata, the world's longest poem.'

'Really?'

'Actually it has two hundred thousand verses. *Bhagavad Gita* means "Song of the Lord".'

'Do you know much about Hindu scripture?'

'Generally I discuss it with my friends. It is containing much beautiful poetry.'

'Haan, yes,' concurred Ramesh. 'I am knowing the Bible,' he said casually as if, picking it up one day, he'd read it from cover to cover.

'What are you all studying?' I asked.

'Commerce,' replied Ramesh.

'Technology,' said Vikrant.

'English,' said John. 'I want to be a teacher.'

'Why?'

'Have you heard of Mister Abdul Kalam?'

'Sure. Your president.'

'He's a veerrry great man,' stated John, waggling his head eulogistically. 'He is champion for our generation. He once said that if the country is to become corruption-free and a nation of beautiful minds, three people can make a difference. The father, the mother and the teacher. That is why I am wishing to teach.'

'And the politician, isn't it?' said Ramesh. 'The politician can make a difference. That's what I want to be.'

'What can they do, ah? The bureaucrats that is holding the power, machaa,' contested Vikrant. 'They run the country; the politicians are having no power without them.'

'Untrue!' said John. 'They're as bad as each other, always covering each others' backs. They're greedy-greedy for power. Isn't that right, Uncle?'

'Why ask me? It's your country, not mine. I'm just a visitor.'

'You're British,' said Vikrant accusingly. 'You are giving us bureaucracies in the first place, isn't it?'

I was beginning to feel on trial. On that point, though, I couldn't disagree.

'True. You certainly love your paperwork,' I said, reminded of the many hours spent completing forms at the railway station, post office and hotels. 'I know we created it but you hang onto it dearly.'

'Oh yes! We are loving it. We deify the great god Bureaucracy,' John raised his eyes heavenwards. 'We worship at the temple of filing, beautifying it with reams of documentation. We offer prayers to...'

'Yes, thank you Shakespeare!' Vikrant pounced on John's oration by playfully pinning him to the ground.

'John is lovely poet,' commented Ramesh, 'but lousy fighter.'

'And we're great legislators, machaa,' John squeaked, 'but such bad implementers.'

I was impressed by the eloquence of these lads. 'You just said "we're",' I pointed out to John once he'd sat up.

'Yes, sir. I cannot disown my citizenship. I'm Indian. The future of this nation is my responsibility too.' His self-awareness amazed me, as did the self-confidence of all three of them.

'Do you really think you guys can make a difference?'

'If not us, then who is, ah?' asked Ramesh. 'We must be positive for the future.' He glanced at his watch.

'Hey, machaas! We should be returning five minutes ago!'

Vikrant and John looked at each other, laughed, and stood up.

'Bye, Mark,' said John, holding out his hand.

'Thanks for talking to us,' said Vikrant.

'It was a pleasure,' I replied, and meant it.

Off they ran.

The park seemed to empty. I felt as if I'd had an audience with every living soul in Tamil Nadu.

I returned to my book. The *Bhagavad Gita* is not the kind of reading material to scan casually. It requires full concentration at the best of times.

A bird chirruped. The air stilled and a piece of tumbleweed, caught by a light gust, flitted across the grass. An eerie silence fell.

Looking around, to my horror, I saw that my lingering friend had returned. He must have been spying from afar, waiting for the golden opportunity to have me all to himself. Having succeeded, he crept up and crouched on his haunches beside me. With hardly any movement of his lips, a few soft words crawled out from beneath his unkempt moustache.

'What profession being?'

'I work in the theatre.'

'Oh, movies,' he said, inching in closer.

'No, the stage. *Live* actors,' I tried to explain.

'I am loving movies,' he remarked, staring intently.

'No. Drama theatre. Real life in front of your eyes.' I tried to conceal my frustration but his gaze penetrated my brusque manner with unnerving precision. 'Not on the screen. On. The. Stage.'

'I know. What movies making you?'

Deep breath. 'Let's see. You know when...'

He patently didn't have a clue and the verbal exchange - it could hardly qualify as a conversation - spluttered to a halt.

'Haan?'

'Er...'

'Ah?'

'!!'

'??!'

An awkward silence. Although he wasn't quite touching me, I felt invaded. I shuffled nervously. He showed no intention of moving. What could be done with a man, his command of the English language only marginally greater

than my knowledge of Tamil, who was practically sitting in my face? I tried really hard, honestly I did -
'Would you like some of my masala bun?'
- but he showed no awareness of personal space. *My* personal space.

So I returned to my book with him, well, just lingering. Between the two of us we must have been a curious sight: an irate Englishman engrossed in feigned concentration, *Bhagavad Gita* in one hand, masala bun in the other, with a wizened little Indian perched on his right shoulder.

Beer, pressure cookers and cuddly Fatamuti aside, I reluctantly decided to search for another hotel. Evening mirth in the bar would have been fine had it transmuted into enough heat to maintain my body temperature above freezing throughout the night. But it didn't.

In my quest for alternative accommodation, cleanliness, decent food or a room with a view figured low on the priority list. I yearned for just two things: warmth and peace. Within my price range. I even visited the five star luxurious Carlton, Kodaikanal's finest. Tempting, but the charge of 30,000 rupees per night was way beyond my budget; I had paid 200 at Yagappa. The central heating, roaring fire, fluffy duvet and guarantee of 24 hour hot water did cause, however, more than a moment's hesitation.

After vetting at least half a dozen hotels, I settled on Greenacres by the lake. I booked for six nights and returned later to the promise of a steaming shower and solitude.

The following morning I would be checking out. I would see no evidence of a single droplet of hot water and a large group of vacationing students would party raucously throughout the night.

In the meantime, something far more disturbing was about to occur.

It was a simple question requiring a simple answer: 'How much is the fare to Greenacres Hotel?' Easy.

The auto driver's crime? Not understanding. A shrug of the shoulders: 'Nahi, sir?'

His eyeballs bled terror as my grip on his shirt collar tightened. Emitting a choked cry, his jaw dropped open. Nostrils quivering, a bead of sweat formed on his smooth upper lip. Further drops trickled down the furrows of his guileless brow.

A passing woman in a dark overcoat paused to stare, the hem of her sari dragging along the wet pavement. An umbrella held high above her dishevelled headscarf bore the brunt of the heavy downpour. Shabby swirls of mist hovered menacingly and the wind carried a biting chill. A sudden gust sent her on her way.

The moment my clenched fist grazed the auto driver's chin I was transported outside myself in disbelief, appalled.

What's happening to me?

I released my hold. The young man bounced back against the steering wheel, its edge jabbing him awkwardly in the ribcage. Air-grasping splutters rose from his strangled throat.

Ashamed, I turned away.

Trudging through the shadows, I pulled my shirt collar around my rain-smacked face. By the time I reached the hotel door, the sky had wrung out its final gobs of spit. The storm had exhumed the contents of the gutter, sating the heaving air with the stench of rotting vegetables, urine and buffalo dung; a thick soup of gurgling garbage. I tripped on a paving stone. My right foot, landing awkwardly, sent a slosh of slurry up my leg.

That's fair, I thought.

Back in my room, I wrenched off my boot and trousers and discarded them in a sodden pile on the floor.

Throwing myself onto the bed I wrapped the pillow around my head and beat down with my fists, bawling. Steady, hard punches. On and on, the mattress muffled my tortured obscenities.

I lay motionless, my face buried in the pillow.

And sobbed. Cloudbursts of tears and self-loathing.

I couldn't erase the image of the young driver's pained expression writhing beneath my raw eyelids.

***

By the time I awoke, early evening had sucked away the remaining light. A thin film of sweat coated my skin, my mouth was dry, my head muggy. I sat up. The sight of the soggy pile of clothes on the floor launched me straight back into reality with alarming clarity.

Perhaps it's time to go back to the UK, I considered. Bubbling beneath my skin, rising to the surface at the slightest provocation, were abhorrent qualities that I despised in myself. This place was making me behave entirely out of character. With all sense of propriety ebbing away, I was fearful of what I might do next.

The storm over, I decided to go for a brisk stroll around the lake to clear my mind. Although I found a fresh pair of trousers to wear, my feet squelched as I tried to squeeze them back into my clammy boots.

By day, the path surrounding Kodaikanal's vast, amoeba-shaped lake bustled with pedestrians, cyclists and horse-riders. At night, it was relatively deserted and peaceful, save the occasional bird warble or flutter of bat wings. I walked quickly; the rain had left a sharp chill to the evening.

The moment that I breathed in the cool mountain air, my nerves felt soothed. *Go home? What am I thinking? I haven't trekked in the Himalayas yet. Or travelled very far at all in this incredible country.* I'd barely scraped the surface. Going home would be chucking away the opportunity that I had worked so hard to create.

I had made my choices and, perverse though it might sound, deep down I was relishing the adventure. I never signed up for a cosy package tour.

Hang in there, Mark.

Unable to warm up externally, I went in pursuit of a hot meal in the hotel restaurant. As welcoming as a drab school dinner hall, it appeared deserted.

'Hel-lo-o!' I called. And waited.

Eventually a nondescript waiter appeared and begrudgingly handed me an uninspiring menu.

'Good evening,' I forced a smile.

Failing to respond verbally, he offered a reluctant wobble of his head. Although, to my relief, the surly youth exhibited no desire to practise his English, an understanding of the menu may have enabled him to produce the dish I'd ordered, rather than the plate of insipid vegetables he presented fifty minutes later. By the time it arrived, even the surface of my lime soda had frozen over.

It wasn't long before my self-pity re-emerged. Notwithstanding my earlier pep talk, I sulked. *Please let me get through this meal without incident and into bed.*

Swinging wide the glass door, in burst a group of eight ebullient students. I tried to hide behind my chapati but the English-detection-radar homed in. The spacious restaurant contained at least twenty Formica-topped tables, one of which I discreetly occupied at the far end in the corner. What compelled them to walk the full length of the room and choose the table *next* to mine, turn the chairs round towards me and stare, I don't know. Not just a casual glance, either, but a full-on gawk; eight pairs of dark brown inquisitive eyes.

I felt like a freak show exhibit; a novelty act, wheeled in for their amusement. But they neither pointed or jeered. Instead, their quizzical expressions displayed integrity, wonder. Though this may have been a perfectly natural way for them to behave, it was way off the scale for me. Tearing off a strip of chapati, I let the rest of the bread fall onto the plate. The gaping continued.

'Sir, what name, what country, where's your wife and sir, please be telling us, kindly good sir, please, what you are thinking of our fine country?'

For the second time in as many days, an uncanny stillness stifled the atmosphere.

A piece of tumbleweed darted across the floor.

A red-hot scream rendered the air blue.

Several choice phrases defiled eight pairs of impressionable ears.

In one foul swoop, Anglo-Indian relations were in tatters. Chairs apologetically shuffled back to their table. Conversation dropped to an inaudible level of muttering. Occasional, over-the-shoulder glances checked to see whether the fuming *Angrez* still had smoke coming out of his ears.

All I needed at my side was Fatamuti, the human pressure cooker. Between us, we would have generated enough heat to brew up the mother of all curries as well as sufficient hot water for *all* the hotel guests to have a decent shower.

In a strange sort of way, though, I was content. For the first time in three days, I had gotten warm.

On the way out, I apologised to the students for my outburst.

'That's OK, sir, you are English. We are understanding.'

I like to think that I believed them.

But inside and out, every sense was being bombarded to the point of exhaustion. As each day dawned, a rejuvenated energy supply was required. My personal space had become public property. Deprivation of sleep at night served to intensify the noise by day. Utterly relentless, the external racket had started to seep into every pore and gnaw at every nerve, pulse-pulse-pulsating internally, infernally.

ting ting, bang bangra boom bang bangraaaAGH!!

7
Logic Vs Emotion

Truth is a relative concept, as oily as a pan of ghee and sometimes as murky

Imagine climbing into an oven with a dozen people and a radio. Raise the temperature, pump up the volume and take a deep breath.

Two months into my travels, my head was dizzy. Each sense throbbed with *exhaustion* and every nerve bristled with irritation; too much **NOISE**, too little space and reams/reams/reams of unyielding bureaucracy. The simplest of tasks tramped tediously towards eternity: posting a letter, booking a train ticket, checking into a hotel. Corruption and oppression skulked around every corner. **EXTREMES** and **excessexcessexcess** - hot, cold, spicy, sweet, loud and crowded - roared down the streets.

Nothing existed in moderation: children pushed, shoved and questioned; men hacked, spat, burped and slurped...

...but the jasmine-adorned hair that sweetly scented the air as the women breezed past?

That I adored. I revelled in the unrestrained generosity that flowed from the most unexpected of places. I rejoiced that each day presented an opportunity for celebration. I relished having to slow down and open my eyes to the bigger picture.

Nevertheless, India was getting under my skin. I craved peace, space and enlightenment.

Why were people behaving so extraordinarily? Why was everything teeming with antitheses: externally loud *but* internally serene; systematically efficient *yet* shambolically disorganised; furiously materialistic *though* profoundly spiritual; brazenly affluent *and* disturbingly poor?

Most intriguingly, how could it be *all* these things *at the same time*?

I'm no different. Almost every word written about India from a western perspective conveys a similar bewilderment. Yet, like many people, I was hooked.

What was India's secret?

During one particular session on the professional development programme that I undertook two years earlier, Hazel, my mentor, and I discussed the knotty issues that surrounded leaving my job, selling my house and embarking on a new venture. Wobbly moments occurred daily as the judicious voice in my head nagged at the appetite of my heart. The internal dialogue between brain and gut triggered frequent spasms of mental indigestion.

Hazel talked about finding equilibrium between my critical and nurturing side, the pragmatic adult and the intuitive child within. It sounded slightly psycho-babble.

'Which do I listen to?' I asked.

'Both,' she replied cryptically.

Referring to the theories of an American management consultant, James Collins, Hazel explained that choice is often perceived as a decision between incompatible alternatives: should I follow my head *or* my heart, for example? One OR the other.

Collins calls this the "Tyranny of the OR"; the rational belief that it is impossible for two seemingly contradictory ideas to exist concurrently. In business, companies often face the dilemma of choosing between stability OR change, conservative aims OR "Big Hairy Audacious Goals".

Although big hairy audacious goals are good, I'll use an analogy closer to my heart: Marmite.

The product's famous marketing campaign has always proved successful because it's true. Love it or hate it, no one likes Marmite "a bit." I've never heard anybody say, 'It's alright, I suppose'. Marmite is divisive. It elicits an either/or response.

Likewise, India is *marmitical*. Love it or hate it, I defy anyone to express indifference towards it. India provokes an either/or reaction.

Marmite aside, Collins goes on to propose that it's entirely possible for two diametrically opposed ideas to live together as one. This he calls the "Genius of the AND." A visionary company can be both value-driven AND profitable. What's more, the Genius does not imply balance or compromise; 50% value, 50% profit. It means a full 100% plus 100%; a visionary company can be both *highly* value-driven AND *highly* profitable.

With this model in mind, Hazel suggested that, by listening to both my head AND my heart, I could forge a bold synthesis of the two. My decisions could be pragmatic AND intuitive; head and heart working together as a team.

But India? Here's the absolute genius. I was finding India both marmitical AND antithetically marmitical; gloriously loveable AND deeply detestable. *Simultaneously.* 200%-worth. Try putting that in a jar and marketing it!

Actually, someone once did.

A seventeenth-century Britisher, observing a small fish called a bomelon swimming off the coast of Bombay, commented that it looked remarkably like a duck. He caught the creature and hung it up to dry in the sun. The desiccated delicacy became known as "Bombay Duck" and was served in Indian restaurants throughout the UK until banned by the European Commission in 1997.

In my pre-vegetarian days, I could never resist ordering Bombay Duck at my local Indian restaurant. Although its pungent saltiness never failed to cloy my palette, once swallowed, I always craved more. My taste buds were both charmed AND repulsed by the enigmatically addictive dried fish.

Bombay Duck embraced the "Genius of the AND".

I wondered what Indians thought of Marmite. Indeed, was it possible to love India AND Marmite simultaneously?

Delirious musings such as these teased my imagination as I sat squashed in a clammy bus humming with a medley of ripe body odours. The breeze through its window tickled my face like an ineffectual hair dryer as the vehicle careered through the coconut groves. No one seemed perturbed by the stifling atmosphere except me.

Having trekked part of the route across the Western Ghats from Kodaikanal to the tea plantations above Munnar, I was now on my way to Cochin. A couple with a young daughter were seated across the aisle. Aged about six, the girl was well-dressed in a fussy brown and green frock. White bracelets jingled on each arm and a gold charm dangled around her neck. Her pinch-faced mother sat cross-legged, swathed in the rich folds of a burgundy sari.

As we pulled into a bus station, two weathered hands appeared at the window clutching a basket of fruit. Reaching through the rusty bars, the mother exchanged a few coins for six small oranges, the whole transaction conducted in perfunctory silence.

The girl's eyes widened as her mother handed her an orange. She then offered one to me. Father dozed.

With a deft movement of her fingers the woman peeled the fruit, letting its skin fall to the floor. She then delicately spat the pips in rapid succession through her pursed lips like a pop gun firing corks: swift and precise. Attempting to copy her mother, the child merely succeeded in making a sticky mess of her mouth, fingers and dress. Within minutes, a scattering of skin, pith and pips littered the bus floor.

The mother's impassive attitude towards her rubbish fascinated me. But why should she worry? Someone else would clean the floor later.

How refreshing, I thought. Her simple activity had created both a mess and an employment opportunity. Tightening the grip on my own orange peel, however, I was unable to let go, restrained by my head's exhortations to 'do the right thing'.

'Tidy up your litter!' it commanded.

'Go on, live dangerously,' counter-attacked my heart. 'Just a pip or two.'

'It's irresponsible,' rebuked my head.

'Everyone else does it.'

'I know, but...'

Head and heart continued to wage their petty civil war as the bus rattled towards Cochin.

I envied the people I met: intuitive, creative, responding to their hearts' impulses as instinct led the way.

Inevitably that posed a puzzle as west encountered east.

Only an Indian, for example, could cloud two of the most straightforwardly opposite words in the English language, "Yes" and "No", with so many layers of equivocation.

In my quest to find alternative accommodation in Kodaikanal, I asked the manager at one particular hotel if the room he was offering me had hot water.

'Yes, sir,' the manager responded, 'of course.' After a number of supplementary questions it became clear that, yes, the room was indeed supplied with hot water, provided that I ordered it twelve hours in advance. A porter would then deliver the water in a bucket between six and six-thirty the following morning.

The room certainly contained what I requested, but I had to conduct a step-by-step analysis to elicit the full story. The manager's initial 'Yes, sir' was contingent on my perceived need and the information that he believed I wanted to hear. It had no bearing on the reality of the situation.

A request starting, 'I'd like...', would often be interrupted with 'Yes, yes, very good, sir.' Whatever I wanted would be granted, even if a hotel manager or waiter had no idea what it was. Truth never stood in the way of an over-imaginative disposition to please.

I found "no" equally maddening. When occasionally lured into a shop, I usually agreed to 'look, but not buy'.

'Yes sir, I am understanding. How about this shirt? It is beautiful. The colour is so, so liking you.'

'No thanks. I have enough shirts. I don't need any more.'

'But sir...'

'No!'

Yet the shop owner still felt she could charm me, woo me, and tug at my heartstrings to fall in love with the silk fabric running through her fingers. Hoping my intuition would prevail over my pragmatism, she failed to grasp that "no" actually meant "No!" As with many of the people that I met, she was gifted with the ability to *expand* straight talk into a baffling art-form in which "no" could mean "yes" *and* the whole gamut in between.

What was the root of this kind of thinking? Why were the shop owner and I approaching the same situation from entirely opposing directions? The obvious answer was that she ran a business, I carried a wallet; she sold shirts, I possessed cash. Ergo, a transaction. Similarly, the hotel manager probably presumed that, had I known the reality of the hot water situation, I wouldn't have booked the room. He was right. But I think it was more complex than that.

Whereas I exhibited the terribly English trait of excessive analysis, pedantic categorisation and interminable list-making, the average Indian demonstrated an extraordinary propensity for synthesis. Grasping the whole picture, she could hold together yes and no, right and wrong, entire opposites AND everything else in between, as one unified whole. With the compound image in mind, she acted. I dissected, considered, weighed up the pros and cons... made a decision... changed my mind again... She just did it. Unencumbered by the detail, she appeared driven by a greater cause. How much I wanted to be like that!

Conflicting forces brawled inside me, one representing order and security, the other promising freedom and adventure. As the clashing blades thrashed around, the duel regrettably manifested itself in the occasional, and inexcusable, outburst of rage. Unfortunately, other people, including the poor auto driver and the well-intentioned students in Kodaikanal, found themselves caught in the flak.

I conformed to type. Self-analysis provided a circumspect justification for my own, otherwise indefensible, behaviour, although no resolution. But what about those around me?

True to Collins' definition of a visionary company, the Indians that I met seemed to embrace the genius of the AND. Assuming that they represented the India Inc corporate consciousness, what inspired them to behave in a way that was so alien to my comprehension? Could they teach me the genius of the AND too?

In the meantime, I neatly transferred the orange peel to a plastic bag, placed it in my pocket and wiped clean my sticky fingers.

"The venerable city of Kochi, long known as Cochin, is Kerala's prime tourist destination, spreading across islands and promontories in a stunning location between the Arabian Sea and the backwaters. Exotic spice markets, Chinese fishing nets, a synagogue, Portuguese palace, India's first European church, Dutch homes, and a village green that could easily have been transported from England's Home Counties can all be found within an easy day's walk."

In the cooling sea breeze of the late afternoon, armed with my *Rough Guide*, I left my hotel in Ernakulam, the more modern, mainland district of Kochi, to explore the neighbourhood. On foot.

As if by magic, a number of taxi and tuk-tuk drivers materialised to enquire where I was going.

'For a walk.'

'Where?' a tuk-tuk driver asked.

'Nowhere especially, just a walk.'

Mistake. I should have known by then that the concept of walking anywhere in the city was anathema to many Indians, particularly if I could clearly afford a tuk-tuk. Being a white male, I could. Why use two legs when God made a tuk-tuk with three wheels?

'Let me take you.'

'What, to nowhere? I can walk there myself.'

Uh-ho. Mistake number two. I didn't have a particular destination in mind. By stating 'nowhere especially' I was inviting an offer to be taken 'somewhere specifically'.

So, of course, the driver suggested that I needed his service.

'I am taking you to ferry port for Fort Cochin. See Chinese fishing nets.'

'No thank you.' I could see the port across the road from where I was standing.

'Book ticket for Kathakali dance?'

'I'm going later.' Kathakali is a unique form of dance-theatre only performed in Kerala. I had every intention of attending a performance, but not then.

'Temple festival?'

I declined.

'Please sir, get in. I am offering good price'.

'But I don't want to go anywhere.'

'Then let me take you.'

I shrugged and walked away.

With the tuk-tuk driver gone, a young boy started pacing beside me.

'Hello, sir, my name is Satish,' he announced, offering a variation on the usual dialogue routine by volunteering his name before asking mine.

'England,' I replied in response to statutory question number two. Satish had soon slipped back into conventional interrogation mode.

'I have friend in Manchester,' he informed me.

'Really?' I smiled, somehow doubting his claim. I also suspected that, unlike my walk, the conversation was going somewhere in particular. But I played along.

In response to question number five relating to my occupation, I had learnt from my experiences in Kodaikanal not to say I was a theatre director. I decided to become a teacher.

'Ah, English teacher. Very good job, sir.'
'If you like.'
Satish then lobbed the real purpose of the chat into the dialogue.
'Actually there is temple festival around corner. Today only.'
'Good to talk to you, Satish. I must get going though...'
'...It is starting in five minutes. We take auto.'
Since when did anything in India ever begin 'in five minutes'? I politely declined and dashed across the road...
...straight into the outstretched arms of a jaded gentleman selling a miserable set of postcards of the afore-mentioned temple, over-exposed and poorly photographed from every conceivable angle. Automatically, and wrongly, he assumed that I was liking his 'veee-rrry beaut-eee-ful pictures' and began to barter. Though charming, his unorthodox negotiation technique was entirely one-sided. With no input from me, he dropped his price from 400 to 20 rupees within seconds, completely oblivious to my insistence that I had no intention of purchasing any of his produce, at any price, ever.
'Bangles, sir? You are only best customer today.'
Another guy came alongside. Called Rajish, he also had a friend in Manchester.
'Do you know Satish?'
He started to tell me about the temple festival around the next corner...
'You do know Satish.'
...and so it continued. Men popped up from cracks in the pavement, boys appeared mysteriously from behind lamp posts. Despite my desire to go nowhere-in-particular, I felt like the four children stepping through the wardrobe into Narnia. Following a mysterious tree-hopping robin, they were being led *somewhere-for-certain*.

My interest was sufficiently aroused though. Perhaps the festival could be worth a visit after all? Consulting my map I discovered that the Shiva Temple was only a few streets away.

After a short walk, I found myself standing on the pavement opposite the temple gates, separated from my destination by a dense flow of traffic that showed little sign of abating. Dodging between a truck, a bicycle and an erratic tuk-tuk, I eventually reached the central reservation where I waited patiently for a lull.

Prompted by a middle-aged man waving in my direction, I glanced over my shoulder. Looking back, I realised he was signalling to me. Without warning, he stepped in front of an oncoming bus, giving it no choice but to blast its horn and screech to a halt. He then beckoned for me to walk safely to the pavement.

'Thank you,' I said. 'I thought I'd never get across.'

'Tea?'

'I beg your pardon?'

'You would like tea?'

'I'm actually on my way to...'

'...the temple?' he caught my bemused look. 'Why else would you be here?'

He had a point.

My timing was perfect. I had arrived during a break in the festival programme.

'We are having tea,' Krishna confirmed, as if our chance encounter had been predetermined, 'and then we are visiting the temple festival. The chief priest is my friend. He will make you very welcoming.'

Well... what to do?

Thirty minutes later, seated at the back of a long, cramped, *Udipi* canteen, we were sipping our second cup of chai. Elbows on the wooden table, hands clasped, Krishna held court. I was a willing captive.

Unlike the god of his namesake, Krishna possessed neither a blue face nor played the flute scantily clothed. His seasoned complexion was sallow, his receding hair flecked with silver, and he wore his dhoti full-length. My Krishna was a Brahmin priest, the next best thing.

'So you're saying Hindu and India mean the same thing?' Prompted by my questioning, our conversation had soon strayed into the fundamentals of Hindu history and philosophy. Krishna was an engagingly well-read man, as a Brahmin ought to be. Exhibiting tremendous patience, he became very animated, his banjo eyes dilating fervently, whenever I grasped a point he made.

'Yes, yes! *India* and *Hindu* are deriving from same root,' he replied. '*Indos* was the Greek name for the River Indus in the northwest of the subcontinent.'

Dipping into the breast pocket of his white shirt, he extracted a folded sheet of paper. He flattened it out, face down, on the wooden table. 'Let me illustrate.'

He continued to speak as he drew. 'The Greeks and Persians were giving the name to describe the land and people living to the east of the river. Nowadays that same river is flowing from Tibet through the land of Kashmir and Pakistan and out to the Arabian Sea.' I followed his inky line as it trailed across the paper. 'See?'

'I'm with you so far.'

'The Sanskrit name for the river was *Sindhu*. But, in spoken Persian, words starting with "s" were said often like "h". So people were known as Hindus. Actually, before Mogul empire, Hindu was geographical term for anyone living in Indian subcontinent.'

'No matter what they believed?'

'Haan. But then, during Mogul rule, the Muslims started naming them Hindustanis to distinguish them from people of their own Muslim faith and culture.'

'I see.'

'Then you Britishers came along,' he said with a twinkle. 'In so typical colonial fashion, you put everyone in boxes for making easy administration!' That sounded familiar. 'Same-same as Muslim and Christian categories, all the wide range of local beliefs and practices were gathered under one banner. That is Known as Hindu Religion.' In rhythm with his sing-song voice, he tapped his pen on the table as he spoke the final sentence.

'Even though the beliefs were so diverse?'

'Quite so. You Westerners are smart at generalisation.'

'I beg your pardon, if that's not…'

'Curry!' Krishna interrupted, chortling at his deliberate provocation. 'I am giving as example. That's a European concept.'

'Oh!' I hesitated. 'It's an Indian word, though, isn't it?'

'Yes. Actually, two. *Karil* in Kannadan and Malayalam languages and *kari* in Tamil are referring to spices for certain South Indian dishes. In British and Portuguese hands, however, they became any spicy dish eaten throughout the land! But I am digressing. Within India, you know, few people are calling their belief as Hinduism. To us it is *Sanatana Dharma*.'

'Meaning?'

'It could be translated as "the eternal truth or law". Generally, most people are not having concept of *India* or what it is meaning to *be Indian*. We are referring to ourselves in terms of our village, region or state.'

'You say you're Keralan, not Indian?'

Krishna scratched his stubbly beard. 'Actually, I'm from Tamil Nadu, but I am making same point. We are having no real notion of unified India in a political sense. Neither is it un-unified. This is not an issue most people are considering.'

'So you're saying that an Indian rarely calls himself an Indian? Nor says he's from India, refers to his religion as Hinduism or eats curry - they're all labels imposed from outside?'

'Generally, yes! To be Indian is to be Hindu *and* vicky versa. There are Indian Muslims, Jains, Buddhists, Christians, that and all. Being Hindu is as much about being

Indian as about following one kind of religious belief. *Being a Hindu is bigger than Hinduism,'* Krishna stated emphatically. 'Anyone living in Indian sub-continent is Hindu.'

I let that statement settle briefly. 'Including people of other faiths?'

'Haan. It's central to our history, our heritage. It's in our blood.'

'But...'

'You must understand that, culturally, spiritually even, *all* Indians are Hindus. But not all practise Hindu-*ism*. That is where people are obtaining their mixing-ups.'

I loved the way Krishna talked. Although he was clearly a highly-educated scholar, his occasional choice of words and faulty grammar made him an entertaining, as well as informative, teacher.

'Ok. So what do those who practice Hindu-ism believe?' I asked.

He wobbled his head. 'That is not being an easy question.'

'Why?'

'You are so-so English! Hinduism is not a religious system with one set of principles. It is representing many faiths and traditions evolving over long-long time.' Responding to my blank face, he added, 'Try thinking of Hinduism as an extended Indian family of beliefs. Each individual is finding his own way.'

'To where?'

'God.'

'You believe in *one* God? I thought tha...'

'The Ultimate Reality is *Brahman*, the supreme essence of the universe,' Krishna interrupted firmly. 'The Absolute. Brahman is all and all is Brahman. Everything and nothing. Life and death.'

'Health and disease?' I ventured.

'Correct!'

'Good *and* evil?' More daring.

'Haan!'

'Yes *and* no?' *Go for it!*

Krishna bounced on his plastic chair. 'Yes, yes!'

Yes! I punched the air. *Genius*.

Krishna's pouchy cheeks quivered with laughter.

A young boy, seated with his family at a nearby table, turning around, stared in amusement at Krishna's jocularity.

'How does that work then?'

'Meaning?'

'What you've just said.'

I didn't want to deflate his enthusiasm but how could *something* be *everything* AND *nothing*?

'Is a mosquito knowing what it is like to be human?'

'I guess not.'

'In same way, Brahman is inaccessible to human comprehension,' he rebuffed with the ultimate cop-out. Yet, keeping the all-and-nothing theme in play, it was the ultimate answer. If I could figure out Brahman, Brahman would no longer be Brahman. This man was good. Yet, I was still baffled.

'I am helping you,' Krishna said, reading my mind. 'There is a word in the *Upanishad* scriptures that is explaining it best: *neti*. Sarvepalli Radhakrishnan, a great philosophical writer, translates it as "not this".'

'You mean the best way to describe Brahman, is to say what it isn't?'

'Neti, neti are appearing many times in our scriptures following a description of Brahman. Some scholars are preferring the translation "not this *alone*".'

'Is that more accurate?'

'It is implying that any attempt to describe the Ultimate in human words will never-never be complete. It is not this, not that, nor anything that we are capable of understanding.'

'Hmm.'

I had noticed that, as we'd been chatting, the Udipi had been filling up with chattering festival devotees in need of refreshment before the next stage of the programme. One single waiter dashed between tables, taking orders, and returning a few minutes later precariously carrying a tray laden with aromatic cups of chai above his head.

'Now, kindly remember I am saying Brahman is the Ultimate Reality? Actually, in truth, Brahman is the *only* Reality.'

'Which means...'

'...all other finite manifestations, including our human capacity to think, are stemming from this infinite reality. This is a mystery we are calling *maya*. It is explaining the existence of the universe *as humans experience it.*'

'Can you give me an example?'

'Haan. In this world, light and dark, right and wrong are relative. Opposition is an illusion. But in the grand scheme of the Absolute, no such polarity is existing. Brahman is both good *and* evil, everything and nothing.'

'So love and hate can co-exist *and* sit on the same side of the *same* coin?!'

'Yes, yes!' he exclaimed.

But if all human experience is an illusion, I thought, *what's the point in taking life seriously? Is Brahman playing a sick joke on humankind? Are we all players in some sort of puckish divine comedy?*

'I'm sure a beggar would feel much better knowing that his hunger pangs were just a figment of his imagination,' I observed sceptically.

Krishna tutted. 'You are missing the point. I'm not saying that our experiences are imaginary. If something is appearing real, that is what it is. Pain *is* having a reality of its own.'

'Especially for the poor beggar!'

'Listen!' Krishna retorted. 'You have seen that old-old movie clip of a cinema audience watching a steam train speeding towards them?'

'The one where people scream and duck out of the way because they think the train's about to burst through the screen?'

'Haan! The train is an illusion, yet the people react as if it is real.'

'Of course they do! They've never experienced anything like it. But *we* know it's only a film image.'

'Do we?'

'What's your point?'

He smiled and finsihed his tea. 'Imagine a coil of rope lying all twisty-twisty on the ground. Supposing I trip over it in the dark. I am mistaking it for a snake. "Aagh!" I shout, jumping through my skin. "What a fool!" you might say, "It's only a piece of rope." Looking at it more closely I would be agreeing: "Yes, yes! You're right! There is no snake." Yet it is not a complete illusion because the rope actually exists. The snake is neither real nor entirely unreal.'

'So?'

'I am saying that the rope is Brahman and the snake is the world. Just as the reality of the snake is depending on the existence of the rope, the world both *is* and *is not* an illusion based on the absolute reality of Brahman. That is what I am meaning by maya. Clear?'

'As mud.' I tapped the rim of my metal beaker.

'It is for thinking about.'

'I will.'

He looked reproachful. 'But do not be falling into the trap of believing that Hindu philosophy teaches that every human experience is imaginary and therefore of no significance. People may *act* as if the external world is an illusion,' he paused, 'but that is another matter.'

'What are you getting at?'

'Sir, I am sensing your misgivings.' Krishna's eyes narrowed.

'I'm just trying to understand.' Leaning forwards, I rested my forearms on the table. A line of sweat dribbled down my back between my cotton shirt and my skin.

'You must be opening your mind,' he cautioned. 'You may be seeing many strange things on your travels that you are wishing to question. You will witness behaviour, justified by people's religious conviction, which is defying explanation. But kindly remember: there are no problems with Hinduism itself. Hinduism is perfect Sanatana Dharma. It is only over time that human nature has perverted and corrupted the eternal laws. The problem is Hindu society.'

'Will you help me, then?'

His expression lightened. 'I am enjoying your questions. It is very providential that you are here,' he said, bending down to retrieve a worn, leather satchel from under his chair. Undoing two metal clasps, he fumbled around inside.

'Aha!' he exclaimed, brandishing a small, well-used paperback. 'The great man!'

'Who?'

'Sri Aurobindo. A very wisely astute philosopher.' He started flicking through the creased pages. 'Please be bearing me a minute.'

The windows of the canteen were beginning to steam up with hot air from the pans of chai bubbling on the stove to meet the demand of the customers. Streaky patterns of condensation trickled down the grimy walls.

'Yes, yes.' Krishna tapped me on the arm. 'Listen. "There are two Hinduisms; one which takes its stand on the kitchen and seeks its Paradise by cleaning the body; another which seeks God, not through the cooking pot and the social convention, but in the soul."'

'He's saying that Hinduism has lost its way?'

'No, listen, I am reading more.' He flicked back a few pages. 'Here. "In practice this resolves itself into certain observances and social customs of which he" – the Hindu – "understands neither the spiritual meaning nor the practical utility. To venerate the Scriptures without knowing them and to obey custom in their place; to eat nothing cooked by a social inferior; to do one's devotions twice a day without understanding them; to observe a host of meaningless minutiae in one's daily conduct..." and so forth!'

'Cooking pot Hindus!' I laughed.

'Yes, yes, very good! Cooking pot Hindus – I am liking it! They're full of outward showing. They are not seeking God in their spirit. The soul of Hinduism, Sri Aurobindo is saying, languishes in an unfit body.'

'When did he write these things?'

'Since one hundred years. How true he is.' Krishna nodded sagaciously. 'Now,' he added, 'time for more tea.' Catching the waiter's eye, he pointed at our empty cups.

I was intrigued. I wanted to quiz him further about "Hindu society", but his talk about the unity of Brahman had sparked my interest. Was this a clue to discovering India's genius?

'Do all Hindus believe what you've told me about Brahman?' I asked.

'I will answer in one minute. But first, the belief that the world is not existing separately from Brahman is the essential message of the *Upanishads*,' said Krishna. 'This we call *Advaita*, non-duality.'

'Upanishads?'

'Haan. I am explaining. There was an ancient Vedic civilisation in northern subcontinent from about one thousand five hundred BC, maybe earlier. They had a religion called Vedism which believed in many gods. Because the people were illiterate, their sacred texts, called Vedas, were passed down orally over many centuries by the priests.'

The waiter placed two steaming cups of chai in front of us.

'What does Veda mean?' I asked. Lifting my cup a few inches, I sipped from it gingerly.

'It is meaning "knowledge". Slowly-slowly, their polytheistic beliefs were giving way to monotheism and the idea that the universe is One came into being. The doctrine of the Brahman was appearing in the Upanishads by about 800 BC. We are believing that these Vedic teachings are revealing the fulfilment of the other Vedas and our ultimate understanding of Brahman.'

'In that case,' I asked, 'why are there so many gods in the temples?'

'"Truth is one; men call it by different names",' says a verse from the Rig Veda.'

'OK, so why are there loads of them?'

'Ishwar Aik Hai. God is One.'

'Yes, but there...'

'*One* God,' he said emphatically, 'worshipped in many ways.'

My metal beaker, clanging on the table, spilt a few drops of chai.

You're not alone,' he continued, sensing my frustration. 'It is a commonly held, but misguided, belief that Hinduism is polytheistic. You were going to tell me that there are over three million gods. Haan?'

I nodded.

'I understand. It is not surprising that people are confused.' Krishna shook his head. 'As Hindus, we are being partly responsible for that misconception.'

'What do you mean?'

'The Upani...'

'Excusing me, good sirs,' interrupted a voice, 'but may I kindly be taking this chair?'

I looked up at an uneven set of yellowing teeth protruding from beneath a tidy moustache. 'Please,' I said, shunting forward so that the gentleman could get by.

'Thank you, sir. American?'

'English.'

'Very good, sir. Thank you.'

Krishna smiled. 'I was about to say that, although the Upanishads teach that God is One, later scriptures are acknowledging that God may be reached in a number of ways. "All paths lead to me," Krishna tells Arjuna, for example, in the *Bhagavad Gita*.

'Every path?'

'Actually, there are three main paths. Although Advaita Vedantists, like myself, are following *Jnana*, the path of knowledge, most Hindus, the less-educated, follow the *Dvaita*, dualistic, paths of *Bhakti*, devotion, or *Karma*, action.'

'Where do they come from?'

'These are deriving from beliefs and customs of the non-Vedic traditions. They are believing that the human soul and the deity are separate, yet connected, entities. Over time they have been bringing many gods and goddesses into the pantheon. That is why it is confusing! In popular Hinduism, God may be reached in many ways through many gods.'

'Surely that's licence for people to believe whatever they want?' I asked.

'Yes, yes, that is why Hinduism is of so much beauty. It is allowing space for all philosophies. An individual is choosing to be a Hindu monotheist, dualist, polytheist, pantheist, agnostic or even an atheist.'

I shook my head.

'Imagine a sculpture,' Krishna suggested. 'You can walk around it and snap-snap from many angles. In same way, Hinduism is presenting many ways of looking at one single object. Just like a series of snapshots. None is offering a complete picture but each is being equally valid.'

'That helps.'

The noise level had risen quite considerably over the past few minutes, as every seat in the Udipi was now filled. Some people stood leaning against the wall, balancing their drinks on the edge of a nearby table as the metal beakers were too hot to hold.

'It's getting busy,' I commented.

'Yes, yes. It is a very popular festival. Actually, you see these other Hindus? If you talk to them, they are explaining things differently to me. I am believing that Brahman is the only reality, while others here are worshipping at the feet of Shiva. That is fine. There is of much room for many schools of thought. Certain philosophical tenets, however, we are universally sharing.'

'Such as?' Krishna picked up his pen and drew a straight line on the paper.

'Many Westerners are seeing life's journey like this?'

'As in, we are born, we live and we die?'

'Haan. To me that is having no logic.' He drew a large circle. 'All processes of the world, including human existence, are cycles, not lines. We are calling cycle of birth, life, death and rebirth *Samsara*. It is meaning "wandering".'

'Reincarnation?'

'Yes, yes!' Krishna bobbed enthusiastically. 'Within this wheel of life, humans are reincarnated according to their karma. That is the driving force behind rebirth. It is often translated as "action". All our thoughts, words or deeds are producing an inevitable result. Our present existence is determined by our performance in a previous life. Then what we are doing in this life will be having consequences in the next. Nothing is happening by accident. Understand?'

'Yes. It's all down to fate.'

'NO!!' Bouncing higher than ever, Krishna slammed his palm down on the table. 'Piffle! You are missing the point! Many people are confusing karma with fatality and using it as excuses for laziness. It is *not* permission for inactivity.'

'You don't believe our lives are predetermined then?'

'No.' He winked. 'And yes!'

Here we go again.

'In life's game, our cards are dealt. We are not choosing our hand; it has been decided by our past karma. But, we *are* free to play the cards as we are pleasing to live a productive and meaningful life.'

I frowned.

'I am confusing you with the doctrine?'

'Kind of.'

'No matter. Let's get down to practicals. What a Hindu is *doing* is far more important than what he is *believing*. I am going to tell you about the four fundamental goals in life, named *Purusharthas*.'

Picking up his pen, Krishna continued to talk.

1. Artha – the acquisition of wealth

2. Kama – the pursuit of desire
   <u>Not</u> to be confused with Karma

3. Dharma – obedience to the cosmic law

4. Moksha – the path to salvation and liberation from the cycle of rebirth

As he wrote, I noticed a mottled liver spot on the back of his right hand. Despite his youthful vigour, Krishna was obviously a man of considerable maturity.

'Each Hindu is aiming to achieve these four aims before leaving his current life.' Firstly, the pursuit of *artha*, wealth, is an important duty for the Hindu.'

'Really?'

'We are not keeping our necks in the clouds, you know! Have you ever seen a poor god or goddess in the temple?'

I shook my head.

'Of course not! Possessions and money are necessary for happiness and salvation. But they are to be achieved *by honest means*,' he said, laying heavy stress on his last three words. 'Kama is about enjoying the pleasures of life. Most specifically, it is referring to' – he lowered his voice – 'sexual desire.'

'As in kama sutra?'

He coughed. 'Haan. But sexual freedom,' he added quickly, 'like all else, is permitted if it is in accordance with the laws of *dharma*.'

'Dharma?'

'Please be having patience. I am coming to that!' He slurped his tea. 'Now dharma and karma are two most important principles in Hinduism,' he said. 'You remember I am saying that Upanishads teach that all things are interconnected and interdependent.'

'Of course!'

'You are a good student! Imagine a system of cosmic rules that is governing all processes in the universe. That is dharma, the absolute *law* of the cosmos, inherent in all things.'

'You've just lost your good student again!'

'Basically, dharma is the essential essence that is making something what it is. It is bedrock to human morality. This is why we are referring to what we believe as Sanatana Dharma, the eternal law.'

'I still don't…'

'OK. Everything has dharma. The sun's dharma is to shine, the rain's is to fall. Dharma is like a cosmic benchmark against which all actions are being measured. How its principles are followed is determining a person's status in their next life.' Picking up his copy of Sri Aurobindo's book, he started to waft it absentmindedly in front of his face.

'A teacher's dharma is to teach,' he continued, 'a dhobi's to wash clothes. Performing in harmony with the universal laws is what is counting. A teacher should not be scrubbing linen shirts, nor should a dhobi be wishing to educate others.'

'What! By doing the laundry the best way he can, a dhobi will be assured of a better lot in his next life?'

Krishna stopped waving the book and tipped his head with a mild look of despair.

'Your English over-simplification is bewildering at times! The dhobi should be performing his duty and then he is leaving the consequences to God.'

'Even if he'd rather be a teacher?'

'He should be accepting his dharma without complaining or desiring for change. He is only responsible for carrying out his duty, not for its outcome.'

That sounded dubious to me. 'How does an individual know what the right action for their assigned station is?'

A sudden burst of laughter from the next table cut into our conversation.

'For their what?'

'Assigned station,' I repeated.

'That's a too good question.'

'And the answer…?'

'Is a matter for individual interpretation,' he replied, raising his voice above the bustle. 'I am not concerning myself with detail of this life. Preparation for the next is what is important.'

With Krishna's eye focused resolutely on the bigger picture, I realised that he was not going to be drawn into the minutiae of my probing.

'Are you getting tired of all my questions, Krishna?'

'Not at all. I'm a Brahmin; I am loving to teach. But it is becoming noisy-noisy in here for my ears. Perhaps if we wander back to the temple, the festivities may be underway?'

We stood up and started to squeeze between the tables towards the door. Glancing over my shoulder, I noticed that

Krishna had left Sri Aurobindo's book on the table. I went back to retrieve it just as another couple were dashing for our vacated seats.

'Here,' I said, once we were out in the street. 'You left this behind.'

'Thank you,' Krishna said, about to take it. He hesitated. 'I'd like you to keep.'

'No, I can't...'

'Please,' he insisted. 'I am gifting it to you.'

It was dusk by the time we deposited our shoes at the gate to join the mass of Hindu devotees pushing their way through the courtyard. Strings of ruby and emerald fairy lights twinkled brightly from the rooftops of every building within the temple compound. Two priests were ceremonially preparing an elephant under a tall canopy. An enormous gold and jewel-encrusted headpiece ran between its ears and down the length of its trunk. A third priest sat astride the elephant's back, dwarfed by the beast's broad physique.

In front of the elephant stood eight bare-chested, dhoti clad men, each beating a large drum suspended on a thick cord around his neck. They were being led by a ninth musician who, raising a long, curved wooden instrument to his lips, emitted a horn-like tone. The rhythmic pulse of their strains trembled above the hubbub. Boys in pristine shirts, shorts and neatly-combed hair and girls in buttoned-and-bowed party dresses skipped about excitedly while their parents, grandparents, aunts and uncles, mingled and exchanged pleasantries. Whitish wisps of smoke, rising from bronze bowls of burning incense, twisted towards the sky, diffusing a sweet, heady concoction of jasmine and myrrh.

In the centre of the courtyard stood another ornately-carved stone building into which people were filing one at a time, bowing their heads as they entered.

'What's in there?' I shouted, raising my voice above the drumming.

'That is the Sanctum Sanctorium. Inside are the *Linga* forms of Shiva and Parvati, his wife. Devotees are coming to the temple to make *puja* to them.

'Puja?'

'Meaning worship. But you cannot go in. You may walk everywhere else, though. Come!'

I followed him through a doorway into a vast room behind the temple precinct. Down one side ran a row of tables and benches. 'Please sit!'

Before I realised what was happening, a boy had placed two plates made from several palm leaves sewn together in front of us.

'We eat and talk?' Krisha suggested.

Two further boys plunged wooden ladles into a series of pots, filling our plates with rice and small mounds of vegetables, pickles, two small, crispy papads and a spoonful of steaming dal.

'So, this is a Shiva Temple?' I asked, squelching the rice and dal between my fingers.

'Yes, Shiva was originally a folk god. Over time he was elevated to personify an aspect of Brahman itself. He is a complex character because he is bringing both destruction and blessing.'

'I thought Shiva was an evil deity?'

'Nahi. He is destroying to re-create. He is also having a third, all-knowing eye in the centre of his head. This is a common symbol of spiritual vision.' Krishna crunched a papad between his teeth. It disintegrated in pieces down his shirt. 'How is your food?' he asked.

'Good, thank you.'

'You eat like an Indian!'

While we were talking, several men had entered the room and started to apply brightly-coloured make-up, exaggerating their moustaches and eye-brows into almost cartoon-like features. They rouged their lips and painted ornate, white symbols on their foreheads. A number of beautifully-stitched costumes were draped over the backs of the wooden chairs.

'They are preparing for the dance programme. They will be performing various tales from the epics. They will also be acting out the legend of the Linga, the phallic symbol representing Shiva, coming to this place. Total devotion to him is achieving the ultimate goal, *moksha*.'

'Number four of the fundamental life goals?'

'I am gratified that you have been paying attention! Yes, moksha is liberation from cycle of rebirths and freedom from all worldly ties. It is the ultimate union of our soul with Brahman. And before you are asking,' he added in anticipation of my interruption, 'here is biggest paradox. I have said that Brahman is inaccessible to human comprehension. But salvation for the Hindu is the ultimate realisation that he himself *is* Brahman. He and the universe are one.'

'Am I and the universe and Brahman one?'

'Haan.' He grinned. 'You are just not knowing it yet!'

Hmm. 'That might take a while!' I joked.

'Moksha is rarely achieved in one lifetime. This is why a Hindu is finding the concept of a single life an impossible idea. As we are performing righteous acts, each subsequent life is moving us towards liberation from the cycle of karma. And oppositely, evil deeds are removing us further away from liberation.'

'Is there no notion of forgiveness in Hinduism?' I asked.

'Nahi. A Hindu must suffer, or be rewarded, for his own deeds.'

'Then the cycle could be endless?'

'Yes. yes. Rebirth is only unnecessary when moksha is attained and he and Brahman are becoming One.'

I was about to open my mouth.

'Enough questions. Come! It is time for the programme.'

It was almost three in the morning when I slumped into an auto to drive me back to my hotel. Although the performance was still in full flow, I was shattered. Elegant changes of costumes, elaborate dances and florid backdrops of mountains, valleys and battlefields had held me enchanted for hours. Krishna translated the stories throughout the programme, his words vying with the meandering sitar and pounding tabla for space in my already cluttered head.

I was enthralled most of all by the response of the audience. From young to old everyone was transfixed, engaging with each legend as if their own lives depended on its outcome. The spiritual union shared between audience, actor, dancer and the great universal themes expressed by the performances, was remarkable.

The temple was a holy place AND a normal part of life.

Though exhausted, I took out my notebook, lay on my bed and started to scribble.

1. Brahman, the Ultimate Reality, embraces both everything AND nothing.

2. The world both is, and is not, an illusion based on the absolute reality of Brahman. All truth is _relative_.

3. Life's a cycle of rebirths, governed by the law of Karma. Every thought and action has an inevitable result.

4. Every Hindu has a duty to act appropriately to their assigned station in life; the end justifies the means.

5. The pursuit of material gain, BY HONEST MEANS, is a fundamental goal in life.

Thanks to Krishna, I now have the definitive guide to Hinduism, I thought.

Uh-oh. Mistake number three of the day.

Logic Vs Emotion

The size of the reward seemed disproportionate to the amount of effort expended.

Seated in a restaurant on the shore of Fort Cochin I was watching six fishermen haul, via an ingenious system of cantilevers and stone weights, the twenty-metre wide Chinese nets out of the sea. Suspended from four lengthy bamboo poles, secured together at the top like a tepee framework, the nets sagged with no more than half a dozen fish. By the time one of the fisherman had climbed stealthily along the central beam to retrieve the catch, the fish had been snatched away by the circling gulls.

Maybe I caught them on a bad day, but the arduous exercise confirmed my evolving theory that if an Indian could make a task ten times more difficult than it need be, he would. That said, the rhythmic process was mesmerising to watch.

I poured myself another cup of "special tea". Due to the quirks of the local licensing laws, some restaurants were prohibited from serving alcohol at lunchtime. Consequently, I was supping beer from a china cup and saucer.

As I replaced the teapot on the table, a young woman approached me. Smiling nervously she thrust a crumpled piece of paper into my hand:

> Hello
> My name is Sarah.
> I am deaf and dumb.
> Caste - Christen
> My mother abandoned me at age 2.
> Please give or pledge money.

I indicated that I had no loose coins and, without any fuss, she wandered over to another table. Suddenly I heard a shrill whistle. The restaurant manager, having noticed her, was ordering the woman, Sarah, to move on. She, however, hadn't seen him. He whistled a second time. Again, no response.

On the third call, clearly annoyed, Sarah turned her head and betrayed her guise. There was obviously nothing wrong with her hearing. She was soon on her way, sporting a contemptuous glint in her eye.

Recalling our conversation the previous afternoon, I reflected on Krishna's suggestion that Indians shared a collective consciousness of culture, belief and values that transcended Hinduism. Might this influence the way Sarah, a Christian, thought and behaved?

Perhaps he was right: the Hindu paradigm touched everybody. A Christian didn't have to believe in Hinduism to *think* like a Hindu. Although she may not publicly subscribe to the concepts of karma and dharma, Sarah might act as if they existed because, deep down, she couldn't help herself. It was in her genes.

Maybe the poor woman had no choice but to beg? Determined by her karma, this was her assigned role in this life, her dharma. How she conducted herself, though, was an entirely different matter. Whether Sarah was actually deaf, dumb or abandoned by her mother was immaterial. The end justified the means. The following day she may have carried a small child or affected a different form of disability. That was admissible; as long as she continued to beg. Sarah's material urges were justified by a spiritual drive.

Recalling the events in Mamallapuram, the demanding women that I'd met on the beach *may* have been genuine victims of the tsunami. Or their stories may have been a complete ruse. I subsequently discovered from other travellers that women such as they were always hassling the tourists, tidal waves notwithstanding. Although their ultimate aim may have been liberation from the cycle of rebirth, their immediate goal was survival. Even if that meant weaving a couple of white lies.

From their perspective the women possessed very little. Along the beach they encountered tourists who, relatively speaking, appeared affluent. What did it matter if a few tall tales were spun to service their needs?

'It's morally reprehensible,' we cried in disgust. 'These women are exploiting the real tsunami victims for their own personal gain.'

Purpose, not principle, prevailed. They prospered by whatever means possible, particularly if their short-term act was legitimised by a long-term religious conviction.

The stoicism that I encountered never ceased to amaze me. Street cleaners, porters, beggars even, appeared to accept their lot in life with resignation and resourcefulness, but with little complaint. This was frustrating to witness. Rarely did anyone want to move above or below their station. If they were poor, they were satisfied, for it was no less than they warranted. If they were wealthy, they were certainly satisfied; it was no more than they richly deserved.

I'm not sure that people were reluctant to better themselves per se. Self-improvement appeared admissible, *provided it was within their assigned dharma*. A university degree, for example, functioned as both a means to acquire an education and as a visible demonstration of an individual's social standing.

'What do you do?'

'I am driving an ambulance.'

'Do you enjoy it?'

'Yes. Actually I am also having a degree in commerce. That makes me a very good ambulance driver.'

I've often heard India described as an extremely tolerant nation. I'm unconvinced. The tolerance that I encountered seemed more related to people who, acting in accordance with their dharma, harboured a preoccupation with status and social standing.

On so many occasions I was besieged by a bewildering number of questions relating to my name, age, occupation, family and marital status. Yes, people wanted to impress me with their knowledge of English but their obsession with rank kept peeping through the amiable veneer.

The duo of karma and dharma, as defined by Krishna, was a great ideology. It seemed to give everyone a clear, identifiable role. Yet I discovered that it wasn't always interpreted in the way that he meant.

Although dharma embodies a certain degree of aspiration, once a person has realised their assigned station, what remains for them to do but maintain the status quo? A teacher's dharma is achieved once they've gained their teaching qualification and a job. Though they may have another thirty years left on the earth, they've reached where they need to be *in this life*. Their sights are set on the next.

India's Rebirth, given to me by Krishna, was fascinating to read. "Many Indians," Sri Aurobindo writes, "are utterly overcome by *Tamas*, the dark and heavy demon of inertia."

Maybe those that describe India as a tolerant society are correct; tolerant of mediocrity and things never done quite as well as they could be. Inert. An Indian, theoretically, could live the whole of his life according to his dharma without having to take responsibility for one single decision. The desire to do any more than he *need* do is rendered superfluous.

Sri Aurobindo depicts the condition superbly:

> If the amount of force that is spent on India were spent on a European nation, you would find it full of creative activities of various kinds. But here, in India, it is like sending a current of electricity through a sleeping man: he suddenly starts up, begins jerking and throwing his arms and feet about and then drops down again; he is not fully awake.

So much creative potential, realised by the minority, lies dormant elsewhere: "That bucket is made for washing, so wash with it we will. That hose is intended to irrigate the fields. Combine the two to make a shower? Why would we want to do that?" Sri Aurobindo calls it "thought-phobia."

This enigma confounded me. While an Indian seemed to focus on the long-term, he exhibited an incapacity to think ahead on a *daily* basis. Though his life was governed by karma, the ultimate law of cause and effect, he failed to grasp the idea, for example, that if he didn't fill his vehicle with petrol (cause) it would stop (effect). The practical implications of this were mind-numbing.

'What's the problem?' I asked one morning as my taxi spluttered and stalled.

'No petrol,' replied the driver as if this was an everyday occurrence.

'Why not?'

'Empty tank.'

'What are you going to do about it?' I asked, beads of sweat dripping onto the back seat.

'Garage is down road,' he said, producing a small well-used bottle from under his seat. 'I go and come.'

Thinking through the consequences of an action never entered into it. The taxi driver lived for "now", for the moment.

This possibly also explained why shopkeepers never had any small coins. Purchasing something for seven rupees with a ten rupee note was always asking for trouble.

'Correct money, please!'

'Do you not have any change?'

This prompted a shrug and a quick dash to a nearby store to borrow enough coins for me. *Just* me, mind you. On leaving, I noticed his neighbour then scuttle out of his shop. He now had no change. Cause and effect, but the way it was designed to be?

That's one explanation. Of course, the shopkeeper may have hoped I'd say: 'Don't worry, it's only three rupees. Keep it.' The pursuit of artha, by honest means or otherwise, manifested itself at every opportunity.

Generalisation, though, is unhelpful. In 1959, seven semi-literate women borrowed 80 rupees to start a poppadom business. By 2004, Lijjat Papad in Bombay was employing

40,000 women in sixty branches across the nation with a turnover in excess of US $60 million.

Sunil Mittal started a small business selling bicycles in 1970. Thirty-five years later, Bharti Enterprises, his company, controlled over 20% of India's mobile communication market with sales of US $300 million.

India boasts many examples of entrepreneurial success such as these. Yet, even today, they are realised by a tiny proportion of the population.

'The Brahmins used to run the temples. Now they run the country!'

Outlandish statements were bouncing off the walls of the back street bar. Their author, Dilip, was a lanky non-resident Indian with a strong, angular jawbone and hungry eyes.

'The pundits who originally demanded temple money are now the police, the legal institutions and government departments.' THUD.

The night was sticky, the sultry atmosphere spoiling for contentious talk. Swinging wide the door a few minutes earlier, Dilip had sauntered in and slumped onto a barstool near to mine.

'San Miguel,' he'd ordered brusquely, clicking his fingers in the waiter's face.

'Finished, sir,' the barman had replied.

Looking in my direction, he'd rolled his eyes.

'They have Sandpiper,' I'd suggested helpfully.

'Any good?'

'Well... it's cold.' And we started to chat.

I learned that, though his family lived in Cochin, Dilip had emigrated to Sydney over twenty years ago. Now in his mid-forties, he returned every summer to spend a few weeks in Kerala, the only part of India for which he held any real affection.

'The rest,' he'd dismissed with a waft of his hand, 'I tolerate.'

It soon became evident that Dilip delighted in lobbing huge statements into the air, leaving them to plummet to earth under the weight of their own provocation. He rarely provided any justification to keep them buoyant. If anyone else wanted to pick up his argument; that was up to them. I imagine he'd have made a lousy juggler.

Dilip's little tirade had been ignited by my innocuous reference to 'a fascinating conversation with a rather erudite Brahmin called Krishna the previous evening.' Touch paper lit, he was off.

'He was a Brahmin!' SLAM. 'Naturally he's only going to offer one view of Hinduism.'

'Why?'

'Three per cent of the population control between fifty and seventy per cent of the country's key positions. The ideology of karma has great sway over the masses if you convince them to buy into it. And they have.'

'What are you getting at?'

'India became a democracy nearly sixty years ago. The Brahmins loved that. It was a perfect model post-independence because of the freedom it afforded. It allowed all their systems to flourish.' Grabbing a fistful of peanuts from a glass dish on the bar, he tossed them into his mouth one at a time as he continued to speak. 'Democracy is one of the most effective systems to aid upward mobility and the acquisition of power and wealth.'

'That's a bit cynical, isn't it?'

'Is it? You know what Krishna told you about the British labelling Hinduism?' he said, wagging his finger. A few nuts fell onto the floor. 'That's only half the story. I bet he conveniently forgot to mention that Vedism was also known as Brahminism?'

'I don't remem...'

'A-ha! Thought so. The Brahmins had already pulled together the popular village and folk gods into their man-made hierarchy centuries before the British came along. Maybe they didn't call it Hinduism, but they certainly held the masses under their control. What's become erroneously known as the caste system was a social order in which the Brahmins set themselves apart from everyone else.'

'It seems to work at a certain level,' I argued, suddenly taken aback by the sound of my own voice defending the system. That was the thing I soon discovered about Dilip: such was the force of his opinion that I found myself adopting a contrary position, even if I didn't believe what I was saying.

'Apart from the starving millions,' he rebuffed. As he leant forward, a waft of expensive cologne cut through the smoky air.

'Fair comment.'

The sound system, situated behind a sorry-looking pot plant in the far corner suddenly whirred into life, pumping a shrill Bhangra dance track into the bar.

'Hey!' Dilip bawled at the barman. 'We're talking!'

'Sorry, sir, sorry!'

Dilip shifted his stool closer to mine.

'Look, the British occupied the highest positions in the land. They treated the Indians as inferior beings, politically, culturally and morally. They gave them no real responsibility for self-governance. When they moved out, the Brahmins moved in.'

'Hmm.' I picked a few nuts from the dish. The music dropped to a tolerable level.

'Actually they were already there, hand-in-glove with you guys. At partition, eighty-five per cent of the population was rural and predominantly lower caste. They were helpless! The guardians of the sacred texts emulated the British elite and all India got out of it was a transference of power under a different name.'

'It's a point of view.'

'OK. Maybe I don't mean the Brahmins literally,' he conceded. 'But the ideology was inherited. Perhaps what the country initially needed in 1947 was not democracy but a benign dictatorship.'

'You don't mean that!'

'Too late to tell now. But just for a while it may have helped the country get back on its feet. Partition was pushed through pretty damn quickly...'

'So you're blaming the British for all...'

'Certainly not.' Turning his head, Dilip took in the bar's clientele in a single swooping glance. It wasn't busy: just a few other westerners and one or two local-looking lads. His eyes then flicked back and caught my expression. 'Others might though. Some Hindu fundamentalists, for example, peddle a fantastically revisionist take on history which lays the blame of most of India's problems on your doorstep.'

'They could be right!'

'Hang on, you guys may have your faults, but after ninety years of colonial rule you can't be held entirely accountable for the way the country is now.'

Phew. I felt my baggage of post-colonial guilt lighten slightly.

'Neither can the Muslims. They governed the nation for much longer than the British. Today they make up nearly fifteen per cent of the population. Yet even if a tiny proportion of them, say 0.1%, decided to become reactionary - that's 165,000 people - the effect on India would be devastating.'

'It may yet happen.'

'Indeed. That's possibly what this country needs.'

'What, a revolution? You've said some outrageous things but...'

'...No, calm down, I don't mean in a militant sense. The Hindu masses need to get their voices heard somehow. But they won't.'

'Why not? Surely there's enough of them? India's the largest the democracy in the world.' Draining the warm dregs of my beer, I placed the empty bottle on the bar.

'Yes, but democracy should allow free and equal representation of the people. In India it's neither free nor equal.'

'Isn't it?'

'One man, one vote, is a great ideal but useless when such a high proportion of the population is illiterate. Or living in rural parts without access to voting facilities. As I say, the

Hindu hierarchical system was transferred neatly into the governance structures.'

'But India became a democracy sixty years ago!'

'I agree, but the nation continues to be governed by an elite who can buy their way into power. That's if they're not there already by default.'

'More beer?' asked the barman. Pre-empting Dilip's response, I nodded. 'Two Sandpipers, please. Cold.' I turned back to Dilip. 'But the situation's improving, isn't it?'

'Undoubtedly,' Dilip conceded. 'The appetite for change is rising rapidly in some quarters. But there's still a long way to go.'

The barman placed two bottles in front of us. 'Cheers,' said Dilip.

'You're welcome.' I took a swig. 'I've read that increased representation in government from the scheduled castes is making a difference.'

'Indeed, and a number of recent economic reforms are restricting the self-seeking meddling of certain politicians. But one of the main stumbling blocks continues to be the belief system of the masses.'

'You're suggesting that Hinduism is holding back the nation?'

'What I'm saying is that most individuals have very little to say about communal matters for the simple reason that, on the whole, they're content. If they weren't, there'd be a massive uprising.'

'There's no strong corporate voice?'

'More than that. I'm saying it's neither permitted, nor desired. That's why karma is such a splendid controlling device. What other belief system allows the minority who have worked their way up the karmic ladder to control the majority who, not only stand on the bottom rung, but are perfectly content to remain there? Until the next life that is.'

'That's a bit harsh, isn't it?'

'Is it?'

'Hinduism's an easy target...'

'Because it gives license for the most outrageous behaviour. It's part of life – you must have seen it!' A vein twitched in his forehead.

'Tell me about it. I had a run-in with a dodgy Ticket Examiner a few weeks ago.'

'What happened?'

'Well, the short version is he sold my train reservation to another passenger. I couldn't believe it.'

'They'll get you whatever way they can.' He slapped his palm down on the bar. 'Get stopped for speeding and you're offered a choice: a court summons or a bribe to the police officer who'll turn a blind eye.'

'I'm amazed they can get away with it.'

'Well, it's partly because you have to pay to become a police officer.'

'No way!'

'Sure, it costs about six lakhs. Once you've got your badge you've got to make your money back somehow.' He grabbed another handful of nuts.

'It might be better if they were paid a decent wage in the first place.'

'Fat chance. Foreigners are always a good bet. If you're caught hiring a bike without an international driving license, give the officer one hundred rupees, simple - the transgression's ignored.'

'But that kind of thing happens in other developing countries too. Why is it any different here?'

'Because everyone accepts it.'

'What, the belief system again? You can't keep blaming…'

'No?' The vein above his left eye twitched again. 'Listen, most people like to live in their own world. They deliberately avoid any grip on reality.'

'What do you mean?'

'Surely your Brahmin friend told you about maya, the world being illusory and all that?'

'Yes he did. He also said the concept is often misunderstood.'

'Exactly. Look around you. On the streets. What do you see?'

'People.'

'Yes, and..'

'More people and...'

'Rubbish!'

He was right.

'You see it. I see it. Your average Indian doesn't. What do you hear?'

That was easy. 'Noise.'

'But he doesn't. The rubbish, the noise, the smell – it all belongs to the external world of maya. It doesn't exist. And even if it did, no one could do anything about it, apart from resign themselves to its existence.'

'Karma and dharma?'

'You got it. Hindus go through the ritual of cleansing their bodies and purifying their souls on a daily basis, but they have no concern for the "exterior" world, or environment, as they see it.'

'I'm not sure that's what Krishna meant by maya.'

'Maybe he didn't, but I'm sure that's what many people have turned it into.'

'Or a canny excuse for laziness?' I suggested, remembering the orange-peeling mother and daughter on the bus: 'You know, "Why shouldn't I throw my rubbish on the street if someone else will pick it up?"'

'I'm not sure that rationalisation crosses most people's minds. Hindus have a strong sense of personal accountability. But communal responsibility?' Dilip shook his head. 'I can't remove you from the cycle of rebirth. You're on your own, mate.'

'So Hinduism allows space for people to make up their own rules as it suits them?'

'Yes. Forget the philosophical hypothesis. In practice, the average Indian is acutely pragmatic. He believes he's telling the truth because, in his own way, he is.'

Memories of Ishita and the tsunami beach women came flooding back.

'Their reality is another's fantasy?'

'Yes. Truth is a relative concept, as oily as a pan of ghee and sometimes as murky. The net result is a slippery slope of practical relativism in which there are no absolutes. At one end you have the tailoring of an answer to suit any occasion, at the other, plain unequivocal corruption. No universally accepted code of conduct distinguishes between good and evil, right and wrong.'

Highlighted by Dilip's obvious scepticism, I was beginning to see what Krishna may have meant when he said that the problem was not Hinduism per se, but the way it manifested itself in Hindu society. The difference between the philosophy and the practice was plainly evident. Making money by honest means was sanctioned by Hinduism for the achievement of a higher purpose. Artha, the acquisition of wealth, was paramount for the well-being and happiness of the individual.

'Another beer?' I asked Dilip, noticing his bottle was almost empty.

'No, thanks. I must go soon.'

'OK. Tell me, if the moral continuum is as greasy as you suggest, then honesty must slide up and down the scale alongside every other value?'

'One thing Krishna probably didn't tell you about dharma is that a man commits no transgression if *he believes* he is acting according to his allotted station in life.'

'So a police officer can justify taking a bribe if he believes it goes with the territory?'

'You tell me.' Dilip shrugged. 'A person is not personally accountable if their conduct fulfils *their own sense* of religious and social duty.'

'If the system of cosmic rules embodies both good and evil, it's hardly surprising that distinguishing between right and wrong is problematic,' I said.

'Yes, but most Indians don't even go there in their thinking,' Dilip replied.

'Correct behaviour is not about doing right or wrong in the present. It's the final outcome that counts. A deed is only wrong if it doesn't produce the intended result.'

He stood up.

'Why have you been telling me all this?' I asked.

'Listen! I've lived abroad for many years. But my family is here. So is my heritage. Every year I come back and every year it gets to me. It's in my blood.' Sticking out his jaw defiantly, he snatched a sharp intake of air. 'This nation could be so great.'

'Do you believe it *will* be?'

Curling his thin lips, he shrugged.

'I'm a nihilist. I don't believe in anything.'

Back in my hotel room, I dug out the notes I'd made the previous evening. They needed qualifying:

- Concepts of "right" and "wrong", "yes" and "no" are fluid. They sit on a different continuum to the one with which I'm familiar. Get used to it.

- Opportunities for flexibility, negotiation and equivocation are limitless. The stark exception is the endless bureaucracy.

- Filth, noise and lack of personal space are tolerated. This is because they don't exist. Get used to that, too.

Cochin was blessed with many bookshops. Earlier in the day I had purchased a slim but incisive volume by Gita Mehta called *Karma Kola*. Skimming through it in bed that night, the title of chapter twelve leapt off the page:

"Being Hindu means never having to say you're sorry."

I could see where Mehta was coming from.

Still irked by Ishita's deception in Mamallapuram, I recollected her *public* maxim with reference to her children: "Their joy is my joy." Flipped on its head, the rearranged words probably rang closer to her *private* conviction: "*My* joy is *their* joy." By furthering her own interests, she was ensuring the children's happiness; integrity was abandoned by the wayside, right and wrong discarded somewhere along the path of relative values. Perverse, though it was, I could grasp the reasoning.

Ishita demonstrated a conviction that her behaviour was appropriate to her station in life as a businesswoman. Exploitation, extortion and deceit didn't come into it. Truth was like modelling clay in the hands of one of her children; it could be shaped into whatever the situation demanded. She was perfectly self-deluded by a morality of her own fabrication and, when confronted, remained unremorseful. *How long would she get away with that back home,* I wondered?

Even though by religion she was a Catholic, *culturally* Ishita was a Hindu. She had no need to apologise.

I was beginning to appreciate how the Hindu paradigm permeated so many aspect of Indian society. Politics, education, business, healthcare and even other belief systems; nothing eluded its influence. Auto drivers displayed shrines of flashing Vishnus and twinkling Jesuses on their dashboards. Shopkeepers turned their counters into altars and mountain buses burnt incense sticks to invoke protection on the treacherous roads. Anywhere and everywhere could be a holy place: a vehicle, a rock, a shop.

This holistic approach to life fascinated me. On the one hand, I observed the distinction between the non-dualistic Vedic doctrine of the Brahman and the heartfelt, dualistic devotion to deities such as Shiva of non-Vedic origin. Though not positioned at opposite ends of the philosophical spectrum, the beliefs sat significantly apart.

On the other hand, spanned by the duo of karma and dharma and the conviction that all paths led to God, I marvelled at how so many diverse beliefs could be synthesised into the one, broad arch of Hinduism. Genius!

In the doctrine of Brahman, the Absolute, there was no polarity. Brahman was everything AND nothing. Morality couldn't be compartmentalised into value-proof boxes of right or wrong, yes or no. The "Tyranny of the OR" had no place. Brahman expressed the *Ultimate* genius of the AND, the same genius that unified an entire nation of contradiction.

But Krishna's cautionary words rang true. Distorted values, corruption and oppression were prolific. Behaviour defied explanation. Whatever an individual believed seemed to be tolerated.

He was right. The problem wasn't Hindu philosophy but Hindu *society*, the bustling market place where the genius of the doctrine's unity was traded for personal taste. People selected the items they desired and overlooked the rest.

A system of spiritual Pick 'n' Mix, in which everyone is permitted to choose their own moral stance, is ripe for exploitation. Hindu scriptures acknowledge that the craving for power and wealth is a legitimate human aspiration, but exhort that it should be pursued in righteous ways. The appeal of material acquisition at the expense of any ethical necessity, however, seemed too beguiling for many. People believed, or were self-deluded into believing that, whatever they did, they were doing the right thing.

The same applied to karma and dharma. The unprincipled Brahmin enjoyed the latitude the duo afforded while lesser mortals dodged their personal responsibility. In so doing, both strayed from the path of spiritual discipline.

In fairness, though, show me a religion that isn't guilty, to varying degrees, of the same charge. Many of us capitalise on personal conviction to justify our actions. That's human nature.

Stalemate. While Krishna challenged the integrity of other Hindus abusing the philosophy and Dilip distrusted Krishna's impartiality because he was a Brahmin, I conceded that my analysis was barely skimming the surface. Like Krishna's description of the many Hindu gods, my encounters amounted to a handful of snapshots, never the complete picture. I could live the rest of my life in India and never see it all.

I realised that my quest for rational, neat answers was fruitless. Nothing was definitive. Unlike Marmite, I couldn't package India in a jar and say "love it or hate it, it tastes like this because..."

There is no absolute recipe. Just as "neti" implies that it is impossible to formulate a complete definition of Brahman, the same could be said for the land itself. India is "neti, neti". Not this, not that.

Although the noise raged on relentlessly, the lack of personal space bugged me to distraction and the voices in my head and heart continued to bicker, I had to accept that wallowing in self-pity and over-analysis would get me nowhere. *Deal with it!*

Further into my travels I would question whether India did actually embrace the genius of the AND. In the meantime, the best I could do was venture forth with

- An open mind
- An eye on the bigger picture
- The realisation that my journey would never be complete

From South to North

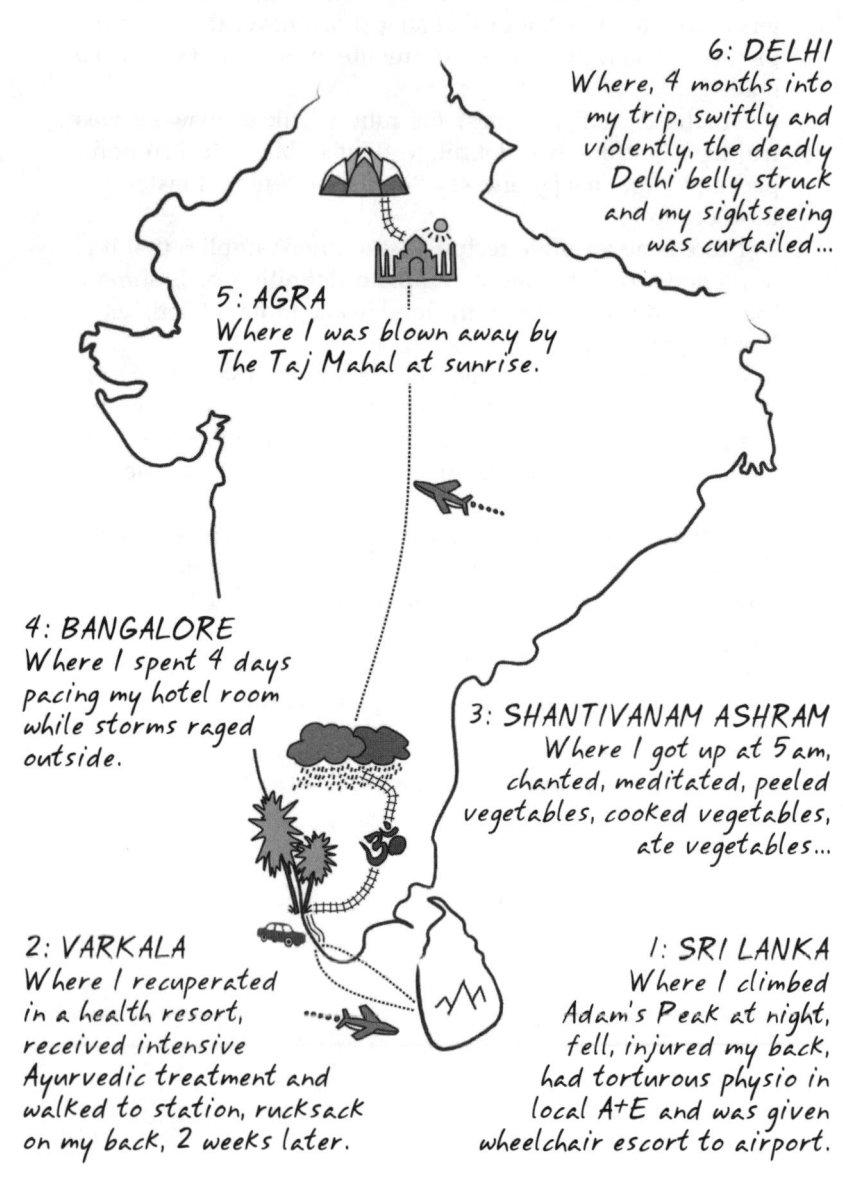

6: DELHI
Where, 4 months into my trip, swiftly and violently, the deadly Delhi belly struck and my sightseeing was curtailed...

5: AGRA
Where I was blown away by The Taj Mahal at sunrise.

4: BANGALORE
Where I spent 4 days pacing my hotel room while storms raged outside.

3: SHANTIVANAM ASHRAM
Where I got up at 5am, chanted, meditated, peeled vegetables, cooked vegetables, ate vegetables...

2: VARKALA
Where I recuperated in a health resort, received intensive Ayurvedic treatment and walked to station, rucksack on my back, 2 weeks later.

1: SRI LANKA
Where I climbed Adam's Peak at night, fell, injured my back, had torturous physio in local A+E and was given wheelchair escort to airport.

8
In Pursuit of Happiness

*Before you are through,
your destination has arrived*

If ever an Indian train existed that could meet the above claim, the Shatabdi Express would be it. Translated from Hindi as "centenary", the Shatabdi was introduced in 1988 to commemorate the birth of India's first Prime Minister, Jahawar Lal Nehru. Indian Railways operates twelve pairs of Shatabdi express trains, eight of which originate from Delhi. Inside, they are more like a budget airline than a conventional carriage, complete with reclining seats, air conditioning and a meal service.

I was waiting patiently on the crowded platform at New Delhi Station for the mid-afternoon Shatabdi to Dehradun. With half an eye on my rucksack slouched against a concrete pillar, I squinted to read the electronic display board further along the platform. In accord with the sluggish mood of the waiting passengers, it wasn't working. I took a large gulp of water from my plastic bottle, then wiped my forehead. The dry Delhi heat was punishing.

A few weeks earlier, I had called Mark Thomas in the UK to say that I was planning to head north by mid-April. He suggested that I emailed JP Singh, the director of KHW, a development organisation based in Rajpur, Uttaranchal. Following his advice, I received the following reply from JP a couple of days later:

> Dear Mark,
> You would be most welcome to stay and use KHW as a base.
> Perhaps you would like to get involved in some of our projects?
> Yours, J. P. Singh

With my itinerary wide open, how could I refuse? In a subsequent email, JP Singh instructed me to catch the Shatabdi to Dehradun. There he would meet me and drive us to his home in Rajpur, a few kilometres further north.

I looked at my watch. With the train's scheduled arrival time imminent, I felt slightly concerned that I was waiting on the wrong platform. I hadn't heard any announcements and the display board still wasn't functioning.

'Shatabdi Express?' I asked a trio of young men, two of whom responded with a vacant shrug.

'Yes, yes,' the third said, wobbling his head confidently.

Hmm. Unconvinced, I picked up my rucksack and approached a middle-aged couple who were standing further along the platform.

'Excuse me, is this the right platform for the Shatabdi Express?'

'Actually,' replied the woman in a homely Yorkshire accent that caught me by surprise, 'we were just wondering the same thing.'

As we chatted, it transpired that Jan and Dave Carpenter were English teachers returning to Mussoorie after a long weekend in Delhi. I was reassured by the fact that we were all in the same boat.

'Where are you heading?' Jan asked.

'Visiting a friend in Rajpur.'

'Oh?'

'Well, when I say "a friend", I actually mean a friend-of-a-friend. He's invited me to stay. At some point, I'm hoping to go trekking in the Himalayan foothills.'

'I'm envious!' said Dave. 'If you have time, I recommend the Char Dham pilgrimage. The landscape is incredible.'

'Have you done it?'

'Many years ago. I'm not sure my legs are up to it now!'

'Parts of the route are much more accessible by road nowadays,' added Jan.

'Thanks. I'll mention it to...'

I was interrupted by the tannoy system crackling into life.

'The Shatabdi Express will shortly be arriving on platform four.'

Relief: we were in the right place. All around, people started to gather their bags, crates and luggage and move towards the platform's edge.

'Which school do you work at?' I asked Dave and Jan, hitching my rucksack onto my back.

'Woodstock International. It's a mile outside Mussoorie, overlooking the Doon Valley.'

'Sounds idyllic.'

'It is. You should come and visit! On a clear day you get a fantastic view of the Himalayas.'

As the train rolled in, I exchanged email addresses with Jan and Dave and we parted company. They were booked into another carriage.

The following evening I was sitting in JP Singh's garden, browsing through a colour-plated book on the region's history that I'd found on his shelves.

"The Goddess Ganga first descended to earth as a life-sustaining torrent of water," I read. "Showering onto the head of Shiva as he meditated, she trickled through the matted coils of his hair to form countless tributaries. Weaving their way through the mountainous landscape they eventually converged to form the great river renowned throughout India as Ganga Mai. To the rest of the world it is known as the Ganges. Venerated as home to the source of the nation's holiest river, Garhwal is often referred to as *Dev Bhumi*: land of the gods."

Looking around, I could appreciate what the author meant. The back of JP's house commanded a tremendous view of the neighbouring Garhwal foothills. Rolling down the valley and then up towards the Mussoorie Ridge, majestic sal trees darkened the hillside in the failing light.

Serenaded by the songful tick-tick of the waking cicadas in the undergrowth, I breathed in a draft of balmy evening air. It felt so refreshingly clear after the polluted haze of Delhi. A crimson-winged butterfly bumbled towards me. I ducked. Blessed with the wing-span of a sparrow, but the clumsy coordination of a crane fly, it barely missed my forehead before continuing its random flight path across the garden.

'Here you are, Mark! Something to aid your concentration.' JP emerged from the house clutching two bottles of ice-cold Royal Challenge beer.

He had been director of KHW since 1998, an organisation committed to projects that work towards "a poverty-free and just world where all children have equal opportunity and access to develop their full potential." JP lived with several members of his family on the KHW campus, a two-story building situated in Rajpur, a few kilometres north of Dehradun. Surrounded by immaculately-maintained gardens, the site included the KHW offices, a kindergarten, a number of workshop spaces and ensuite guest accommodation.

JP was the most un-Indian Indian I had met so far on my travels.

'That's because I'm not,' he argued. 'I have Nepali ancestry.'

By describing him as un-Indian, I'm not referring to his appearance. Like many men, JP sported a tidy moustache and thick dark hair. I'm talking about his demeanour and sense of humour. JP possessed an uncanny ability to step outside the Indian paradigm and scrutinise it with an objectivity seasoned with a healthy sprinkling of scepticism. He viewed the world with an ironical glint which, I imagined, helped him keep the demands of his work in perspective. In the morning, for example, he might be talking to the mother of a young girl in desperate need of corrective surgery; that afternoon, he might be negotiating with the bureaucratic red tape that hindered the same child from receiving an operation that could so radically change her life.

I looked at him, relaxing, enjoying his beer, relieved that we had immediately connected. JP was a big-hearted guy whom I would grow to admire immensely.

'What is JP short for?' I asked.

'Jaywant Pratap,' he replied. 'But everyone calls me JP except my mother!' He laughed. 'Oh, and in case you're interested, Singh means "lion".'

'Cheers!' I said before taking another swig of beer. Tasting good, it served to lubricate the potentially dry conversational wheels concerning the region's history.

Sharing its borders with Tibet and Nepal, Uttaranchal state has a population of eight and a half million, 77% of which is rural, living in over 15,000 villages. Over 90% of the land is hill country and just over 60% is covered by forest. Administratively, Uttaranchal has thirteen districts governed by the two divisions of Garhwal and Kumaon.

'This book claims that Uttaranchal is the newest mountain state in the world,' I observed.

'Correct. It didn't receive separate statehood until the millennium.'

'What was it before that?'

GARHWAL

Map showing districts: Uttarkashi, Chamoli, Rudraprayag, Dehradun, Tehri Garhwal, Pithoragarh, Haridwar, Garhwal, Bageshwar, Almora, Nainital, Champawat, Udham Singh Nagar. Bordered by TIBET, NEPAL.

KUMAON

'Between 1947 and 2000 the region formed part of the northern province of Uttar Pradesh state, commonly called Uttarakhand. That's Sanskrit for "North Country". In population terms, Uttar Pradesh is the biggest state in India. If it were a country, it would be the sixth largest in the world. It's inhabited by more people than the whole of Russia!'

'Really?'

'Oh yes. For centuries, Uttarakhand consisted of two rival kingdoms, Kumaon in the east and Garhwal, where we are, in the west. In the 1990's, a number of political groups started campaigning to unite them as one separate state. Arguing that Uttar Pradesh's capital administration in Lucknow had failed to develop Uttarakhand adequately, they presented a legitimate case for change.'

'Such as?'

'Actually, Lucknow was located twice as far from the Uttarakhand borders as Delhi. Almost five hundred kilometres.

A merge of the two rival kingdoms of Garhwal and Kumaon made geographical and political sense. Decisions over where the spoils of the new statehood should go, however, caused much heartache.'

'Why?'

'Both regions, for example, staked a claim to be the capital. The Kumaonis were displeased when Dehradun, the largest city, was provisionally selected. They wanted Gairsain, a tiny hamlet in the centre of the state.'

'I've never heard of it.'

'Nor has anyone. You'd struggle to find it on a map! Strangely, though, it's still mooted as a viable contender, just because of its geographical positioning.'

'So Dehradun is still only the provisional capital?' I asked.

'Yes, permanently provisional!' quipped JP. 'But that wasn't the end of the debate. With the capital selected, the next source of controversy was the choice of name. Although the final decision to grant separate statehood was made while the BJP was in power, in many ways, the party had been against the idea. But that didn't stop them trying to gain political mileage for the deed. The politicians called the new state Uttaranchal, I feel, to claim that they had fulfilled the political demands of the hill people. But in so doing, they trod on the sensibilities of others.'

'Why?'

'The name Uttaranchal, I suggest, had less sectarian connotations. The opposition, however, accused them of coining the name to further the party's wider ideological cause. They felt it should remain Uttarakhand.'

'What was the big deal?' I asked.

'Basically it's a matter of definition,' JP replied. 'Both *khand* and *anchal* mean "land" but khand has a far more militaristic connotation. In meaning it is closer to "territory". Anchal, translated literally, is "lap of a mother". As it gives an impression of nurture and care, it suited the softer image that the BJP wished to communicate. The party wanted to move away from its harsh, fundamentalist perception.'

'I see.'

'Yes, but those who had struggled for a separate state regarded the decision as a slap in the face. Uttarakhand enjoyed a strong identity and had featured prominently in Hindu legends and scriptures for thousands of years. The activists, though not fooled by the BJP, decided not to push the issue too far.'

'Best to quit while ahead?'

'Yes their goal of statehood had been achieved. Although Uttaranchal officially became India's 27th state in November 2000, it will always be Uttarakhand in the minds of some.'

'Because of its historical significance?'

'Yes. For the majority, though, the controversy is no more than a quibble over words. It has little impact on daily life.'

'Is that what you think?'

'Come, it's getting chilly,' JP replied evasively. 'Let's go inside.'

During dinner, we mulled over my options for the following weeks. JP's mother, though she repudiated it, was a superb cook. Her chapatis, smaller and softer than I had tasted anywhere else, were a good accompaniment to the vegetarian dishes she prepared, often especially for me. JP was an unashamed carnivore.

'Mama!' he would bellow if he hadn't eaten his daily quota of meat. 'Why just vegetables again?'

Shanti Singh would look at me, smile, and return meekly to the kitchen. A forbearing woman of few words, like many wives and mothers, she rarely dined with the men. This Indian practice, along with her embargo on washing-up, I found mildly perplexing. Two weeks elapsed before my hands reached the sink. Even then, I only managed to clean one plate before she scuttled over and flicked me with the dishcloth.

'Shoo, shoo, Mark. I do not like to cook. The washing, I love,' she rebuked playfully, as if I was denying her one of life's great pleasures.

'I'll cook for you, then.'

'Shoo!' Cooking was woman's work. Mrs Singh found it a chore, but it was her duty. I couldn't win. Neither, dare I say, could she.

After she had cleared away the table that first evening, JP quizzed me about my plans.

'I'm keen to go trekking,' I said.

'Fine by me,' he replied scornfully. 'You trek, I'll take the jeep.'

It was on the issue of walking that JP disproved my earlier observation about his lack of Indian-ness. As far as his reluctance to use his feet to travel any distance was concerned, he was as Indian as the next man.

'Seriously,' he continued, 'I have an idea. My good friend, Shailender David, runs an educational project called SASA for people living in the Garhwal interior. He travels there once a month. Perhaps you would like to go with him on his next trip?'

I'd heard Mark Thomas talk about Shailender. SASA was another project that CHILD's Trust supported. 'Sounds good to me. What about the trekking?'

JP stood up and wandered through the open doorway into the kitchen. 'Let me speak to Shailender,' he said, peering into the refrigerator. 'As he was born in the area, he's familiar with many of the trekking routes. In the meantime, how about visiting Dehradun Public School, one of KHW's projects in Kandoli?'

'I'd like that. I'd be interested to see how North Indian education compares with my experiences in the south.'

JP returned to the dining room. 'I think you'll find Dehradun Public school rather unique. Remind me to give you a copy of our most recent annual report. It contains information about some of our projects, including the school.'

'Will do.'

'So, enough business. How about a mango?' he asked, placing a plump fruit in front of me. 'They're just coming into season.'

9
The Booklovers

- *40% of India's population is below the age of 18 years*
- *India has the largest child population in the world*
- *It also has the highest number of "out of school" children in the world*

Had I ventured into the woods fifteen kilometres west of Dehradun in 1994 I may have met, seated under a mango tree, a dedicated teacher and five young children hungry to learn. With the Himalayan foothills sweeping the horizon and a light breeze nudging the green dangling fruit, kernels of knowledge were being sown into their keen minds.

But I didn't. I visited eleven years later. By then, Dehradun Public School boasted 338 students, 183 boys and 155 girls, sixteen teachers, eleven non-teaching staff and a part-time cleaner. It provided classes up to year eight but would soon be starting classes nine and ten. The clean, stone-built school building contained a well-equipped computer lab, a library, two floors of well-resourced classrooms, a kindergarten and a new, three-storey teaching block nearing completion.

Pupils learnt all the core subjects in the English Medium curriculum and were encouraged to engage in a wide range of other activities: cultural programmes, music, painting, stitching, embroidery and educational excursions. The school owned two buses, a 32 and 42 seater, which daily transported many children and teachers the long distance between their homes and the school.

On arrival, I was welcomed by the cheery watchman who swung wide the security gate to allow my Ambassador Taxi to drive into the school grounds. Smartly-uniformed children, playing contentedly on the steps of the white-pillared portico, looked up and waved, their teeth gleaming.

This was an idyllic academic scenario. First impressions may have led me to believe that Dehradun Public School was only enjoyed by the privileged; those children whose parents could afford a private English Medium education.

An invitation to visit to some of their homes after school revealed a very different story.

☼

Saira Bano-Deen lived in Upper Kandoli Village with her five sisters and two brothers. She was a shy, but industrious, young woman of fourteen who was extremely healthy and loved athletics. Neither of her parents was employed. Naeem Ali, one of Saira's brothers and the family breadwinner, worked as a guard at the recently completed nearby Petroleum University.

On a summery afternoon, accompanied by Ajay Issachar, the school's senior teacher, we rolled up in the conspicuously shiny white Ambassador outside Saira's home. The only other vehicles in the neighbourhood were a wooden cart and a couple of scrawny buffalo. Although her family's plot was surrounded by fields and forest, I couldn't discern much difference between the cultivated land and the open bush.

A man in dark trousers, a thick pullover and woollen hat greeted us with a solemn nod.

'That is Saira's father,' Ajay pointed out. He was working barefoot on a patch of land adjacent to the house, one *bigha* in size, an area of 90 x 90 feet. Onion, garlic and spinach plants were struggling to push their straggly green heads through the bed of stony, scorched earth.

Saira's mother appeared in the doorway and beckoned us into the main room of the house. A tangle of wires, festooned like Christmas decorations across the chalky walls and ceiling, supplied electricity to a bare light bulb in the centre. A portable black and white television, on which two crackly channels intermittently transmitted the news, balanced on a wobbly table covered with a purple cloth.

In addition to the random cabling, a few genuine festive ornaments drooped gaudily from the central wooden beam. Creating the ambience of a neglected Santa's grotto, they enlivened what was otherwise a miserably small and cluttered living space for a family of ten. The other two rooms, without electricity, were dark and chaotic. I sensed that Saira's mother, concealing her face in a flamingo pink headscarf, was mildly embarrassed at what I saw.

A small fire burned in the corner of the kitchen, a separate building. Pots, pans and other cooking utensils were piled on a concrete slab that ran the length of the wall. Serving as a shelf and food preparation surface, its corners were chipped and dirty.

Outside, Saira's father pointed to a small, fence-like construction about twenty feet from the house. Standing about four feet high, it consisted of four vertical lengths of wood supported by two cross-beams, between which large wads of dried grass were stuffed to form a modest screen.

'This is the toilet,' he proudly announced, translated by Ajay, 'but only for the women of the house and guests.'

'What do the men do?' I asked.

'We go to the jungle,' he replied, pointing to a clump of trees about 200 metres away. I later discovered that this flimsily-enclosed patch of earth was considered a luxury. In other homes, the entire family, including the girls and women, used the trees.

In reality, the jungle was possibly more sanitary than Mr Bano-Deen's closet. Comparison, however, was academic; neither option was an ideal scenario. But it highlighted the inherent challenges faced by a fourteen year old girl growing up in such an environment.

'It is extremely unpleasant and embarrassing when they are ill,' explained Ajay, 'especially in the rainy season. Walking to the woods alone, particularly in the dark, presents a number of safety issues. There are threats from both wild animals and dangerous, drunken men.'

I couldn't imagine what it would be like to have a stomach upset in the middle of the night in the dead of winter, the only relief located 200 metres away across a pitch black, sodden field in which anything, man or beast, could be lurking.

The Bano-Deens were a Muslim family living in a predominantly Hindu area that contained about 25 houses, seven of which, unusually, were owned by Muslims. Characteristically, the families were all inter-related and had been residents of the village for two or three generations. Most of the school's pupils, comprising about 95% of its enrolment, were Hindu. Ajay told me that issues of cleanliness, health and hygiene were less of a priority to Muslim families, an observation confirmed by my own experience.

Saira's family was larger than some but not as sizeable as it could have been. Traditionally, Muslim husbands may wed up to five wives. Saira's mother was her father's second wife, married after his first spouse, having passed away, had left him childless.

'We are very proud of Saira,' her mother told me. 'She is very motivated and hard-working. She is also a good sportswoman.'

'What have you achieved recently?' I asked Saira.

'I ran a two kilometre marathon. And won!'

Although Saira had made good progress in her studies over the last two years, that had not always been the case. When she was eleven, her parents had wanted to withdraw her from the school. Because she had twice failed her exams, they thought it best that she should marry. Through the teachers' gentle, but firm, encouragement, they were persuaded to let her stay. Since then, Saira had flourished and was keen to learn. Her parents' low expectations had also been raised.

'Habits and tradition die hard,' said Ajay.

'What do you mean?' I asked.

'Prospects for someone in Saira's position are far from certain. She faces family and cultural pressures to marry and raise a family as soon as she leaves school. But her schooling has given her a head start. She certainly has a far greater opportunity to broaden her horizons than if she had married three years ago.' Ajay, an astute, self-effacing man with a fervent passion for education, was expressing a concern shared by all his colleagues: would the older girls, like Saira, return after the summer holidays or would they be coerced into a marriage over which they had no control?

'What about your future?' I asked Saira.

'I do not wish to get married yet,' she replied. 'I want to complete my studies. After I finish school I will pick a job to help my family.'

'What will happen if you fail again or have to discontinue your studies?'

'I will learn some knitting, stitching or something like that,' she replied. 'I do not want to waste my life.'

Despite an erratic dial-up connection, Google came up trumps. Prompted by my visit to Dehradun Public School, I wanted to find out more about the Indian education system.

'May I use your office computer after dinner?' I asked JP one evening.

'Sure, you know where it is.'

Google: garhwal education

Mountain Voices: oral testimonies from Garhwal and Kumaon,
The interviews were gathered in the high valleys of **Garhwal** in Uttaranchal and Kinnaur ... The impact of **education** and increased migration are key issues, ...
Children have to travel up to 8 kms even to get primary **education** in many ....
www.mountainvoices.org/i_th_education.asp - 28k - Cached - Similar pages

A few minutes later I was transported, via the Panos Institute in London, to *Mountain Voices*, an oral testimony project that aims to amplify the voices of individuals and communities living in some of the world's most mountainous regions. One of the two areas on which the India collection focused was Garhwal.

Gathered over several years by the Himalaya Trust, the testimonies made illuminating and, at times, contentious reading.

"I feel that girls should not be educated. If they have to slog, cut grass, till the earth, then what use is education?" commented Attar, a sixty year old midwife and farmer. Her scepticism was tempered by the views of Sudesha, a farmer and activist in her fifties: "In my opinion, an understanding girl will remain so, even if she becomes educated."

After reading a few more testimonies, I made a note to return to the site at a later date.

Dehradun Public School bucked the trend by providing good quality education to needy children from poor, underprivileged backgrounds. Ordinarily they would not have received the opportunity to attend *any* kind of school, government or otherwise, let alone one of that standard. Regardless of caste, religion, gender or race, it was evident that the pupils benefited greatly from a holistic ethos that included not only a solid education but also a nutritious mid-day meal and regular health checks.

The journey from the early days of lessons under a tree was paved with obstacles, JP later told me, and not necessarily for the reasons that I might have expected.

'Despite KHW's financial commitment to develop the school,' he said, 'resistance from the immediate community proved to be the main stumbling block. Villagers treated the endeavour with suspicion and were reluctant to send their children.'

This reaction was characteristic of the attitude towards similar projects where local people defied change. They regarded intervention with scepticism, even from their fellow-Indians up the road. Having experienced far too many instances of government officials promising the earth but delivering nothing, people preferred to maintain the status quo than allow the bureaucrats persistently to boost, then quash, their hopes. Perseverance and integrity were the only effective weapons against the barriers of cynicism and distrust.

'As time slowly ticked by,' JP continued, 'parents witnessed the positive impact the school was having on individual lives. More families came forward to enrol their children. Determination eventually triumphed and, in 1997, construction of the present building was sanctioned.'

From the onset, Dehradun Public School placed a strong emphasis on the education of girls. I asked JP why this was considered so important.

'Most parents direct a disproportionate amount of help and effort towards their sons,' he explained. 'Our philosophy is to redress that imbalance. By educating one girl child, the whole family benefits. When a young woman eventually brings up her own children, she will know about health, hygiene and how to address other social problems.'

Given the sanitary conditions of many of the homes, his rationale made sense.

'Intransigent attitudes towards female education still exist in some instances,' he continued, 'but many parents regard it as an opportunity to empower their daughters with a stronger voice, thus enhancing their position within society.

'The teachers are aware that many of the girls may marry as soon as they leave school. It is important, therefore, that they learn how to set up and maintain a clean and healthy home as well as cope with the changes happening around them.'

I began to appreciate the value of such a positive intervention; a strong education could launch a child's life in a completely opposite direction to that which fate might ordinarily dictate.

Google: education system india

	THE INDIAN EDUCATION SYSTEM	
Age	**Class**	**Education Stream**
18+		Higher Education: Academic & Professional Degree Colleges & Technical Universities
	Board Examinations	
17-18	Class 12	Senior Secondary Schools / Colleges, Vocational Training Institutions
16-17	Class 11	
	Board Examinations	
15-16	Class 10	Secondary School
14-15	Class 9	
13-14	Class 8	Middle School
12-13	Class 7	
11-12	Class 6	
10-11	Class 5	Primary School
9-10	Class 4	
8-9	Class 3	
7-8	Class 2	
6-7	Class 1	
3-6		Pre-primary, Kindergarten

I discovered that the many different types of school in India fall broadly into two categories: government schools and the rest. The latter includes private (government aided, unaided, recognised and unrecognised), charitable and international institutions.

As in England, terminology is confusing: "private" and "public" are used interchangeably. Dehradun Public School, for example, is a charitably-funded private establishment. The school at SKCV in South India, by contrast, provides a non-formal education for its students, should they choose to attend.

The class number, particularly in rural areas, corresponds more to ability than age. Children in Class Two, for example, could be aged anything between seven and eleven. A child starting school for the first time at the age of nine might enrol in Class One to receive a basic foundation, rather than automatically join Class Three.

The term "Medium" refers to the main language in which the curriculum is taught. Most government schools, and some public and charitable, teach in the state language. The older girls at Hebron Hostel in Andhra Pradesh, for example, follow the Telugu Medium curriculum. Within the non-government sector, the English Medium curriculum tends to be the norm.

NATRAJ BOOKSTORE was the booklover's nirvana. Situated on the busy Rajpur Road in central Dehradun, its rambling shelves offered a tranquil reprieve from the heat and noise of the bustling main street. It was a pocket-size version of London's Foyles in its heyday before the store surrendered its haphazard charm to a regime of refurbished efficiency.

A solid oak desk laden with leather-bound ledgers dominated the centre of the shop, presided over by, I presume, Mr Natraj himself, a spindly, stooping gentleman with a pair of silver pince-nez balanced on the bridge of his angular nose.

With its logic-defying classification system, the bookshop was competently staffed by a team of eager-to-please scuttling assistants who could identify the whereabouts of any particular volume within moments. Yogic aerobic manuals rested against philosophical pamphlets of the BJP; gymnastics of a more cerebral kind.

The Booklovers

I was scanning an area where I imagined books on the education system might be located. As I reached out to pluck a likely publication from the shelf, another hand grabbed its spine at the same time. Turning around, I found myself nose to nose with a well-upholstered female Britisher, dashingly attired in a pair of flapping khaki culottes.

'Sorry.'

'No, I'm sorry.'

'Please, I am.'

Naturally, with our fingers clasped around the same volume, we started to talk.

'Ralph and I have been sojourning in Delhi with friends,' she informed me. 'But, as the city heat is simply too much, we're fleeing to Mussoorie for gin and a cooling respite'.

'Funnily enough, I've just spent a couple of days there myself,' I said.

'How did you find the weather?'

'Chilly,' I understated. But, given her ample natural lagging, I suspected she wouldn't find it a problem. An opinion, of course, that I kept to myself.

During the ensuing conversation, I discovered that Ralph's wife was a retired Schools' Inspector from Kent. With a vested interest in education, she was keen to hear about my recent experiences. So I told her.

'I wish to take issue with something you've just said,' she challenged me a few minutes into our conversation.

'Oh?'

'Yes. You said that more than half of India's children between the ages of six and fourteen do not go to school.'

'That's my understanding.'

'Well, the government official with whom we've been living in Delhi informed me that every child in the country receives an education.'

'Our experiences obviously differ. With whom did you say you were staying?' I asked slightly naughtily.

I left the shop with a few books under my arm, including a slim publication on the Indian education system that I discovered leaning against *Flyfishing in the Ganges*.

Around the corner from the bookshop stood KUMAR'S GROCERY AND GENERAL PROVISION STORE. Pushing open its polished glass door, I discovered that Kumar's was not any old grocery and general provision store. It specialised in imported produce: Cheddar cheese, Bird's Custard and my mate, the growing-up spread.

KUMAR'S was the Marmite-lover's nirvana.

JP's in for a treat, I thought as I left the shop, gleefully clutching my yellow-topped purchase.

※

Sandhya, also a pupil at Dehradun Public School, invited Ajay and me to her home after our visit to Saira's family. Her name means "dusk time". Aged fourteen, she was a Hindu, living in Bidholi village about two kilometres from the school on the edge of the jungle. There was a sizeable age gap between Sandhya and her older siblings, one brother and two sisters, who no longer lived at home. Consequently, she did much to help her elderly parents: preparing food, cooking and other household chores. Awake and working around the house by seven o'clock each morning, Sandhya didn't go to bed until eleven at night.

Although her home, a two-storey building, appeared deceptively large, she told me that it was subdivided into units.

'My parents and I live in the middle portion,' Ajay helped her explain. 'On the right are my grandparents' rooms and on the left, my uncle.'

'How many people live here altogether?'

'Ten people in three rooms.'

Other families lived on the second floor. The building was constructed out of stone and rendered with white-washed plaster. Five, rectangular concrete pillars supported a corrugated iron lean-to that ran along the front of the house. Part of the back wall had collapsed; the remainder tilted precariously against the supporting stonework.

The room in which Sandhya's family lived was similar in size to Saira's, but far less cluttered. Two *charpoys*, or string cots, covered with coarse, green and white bed sheets were pushed neatly into the corners. A portable radio sat on a small table and several items of clothing were draped across a pole suspended from the ceiling at either end. A frayed-edged poster of the goddess Lakshmi hung on the wall; her two benevolent eyes and four outstretched arms invited good fortune into the home.

At the side of the house stood a small area enclosed by stone walls but open to the elements.

'That is where we take bath,' explained Sandhya.

'There's no toilet?' I observed quietly to Ajay, not wanting to embarrass Sandhya or her mother.

'No, they have to go to the jungle,' he replied, pointing to the edge of the woods about two hundred metres away behind which the Himalayan foothills started to ascend. An electricity pylon indicated that they weren't entirely bereft of amenities and I spotted a small calor gas stove on the floor of the tidy kitchen.

Sandhya's mother saw me looking and smiled.

'She says that, although they have a gas cylinder, Sandhya collects dry wood from the jungle after school every day. It saves money.'

She softly uttered a few more words. 'She says Sandhya is a good girl.'

Standing side by side, the strong bond between mother and daughter was clearly evident. In terms of appearance, however, they stood generations apart. Sandhya proudly wore the school's pale blue uniform, stripy tie and knee-length grey socks, while her gaunt mother was clothed in a length of crimson and black fabric embroidered with tiny yellow flowers. Flowing from her waist to the ground, it draped around her back, over her head then down her right shoulder like a shawl. The only feature that the two women shared was a silver stud piercing each of their left nostrils.

Having met Sandhya, Saira and some of their friends, I later asked Ajay if they would be willing to write, in English, about an aspect of their lives that was important to them. This is what Sandhya produced:

> *I want to become a successful and a good person and with this I want to become a very good doctor. My father is not a rich person but he struggle with this life for us. I like to study in English schools. If I work hard in my studies I will definitely meet with success. For this I pray to the Lord that he give me energy.*

Slightly concerned that the school was encouraging false hopes from young people with such poor backgrounds, I quizzed Ajay if Sandhya's aspiration to become a doctor was achievable.

'Yes it is a realistic expectation,' he responded, 'but she will have to work hard, pass an entrance exam and possibly have additional coaching. The school will ensure that she has the required educational resources but four hours a day is not really enough. She will have to continue her studies at home, outside of school hours. For that she will require the support of her family.'

'Surely she will find that difficult, given the increasing pressures to assist her elderly parents with the household chores?' I asked.

Ajay nodded. 'Yes, and that is not the only barrier. At school, the children are educated in Hindi and English. At home, the family probably communicates in a local dialect or a form of broken Hindi. Speaking only Garhwali, for example, is not going to help Sandhya become a doctor. She needs the opportunity to speak the more mainstream languages on a regular basis.'

More positively, though, the school was blessed with a dedicated team of teachers who frequently worked beyond their contractual requirements to support the children. They patiently invested additional hours to assist with homework when required, motivated by the knowledge that they were effecting a positive change in each child's life.

In response to the writing task, Sonia, one of Sandhya's classmates aged fourteen, composed the following poem.

Last Night's Dream

Last night I saw a dream,
In which there is a beautiful scene,
Somewhere is a stream and somewhere is green.
Last night I saw a dream,
In which there is a beautiful scene.
There is a pond, there is an open gate
From which a beautiful girl came.
She came with a king,
We know she is a queen in a beautiful costume.
They went back from where they came.
Last night I saw a dream
In which there is a beautiful scene.

These words triggered several thoughts about the young women I'd met: what were their dreams? Would Sandhya, for example, become a doctor? And Saira: a career, marriage... both?

I wondered what the future held for those other young people, the majority living in this area not fortunate enough to attend an establishment such as Dehradun Public School. What hope did they have?

My encounter with the bureaucrat's friend in the bookstore had aroused the sceptic in me.

Google: | india education reality |

Indian education: what's really going on ...
Rhetoric and **reality**... **education** system... view of the **doubter**...
www.what-they-dont-tell-you.org. - 42k - Cached - Similar pages

---

As I searched the Internet for information, my head was soon spinning. Ascertaining verifiable, accurate facts was like eating dal with a fork: time-consuming, with very little substance reaching the mouth. Take literacy, for example.

The 2001 Census claims that 54% of women and 76% of men are literate: a total adult literacy rate of 65%. By contrast, the 2005 Human Development Report measures the literacy rate for women as 48% and 73% for men, making a total literacy rate of 61% for people over the age of fifteen. Although that's only 4% difference, it represents a discrepancy of over 41 million people.

Much depends, of course, on the definition of literacy. Within India there appear to be many variations, ranging from a person's capacity to read and write with understanding, simply to being able to write their own name.

A research paper, citing a survey conducted in 2003 by ORG-CSR in rural villages across five northern states, revealed that 68% of the people questioned believed themselves to be literate. Only 12%, however, could read a simple passage in Hindi with ease, 36% could read with varying degrees of difficulty and 52% couldn't read at all. 47% were unable to write their name and only 38% could write it without error.

On a subsequent visit to Natraj's store, I discovered another book: *The Great Indian Dream.* One of its co-authors, Dr Malay Chaudhuri, suggests that out of the 700 million people living in rural India, only 210 million are functionally literate: capable of reading simple instructions to operate a machine. The *functional* literacy rate of the entire nation, he proposes, is not much above 37.5% in reality.

The census claims that 65% of the nation are literate, Chaudhuri says 37.5%. That's a difference of 27.5%. Others suggest something in between. It seems that no one knows for sure whether almost a third of the population are literate or not.

There does, however, seem to be agreement on one matter: India has the largest illiterate population in the world, a fact that ought to be placed in its historical context. In 1947, the nation inherited a substantial legacy of illiteracy. According to the first post-Independence Census of 1951, only 9% of women and 27% of men were literate. The reality was probably much worse.

Synonymous use of the words "literacy" and "education" serves to compound the problem. One does not imply the other. A child who can write her own name is not the same as one who can write, read with understanding, and then act on her acquired knowledge. Using the government's definition, they are both literate, but only the latter could be described as educated.

Article 45 of the Indian Constitution, 1950, affirmed that "the State shall endeavour to provide, within a period of ten years from the commencement of this Constitution, *for free and compulsory education for all children until they complete the age of fourteen years.*" The italics are mine.

Thirty-six years later, the 1986 National Policy of Education stated that "it shall be ensured that *free and compulsory education* of satisfactory quality is provided to all children up to fourteen years of age *before we enter the twenty-first century.*"

In November 2000 the government launched a flagship programme Sarva Shiksha Abhiyan – "Education for All". Its mission is to make "in a time-bound manner, *free and compulsory education to the children of 6-14 age group a Fundamental Right... by 2010*".

Two years into the millennium, an estimated 82% of children in this age group officially *enrolled* in school. Yet, according to CRY, the Seventh All India Education Survey conducted in 2002 revealed that less than 50% of the population aged between six and fourteen actually *attended* school. That's about 90 million children.

Enrolment rates taken at the beginning of an academic year mask the attendance figures of those students who drop out of school during the course of that year.

The organisation iWatch claims that there is a 90 to 94% drop-out rate of children between kindergarten and year twelve, including those children who have never been to school.

A little "Policy and Practice" puzzle. Identify the words below and re-arrange in the correct order.

A	B	C	**L**	D	E	F	G	H	I	J	K	L	M
N	O	P	**E**	Q	R	S	T	U	V	W	X	Y	Z
A	B	C	**G**	D	E	F	G	H	I	J	K	L	M
N	O	P	**I**	Q	R	S	T	U	V	W	X	Y	Z
A	B	C	**S**	D	E	F	G	H	I	J	K	**L**	L
I	**M**	**P**	**L**	**E**	**M**	**E**	**N**	**T**	**A**	**T**	**I**	**O**	**N**
M	N	O	**A**	P	Q	R	S	T	U	V	W	**U**	X
F	**A**	**N**	**T**	**A**	**S**	**T**	**I**	**C**	Y	Z	A	**S**	B
C	D	E	**I**	F	G	H	I	J	K	L	M	**Y**	N
O	P	Q	**O**	R	S	T	U	V	W	X	Y	Z	A
A	B	C	**N**	D	E	F	G	H	I	K	L	M	N

Now locate the holy herd of cows to steer between the rhetoric and reality.

Translating policy into practice is a major challenge in India, a nation that has 46% of the world's illiterate population yet nearly 50 million degree graduates.

How can this be?

The answer lies partly in the fact that, despite the wellmeant commitment of the Constitution and its ensuing policies, the government's promises were never going to be fulfilled; it had an alternative agenda to shore up the provision of tertiary and further education. Investing in the brains of the privileged elite appealed far more to the governing meritocracy than basic provision for all.

Over the last 50 years, the budget allocation for higher technical education has grown disproportionately higher than that committed to primary schools. This disparity remains.

The MHRD, India's Ministry of Human Resource Development, has estimated that an additional Rs 100,000 crore, an excess of £11 billion, is required per year to fund Primary and Secondary education to reach the 100% attendance targets of children up to Class Ten.

Another quick game. I'll start.

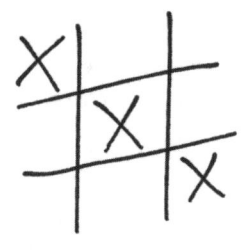

```
X |   |
--+---+--
  | X |
--+---+--
  |   | X
```

Your turn.
Well, it is my book...

10
Don't Look Down

The Himalayas are one of the youngest and most fragile mountain ranges in the world

'Eeeaa-yuk!' JP grimaced, gulping down a huge mouthful of water. 'Where did you get *that*?'

'Kumar's store,' I replied.

'Mr Kumar has much to answer for.'

He was referring, of course, to the Marmite. I had just persuaded him to sample a dab on his chapati.

'It's food of the gods,' I said. 'Lord Krishna eats it every day for breakfast.'

'That's why I'm a Christian,' JP retorted.

'I thought you liked strong tastes? You complained the other day that English food is too insipid.'

'It is,' he replied, reaching for the cornflakes.

'Actually, it's better on toast.'

'It's better in the bin.'

'I don't…'

Just as Anglo-Indian relations were about to nose-dive into the sugar bowl, the front door swung open. A man in his mid-thirties wearing a pale blue polo shirt strolled in.

'Ah, Shailender, *su prabhat!*' JP exclaimed. 'Excellent timing. The Angrez is trying to poison me.'

"Angrez" was a term used for foreigner, usually English. JP knew it wound me up.

'Mark, this is Shailender, Director of SASA and a good friend.'

We shook hands.

'So, you're the guy who's going to take me up to the mountains?' I asked.

'What's JP been saying?' He grinned.

'Don't worry. He's been singing your praises.'

'Would I do otherwise?' said JP sweetly.

'I understand you know the area well?'

'My family is from near Tehri. I grew up in the foothills.'

'Sit, Shailender. Mama!' JP called to the kitchen. 'Bring my friend some coffee!'

'You wish to go trekking?' asked Shailender.

'Having come all this way...'

'What I am thinking is this,' interrupted JP. 'You're going up to Akori soon. Right?'

'Yes. After the weekend,' replied Shailender, turning to me. 'Akori is the nearest village to Dhung, where our main SASA project is based.'

'Mark could go with you and spend a week or so teaching at the school. You want to see life in the mountains, yes?' JP turned to me.

'Ye-es,' I responded hesitantly, unsure to what I might be agreeing.

'I could then come and join you and we could travel on from there. What do you think?'

'*Acchha*,' replied Shailender, 'The teachers would welcome your support in the classroom, Mark.' Like the infamous head wobble, acchha could mean many things: good, a-ha, whatever or really? It was a Hindi word that I only heard for the first time after I'd travelled north.

Another phrase which peppered many North Indian conversations was *theek hai*, pronounced tee-ker. Literally translated as "fine is", it was usually abbreviated to "TK", the equivalent of "OK". Although JP and Shailender rarely used these words when talking to me, they continually littered the conversation when speaking to each other.

'Some guys I met while waiting for the Shatabdi recommended the Char Dham pilgrimage. Is that possible?'

JP looked at Shailender and smiled. 'It would take weeks to do that!'

'We could go to the temple at Kedarnath,' suggested Shailender.

'It's a thought,' replied JP. 'You know what I think about walking, though!'

'We'll hire you a mule!' Shailender laughed.

'TK. Leave it with me for a few days.'

'Great. In the meantime, how long will it take to reach Akori?' I asked.

'It can be done in a day. However, we could stop overnight and visit a few places on the way,' said Shailender.

'I'm in your hands.'

'I'll stay a few days to meet with the teachers, check everything is running smoothly and then return to Dehradun.' As he and his wife, Jyoti, had recently had a baby daughter, Shailender didn't like to stay away from home for too long.

'Thinking about it,' JP mused, 'Robert might like to come with us as well.' Robert was KHW's Finance and Personnel Manager. 'He could do with a break.'

'What about Ramesh?' asked Shailender.

'TK. There's an idea. We could also visit some of the Samvedna villages.'

'Samvedna?' I asked.

'I'll tell you about it later. That's more than enough for now.'

'OK.'

'*Chal*, I must get up to the office. I have a meeting in a few minutes.' The KHW office was situated on the first floor above the room in which I was staying. Although it was accessed by an outside staircase on the other side of the courtyard garden, the fact that the home and office were physically separate had no bearing on JP's work ethic; the two merged into one. Perhaps that's why he, too, was secretly looking forward to a short break.

'Shailender, perhaps you and Mark could start making plans for the trip?'

'Accha.'

'Maybe tell him about the region we're going to visit,' he said, leaving the room.

'That would be very helpful,' I added.

'Accha.'

'Oh, one more thing.' JP reappeared in the doorway. 'He has a tasty English delicacy you might like to try.'

In its earliest days, Garhwal was known as Kedarkhand, the region of Kedarnath, one of the main pilgrimage sites where Shiva was worshipped. Over time, it was sub-divided into small *garhs*, or forts. By the 9th century AD, a loose federation of 52 states, ruled by independent kings, had evolved.

Although historical documentation is both hazy and contradictory, it appears that, at some point towards the end of the first millennium, a certain Kank Pal of Malwa visited King Bhanu Pratap of Badrinath. The Rajput prince succeeded in charming the King into offering not only his daughter's hand in marriage but his entire kingdom as an inheritance. Ever the opportunist, Kank Pal and his descendents went on to conquer all the garhs and extend their empire, the Pal Dynasty, to cover the whole region.

Moving on 400 years, the next significant player in the development of the region was Ajai Pal who, in the mid 14th century, acquired a large part of Garhwal. Seizing all 52 garhs, he brought together the scattered states under a single authority.

There is a legend that Emperor Buhlul Khan Lodhi, Sultan of Delhi, travelled to Garhwal one summer in the latter years of the fifteenth century. So impressed was he by the reception offered by Balbhadra Pal, the Raja of Tehri, that he conferred the title "Shah" upon him. Dropping the suffix Pal, the house of Shah flourished. By mining its rich mineral fields of copper, lead and gold, the region began to enjoy great prosperity throughout the late 16th century.

In 1640, Emperor Shah Jahan, famed creator of the Taj Mahal, sent his forces to invade the region. Greeted by the formidable Queen Mother Karnavati, the soldiers returned post-haste, humiliated and minus their olfactory senses. The sovereign became known as *Naki-Katti-Rani*, the "Queen Who Cuts off Noses".

The rulers of Garhwal successfully continued to defend their land from a number of subsequent attacks, notably a Mogul invasion in 1654-55. An ongoing feud with the neighbouring Kumaonis persisted for almost 200 years, with raids and counter raids into opposing territories, until Pradip Shah, one of the most important rulers of Garhwal, acceded to the throne in 1717. Though he brought relative peace and prosperity to both regions, tension continued to rumble beneath the surface.

Invasion from outside forces was inevitable. Taking advantage of a devastating earthquake in 1803 that, killing almost a third of the population, weakened the state's administrative and economic infrastructure, the Gurkhas from neighbouring Nepal successfully launched an attack on Garhwal and Kumaon. Capturing Dehradun, they began a twelve year occupation of the region.

Although the Gurkhas had made several previous attempts to conquer the land, they had failed to secure any lasting impact. On this occasion however, compounded by a severe famine a few years' earlier, the people of the region were unable to challenge their advances. Neither could they withstand the exploitative measures exerted by the ruthless Gurkha government. Over 200,000 people, unable to pay the heavy taxes, were sold as slaves to Nepal and other kingdoms. The occupying magistrates and officers, on condition that they met their income targets, were granted an entirely free hand. Unsurprisingly, much of the collected revenue found its way into their pockets.

A combination of corruption, appalling conditions and low morale forced many of the remaining population to flee to the adjoining kingdoms, leaving behind deserted villages and an agricultural infrastructure in tatters.

Once the Gurkhas had established their hold over Garhwal and Kumaon, they began to raid the neighbouring, British-controlled, territories. Although the British army responded by attacking Nepal from a number of directions, the campaign proved ineffective, serving only to compound the ambition of the British to gain a foothold in the Kumaon hills.

Urged on by Raja Sudarshan Shah, the deposed ruler of Garhwal, to intervene, the British forces eventually invaded the southern border in April 1815 with success. The Gurkhas were compelled to retreat, but not before the Garhwalis had exacted full payment in blood for the way that they had been treated in the preceding years. Large numbers of Gurkhas were massacred or driven away to the hills to die of exposure and starvation.

Although Sudarshan Shah was a wealthy young man prior to the Gurkha invasion of Dehradun in 1803, he subsequently lived in great poverty under British protection at Jwalapur near Haridwar. Following the crushing Gurkha defeat, the enterprising East India Company offered him a settlement proposition: the company would return his kingdom in exchange for five lakh rupees, about £5,700. With his financial resources totally exhausted, Sudarshan Shah couldn't comply. Left with little choice, he agreed to an alternative deal; that of carving up his inheritance, the land of his forefathers. The British assigned him jurisdiction over the rugged interior western area of Garhwal between the Alaknanda and Mandakini Rivers but maintained control of the rest.

In a further act of largesse, the East India Company offered the Shah the neighbouring area of Rawain Pargana, a barren, inhospitable piece of land. The fact that it was inhabited by bandits with an insatiable appetite for assaulting pilgrims en route to Badrinath and Kedarnath may have figured in the British decision to relinquish all responsibility for its governance.

Caught between a rock and a hard place, Sudarshan Shah accepted the proposal, founded Tehri as the capital of his kingdom and ruled as the Raja of Tehri State or, more popularly, Tehri Garhwal, until his death in 1859. The bordering areas of Kumaon and the rest of Garhwal remained under British administration until independence.

Map showing Tehri Garhwal, British Garhwal, with labels: Bhagirathi, Kedarnath, Badrinath, Mandakini, Alaknanda, Dehradun, Haridwar, Ganges. Legend: Kingdom of Tehri Garhwal; Tehri Garhwal as it is now.

The Shah's initial relief at the departure of the Gurkhas was cruelly dispelled when he realised that he didn't have the resources to administer a kingdom troubled by a depleted, demoralised population and a shattered economy. The land was arduous to work and traditional agricultural practices were all but destroyed. It's no wonder that many inhabitants had become unruly and took to plundering the passing pilgrims.

An extraordinary catalogue of events, therefore, has defined Garhwal's development and, in particular, the district of Tehri Garhwal:

1 A relentless series of invasions from the end of the twelfth to the beginning of the nineteenth centuries

2 Unprecedented loss of life following the devastating earthquake of 1803

3 *Tyrannical Gurkha exploitation*
4 *Thousands of inhabitants sold into slavery or forced to flee as refugees*
5 *Economic, administrative and agricultural ruin*

By the mid-nineteenth century, Tehri Garhwal had become an independent Raja-governed island adrift in a sea of colonial rule.

It might be poetic to complete the metaphor by suggesting that the kingdom drowned. But that would be untrue. Although Tehri Garhwal struggled with its distinct autonomy, relations with the British remained civil, albeit restrained. The dawn of independence in 1947, however, exposed a significant contrast between the development of the kingdom of Tehri Garhwal and that of the rest of Uttarakhand.

To take

- *Chocolate*
- *Marmite*
- *Thermal underwear + waterproofs*
- *Insect repellant*

Shailender and I left Rajpur early on a mild May morning. We drove via Mussoorie to catch a glimpse of the snow-capped mountains visible from Camel's Back Road, but a combination of natural mist and man-made pollution obscured the range from view.

Our route continued through hills clothed with majestic *deodars* and silver firs glinting in the early morning sun. Resilient in all seasons, the deodar is derived from *devdar*, meaning "tree of the gods". My calm admiration of their sweeping, blue-needled branches gradually turned to unease as I became aware of the increasingly precipitous drop below the road edge.

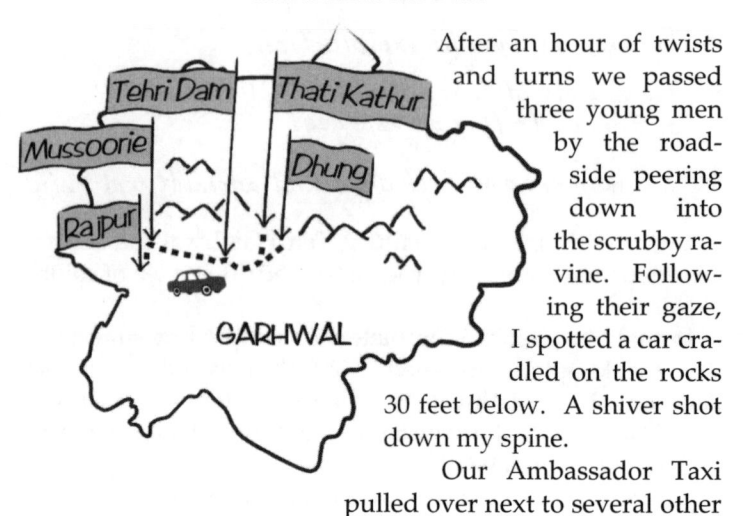

After an hour of twists and turns we passed three young men by the roadside peering down into the scrubby ravine. Following their gaze, I spotted a car cradled on the rocks 30 feet below. A shiver shot down my spine.

Our Ambassador Taxi pulled over next to several other vehicles. Clumps of bystanders dotted the scene, deep in discussion. Indians, the men in particular, relish a healthy argument. They are commonly seen around the chai stalls, in the street, outside their houses, drinking tea and debating at length, each man holding forth his opinion in turn. Speculation on the fate of this vehicle would fuel conversation for the rest of the day.

'Actually, it looks as if the accident happened a day or so ago,' suggested Shailender as he strolled over to discuss his theory with the audience staring down the gully. Suspecting it had occurred more recently, I remained in the car, uneasy about intruding into someone else's tragedy. After a few minutes, Shailender wandered back. It transpired that the calamity had indeed only struck a few minutes earlier.

'The driver told me they stopped to have a pee,' he explained, 'but he forgot to put on the handbrake. While they were doing their business, the car rolled backwards over the edge. There was nothing they could do.'

Although no one was inside the vehicle, the misfortune was proving to be a salutary lesson to the shaking, tutting heads congregated by the roadside. Relieved no one had been harmed, I was less reticent to join the crowd. Looking down, I saw that the car was a wreck; anyone inside wouldn't have stood a chance of escape.

This accident, sadly, was nothing in comparison with the many others I would witness and would read about over the coming weeks. As we returned to our taxi I recollected reading in *The Hindu* that the district's Chief Medical Officer had been killed a few days earlier on the same road on which we were about to travel. My spine tingled for a second time.

India is one of the world's biggest dam building nations. It is estimated that, since 1947, over 4,000 reservoirs have submerged an estimated land area of 40,000 square kilometres, displacing at least 42 million people. Dam construction, a major source of controversy for many decades, has always been greeted with considerable local opposition. Despite the fact, it has been argued, that dams rarely meet their expected benefits of power generation, irrigation and flood control, the government is committed to a comprehensive construction programme with plans to increase hydropower capacity by 50,000 megawatts before 2013.

Earlier in the week, overhearing Shailender and JP discuss the Tehri Dam, I had failed to register the significance of their conversation. Driving past the construction site on the way to Akori, Shailender told me more about the project.

At a height of 260 metres, the dam, when completed, would be the fifth largest in the world. Old Tehri and at least 40 neighbouring villages would be submerged beneath its reservoir, with up to 100,000 people requiring new homes.

Over 25 years in the construction, the project, managed by Tehri Hydro Development Corporation was conceived as a partnership between the Indian government and, as it was then, the state of Uttar Pradesh. It received a massive boost in 1986 when an Indo-Soviet agreement secured Soviet expertise and aid valued at over $400 million.

'Many campaigners are opposing the project,' Shailender told me. 'They have condemned it as an economic, humanitarian and environmental disaster waiting to happen. There is a staunch Gandhian activist, called Sunderlal Bahaguna, who has been its most vocal opponent since its approval in 1972. He once described it as "a dam built with our tears".'

As we approached the colossal construction I could appreciate his concern. Looming before me, soared the highest man-made rock face I've ever encountered. Diggers and dumper trucks dotted the towering barrier like tiny robotic ants preparing for the cataclysmic climax of a Bond movie. In the valley below nestled Old Tehri, a virtual ghost town; most of its inhabitants had already re-located to New Tehri in the hills above us. It was hard to imagine that all the surrounding land, including where we were driving, would be submerged under billions of gallons of water within twelve months. Given Tehri Garhwal's turbulent history, it felt like the final nail would soon be driven into the coffin.

The taxi stopped. I climbed out and took a deep breath. Too late: the hazy air was swarming with dust particles. I spluttered uncontrollably as they caught the back of my throat.

'Are you OK?' laughed Shailender. 'I should have warned you.'

'I'm fine,' I choked, pulling my handkerchief from my pocket to cover my nose. The rhythmic clunking, pounding, clank-clank-thud of the machinery reverberated between the dam face and the surrounding hills.

Shailender saw me take my camera from its case.

'No!' he called. 'You mustn't.'

'Why?'

'We'll be in trouble. This is government property. We're being watched.'

The thrill of the Bond movie suddenly seemed very real.

'Don't worry. We're not breaking the law. We just need to be careful. Time to get going anyway.'

The dam project was intended to supply water to Delhi and to irrigate the sugar cane growing land of western Uttar Pradesh.

'The problem is that those who stand to gain least are the people of Tehri Garhwal themselves,' explained Shailender. 'It's already one of the poorest districts in the country.'

As we continued our journey towards Akori, he talked more about the dam's potential impact on the region. Immersing over 4000 hectares of fertile land, it would turn the valley into little more than a glorified swamp in 30 or 40 year's time once it had outlived its function. Higher in the hills, the effects of deforestation had already upset the delicate ecological balance, depleting the water resources and limiting the potential for future tree growth. Transferring water away from the region, the dam would leave it even more barren than at present.

Later, on my return to KHW, I revisited the *Mountain Voices* website to read what local people had to say.

"If we can get facilities for irrigation, and if we get good grain harvests in our hills, then we have no need to go anywhere else. These are the reasons why I oppose the Tehri Dam," said Sudesha, the farmer and activist from Rampur Village in Tehri Garhwal, that I quoted earlier. "Since there is water in our river, they are transporting it to Delhi. The people of Delhi are rich; they can do whatever they like. We are poor people."

More alarming, was my discovery that the Tehri Dam was being constructed in the middle of a Himalayan seismic fault zone. The Himalayas are one of the youngest and most fragile mountain ranges in the world. Still growing, they currently rise at a rate of five millimetres per year. Garhwal has experienced eighteen major earthquakes since the devastation wreaked in 1803. The most recent, the Uttarkashi tragedy in October 1991, reached 6.6 on the Richter scale and killed over 2,000 people. Most of those who died were crushed under the collapsed slate roofs of their homes.

Based on damage evidence, the 1803 earthquake that wiped out a third of Uttarakhand's population was assigned a magnitude of 7.7. The Tehri Dam has been designed to withstand tremors of up to 7.2, though some scientists have predicted that a future quake of magnitude 8.5 is not inconceivable. Earthquakes of this scale notwithstanding, they have also suggested that the mountains cannot sustain the construction of such an enormous dam.

With diminishing vegetation cover and continuous blasting, landslides are a frequent cause of widespread damage. One expert has predicted that, should the dam collapse, the reservoir would empty in 22 minutes. Rishikesh, a town forty kilometres away, famously associated with the Beatles, would drown under 260 metres of water within the hour. Other major towns would also be submerged and over half a million people washed away.

Though many local people didn't disagree with the principle of the dam construction, they argued that it should have been built in a way that benefited *all* the regional villages. "The water should reach the people whose land it goes through. It should only be allowed to go further when everybody's stomach is full," said Sudesha.

Sunderlal Bahuguna contested for many years that it would have been more advantageous for the government to have constructed several smaller hydro-electric projects throughout the region rather than one massive dam. Working with the local people as partners rather than riding roughshod over their concerns, the government could have provided an appropriate irrigation system that produced good grain harvests *and* maintained an environmental balance.

Instead, the hill areas have been stripped of their resources, natural and human, leaving people angry and resentful. Their accusations of corruption and mismanagement, targeted at the government and the Tehri Hydro Development Corporation, have frequently appeared in the press. Feeling vulnerable and exploited, local people claim to have suffered at the hands of the wealthy.

Sunderlal undertook a number of fasts to amplify his concerns. In 1996 he embarked on a hunger strike to force the government to reconsider the environmental, seismic and rehabilitation implications of the project. After 74 days, and with his health very much in danger, the government conceded. A review committee was established which made a number of recommendations. Most of them remain unimplemented.

When I was to return to the region in January 2006, ten years after the government's assurance, I was informed that flooding of the valley had commenced. Tehri was under water. The only remaining visible landmark was the top of the clock tower. That, too, would soon be submerged for ever.

The clouds darkened. Heavy splats of rain soon started to smatter the windscreen and mix with the construction site dust. Visibility became difficult. Having turned off the main road above the town of Ghamsali onto a much narrower track, the higher we drove, the more our trusty Ambassador's suspension and balance were put to the test. The vehicle's tailgate frequently jutted over the edge as our driver negotiated the tight hairpin bends.

'I hope we're going to get there OK,' I commented in a half-joking attempt to hide my genuine fear.

The taxi driver, sensing my apprehension, laughingly muttered something to Shailender.

'What's he saying?' I asked.

'He says that "If God wants us to arrive safely, we will. And if He doesn't..."'

'I'm not sure I buy that theological point of view,' I interrupted nervously.

Throughout my travels, especially in North India, I was struck by the number of people who clung to an incontrovertible fatalism as if their life depended on it. Absolutely convinced that every eventuality was beyond their human control, phrases such as *Inshallah*, "It is God's will" or "God willing" were never far from their lips, irrespective of their religion. It was tempting to question the sincerity of the sentiment, particularly when the hollow words rolled off the tongue with ease.

At worst, it seemed a blatant negation of personal responsibility; at best, an infuriating excuse for inactivity, apathy and a feeble source of false comfort. The attitude seemed to be: "What's the point of doing so-and-so? What will be, will be…"

On this occasion, given the carefree attitude of the other road users, I wasn't convinced that God would reach out His hand to save us if an approaching bus decided to shunt our taxi over the edge. Even if it wasn't on His agenda that we should die that afternoon.

To be fair, many westerners share a similar philosophy, saying "it was meant to be" or "*que sera sera*" when things don't go according to plan. Rarely, though, does it represent the extreme denial of accountability that I experienced in India. If fate decreed, so be it.

Further into the mist we ascended.

Without warning, the driver hastily slammed on the brakes.

'What's the matter?' I asked.

'We must get out. Look!'

A few metres ahead, the road had partially subsided, the solid ground having yielded to a russet rivulet of water gushing from the rocks.

'Not a problem,' said Shailender. 'He's a good driver. We must lighten the load and push!'

Though my heels squelched and slipped in the silt, the taxi's tyres gained a better grip. After several hard shoves we suddenly lurched forward and were soon on our way.

As the skies cleared, we arrived at the Lok Jivan Bharati Ashram, a rambling complex of one-storey buildings situated on a bend in the river just below Budha Kedar. This was the home of Bihari Lal, a prominent Sarvodaya activist, his wife and other residents of the *ashram*, a centre for spiritual learning and practice.

'This is where we're spending the night,' said Shailender. 'Come!' He evidently had everything planned.

Two young men, neatly-dressed in chequered shirts, took our bags and escorted us through a quadrangle of peacefully deserted rooms. A little girl poked her head around the corner, stared at me, giggled and scampered off.

Dressed in a white kurta, a loose-fitting collarless shirt, down to his shins and a cream Garhwal waistcoat, Bihari Lal received us with beakers of home-made orange squash and a plate of mulberries from his orchards.

'Please, sit! Eat!' His mop of wavy white hair, boyish face and toothy grin made me feel extremely welcome.

Unlike the bare terraces through which we had just driven, the land surrounding the ashram was lush, green and burgeoning with several types of fruit trees: lemons, peaches, plums and oranges. Watered by a sophisticated irrigation system, it was an Eden of tranquillity. As Bihari Lal and Shailender conversed in Hindi, I tried to remain politely attentive. Though my head kept nodding, the small insects buzzing around my ankles prevented me from dozing off entirely.

'Watch those flies, Mark,' advised Shailender, 'they bite!'

'Now you tell me.' I was only wearing sandals.

Little did I anticipate the aggravation that those deviously evil nibbles would eventually cause. Two days later, the bites disappeared, only to return 24 hours later as an outbreak of itchy red marks erupting over both my feet. As each lump swelled into an inflamed, bleeding mound, the urge to rip off my boots and scratch became irrepressible. The more I rubbed, the greater the irritation, the more the blood flowed.

Observing that the flies were troubling me, Shailender suggested that we walk along the grassy river bank into the village. But the damage had already been done.

Though commonly referred to as Budha Kedar, the village's actual name is Thati Kathur; Budha Kedar is the temple situated on the old pilgrim trail from Gangotri to Kedernath.

Just as we turned into the main street, the temperature dropped and the skies opened with a vengeance for the second time that day. We dived into the nearest village tea shop.

While "grassy river bank" and "village tea shop" might conjure up images of jam, Jerusalem and the WI, forget the china plates, doilies and sugar lumps. Think corrugated iron shack, wooden benches and a large pan of tea brewing on a smoky, open fire. But no flies; how good that was.

When the rain subsided we strolled through the village up to the Budar Kedar Temple. Remarkably, it was surrounded by a graveyard of interred priests. Although burial of the dead is rare in Hinduism, this small cemetery was doubly unusual; each priest was buried upright, crowned with a small pile of rocks on his head.

As if by magic a curious beanie-headed little fellow, the present incumbent, appeared mysteriously from behind a grave. Eying us shiftily, he would have looked more at home outside a second-hand car showroom than a revered place of worship.

'Please!' he shuffled, insisting on taking us inside the dank ancient building constructed around a large rock engraved with images of several indistinguishable gods. A cleric of few words, he then demanded remuneration for his unsolicited tour by holding out his palm. Silently snatching a few coins from Shailender's fingers he promptly made an exit every bit as baffling as his appearance.

Bihari Lal had grown up in the area and attended the ashram school in nearby Siliyara run by Sunderlal Bahaguna, his guru. Becoming a teacher, he worked at several Gandhian centres throughout India before returning to Thati Kathur to start an education programme of his own.

Like many people in this region, Bihari Lal's strong convictions had been influenced by Sarvodaya, a movement founded on Gandhian principles. Literally translated, Sarvodaya means "compassion for all". The belief is simple: everyone is equal. In practice, this means promoting equality and justice for all those who are considered unequal within Indian society, particularly girls, women and the scheduled castes.

Later that evening, as I sat cosily wrapped in an eiderdown in the communal bedroom, I quizzed Bihari Lal about the history of the ashram and the principles on which it was founded.

'All we are doing is providing for the basics in life; food, shelter and clothing, which every human should have,' Shailender, translated, his bushy-moustached face peering above the white bedclothes in which he was also cocooned.

'We built the ashram ourselves,' he continued, 'and it now operates as a commune and school. When it is open, we educate about 100 students. We follow the government curriculum and teach Gandhian principles. We encourage the students to put their understanding into practice by helping with building work, in the gardens and the orchards.

'We have also developed a number of training programmes for members of the scheduled castes, equipping them with new skills including masonry, carpentry and weaving to increase their long-term employment prospects. I will show you some of our work in the morning.'

Following a good night's sleep and a plastic bucket-and-jug bath, we ate a hearty breakfast of curried nutrient substitute. The dish of brown lumps floating in an anaemic sauce tasted better than it looked. We then walked to the river to inspect progress on the flood protection development. Though only a few hours of rain had fallen the previous day, the speed of the river tumbling over the large boulders demonstrated how quickly the water level could rise to potentially destructive heights.

'I cannot control the course of nature,' Bihari Lal commented, 'but I can do my best to safeguard the welfare of the community.'

'A cloudburst a few years ago caused much damage,' said Shailender. 'The river rose much higher than its normal level.' He then pointed to a small, but impressive-looking construction.

'What's that?' I asked.

'A water-powered generator. SASA provided the money to build it.'

'Self-sufficiency is an important principle of the Sarvodaya movement,' said Bihari Lal.

'There's another water mill further upstream,' Shailender pointed.

'You wish to go see?' asked Bihari Lal.

'Actually, it's time we were on our way,' said Shailender, keen to hit the road.

'You must have lunch before you go,' offered Bihari Lal.

I looked at my watch. It was nine-thirty, an hour after breakfast. Indian generosity knows no bounds.

11
Note to Self

If you don't stick your neck out you're not likely to achieve anything

Raindrops pounded on the corrugated tin roof with a deafening vehemence as if spat from the mouth of a raging god. Clutching the hillside, my little cabin was enveloped in a biting, swirling emptiness of dense cloud. All evidence of life had been wiped from the planet.

My pen quivered. Wrapped in an itchy blanket, I listed my expectations, peeved that the air was much warmer just a few kilometres down the valley. Had the mountains not peeked politely through the mist on our arrival, Dhung would have received my vote as the bleakest place on earth.

Only hours earlier I had observed that the SASA centre could not have been positioned in a more striking environment. Perched high in the foothills, enclosed by the Himalayas, it straddled either side of the road running between Ghamsali, Akori and the neighbouring villages. Patchworks of terraced land quilted the hamlet-dotted hillside in myriad shades of yellow and green.

Walking up the short steep path from the road, the first building I saw was the toilet: a brick-built, iron-roofed, lockable hole in the ground. Luxury.

On one side of the school's courtyard stood a red-brick building that comprised three classrooms, each one large enough to accommodate about twenty children. Examples of their artwork decorated the grey concrete walls. Simple, functional wooden benches and desks were arranged in neat rows.

At the end of the classroom block were two small rooms, one used for cooking, the other for bathing. Steps led up the side of the building to the flat roof, at the far end of which was the room that Shailender and I would share until his return to Dehradun. Sparsely furnished, it contained two beds, a bookcase, three plastic chairs, a wooden table and a small gas stove. On top of the hill above the school stood another concrete classroom used by the older pupils in Class Four. Each of the separate buildings was linked by steps hacked haphazardly into the hillside, up and down which the children fearlessly leapt.

Apart from a small tap which spurted and dribbled with a mind of its own, the centre had neither electricity nor running water. Just two solar-charged lanterns and plenty of buckets.

A breath of wind wafted up the sound of children's laughter from the schoolroom below. They probably loved the rain. Tired of my western baggage, I ached to be so easily pleased.

As dusk seized the remaining light, I contemplated the coming days.

> 1 Make lesson plans
> 2 Find more blankets
> 3 Learn to be content with very little
>   — it'll be good for me

I noted to myself, gripping the pen tightly. The gods launched another deluge onto the tin-roof.

SASA, Serve and Share Association, was established by Shailender in the late 1990's. Its first project was a programme to train 30 young people on a number of social issues to benefit their village. It also opened two libraries and two small clinics in the villages of Choura and Jakh.

NOTE TO SELF

In 1999 an earthquake struck the Garhwal interior. While undertaking aid work with various organisations including KHW, the board of SASA felt it was appropriate to build a relief and rehabilitation centre to sustain the community following the disaster. Aware of the desperate educational needs in Tehri Garhwal, the organisation decided that a school would be most appropriate. Shailender approached JP Singh, who was on the SASA board, for assistance. He agreed to direct a proportion of KHW's funding from International Needs to support the plans.

'If you don't stick your neck out you're not likely to achieve anything,' JP later told me. In addition to KHW's major financial support along with other partners, JP acted as an advisor to Shailender. 'He was a man with a great vision. I wanted to encourage him to achieve great things.'

The school, situated in the hamlet of Dhung, opened in 2000. Initially, fifteen children were sponsored by SASA and a further twelve by KHW. Over time, JP introduced Shailender to CHILD's Trust in the UK. At the time of my visit, the school, supported by various partners, provided education for nearly 120 children in the surrounding communities.

The Garhwal "interior" is so-called because that's precisely what it is. Many of its villages nestle *inside* the high valleys of the Himalayan foothills, overlooked by dramatic mountain ranges including Nanda Devi, India's highest peak.

Although the people of this region are Garhwali, colloquially, those living above the plains refer to themselves as *Pahari*, meaning "of the hills". The transitory population over the centuries has resulted in a broad ethnicity among them including Tibetan, known as the Bhotiya, Nepali, Punjabi and Bengali. In this respect, Garhwal is similar to other parts of the Himalayas where various ethnic groups live side by side. In some of the villages I visited, the extensive range of facial complexions and skin tones was highly noticeable. Out of context, some of the paler-skinned children may easily have been mistaken for Eastern Europeans.

People living in towns and cities on the plains generally conversed in Hindi, whereas those in the interior areas spoke the Garhwali dialect. On most occasions someone was available to translate for me.

The number of out-of-school children in the Garhwal mountains is considerably higher than the national average. Shailender gave me further information about the region which helped to explain why this may be the case.

Follwing the sub-division of the hill areas in 1815, the land and people assigned to British jurisdiction developed in relative freedom. Progress for the Pahari living in the newly-formed independent kingdom of Tehri Garhwal, however, was severely impeded by poor natural resources and inconsistent governance.

The main encumbrance to educational progress in the first half of the 20th century was, allegedly, the King himself, Narendrah Shah. Unlike some of his predecessors, he regarded himself as the autocratic ruler of his kingdom, not as a man of the people.

Shailender intimated that King Narendrah was an extremely literate but, possibly, insecure sovereign. Fearing that an erudite population might wake up to his tyrannical tendencies and rebel, he suppressed access to education throughout the kingdom in an attempt to keep his subjects uninformed and restrained.

He was not, however, quite as wise as he thought. Though they may not have displayed great academic prowess, the Pahari did know about forest management. King Narendrah's support of the government's draconian forest management polices inflamed a number of protests, the most violent occurring in 1930 when he commandeered a force of 300 soldiers to restrain the Pahari upsurge. Several people were killed and wounded. A further 65 were sentenced to imprisonment.

By the time King Narendrah died in a car accident in September, 1950, he had already relinquished the throne to his son, Manavendrah Shah, in May, 1946. His reign, however, was short-lived. In August, 1949, congress and peasant activists forced him to abdicate and Tehri Garhwal was merged into the new, independent India as a district of Uttar Pradesh. British Garhwal had already become part of the Indian Union in 1947.

With its new-found freedom, Tehri Garhwal had to play a swift game of catch-up with its neighbours. Relatively speaking, they were far more socially and economically developed. As a consequence, many of the pupils at SASA Academy were among the first generation ever to attend a school in the district.

※

Ankit, a tubby ten-year-old with a constantly runny nose and dirty sleeves, was a regular visitor to my room after school. Tap, tap on the door, sniff, sniff, there he'd be standing - twang, twang, 'Uncle!' twang, twang - strumming the air.

'This is a little number by The Divine Comedy I've been practising,' I told him one afternoon, as we sat cross-legged on the roof. 'It's called Songs of Love. Otherwise known as the theme tune to Father Ted.'

'Uncle-ji?'

He was unimpressed. Before I'd even reached the end of the first phrase, he was tugging the mandolin from my hands.

'Me, me!' he demanded.

'Gently!' I said handing him the instrument. I stroked its neck to indicate what I meant.

Of course, my instruction made no difference. He struck his fingers across all the strings at once, 'la-la-la-ing' tunelessly. A broad grin lit up his round face and his nose dribbled with glee.

Ankit won my award for THE LEAST MUSICALLY-TALENTED CHILD IN GARHWAL. He also held another record: THE BOY WHO WALKED FURTHEST TO SCHOOL. He lived in a village far across the next valley that necessitated a three-hour round trip each day.

Mountain schools were such a rare and valued commodity that children and families sought them out with determination. History aside, the cost of material and human resources significantly affected the availability of education.

On our journey to Dhung, Shailender had quipped about the price and quality of building materials and labour in the mountains.

'Take an ordinary brick,' he joked. 'It costs one rupee in the city. By the time it reaches Dhung it's worth five rupees. Take it further up to Sumari and you could exchange it for a herd of buffalo!'

The figures may have been fabricated but Shailender's point was well-served; the mountains are a costly location in which to build a school. Due to the shortage of men, quality labour is thin on the ground and then only available at a price.

The same is true for teaching staff. Required to relocate to a basic rural environment far from home, good teachers may command a high salary as compensation for the lack of running water, electricity and other conveniences. Recruiting qualified, but affordable, employees prepared to work in poor mountainous conditions is problematic; few fully-trained teachers wish to live in a bleak, unfamiliar environment for any length of time. Charity schools such as SASA, therefore, are frequently obliged to employ well-motivated, but relatively unskilled, teachers.

By contrast, the small government primary schools pay a decent salary, but often neglect to provide a good education. Many establishments are typified by low standards that fail to reflect the high wages commanded by their employees in comparison with those engaged in the private sector. Throughout India it is generally true that teachers' salaries in private schools are lower, often by as much as two-thirds, than those of teachers employed in government schools. Yet the quality of education is considerably higher.

Teacher absenteeism is also a major issue. A research paper produced by Michael Kremer of Harvard University concludes that one in four government primary school teachers is absent on any given day and only one in two is actually teaching. The motivation and creativity of the government teacher plays second fiddle to routine and a pedestrian duty to complete the job. A teacher is not accountable to the child but to the system.

Throughout my travels, I met many people who dreamed of acquiring a government appointment, whether in education, health, the police, the railways or the post office. 'Why?' I asked.

'It is my dharma,' some replied whimsically.

'It's a regular salary, a pension and job guarantee,' the more pragmatic asserted. 'Once appointed, dismissal is not possible.'

Dharma or security, it amounted to the same thing. Once acquired, a government contract invites complacency. There is little incentive to perform well.

Maybe that's why I found the simple act of posting a letter abroad so time-consuming. The stamp had to be purchased at one counter, the letter weighed at the next, franked at another and the details entered into a log book at a fourth. This was followed by a search for the little pot of lumpy glue in which to dab my index finger to stick the stamp to the letter. Served - I use the term loosely - by a succession of disinterested, eye-rolling clerks who would rather have read the newspaper than offer a prompt service, my patience was occasionally stretched to its limits.

Eliminating all the bureaucratic paper-chasing, however, would render millions of workers redundant. The procedures, though grossly inefficient, at least keep people in employment.

Unfortunately, government education doesn't fare any better. Teachers are driven by a system obsessed with results, percentages and certification. Like my letter, the child is an item to be processed, stamped and thrust into the post box of life. A strict syllabus, uniformly followed, reduces subjects to a set of questions and answers that may be conveniently duplicated in the examination papers, thus ensuring a commendable pass rate, a good quota of figures and a pat on the back for the teacher. Job well done.

Thankfully, the well-motivated team of staff at SASA wasn't like this. Though they lacked experience and qualification, they treated the pupils as young adults, not numbers in a system.

Rajeev was the school's principal, a slight man with a fantastic head of wavy black curls and a small, neat moustache. Healthily feared by the pupils, he traded his imposing daytime authority for a mischievous sense of humour in the evenings. He taught English alongside Sandeep, an easygoing guy whose enthusiasm made up for his shortage of classroom expertise. Recently married, he and his Tibetan wife, Tsering, were expecting their first child at the end of the year. All three of them came from Dehradun. None of them had been teaching for very long.

Then there was lofty, sincere Samuel and his level-headed wife, Neema, recent additions to the staff. Neema worked alongside Tsering with the younger children while Samuel was responsible for the extra-curricular activities, an important aspect of school life. The social and spiritual development of the children was encouraged through games, stories and songs. Two of the other regular teachers were away on a training course.

Pratap was the odd-job man. He cooked, cleaned, mended and put his hand to anything that required attention. Although married with a young baby, his boyish looks and wiry stature made him appear about fifteen. The only true Garhwali on the staff, his family lived about three hours away across two valleys.

Like my colleagues, I didn't have a teaching qualification. Thrown into a secondary school, I cut my teeth many years ago when Croydon Education Authority, desperate for drama and English teachers, would employ almost anyone who could control a class of kids. Straight from my training I took the view that, if I was to succeed in the theatre profession, I would have to create the work myself. I taught English, Drama and Music in a number of schools, therefore, in order to finance and direct productions on the London Fringe.

None of this was of any relevance to SASA Academy. For them, my qualification for teaching English was simple: I *was* English.

'Mark, you are not here for long,' Shailender had said, 'but please you will spend much time in the classroom to advise the teachers.'

I often experienced an unnerving response when I walked past the younger inhabitants of the village, particularly from those who hadn't seen me before. As soon as my back was turned, their bemused faces would break into fits of giggles that sent ripples of paranoia through my body. With hindsight, I presumed their laughter was generated by nervous curiosity. I was not being mocked, I hoped. The sight of a white person was a rare occurrence in a hill village where, quite feasibly, most people believed that everyone else in the world looked like them.

Few children had travelled to the nearest town, never mind a city. They may have read the occasional magazine or newspaper, but rarely watched television. Images of the Western world were generally not part of their life. It was hard to imagine.

I only saw one TV in a home near SASA Academy. It was broken. Even had it been working, the house wasn't supplied with electricity. Nevertheless, surrounded by images of Rama and Krishna on a rickety shelf, the hallowed TV occupied a shrine-like position as a proud family status symbol. It was clearly better to have a useless television than none at all.

The lack of not only western, but also Indian, social and cultural references proved a challenge in the classroom. The children's understanding of the world, to an extent, was informed by the immediate environment in which they lived. Class Two displayed a diagram of an irrigation system on the wall; Class One boasted a number of self-portraits and pictures of the children's homes.

During a particular Class Three English lesson, I asked the children to complete the sentence 'My favourite food is...' From a dozen pupils, the responses were limited to four items: rice, chapati, mango and banana. I don't believe that they were copying each other or, indeed, that these were necessarily their favourite items of food. The choices represented a selection from their *only* food. Their world was very small.

An aspect of the education at SASA Academy that I found more exasperating than revealing was the children's lack of self-comprehension when speaking English. They learnt by rote and understood very little, evidenced by their habitual mispronunciation and strange, automaton-like, patterns of behaviour.

As I entered Class Three one morning, the pupils politely stood up, saluted and greeted me with the statutory 'Good morning, sir.'

'Thank you, children. Please sit down,' I gestured with my hands.

With Sandeep translating, I explained that we would continue the lesson outside. As the morning weather was usually clear and warm, I often took the class up to a flat patch of ground above the school. There, beneath a rich blue sky surrounded by peaks and golden terraces, I used drama and games to teach them English. It was the most inspiring classroom in the world.

After about twenty minutes we returned downstairs to write down what had been learnt. Allowing all the children to file in first, I then entered.

'Good morning, sir,' they uttered once more, standing up and saluting. Some of them had barely had time to sit down.

'That isn't necessary,' I explained, 'you said good morning just a few minutes ago. I've been with you ever since. Good morning is a greeting you only need to say the first time you see someone in the day.' Despite their enthusiastic nods at Sandeep's worthy translation –

'Yes, sir!'

- I suspected that they didn't understand.

Turning to write on the blackboard, I couldn't find any chalk. Rather than explain what I needed, I dashed quickly into the next classroom to find some myself. Immediately the children stood up and saluted:

'Good morning, sir,' they chanted.

'Hello children,' I muttered, interrupting the teacher. 'Sorry, Rajeev.' I grabbed some chalk and returned to my own classroom. I'd been gone all of twenty seconds.

'Good morning, sir,' the children rose and saluted once more.

'OK, that really is too much. You've now said good morning to me three times, the last occasion being less than a minute ago.'

The children were performing like programmed little robots. They obediently delivered the whole standing-saluting-greeting routine whenever an adult entered the room, even if it was the same person, several times within the space of a few moments. With no grasp of what they were saying, they were incapable of discerning whether, or not, their words were appropriate.

The language in which a pupil is taught in India is an emotive subject and continually under debate. Should it be the mother tongue, Hindi, English or all three?

On discovering that English Medium was the education of choice for many parents, my initial response was one of sanctimonious, anti-colonial indignation. Lord Macaulay's argument for the use of English, as stated in his 1835 *Minute on Education*, makes uncomfortable reading for the enlightened 21st century:

> Whether we look at the intrinsic value of our literature, or at the particular situation of this country, we shall see the strongest reason to think that, of all foreign tongues, the English tongue is that which would be the most useful to our native subjects.

Calming down, I gleaned that attitudes have progressed. Though dubiously-motivated at the time, Lord Macaulay may have had a point; English is now serving the nation well. Or so it appears.

Many Indians regard English as a golden ticket to increased employment prospects. The choices available to a young person educated in Garhwali alone, for example, are limited to parts of Uttarakhand. Though it is important that he learns the language of his regional heritage, it would prove challenging, but not impossible, for him to find work in another state whose language he did not speak. Nowadays English is not just a passport to opportunity throughout India but the rest of the world.

Hindi, the official language of India, is spoken by about 40% of the population, although predominantly in the north. English, the co-official language, bridges the gap between some of the nation's 22 officially recognised languages and the 1,652 mother tongues. It is spoken by at least 350 million people, almost the combined population of the UK and USA. For 99% of those speakers it is their second language.

On one particular train journey from Madurai to Bangalore, a businessman joined our compartment soon after we had crossed into Karnataka state. Seating himself next to a gentleman from Tamil Nadu, he started a conversation in English, but not, I suspect, because he wanted to include me. He couldn't speak Tamil and his colleague didn't know Kannada; two educated men from neighbouring states but their common language was my own.

A school need only advertise that it follows the English Medium curriculum and parents flock in droves to enrol their children. Which is fine for those that can afford it.

Attempting to negotiate a clear path through the discussion is the *National Curriculum Framework 2005* which recommends that schools adopt the three-language formula: education in the mother-tongue, Hindi and English.

Clearly, English is in India to stay, but contention prevails over its right and proper role within the education system. As I discovered with most things Indian, there are many sides to the same coin.

While on the subject, it would be remiss of me not to mention the re-emergence of Hinglish, the glorious fusion of Hindi and English that once was the vocal domain of the top-hole bureaucrat. Cutting across all caste and cultural divides, it is now the language of the street as well as the cocktail party. It may soon be the pan-Indian, *pucca* way to speak, hain?

In the meantime, back to the lesson. Teaching by rote is problematic. Not only does it leave a trail of misunderstanding and inaccuracy in its wake, it potentially drains a child of her natural instinct and creativity. When a pupil is told what to say, do and believe, that way of thinking soon becomes second nature. When a question *and* answer are drilled in simultaneously - 'What-is-the-capital-of-India-the-capital-of-India-is-Delhi,' - what hope does she have of comprehension?

The danger is that the process is pursued into adulthood. Life becomes mechanical, inefficiencies repeated, routines cloned.

I encountered numerous examples of this "thought-phobia", as Sri Aurobindo described it, the most memorable being the occasion I tried to book a room in Cochin. Many of the hotels were full due to the number of tourists in the city. After several frustrating attempts, I walked up to the reception desk of a hotel that seemed more promising.

Me:	I'd like to book a room please.
Receptionist:	Yes, certainly. But we are only having double rooms available, sir.
Me:	That'll do.

Receptionist:	A double room is being for two people. Where is the other person?
Me:	I understand. I will pay the full price for two (The difference was negligible).
Receptionist:	No, sir. That is not possible. You must be two people.
Me:	Well I'm not. I am one person. But I will pay for two.
Receptionist:	No you are not comprehending. The hotel rules say...

I'm not comprehending!

But I *am* generalising.

SASA Academy was not a government school. The children were not learning and thinking by rote because the teachers couldn't be bothered. Nor were they being educated for statistics-sake. Though, in some cases, they lacked experience, each teacher was motivated, committed and genuinely desired the best for every pupil. Not knowing any different, they possibly taught the way that they were taught. Without their efforts, the children were unlikely to receive an education at all, good, bad or indifferent.

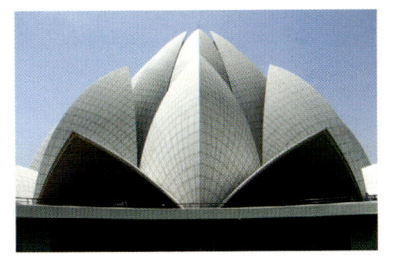

Bahá'í Temple, Delhi

Humayun's Tomb, Delhi

a Delhi street

Qutb Minar, Delhi

Lakshmi Narayan Mandir, Delhi

looking across the Himalayan foothills above Mussoorie

Saira and her family

Dehradun Public School

Saira's village

Sandhya outside her house

assembly at SASA Academy

studying at SASA Academy

the home I visited in which the family lived in one unventilated, pitch-black room

terraces of wheat around SASA Academy

a Garhwali home

en route to Pratap's house

a Garhwali family outside their home

the Kedarnath trek

JP, Robert, Shailender and Ramesh

Sujan

Pintoo and his sister

12
Going Downhill Fast

Of the twelve million girls born in India each year, one million do not see their first birthday

At about four o'clock most afternoons I met Rajeev and Sandeep outside the school. We would then walk several kilometres to visit a number of homes in the neighbouring villages. The primary purpose of the calls was to collect information about prospective pupils. SASA Academy enjoyed a good reputation and, because it offered the best education in the area, places were over-subscribed. Consequently, a simple selection process was required. My role entailed gathering answers from a specially written questionnaire about the parents' background, the size of the family, their monthly income and their attitudes towards family planning. Thankfully, I was not required to assess whether or not a child should be offered a sponsored place. That unenviable responsibility lay in the hands of Shailender and the teachers.

The notion of an Academy with selection criteria possibly conveys a misleading impression of the school. "Academy" is a term used extensively throughout India to describe many kinds of educational establishments, irrespective of size or quality of learning. Means-testing at SASA was purely an administrative exercise, the key criterion being whether an older sibling already attended the school. If they didn't, a child stood more chance of receiving a place herself. The rationale was simple: if one child per family received an education, the whole family benefited. Although siblings were not necessarily precluded, it was prudent to spread the limited resources between as many families in the locality as possible

The questionnaire also asked about caste background. Most families were SC, Scheduled Caste, but a few were classified ST, Scheduled Tribe. I asked Sandeep why this kind of detail was necessary.

'Surely there aren't caste issues among people here?'

'A few weeks ago we were having a situation. Actually a boy's parents were forbidding him from sitting next to his friend.'

'Why?'

'He was from another social group,' he replied. 'They were not even allowed to talk. This is a difficult issue to be managing. So it is helpful to have as much background information as possible.'

I found this incomprehensible. Superficially, there appeared little to distinguish between the two families. Although they dwelt in clearly delineated areas in the village, in effect, they were neighbours. Living considerably below the poverty-line, both families struggled to make ends meet. Neither possessed a toilet or running water. Yet their beliefs fiercely governed their relationship with one another.

Waiting for Sandeep and Rajeev on the Ghamsali road, I scanned the view across the valley. From this vantage point I could see many of the hill-strewn villages in which the children lived: Bajiyal Gaon, Kherkehi, Dhargaon and Choura. They were only accessible by steep, rocky paths that became dangerously muddy the moment it rained. A network of trails led off the main arterial tracks, short-cuts forged over decades to ease the walk between houses.

The rain, having fallen persistently for several hours, had caused the temperature to drop by a few degrees. As usual, though, the skies were beginning to brighten as we set off. Distorted mountain reflections bounced off the puddles and thin wisps of cloud, hovering over the valley, occasionally obscured the terraces of wheat and rice from sight. We followed the tracks up and down for about forty minutes, frequently stopping to have a chat with parents or relatives of children attending the school.

'Who was that?' I asked, after Rajeev had exchanged pleasantries with a man carrying a plastic crate.

'That was the uncle of Vinay in Class Three,' he replied, 'his brother runs the little store opposite the school.'

A few minutes later, a girl skipped past. She waved coyly. 'You know her?'

'Oh, yes. Her sister is in Class Two.' Everyone, it seemed, had a connection with SASA Academy.

As we approached a few houses, a lad, darting around the corner, caught my elbow. Looking up, he grinned awkwardly. He and his friends were playing tag in the *chowk*, the open courtyard outside the cluster of corrugated-roofed stone buildings. In the far corner two young women were husking rice by alternately pummelling two thick wooden poles into a shallow, bowl-shaped hollow in the flagstone called an *ukhal*. The muted thud of their co-ordinated efforts scattered the air with dust from the smattered shells.

Making a fleeting appearance, a little girl greeted us and then disappeared into one of the houses shouting excitedly in Garhwali. Evidently we were expected.

After a few moments, three women appeared, one of whom carried a straw mat and three blankets which she spread over the stone step in front of the doorway. Typifying the cultural integration of clothing worn throughout the area, her waist was wrapped, sari-like, with a traditional thick cloth. On her upper body, however, she wore a more westernised maroon blouse and woollen cardigan. Dark eyes, shining out from a wheatish facial complexion, exemplified her characteristically Garhwali open features. A turquoise scarf, woven around her head, trailed onto her shoulder and a bronze *nuth* ornament pierced her nose.

This was Sulachana, the mother of the little girl who welcomed us.

Smiling tentatively, Sulachana indicated for us to sit. She then murmured softly to the younger of the other two women, who promptly disappeared back into the house. The eldest woman, cradling a small baby, hovered watchfully at a distance.

'The girl who spoke to us is named Vinita. Her family are wishing her to attend the school,' explained Sandeep, 'but first we must assess their needs to see if she is deserving a sponsor place at SASA Academy.'

The family's needs were quite evident as far as I could tell. Apart from the street kids in Vijayawada, I had never encountered such poverty. Nine people lived in a three-by-five metre house with no sanitation or running water.

Not unlike a Garhwali version of Chinese whispers, we worked through the survey. Sitting on the blanketed stone step, I asked a question in English which, translated by Sandeep into Garhwali, was put to Sulachana. After a brief discussion with other members of the family, she replied to Sandeep. He translated her response back into English which I then modified into answers that made written sense. The process was quite laborious.

Bright, chatty Vinita, pronounced Vin-ee-tah, was the fifth of seven daughters. 'What are their names?' I asked Sulachana.

'Lalita, Ponita, Sunita, Anita, Vinita, Mina and Pinki,' Sandeep translated from Garhwali, 'aged between fifteen years and twenty-three days.' The older woman, Sulachana's mother-in-law, was carrying Pinki, the baby.

'No boys?'

'No,' she replied expectantly, 'not yet.' With seven daughters and the obvious longing for a son, it seemed insensitive to pursue the survey questions relating to family planning.

'Is this information relevant to whether or not Vinita should be offered a sponsored place?' I asked Rajeev.

'Not directly. But it is helping us to understand discrimination attitudes in these villages.'

'Is this a problem?'

'Generally in India, yes.'

'And here?'

'That is what we are trying to find out. Our role at SASA is not to educate the child only, but to support the whole family.'

The pressures to produce a son are embedded in social, cultural and religious practices that are widely accepted as the norm throughout the land.

Because India doesn't have a social benefit system, the responsibility invariably falls on the eldest son to ensure material and financial provision for his parents in their old age. The birth of a son promises security, ensuring the family's dynasty for the next generation.

The birth of a daughter, however, presages extreme financial hardship, sealed on the day of her marriage. Due to the continuing practice of the dowry system, large sums of money, property or goods are paid to the groom's family. It is something that many parents seek to avoid, often by appalling methods.

Gender discrimination, rampant throughout urban and rural India, results in girls being deprived of adequate education, medical treatment and other basic needs. Of the twelve million girls born in India each year, one million do not see their first birthday. A third of these deaths occur at birth. Girls are victimised considerably more than boys during childhood and 17% of female fatalities are due to gender discrimination. Innumerable, unrecorded numbers of girls are killed within hours of birth. Many others are destroyed within the womb itself.

Analysis of the 2001 Census data indicates that between 22 and 37 million females are "missing" from India's population. Although some say that this is a result of natural changes in the demographic, it is widely accepted that the predominant causes are female infanticide, a practice that has existed for centuries, and foeticide, a rapidly escalating social evil.

The most recently available figures suggest that around half a million foetuses are aborted in India each year.

In many of the world's countries there are approximately 105 female births for every 100 males.

In India, according to the 1961 census results, there were 98. By 2001, this figure had dropped to less than 93.

In Uttarakhand, according to the same census, the 2001 figure was 91.

As scientific procedures for detecting the gender of a baby in the womb improve, the situation worsens. Early diagnostic methods are becoming increasingly accessible in rural India. It is feared that the female infanticide rate is on the increase.

Traditionally, the Garhwal region does not have a history of female infanticide or foeticide. Discrimination against girls is not evident.

Or so it has seemed until fairly recently.

The 2001 census sparked a widespread debate on the issue by revealing a net decline in the number of girls born between 1990 and 2000. It was once assumed that contraceptive failures were the primary reason for sanctioning abortions for the purpose of family planning. Now it is acknowledged that this may not have always been the case. Other commentators argue that the notion of female foeticide is preposterous: access to the most basic primary health care is unavailable in many interior areas, so where could parents possibly locate an ultrasound scanner?

Quantifying the magnitude of the problem is difficult. Though the practice has not infiltrated all the hill villages, there are indications that female foeticide is on a covert increase in the region. It was evident that the copious demands of this staunchly patriarchal society placed a tremendous burden on families with one girl child, let alone seven.

Thankfully, not all parents succumbed to these pressures. Gender discrimination, for many, was not an issue. I chose not to ask Sulachana about her beliefs. The sight of seven healthy daughters, I hoped, was a positive indication of how she may have responded.

Lalita, the eldest daughter, re-appeared carrying three small metal beakers of chai on a tray. She offered one to me, my first of the afternoon.

Earlier in my travels, I wasn't sure what to make of chai. Once my taste buds had learnt to dissociate the sweet aromatic brew from any resemblance to tea, I grew to like it very much. A cuppa was particularly welcome in moments of despondency when, cold and damp, a boost to my energy and spirits was most needed.

Two cups per afternoon were plenty, three more than enough. By the fourth or fifth I was completely chai-ed out. Despite feeling bad about consuming a family's scarce resources, I knew that refusal would have insulted their hospitality. Thanks to the quirks of Indian generosity, I frequently found myself drinking chai I didn't want from people who could ill afford to give it to me.

The chai ritual, however, served as a useful social yardstick for gauging the relative poverty of the people I visited. Collectively, there was nothing to discern between them; everyone lived so far below the poverty line that any comparison with the west was fatuous. It was enough to observe that an entire household survived for a month on the cost equivalent of a McBurger. Individually, though, the comparison between families proved insightful.

My awkwardness about accepting chai was only the start of the moral dilemma. Although every family wished to be hospitable, some did not have the means to be so. Where chai was not offered, I was presented with a tumbler of water and a predicament: should I drink it and chance an upset stomach, or politely decline at the risk of causing offence?

This was a quandary that never occurred back home. Here it was an issue, particularly when the water was part of the daily consignment that a mother had walked several kilometres to collect.

I didn't relish such decisions. However, whether they involved a cup of murky water in the poorest of mountain homes or an unidentifiable berry thrust into my mouth by a South Indian street kid, I never became ill from accepting food offered with a big heart and the best of intentions. In fact, I didn't experience my first dodgy stomach until nearly five months into my trip. That was in a spotless restaurant in central Delhi.

Occasionally I was welcomed into a home with open arms, but offered nothing. I found that hardest of all because I knew that my hosts were not being rude or mean-spirited. They simply had nothing to give.

Sitting on Sulachana's doorstep, I accepted her chai graciously. By this point the family picture had become clearer, except for one person.

'Where is Vinita's father?' I asked.

'Chandan, my husband, is away working,' replied Sulachana.

He was a labourer and earned between 100 and 200 rupees a month. The family of nine survived on this money to supplement the food grown on their tiny terrace of land and the milk obtained from their one gaunt buffalo. It was not a bad income compared with other families who were living on 70 rupees a month: less than £1.

With the interview finished, Sulachana invited me into the house. A small wood fire burned in the corner of the dark, cell-like room, a few cooking utensils hung on the wall and a scattering of mats, the family beds, littered the floor. Apart from those items, and two wooden trunks in which everybody's clothes and other belongings were stored, the house was bare.

As darkness began to fall we left Vinita's family to visit another home. She followed us to the edge of the chowk then waved goodbye. I watched her skip back to her mother, hopeful that the school would find her a place.

At the next home we were received warmly by a widowed mother. I fumbled through the doorway into a pitch black, unventilated room heavy with eye-smarting smoke. Visibility was impossible. I had to catch my breath in shallow snatches. It was not until I used the flash on my camera that I could make out the claustrophobic living conditions, half the size of Vinita's home. They, too, had a wooden box containing all their worldly possessions. That was all.

We were not offered a chair, a mat, or anything on which to sit. This was an unusually stark indication of the family's dire poverty. The cow dung and mud floor was good enough for us.

I photographed the good-humoured mother and her three young sons embracing each other around the fire. The eldest boy already attended the school; this was just a social call. Neither he, nor his two brothers, appeared dirty or unhealthy, just poor in the extreme. And content.

The smell of smouldering cedar clung to my clothes all evening.

One afternoon we visited a child whose sick grandmother was confined to her bed. Her daughter-in-law was labouring on the terraces, her son employed as a truck driver far away in Chennai.

The family lived in a *dopura*, a traditional two-storey, Garhwal house built over one hundred years ago. The ground floor, the *obara*, stabled two buffalos and stored various tools for working the land. A flight of narrow steps led up the front to the upper floor *dandyala*, a long, narrow space open on three sides. While most of the house's construction was starkly functional, the door into the main living area was distinguished by an ornately carved frame. Crafted from rich brown *thuner*, yew, the intricate workmanship graced the front of the building like the entrance to a temple.

Sadly, this idiosyncratic artform is in decline; the wood is costly and the act of carving time-consuming. Although, nowadays, concrete and corrugated tin are the construction materials of necessity, rather than of choice, those Pahari that can afford the time and the money still build their pucca homes from the more traditional local stone and slate. Regardless of shape and size, most Garhwal houses have small windows, mainly for protection against the harsh winter weather and predatory wild animals.

We sat next to the grandmother as she lay in bed.

'She is not seriously ill,' said Sandeep. 'But she is neglecting many vital chores because of her health. This is making her upset.'

Wrapped in several layers of threadbare blankets to keep warm, she smiled weakly. With the profound insight of a daughter, mother, wife and grandmother, this exhausted, but spirited, lady represented the archetypal older Garhwali woman.

Hill women, like her, form the backbone of the family and village economy. For many centuries, however, complex geographical, historical and social conditions have conspired to ensure that their existence is one of extreme hardship.

Although the mountain terrain is rough and the terraced land arduous to cultivate, Garhwali society is predominantly agricultural. The Pahari are a resilient people, managing to persevere through every trial history has thrown at them.

Traditionally, they have depended on the success of their crops for subsistence, bartering between families and communities for the exchange of goods and services. For centuries, through the trade of complementary skills and resources, a system of mutually beneficial transactions underpinned daily life. The productive mountain eco-system ensured the growth of a healthy variety of crops. Food, readily available to all, provided not only a good nutritional balance but also insurance against the failure of a particular harvest in any given year.

Today, though the hills surrounding SASA Academy remain conducive to growing a wide range of cultivated and wild foodstuffs, including rice, wheat, raspberries, peaches, apricots, walnuts, lemons, strawberries and oranges, the quantity and diversity of resources is diminishing fast. Deforestation and environmental changes have contributed considerably to the shortage of staple foods. Most families can only afford to own a small terrace of land, usually less than half an acre. It is barely enough to cultivate the basics – rice, maize, barley – on which to live, let alone trade.

Due to extensive road construction and the advent of electricity, many villages are becoming more accessible. This has precipitated certain lifestyle changes in some areas alongside the continuation of traditional practices and customs in others. Bartering, for example, still exists on a reduced scale but a person requiring food, materials or labour generally must have the capacity to pay for it in rupees. It has become essential, therefore, for individuals and communities to develop strategies to exist within a cash economy.

Despite the progress in road construction, communication networks remain poor. Even if a farmer can grow sufficient crops to trade at market, most towns are too far away or inaccessible. The journey from Akori to Rishikesh is certainly possible, for example, but the time it takes prohibits a market farmer from distributing fresh produce.

The net result is that the agricultural economy has slowly shifted from a dependence on self-sufficiency, bartering and communal collaboration to a reliance on cash to purchase the fundamentals of food, fuel and fodder. This has given rise to an even bigger issue: how to pay for it?

Opportunities to derive direct sources of income within the interior villages are minimal. Out of necessity, the region has witnessed a large-scale migration of men to the plains in search of employment. This has produced what has popularly been coined the money-order economy: men, seeking work elsewhere, send their earnings home to their families in the mountains.

The female-to-male ratio for rural India as a whole is 946; there are 946 women to every 1,000 men. According to the 2001 census results, Uttarakhand's sex ratio is 1,007. This is considerably higher than the national average. However, in the specific districts of Tehri Garhwal and Rudraprayag, a district that I was to visit later, the ratio increases even further to 1,109 and 1,127 respectively.

At the time of the previous census in 1991, Uttarakhand was not a separate state, nor Rudraprayag a district. No comparable figures exist, therefore, to determine any trend. Circumstantial evidence, however, indicates that the male-to-female margin continues to widen, a movement diametrically opposed to that in most parts of India.

Migration from the interior villages is not a recent phenomenon. Historically, the prospect of engaging in the Indian defence forces has enticed millions of hopeful Pahari boys and young men from the hills. The Garhwal Rifles is one of the most respected regiments in the entire Indian army and military service has always been regarded as a highly valued career. Maybe it is the tough mountain existence that makes them particularly hardy and physically strong or their Mongolian and Rajput ancestral blood, but Garhwalis have earned the reputation for being honest, brave and fearless fighters. Today, over 25,000 soldiers serve in its 23 battalions, many of whom fought with remarkable courage during the Kargil conflict in 1999.

Recently, though, recruitment rates have dropped. Relatively few men now receive the opportunity to join the 2,500 soldiers training at Lansdowne each year. The majority are forced to accept whatever alternative work they may find.

It is estimated that at least 50% of men in Uttarakhand who leave their villages are employed in the hotel and tourism industry, scrubbing pots and pans and portering for a pittance. By tourists, I'm not referring to travellers from abroad. They comprise a fairly insignificant proportion of hotel guests. I mean the many hotels, particularly those in the north, that cater for *domestic* business people and pilgrims, religious tourists, on their annual spiritual quests.

While passing through Delhi earlier in my trip, I checked into a simple business hotel late one evening. No less than four smartly uniformed young men clamoured over each other to carry my rucksack to the room.

'Sir, this is the light switch,' one of them demonstrated.

'Please look, sir!' another pulled me into the bathroom. 'This is making toilet flush,' he said pressing the button in the middle of the cistern.

'Television, sir, look!' said a third, switching it on and off.

A fourth porter pointed to a unit on the wall. 'Air-conditioning,' he declared.

'I didn't ask for AC, though,' I replied politely.

'You are not worrying, sir,' he responded. 'It is not working!'

Having helpfully exhausted all the room's possibilities they hovered en masse in the doorway. I knew what was coming.

'Goodnight sir,' they chanted with one voice.

'Goodnight and thank you for your assistance,' I smiled, as four hands thrust forward. Finding a few notes in my back pocket, I looked up. Two more faces had appeared in the doorway.

'What about us, sir?'

'You haven't done anything! At least the others switched on the light.'

'Oh! But we are here, sir, if you are requiring us.' To which there was no answer.

Six young porters who, arguably, should have been in school, were working in a dingy back-street hotel. They may not have come from the mountains. But supposing they had? I wondered if they earned enough money on which to survive themselves, let alone send any back home to their families. What was their future?

The excessive migration of men from the mountains to the plains was a practice with which I became familiar. I also heard people refer to the "missing men". Intrigued, it took me a while to work out what they were talking about. Gradually I was able to piece together what typified the dominant trends of this peculiar phenomenon.

Characteristically, "missing men" are those sons, fathers and husbands who have migrated from their villages, failed to return *and* are not investing financially in their families back home. Seizing the opportunity to leave the mountains, they are ensnared by the trappings of the big city only to forget about their parents, wives and children. For the "missing men", any outside job, however menial, is preferable to a mountain home-coming.

Uttarakhand has a population of eight and a half million people living in the hills and on the plains. In addition, there is a reputed six million, predominantly men, living outside the state. One and a half million work in Mumbai alone, many employed, as in several of the large cities, as truck drivers.

Across the valley from the school lived Hema, a young mother with two sons but no husband. The eldest boy, Vinod, wanted to attend SASA Academy. As we arrived one damp afternoon she came out of her house, knelt and touched my muddy boots with her out-stretched fingers. Throughout our conversation her head, wrapped turban-like in a blue shawl, remained bowed.

'This family is very, very sad,' Sandeep said reverently. 'Although most men never come back, some husbands would return to assist with ploughing and harvesting. Hema's husband did a few years' ago. He had AIDS. When he died, his wife was already being infected.'

'What about the youngest son?'

'He was born with AIDS.'

This scenario is not uncommon. I looked down at Hema. She blinked; though only a tiny flutter, it was enough to expose an image, not of brokenness, but of incredible resilience.

Then she looked at the ground. I also glanced away, rubbing my jacket cuff across my moist eyes.

Another woman came to join us. Her inquisitive smile revealed a couple of broken teeth. 'This lady, Meena, is living in the next house,' explained Sandeep, indicating a slate-roofed building in front of which two tethered buffalo were grazing. 'She is having three children but none are attending the school.'

'Her husband?'

'Working in Delhi. Her mother-in-law is here also, but she is elderly and sick. Meena must care for her.'

Meena pointed at me and chuckled. She and Rajeev exchanged a few words. 'Don't worry, Mark,' he said. 'She only is wanting to know who you are.'

Despite her youthful laughter, her face was weathered, her hands tarnished with years of toil.

'How old is she?' I asked.

'She is saying she's twenty-eight,' replied Sandeep after a brief exchange. She looked at least fifty. 'She is a strong woman.'

Inevitably, the lack of men, whether through migration or death, has dramatically compounded the hardships faced by the hill women. From before dawn to late at night they are constantly at work. They are rarely idle.

'What time do you start work each morning?' I asked Meena.

'When it is still dark,' she replied, 'I am taking buffalo to the forest.'

Rajeev then added his own thoughts to his translation. 'That is normal for many women. They are tending the cattle at home or herding goats and other animals back and forth to the forest. Then they are collecting and transporting heavy loads of fodder, firewood, manure, grain and flour. In building season they would carry baskets of rocks and clay on their heads.'

I had often marvelled at the women walking barefoot along the track supporting heavy bundles of wood, several feet long, on their head, a baby invariably cradled in their arms.

'I presume there's no running water here?' I asked.

'No,' replied Rajeev. 'Meena is walking two kilometres for one day's supply of spring water. When she is returning she has other household chores to do such as cooking, weaving, sewing and knitting,' he said. 'Then there is working in the fields or terraces. Basically, agriculture is so-so important to their livelihoods. The women are making every stage of the process, preparing the land, sowing, reaping, harvesting and threshing. During harvest-time the women would return to the fields after their evening meal and continue working by moonlight till early hours in the morning.'

'Do the men do anything?' I asked incredulously.

'Yes, ploughing,' said Sandeep.

'And playing cards!' added Rajeev mischievously.

I'd already noticed they were very good at that. From an early age, even the children, it seemed, would help their mothers by herding goats or cattle, collecting water and wood, preparing meals and looking after their younger siblings. The men, those that remained, sat watching. Debating. Smoking.

Early May was wedding season in the Garhwal mountains. During my stay at SASA Academy, I must have witnessed at least a dozen marriages, though never an entire ceremony.

I was invited to a groom's pre-nuptial celebrations one evening, danced in the street with wedding guests the next afternoon, was roused on several mornings by firecrackers and shivered in bed most nights with the mantra of a chanting *pandit*, priest, echoing across the hillsides. Due to the lack of electricity and financial resources, a communal mobile generator and amplification system toured the mountain circuit. As soon as one wedding was finished, the equipment was transported to the next, crooning cleric in tow.

Strung between houses and trees, silver and gold strands of tinsel shimmered in the breeze, winking flashes of sunlight over the valley. Involving not only family and friends, each wedding was an affair for the entire village to celebrate. Typically Hindu, it was all drama and showbiz. A trumpet fanfare and drum beating would announce the arrival of the bridal *palanquin*, a box supported on two poles, in which the bride was enclosed. Usually covered in ornate red cloth, it was carried great distances along the mountain tracks, teetering on the shoulders of four bearers.

The entrance of a bride should herald the beginning of a new chapter in the lives of a young couple. For the wife-to-be, however, the future may hold an existence far more terrifying than she might dare to imagine.

At marriage, girls are commonly displaced from their own village to a home in another valley. There they are compelled to forge a new life in an unfamiliar setting. Even a few kilometres away can seem like a huge chasm for a young woman who has rarely travelled beyond her immediate vicinity for most of her life. She may occasionally return to her own mother, either to give birth or to attend to other family matters but, unless she has married into a supportive household, life can become horrifically lonely and unbearable. A bride marrying into the wrong home may face years of misery and torment, shaped by the discriminative practices inherent in the dowry system.

Over time, the dowry has changed into a cruel and offensive mockery of its original, positive intention. Traditionally, a woman had no right to a share of her ancestral land or property through natural inheritance. At some indeterminate point in history, though, a custom developed by which a daughter was given a gift by her parents at the time of her marriage, known as *streedhan*, to ensure access to some of their wealth. Within an agricultural community this was often land. Gradually it became jewellery, household goods and other portable items over which the bride could have control throughout her life.

The parents also offered second gift. Known as k*anyadaan,* this was the gift of their daughter *herself* to the groom's family.

Then the system degenerated. The bride was eventually overlooked and the dowry, as it became known, fell directly into the hands of the groom and his family. What once existed to safeguard a woman's fortune and future became an oppressive millstone around her neck and an onerous burden to her parents, potentially sending them reeling into debt for years.

The practice was legally prohibited in 1961. To advertise, take, give, or demand dowry is now punishable by law. A husband, or relative, in receipt of a dowry may face imprisonment for no less than five years. Yet the dowry system still prevails throughout the land, both within city families of relative wealth and those living in rural parts. Unsurprisingly, the legislation is largely flouted or unimplemented. Convictions are rare and the guardians of the law, predominantly men, are susceptible to bribery. Reputedly, dowry abuse is on the increase. Many young wives end up taking their own lives, often as a result of mistreatment and abuse.

Physically, Pahari women are incredibly tough. They do whatever is within their power to survive. Emotionally, however, the absence of a husband and father places a woman under an intense inner strain. The physical and emotional support of a husband is usurped by an often tense relationship with her mother-in-law in whose home she has to live and work. Constantly under the watchful eye of her husband's mother, a Pahari woman is rarely permitted to lead her own life.

I imagined meeting a young girl aged no more than thirteen or fourteen. Her name is Gitika. It means "small song".

Gitika is a newly-wed surrounded by unfamiliar people in a strange environment, aware that there is a price on her head. She's a commodity, an object exchanged for goods, a means for others to acquire wealth. Possibly Gitika overhears members of her "new" family whispering behind her back:

'She is worthless,' complains her mother-in-law.

'She's not bringing enough money into the marriage,' says her older sister-in-law.

Gitika starts fearing for her life. She may not have directly heard her in-laws plotting to kill her but she talks to other women and is aware of what goes on.

That's how life is for many women throughout India. But the fear is multiplied in the mountains. Gitika's natal family are remote and inaccessible, living several days' walk away over impenetrable terrain.

A few years into the marriage her husband announces he's moving away. He wants to work in the city. Gitika has become part of his family and now he's off, leaving her and their two daughters to live alone with her in-laws.

There's no question that a Pahari woman's life is harsh. Does it go by unaccounted? Yes. Unnoticed? Possibly. Unappreciated?

Shefali, a fourteen year old Nepali pupil at Dehradun Public School, composed the following poem:

My Mother

My mother,
My mother,
I like my mother,
She is so good,
She loves to me,
She struggles for me,
My mother, my mother,
She is so good,
My mother,
My mother,
I love my mother.

The profundity of her simple words illuminates the essential truth for a Garhwali woman living in the mountains; a life of relentless hardship.

13
The Wreck of the Beautiful

Hug the trees!

'I thought you might be up here!' puffed Shailender. Two boys raced past him down the craggy steps. 'Bhawani Bhai has arrived. He is wishing to talk to you.'

I had just finished a Class Four lesson in my favourite teaching space, the lofty terrace of land situated above the main school building. Though the air was warm, threads of cloud had begun to gather around the highest peaks. 'He is staying for an hour or two. Then I shall travel back to Dehradun with him.'

Shailender had told me earlier that Bhawani Bhai might visit. I felt honoured that he wanted to meet me.

'Come!'

I followed him down the hillside into the bedroom-cum-living room that we shared. A genial, unassuming middle-aged man wearing a crisp, white dhoti down to his ankles and purple kurta rose to greet us. Not having made my bed, I felt mildly embarrassed.

Although he was a famous environmentalist and leading figure in the women's empowerment movement, Bhawani Bhai had chosen to work quietly in the background for many decades, allowing others such as Sunderlal Bahaguna to take the political limelight. His influence, however, had been considerable in a number of key issues.

Beside him, a well-nourished gentleman, finely dressed in a pale blue short-sleeved shirt and tie, offered his hand.

'J. P. Shah,' he announced courteously.

'Would you like tea, gentlemen?' Shailender asked in Hindi.

'Just water, thank you,' Bhawani replied. J.P. Shah accepted the offer.

'Mark?'

'Yes, please, if you're making it.'

Shailender measured three cups of buffalo milk into a pan then struck a match to ignite the calor gas stove.

Bhawani Bhai had been associated with a particular hostel in Tehri, as both student and manager, for almost fifty years. An ardent opponent of the Tehri Dam, he was the only remaining resident to resist its construction, refusing to be bought off by the government's, otherwise successful, attempts to cajole the town's inhabitants to re-locate to New Tehri, a few kilometres up the valley. The hostel would soon be under water, he would be without a home.

Bhawani first attended the hostel as a sixteen-year-old. He was a contemporary of Bihari Lal, whose ashram in Budha Kedar we had visited on the way. As a centre of social activity in Tehri, the hostel was open to students of any religion or caste. Informed by Sarvodaya principles, it worked towards the eradication of social discrimination.

'Our main work at the time was to get rid of untouchability,' Shailender translated. 'The Harijans, or Scheduled Caste, were not permitted to eat in restaurants or enter the temples. The students used to produce street dramas and parade from village to village to raise awareness about untouchability issues. This proved to be an extremely effective form of communication to people who could neither read nor write.'

When he was older, Bhawani moved to an ashram in Delhi to study social service in greater depth. 'I met a number of influential politicians including the prime minister and president. Many people encouraged me to remain in Delhi. The temptation to do so was strong,' he said candidly. 'But I was mindful of the "missing men" issue and determined not to become one of those lured to the city, never to return. Too many concerns about education, superstition, untouchability and other development problems compelled me to go back.' I understood that Bhawani Bhai was subsequently appointed manager of the hostel in Tehri before rising to become a leading figure in the Sarvodaya movement.

'I worked at the hostel for thirty years. In that time nobody ever became ill. We lived on a very simple diet; no meat, eggs or tea. As a result, everyone enjoyed very good health. In the mornings and evenings we prayed and everybody worked together, cooking, cleaning and the like. Very poor children also came to the ashram, with not even any clothes on their backs, but they've subsequently moved on to positions of high power as doctors, magistrates and politicians.'

He continued. 'All of the boys who lived in the hostel under my supervision and care are now successful and influential individuals.'

'To what do you attribute this?' I asked.

'I worked very hard, strictly supervised the boys and gave them good values. These they inherited and carried through into the jobs they now do. This man here,' he said indicating J.P. Shah, 'is one of my ex-students. Now he's a successful lawyer.' Bhawani smiled. 'For today, though, he's my driver.'

J.P. Shah said nothing but nodded his head respectfully.

Bhawani hid any pride in his achievements beneath a soft, self-effacing dignity, refusing to solicit credit for his work. I noticed that his principles and fervent belief in equality governed his actions, never a desire for recognition or glory.

Shailender handed us our drinks. I clasped my hands around my mug of sweet, milky tea. Though the sun shone outside, the room was chilly.

'Is untouchability still an issue in the mountain villages?'

'Actually, nowadays it is worse,' Bhawani replied. 'The fundamental caste problem remains but the government does nothing about it. In fact, it's more complex than it used to be. Now there's an element of jealousy; anyone can go to any place! There's nothing to stop a Harijan entering a temple at Badrinath because no one knows who he is. It's not written on his forehead that he's a Harijan. But still he's not permitted to go into the village temples where people know him.'

'Isn't discrimination on grounds of caste illegal?'

'Yes. But since its prohibition in the 1950 Indian Constitution,' Bhawani added, 'little has been done to enforce the law. Legislatively, enormous progress has been made. But there's still much ground to cover in practice.'

Although casteism is more prevalent in some areas than others, it remains a universal problem passed from one generation to the next. Undeniably, successive governments have adopted a programme of affirmative action to raise the status of the lower castes within society. This includes an allocation of admission places in higher education institutions for students and the reservation of a share of seats in national and state government for scheduled caste members.

Yet despite these efforts, politicisation of the issue has often aggravated, not solved, the situation. Bringing the status of the lower castes into the limelight has compounded discriminatory attitudes by artificially accentuating divisions through special treatment, piling stigma upon stigma. The short-sighted intentions of certain politicians have occasionally backfired, some being found guilty of manipulating the circumstances for personal gain.

I've heard some arguments in defence of the caste system claiming that it has assured social stability throughout a number of invasions and periods of subjugation: six centuries of Muslim rule and two centuries of British authority to name but two. Some people claim that caste engenders a sense of identity between members of the same jati, while others deny its existence altogether; possibly another fine example of Indian self-delusion.

Sri Aurobindo suggests that caste, or varna, was originally a *constructive* arrangement for distributing function and value within society. A Brahmin's varna status was not predetermined by birth alone; he also bore responsibility for the spiritual and intellectual edification of the race. A Kshatriya, assigned with the duty to protect the nation, was required to nurture the appropriate qualities that befitted a warrior or prince. Each person, whatever their varna, was required to work for the common good. Sri Aurobindo argues that a shared sense of communal responsibility and a spirit of equality existed between all four varnas:

> There is no doubt that the institution of caste degenerated. It ceased to be determined by spiritual qualifications which, once essential, have now come to be subordinate and even immaterial and is determined by the purely material tests of occupation and birth... The spirit of caste arrogance, exclusiveness and superiority came to dominate it instead of the spirit of duty, and the change weakened the nation and helped to reduce us to our present conditions.

The debate surrounding caste and untouchability is both contentious and sensitive. I may have spoken to a dozen people and received just as many opinions on the history of caste, its relationship with Hinduism and the system's prevalence, or otherwise, in society. Talking to Bhawani, however, I was left in no doubt that the prejudices that he and his colleagues faced in the mountains were insidiously real.

'How were you able to address the issue practically?' I asked.

'When we were actively involved in the Sarvodaya movement, we physically went from house to house, including the Harijans, and sat down and ate with them. By personal example we demonstrated equality.'

'Does this not happen now?'

Bhawani Bhai shook his head. 'Today the government officials and elected representatives are not doing this. If, for example, there was a Harijan marriage and the local elected representative was to go there and eat, it would be a personal affirmation of equality. But this doesn't exist now. The Sarvodaya members were more effective because they actually went out and became involved.'

'What can be done to raise awareness?' I asked.

'The government allows advertisements in the media for cigarettes and alcohol. Why can't they produce publicity about the law against untouchability in public places such as temples, sources of drinking water, or even on the television?

This would make people aware of the punishment for discrimination.'

Legally, discrimination on grounds of untouchability is punishable by between six months and ten years imprisonment. Yet this is one further example of prolific legislation but atrociously poor implementation.

'The issue will never be solved by the law alone,' commented J. P. Shah, who had remained silent until that point.

'What are you suggesting?' I asked.

'The problem in India is that we are all casteist ourselves. Unless we change our attitudes we cannot change the world outside. Casteism cannot be removed by law, it can only be eradicated by a change of heart.'

As Bhawani inclined his head in agreement, a burst of wind rattled the door. Over the last few minutes the light through the casement window had begun to deteriorate. Distorted shadows from the frame's crosspieces wavered across the concrete floor.

Bhawani leaned forward and smiled, 'So,' he said, 'what have you been doing here, Mark?'

I told him about my work in the classroom and the survey visits to the neighbouring villages.

'This is a far cry from your own world?'

'It couldn't be more different,' I replied. 'Yesterday, for example, a mother told me she had to walk two kilometres to collect water. At home, we turn on the tap without thinking.'

He looked at me. 'She's fortunate. I know women who trek much further to collect spring water and fuel.'

'Why so far?'

'You must understand one thing. Hill women have an intimate relationship with their surroundings. They bear the brunt of any problems caused by environmental damage. When trees are felled, the forest cover recedes. This directly affects the availability of spring water. So they have to walk further each day to locate it.'

Bhawani's insights informed my growing impression that Garhwal was a society in transition; a world where the pace of change had produced a noticeable tension between tradition and development. Indicative of that change were the men who, seizing the day, had migrated in their droves. The women had received no such opportunity. My earlier theory that India, as a nation, embraced the "Genius of the AND" was beginning to fall apart. Certainly, in Garhwal, the "Tyranny of the OR" prevailed.

Over the last few decades the women had become the guardians of tradition, acting directly against anyone or anything that undermined their rights and those of the environment in which they lived.

The women's development and empowerment movements in Uttarakhand are recognised throughout India for their role in affecting social change. A high proportion of effective action in Garhwal has been politically motivated by women who, as a result, now have 30% representation in local government.

The door suddenly slammed against the wall, its catch sprung by a strong gust. Shailender stood up to close it but, distracted, went outside. He soon reappeared, the two portable solar lamps hanging from each hand.

'That's the last of the sun today,' he commented. 'We ought to be going soon, Bhawani-ji.'

'Do you have a minute or two to tell me about the early days of the women's movements?' I asked Bhawani.

He looked at Shailender, who nodded.

'When we started our work, we saw that so much responsibility within the households and villages fell on the shoulders of the women. They were the driving forces for change. So we formed groups of women called *Mahilamundal* to train them in self-management skills.'

'What were the key issues in those days?' I asked.

'Initially, alcoholism among the men was causing so much pain for the women,' Bhawani replied.

'The issue of alcoholism escalated in the late 1960s,' added J. P. Shah, 'an inevitable by-product of change and the worsening economic situation in the mountains.'

'We started a campaign movement,' continued Bhawani, 'and thousands of people, men as well, held processions to protest and close down the liquor stalls. If the women found a drunkard, even if it was their brother, husband or son, they would tie him up to a tree. The presence of their Sarvodaya colleagues made them bold.'

'Bhawani Bhai's support of an activity or campaign was regarded as a sign of its credibility,' said Shailender, looking at Bhawani. 'Though he won't admit it himself, he became a well-respected individual in the region, earning good influence among the villagers as well as government officials. That's how he received his adopted name. It means "brother of women".'

Bhawani nodded. 'Gently, I nudged them to think differently about their status.'

'How did you do that?'

'Small, but important steps. Encouraging them to take a break at least one day a week, for example. Bathe. Relax.'

'Over time, more and more women became aware of their rights. The success of the women's group was, in fact, instrumental in the formation of the Chipko movement.'

'Chipko was an organised resistance to the destruction of the forests in the early seventies.,' explained J. P. Shah.

Drops of rain started to clatter on the tin roof. Shailender looked apprehensively out of the window.

'Come, Bhawani-ji. We must leave for Dehradun!'

All three men stood.

'Thank you for taking time to talk to me,' I said to Bhawani. 'I wish you a safe journey.'

'It has been my pleasure.'

Shailender picked up his bag and a few other items he had assembled earlier.

'I'll see you next week, Mark,' he said. 'You'll be OK?'

I smiled. 'Of course! Drive carefully!'

Saturday evening.

'Do we have to get up so early?' I questioned optimistically. 'Tomorrow *is* Sunday.'

'We must leave by 7.30 to reach the jungle before the sun becomes too strong,' insisted Sandeep.

'Really?'

'Yes. We must wake at six.'

Pratap, the odd-job man, had invited the teachers and me for lunch at his family's house, two valleys away. This meant trekking for three hours down the hillside, across the basin, up the other side, through the jungle before descending into Pratap's village in the next valley.

I didn't have an issue with the length of the expedition. In fact, I was looking forward to it. I was angling for a lie-in because, deep down, I just knew that we wouldn't leave on time.

But Sandeep was adamant.

'7.30.'

'Definitely?'

'Yes, definitely.'

'Are you sure?'

'I'm sure.'

'Really?'

'Yes.'

~~~

Sunday morning.

Oh, it was so predictable.

6.00am. I woke. It was still dark.

6.10am. I crawled out of bed, shivered, and quickly threw on my clothes.

6.15am. Outside, I crouched patiently over the tap as water dribbled into the saucepan. I returned to my room, lit the calor gas stove and waved my fingers over the flame for warmth.

6.25 to 7.25am. I made coffee, went to the bathroom, threw a bucket of cold water over myself, cleaned my teeth, returned inside, cooked a pan of porridge, then ate my breakfast.

7.30am. I stood outside the school waiting for the others. Not a soul in sight.

7.40am. Sandeep appeared, rubbing his eyes.

7.45 to 8.15am. The others slowly followed.

'What time do we leave Sandeep?'

'In twenty minutes.'

8.30am. Tsering, Sandeep's wife, and Rajeev sat down on the concrete steps. Producing a pair of scissors, she began to cut Rajeev's hair.

8.45pm. Neema, Samuel's wife, started to make chapatis.

'What time do we leave Sandeep?'

'After breakfast.'

9.30am. We locked the schoolroom doors. Only two hours late.

I didn't say a word.

☼

The sun was blazing overhead by the time we started our descent to the valley floor, its bright rays dancing on the long needles of the emerald chir pines. Their bowed branches pointed skywards like chandeliers, the tip of each one clutching a cone candle. We brushed past bursts of wheatish red grass, clumps of white-petalled posies and succulent flowering cacti. Ripening lemons and apricots dangled temptingly overhead. Sweet wild raspberries stained our fingers as we grasped the delicate fruit and crunched the pips between our teeth. The warm air swelled with buzzing bugs and the heady aroma of magnolia.

Although their season was almost at a close, the occasional mauve and pink showy heads of the *burans*, rhododendron, flamed the path-side, attracting pollinating insects to their clusters of flowers. A few days previously, we had visited a home and been offered a sweetly fragrant drink made from its petals.

The distant landscape undulated like ruffled silk. Closer, the distinct shapes of the pines pulled into focus; tall slender trunks with cleanly-scented branches dousing the breeze.

Viewed from the school, the staggered terraces of wheat resembled a haphazard patchwork quilt. Now, looking straight across, they appeared golden and erect, like the perky strands of a new toothbrush. Slender rice stalks poked through the puddled paddy fields situated either side of the boulder-littered river running through the valley basin.

As the trail twisted through the dappled forest, branches of the elder deodars dipped gracefully towards the earth, whispering cautionary tales to the green saplings.

***

Prompting an endless demand for quality wooden rail sleepers, the construction of India's massive rail network began in the early 1850s. Because the strong, durable wood of the deodar was ideal material, a wide-spread programme of deforestisation commenced in the northern hill areas. No one could predict the monumental impact this would have on the region in years to come.

Many Garhwalis talk of the legends and stories surrounding Frederick "Pahari" Wilson, a soldier, adventurer and native of Wakefield, Yorkshire. His travelling fortunes led him to India where tales of his early days in Tehri Garwhal remain apocryphal. Some say he entered the "horns and hide" business, nomadically wandering the hills to shoot deer and build his trade. Others claim he deserted the army after killing a man in a duel in Meerut and escaped into the mountains to avoid detection.

Whatever the truth, Wilson, shunned by his fellow countrymen for turning native, gradually assimilated into Garhwali society and adopted the lifestyle of the locals. He introduced potato cultivation and apple orchards to the hillsides, thereby transforming the region's economy. Shedding the links to his mysterious past, he became a much-loved and trusted figure. Given the ravaged condition of the land subsequent to the Gurkha occupation, it is no wonder that the locals took him to their hearts.

Wilson met and married a beautiful Pahari girl named Gulabi, the daughter of a drummer from Mukbha. They settled in the village of Harsil on the banks of the River Bhagirathi. Surrounded by dense slopes of deodars, he hatched the idea of felling the trees and, due to the absence of roads, floating them down the river to Tehri. There they would be sawn up, dispatched to the plains and sold to city purchasers for use, among other things, on the railway construction.

Naturally, the King of Tehri, from whom Wilson had leased the forests as early as 1850 for the sum of 400 rupees, was delighted: he gained enormously from a share of the profits. According to Bhawani Bhai, he once placed his hands on Wilson's head and proclaimed him "my gold mine".

This man who-would-be-king even minted his own currency. Promoted to the status of near demi-god by the Pahari he became known as "Raja" Wilson. The mention of his name among environmentalists today, however, is greeted with disdainful silence. In terms of the widespread felling of deodar, oak and pine forests Wilson set in motion a catastrophic trend that can never be reversed.

The Forest Act of 1878 further eased the exploitation of the mountains for commercial profit to the benefit of the Treasury, while also severely curtailing the rights of the hill inhabitants. Villagers were robbed of the right to manage the natural surroundings to sustain their own way of life. Vast areas of land were restricted from their use by the government and trees were cut down and sold to lumber companies and industries in the plains.

As Bhawani had explained, the Pahari have a strong symbiotic relationship with nature. Deeply rooted in a spiritual respect for all the earth's resources, including the physical landscape, they believe that everything must be sustained and cared for in balance; when one element suffers, so does it all. Understandably, their agitation increased as they witnessed a gradual stripping away of their environmental "family". Though alarmed by the implications, they were strait-jacketed in their capacity to respond. Even when heard, their voice was largely ignored.

The removal of trees from the hillside had an immediate effect: the women had to walk further to collect firewood. The longer-term consequences were far more damaging: as the earth wore away, the springs dried up, landslides ripped gashes in the hillsides and the terrain became dangerous and unproductive. Women were losing their husbands to the plains and their brothers, the trees, to the commercial developers.

The depleting forest also forced a number of wild animals to search out food and shelter in neighbouring villages which threatened the safety of the inhabitants.

To be fair, the Pahari have not been entirely blameless. Their indiscriminate gathering of wood and fodder over generations, although less blatant, undeniably has eaten into the forest cover.

In their defence, though, the mountains have been the Pahari's home for centuries. In one fell swoop, the government's procurement of the land demoted them from manager to caretaker. Feeling that the forest no longer belonged to them, the Pahari's sense of responsibility towards its maintenance may have been undermined; yet another thread woven into the complex tapestry of Garhwal life.

In October 1962, the ongoing border dispute between India and China erupted into a brief war between the two nations. Just as the US military was about to intervene in response to a secret appeal from Prime Minister Nehru, China declared a unilateral truce and withdrew its forces. India, naturally, wished to shore up its frontier defences bordering with China as precaution against future invasion. The move generated a rapid programme of social and economic development for Uttarakhand, even though the region had not been directly involved in the conflict.

A comprehensive road building plan was initiated. Timber companies rushed to the hills, towns swelled in population and the forests became more accessible. British and American military investment over the ensuing three years was worth in excess of $120 million.

Typically, the Pahari didn't gain from the additional employment opportunities; skilled contractors and labourers were brought in from the plains. The local inhabitants were left with the menial, poorly-paid, rock hauling-type jobs. Motivated by avarice and corruption, many contractors bribed the forest rangers to allow them to fell more trees than their entitlement. Other areas of forest were naively allocated to the programme by the Forestry Department with little regard for the longer term implications.

'SMAAAAACK!!' The valley resonated with the sound of pounding rock. Pratap was standing, stripped to his shorts, astride two large boulders, the river gushing beneath his feet. Swinging the mallet above his head he brought it down again – 'CRAAAAAACK!' - onto the slab in front of him. It bounced and pitched slightly. He bent forward and peered into the clear foaming water, holding his gaze intently for a moment. Everyone else's eyes followed his, breaths held.

Suddenly Pratap's forearm darted into the river, re-appearing instantly with a small silver-blue fish tightly gripped in his hand. Placed on the rock, the creature lay motionless. Then, without warning, its tail fin flipped in the air. Before it could flap any further, Pratap's agile fingers seized its writhing body.

A small naked boy scampered over the boulders and handed Pratap a sinewy tree root on which several other fish dangled. He skewed the fish's body and threaded it on.

'Ever seen fishing like that before?' asked Sandeep, grinning broadly.

'No! How does it work?'

'The sound of the mallet hitting the rock is very loud under water,' he explained, 'It stuns the fish for a few seconds. That is giving Pratap time to see it floating and catch it.'

Pratap handed me the mallet. The handle was about three feet in length and its head, which I could barely lift above my waist, weighed a ton.

'That's a lot of effort for such a small fish!' I laughed.

'It's traditional way here. Pratap will catch more for his mother to make a stew for lunch.'

The Bhilangana River, where Pratap fished, ran just below the village. From there, it continued its course through the hills before joining the holy Bhagirathi near Tehri. The steep valley sides at this point provided clear evidence of land slippage.

Not so far away, another river, the Alaknanda, flows through Garhwal before reaching the plains. In 1970, the monsoon rains were particularly harsh, causing it to rise 60 feet and flood hundreds of square miles. Almost 200 people died. After several months of relief operations and investigation, it became evident that the natural effect of the heavy monsoon was severely compounded by the man-made clearing of the forest slopes which allowed the rain water to gush uncontrollably to the river. The topsoil was washed away and dumped in smaller rivers and streams to create temporary dams. The water level rose and the exposed rocks eventually collapsed as landslides.

Disasters of this kind, though not necessarily on the same scale, are replicated throughout the region every year during the monsoon season.

In the upper Alaknanda valley lies the village of Mandal. In early 1973 the villagers petitioned their annual request to the Forest Department to fell ash trees to make agricultural tools. It was turned down. In March, two agents from the Simon Company, a sports goods manufacturer, arrived in town. It transpired that the government had allocated a plot of forest area to the company; the same ash trees, in fact, that had been denied the local farmers. Angry words and unrest soon rippled through the village.

Under the leadership of activist Chandi Prasad Bhatt, the Dasoli Gram Swaraja Sangh, a local NGO, held a public meeting to discuss a plan of action.

'Our aim is not to destroy the trees,' Bhatt reportedly said, 'but to preserve them. When the men go to cut them, why don't we cling to the trees, and dare them to let their axes fall on our backs?'

According to some sources, this is exactly what they did. Others suggest that the lumbermen, on reaching Mandal village, were greeted by a blood-curdling rally of singing and drum-beating villagers. Completely overawed, they turned tail without actually reaching the forest on that, or any subsequent occasion. Despite further attempts, the Simon Company's permit expired and the woodcutters fled without taking a single branch.

Though the precise details of that particular protest are uncertain, the campaigns that it spawned were soon to have a profound impact on the future of forestry planning.

The word Chipko was derived from *chipkana*, Hindi for "to embrace". The idea of hugging trees to prevent them from being felled originated in the early 18th century in Rajasthan when people of the Bishnoi community stood successfully against the Maharaja of Jodhpur.

Two hundred and sixty years later, the same principle was re-employed, although the techniques were different. At some protests, large groups of people linked arms to form circles around the trees. At others, individual trees were embraced by women; a canny move, for it was culturally taboo for a man to touch a woman. The woodcutters had no choice but to withdraw.

"Hug the trees!" became the battle cry of the protestors and the songs of the poet Ganshyam Raturi resounded through the deodars and pines:

Embrace the trees and save them from being felled;
The property of our hills, save them from being looted.

The Sarvodaya campaigner, Sunderal Bahuguna, was heavily involved in Chipko from its early days. Coining the phrase "ecology is permanent economy", he and Chandi Prasad Bhatt were the public face of the movement. Bhawani Bhai operated at a lower-key grassroots level. In conversation he was swift to credit, not his vocal colleagues, but the tenacity and unstinting commitment of the hill women. It was they who undeniably formed the backbone of the movement and saved countless forests from government and commercial exploitation.

The first female "tree-hugger" was a woman called Gaura Devi.

In March 1974 the Forest Department granted permission to fell 2,500 trees on the land above the village of Reni, overlooking the Alaknanda River. On hearing that the woodcutters were coming, Gaura Devi mobilised a number of women and girls to confront the contractor's men when they arrived at the forest.

By coincidence, all the men of the village had travelled to Chamoli, a town several kilometres away, that morning. The government, after fourteen years' procrastination, had suddenly announced that it would be paying out compensation for land taken for military use following the Indo-China war. Not wishing to miss out on the opportunity, the men of the village downed tools and immediately journeyed to Chamoli to claim their payments. The only people remaining were the women and children. Bhatt and several other leading activists had been summoned to Gopeshwar for a meeting with a number of government officials.

Confronted by the delegation of militant women as they entered the forest, a few of the lumbermen immediately acquiesced to the protest. They were hill farmers themselves and sympathised with the situation. Others, however, had been drinking and started to become abusive and physically threatening. Fearlessly, Gaura Devi stood facing the barrel of a shot gun and proclaimed:

'This forest nurtures us like a mother. You will only be able to use your axes if you shoot me first.'

The stand-off lasted three days. Eventually the men retreated and the women triumphed. Gaura Devi, a middle-aged, uneducated widow, becae a role model for countless others after her and was hailed as the leader of the first, all-woman environmental action group.

There are numerous Chipko success stories. In 1980, the government finally introduced a complete, ten-year ban on the cutting of trees at altitudes above 1,000 metres. Although hailed as a triumph for the campaigners, the legislation produced the unfortunate by-products of strengthening the resolve of the timber mafia and further depriving the hill people of their forest rights. Nevertheless it was progress. By 1981, not only had the rate of felling declined massively, but over one million trees had been planted by Chipko workers.

To say that Chipko is about trees alone, however, is too simplistic. 'Our movement goes beyond the erosion of the land to the erosion of human values,' Chandi Prasad once said. The guardians of these values are the mothers and the current generation.

The indigenous right of a community to play an active role in the management of its own resources is the fundamental issue. The Pahari have no desire to monopolise the environment entirely for their own use. They do, however, fervently believe that it is most effectively managed by the people that know it best. Themselves.

But has the environmental intervention already done its worst; has mountain life slipped irretrievably towards total degeneration?

'You liking? Yes?'

A large wooden ladle hovered over my plate of rice. My hand shot out. Two stewed fish heads and four glazed eyes swung back into the pot.

'No, mama!' Pratap stopped his mother just in time. 'Mark is vegetarian,' I assume he said. His wife shyly placed a bowl of potatoes and carrots on the table. In her other arm she carried their eight-month old son.

Pratap took the child from her and bobbed him in the air. As he caught him in his broad hands, the boy squealed with delight, revealing a small tooth protruding through his top gum. His wife's intense expression eased into a smile as her son's podgy fingers stretched out and gripped the hem of her red headscarf. It was heart-warming to see a healthy, intelligent young man who had not gone "missing" to the plains revelling in a rare moment with his family.

Eight of us were crammed into the small living area. I sat cross-legged on a bed covered with a rough wool blanket, my plate balanced on my knee, hungrily shovelling lightly spiced potatoes and rice into my mouth. Voices chattered all around me in Hindi and Garhwali.

During the course of the meal the light had slowly ebbed away. Through the open doorway I could see thick clouds billowing above the trees. The air hung heavy, expectantly.

Just as Pratap's mother started to collect the plates, the sky flashed violently. A colossal crack shook the room. Shrieking, the baby burst into tears and the heavens responded with a barrage of hailstones.

As with many Garhwal houses, the family accommodation was situated on the first floor. Below, lived the animals. Above our heads lay a thin, corrugated tin roof; our only protection from the lashing deluge.

Pratap's father's voice strained above the deafening noise.

'What's he saying?' I asked Sandeep.

'Someone must have offended the *devta*, the god.'

I couldn't tell from Sandeep's expression whether he was amused or fearful.

∽∾

Although the Pahari in this area are predominantly Hindu, their religious beliefs and practices do not correspond easily with those in other parts of India.

The elements that constitute their world view, though disparate, are inter-connected, identified by a diversity and complexity of belief rather than any specific distinguishing features. Worship of the traditional Hindu gods and goddesses is mixed with more localised regional, village and family rituals and cults. Folklore, myth and a varied knowledge of scriptures and other religious books sit alongside a faith in spirits, ghosts, witches, demons and magic.

All these colours and shades of creed are blended on the palette to create a supernatural landscape that is intricately crafted yet completely alien to a global view with which most westerners are familiar. With the benefit of comparative religious studies in school and access to endless sources of media and Internet information, it is easy to take for granted that many of us possess an inherent sense of the bigger picture.

Even if we are uninformed about the specific details of other cultures and religions we are aware, at least, that they exist. These villagers, in the main, are not. Their panorama is informed by the few square kilometres surrounding their home, the earth beneath their feet, the sun, moon and constellations. It is constructed from tradition and the experience of what they see and believe to be true within their isolated lives.

A woman might worship the mountain peak towering above her as Kedarnath, lord of the mountain, unaware that across the valley others acknowledge the summit as one of the many abodes of Shiva. They, too, are oblivious to the countless other names bestowed upon it across India.

Although I'm in danger of gross reductionism, I don't wish to give the impression that the Pahari paradigm is primitive mumbo jumbo. I encountered a firm conviction and sincerity among the people I met, more so than I have witnessed in many western religious institutions. An innate sense of the sacred pervades *all* aspects of life. Inherently aware of the sanctity of their Himalayan surroundings, the Pahari invest every element of the landscape, rivers, trees, rocks and the peaks themselves, with mythological and religious significance.

Even the broadest of brush strokes, however, can be misleading. One Pahari's spirituality is another's superstition.

To differentiate between the two is academic. Even distinguishing between the natural and supernatural is problematic. For many interior village people it amounts to the same thing: this is what they know and this is how they live.

The role of the supernatural is as normal a function of everyday life as the hills and forests. Disease, disability, death, family troubles, sick animals, crop failure and economic difficulties are all attributable to karmic belief or to the intervention of one or more supernatural beings. Accordingly, considerable time, money and effort are invested in practices aimed at influencing these powers for good or evil.

While they accept that life rests in the non-negotiable hands of an impersonal, supreme deity, known in these parts variously as Bhagwan, Narayan or, quite simply, God, the Pahari also believe that this power may be appeased to influence daily life in a very real and tangible way. The weather, for example, is predetermined by an external force over which they have no control. Yet if the monsoon does not come at the expected time, ceremonies are held to encourage specific deities to release rain from the sky.

Although this inconsistency confounded my western sense of logic, for most Pahari the dichotomy is irrelevant. There's clearly some form of causal link between destiny and human petition that's to be accepted, not analysed. Fate is accomplished through the intervention of other forces.

"Our fields are cultivated only on faith in God," states a farmer interviewed for the *Mountain Voices* project.

> We have harvest if it rains, otherwise not. If it does not rain for a long time then we worship our local deities and compel them to bring us rain. The entire village gathers in the temple and we all pray. We all have full faith in our gods and goddesses. When worshipped like this, they will send us good rainfall - and on time! Nowadays the meteorological department gives advance information regarding rain and drought. This helps us to prepare ourselves.

A torrent of rain had washed away the hail but the storm continued to rage, the wind howling through the sodden, stooping branches of the deodars.

A few minutes earlier, some of the family had made a quick dash outside to the kitchen with the pots and plates, leaving Sandeep and I sitting on the bed. Tsering lay stretched out on the other mattress.

'I'm surprised she's able to sleep with this noise,' I said.

'Tsering's expecting a baby,' he replied affectionately. 'She rests anywhere!'

Looking around the room, my eye caught a small, gold lamp that burnt on the shelf above where Tsering lay. Against the wall leant a double picture-frame, each side containing a black and white photograph. One of them, a smiling boy aged about eight, was bent and faded. The other, a handsome young man, possibly in his early twenties, appeared to have been taken fairly recently.

'Who are in the photographs?'

'They are Pratap's older brothers.' Sandeep looked around discreetly. 'They are both expired.'

'Oh?'

'The younger boy died when Pratap was a baby. I'm not sure how.'

'And the other?'

'He was killed last year in a coach accident. It was so tragic. Now Pratap is only son.'

'His parents must have been devastated.'

'Yes. That's why they now like Pratap nearby. Work for him at SASA is perfect. He is earning money and seeing his family every week.'

I reviewed my earlier thoughts about Pratap not being a "missing" man. Even if he wanted to travel to the city for an education or job, he had no choice. Family responsibility, in his case, took priority.

The photographs puzzled me. Surrounded by a garland of flowers and a burning lamp, they resembled the shrines to gods and goddesses I had seen in other homes and temples.

'That's what it is,' said Sandeep.

The most commonly worshipped supernatural beings are known as *devtas* and *devis*, gods and goddesses. Each village has its own devta, distinguishable from that of other villages and regions. The generic term for this local god is *isht devta*, although the specific deity varies from village to village. The isht devta, worshiped jointly by most of the villagers at a central *mandir*, temple under the management of the pandit, is the focal point of communal belief and activity.

Then there is the *kul devta*, or family god. This deity is worshiped within the home by members of a particular household, not jointly with the other villagers or under the supervision of the pandit. Devotion to one particular kul devta is passed down the family line.

In addition to the isht devta and kul devta, certain gods are worshiped over a geographical area which far exceeds the village boundaries. For example, Surkanda Devi, a manifestation of the Hindu mother goddess Durga, is revered all along the Mussoorie Ridge above Dehradun. In addition there are the state gods such as Kedarnath and Badrinath. On a daily basis, though, devotion is directed towards the village and family devtas. A pilgrimage to visit the shrines of the regional gods is only made annually, where great festive gatherings involve worship and sacrifice for several days.

The influence and control of the devtas over people's minds and existence is very strong; daily life is governed by maintaining the right relationship with these deities. Patterns of worship and devotion vary considerably not only from village to village but also in the variety of ways the kul and isht devtas are appropriated. The specific machinations of the devtas are largely irrelevant, the main point being that these beliefs are still widely-practiced today.

The devtas may originate from any number of sources but that is of little significance to most people. They may be linked to the great Hindu gods, ancestral spirits or ghosts of dead relatives. Some may not be traceable to any known source at all. Occasionally a shrine is created in a home in honour of a deceased family member, as in the case of Pratap's older brothers. They are worshipped as a *pitr devta* and their spirit is invoked in times of need.

Taking central place on the shelf, the shrine was no inert memorial to his siblings but an active force in the daily lives of Pratap's family.

'Is this what you believe?' I asked Sandeep.

'No,' he thought for a moment. 'I am Christian. But for Pratap's family, the belief is very real.'

Large sheets of battered corrugated tin scattered the ground. A sheared fragment rested gingerly against a broken wall, another across the pathway. Men stood shaking their heads and rubbing their chins while the women and children transported items of furniture and clothes to a neighbouring home.

A square room, enclosed by bricks, lay ripped open below us, its roof wrenched off by the storm. The sun, low on the horizon, illuminated the rich cobalt sky, not a wisp of cloud in sight.

Having just climbed the steep path above the village, we stood on top of the hill gazing down.

With life so vulnerably exposed to the cruel ploys of nature, I understood why people spent so much time and effort appropriating the gods to deliver good fortune. So much was in their hands.

14
Charmed Life

The public removal of clothes at the breakfast table is just not cricket

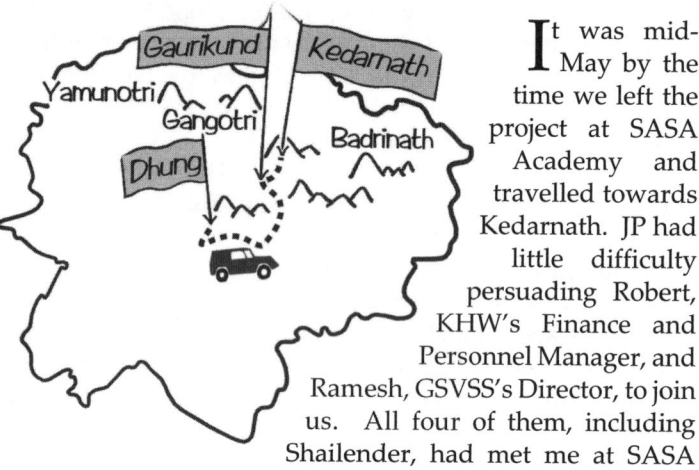

It was mid-May by the time we left the project at SASA Academy and travelled towards Kedarnath. JP had little difficulty persuading Robert, KHW's Finance and Personnel Manager, and Ramesh, GSVSS's Director, to join us. All four of them, including Shailender, had met me at SASA the previous evening. Although our ultimate destination was the village of Tilwara to visit a new initiative named *Samvedna*, we decided to take a few days' diversion en route to join other pilgrims on the Kedarnath Dham.

The four main river sources of the Ganges are known collectively as the *Char Dham*. *Char* is Hindi for four and *Dham* means "abode" or "seat". For many centuries, millions of *yatris*, pilgrims, have travelled from many parts of India to these four pilgrimage centres, the most holy in all the land. Starting at Haridwar, about 200 kilometres north of Delhi, they devoted between two and four months to complete the

Char Dham Yatra by foot. It was a significant spiritual journey demanding time, commitment and stamina. The mountainous paths were often steep and treacherous, frequently rendered impassable by landslides and earthquakes. Perilous rope bridges swung between the valley sides to help pilgrims negotiate the gushing rivers below.

Following the Ganges up to Devprayag they trekked up to Yamunotri and then headed eastwards over the ridges to Gangotri, Kedarnath and finally Badrinath. *Dharamasalas*, rest houses, strategically positioned along the route provided simple accommodation for the pilgrims to recuperate after a long day's walking.

Since the construction of the motor roads, however, most people now undertake the pilgrimage in just a few days by bus, jeep or car. It is possible to drive right up to the temple doors at Gangotri and Badrinath, although it is still necessary to complete the fourteen kilometre approach to the temples at Yamunotri and Kedarnath by footpath. The religious destinations remain as they have been for many centuries but I imagine the spiritual significance of the journey may have diminished considerably.

Traditional Hindu belief suggests that anyone who undertakes the *yatra*, pilgrimage, will achieve moksha, liberation from the cycle of death and rebirth. Nowadays the pilgrimage may be achieved with no more commitment than a few days' holiday and the price of a bus ticket. Nevertheless, the official Uttarakhand Tourism Development Board guide states that, even though the Char Dham are easily accessible through a network of roads, the pilgrimage remains a deeply "fulfilling experience."

Fulfilling maybe, but I suspect the experience has gradually slipped down the spiritual continuum that has sacred pilgrimage at one end and religious tourism at the other. Whether the yatra is sufficiently edifying for the 21st century Hindu pilgrim to achieve total liberation from the cycle of karma, only time and fate will determine.

The pilgrimage season runs between the middle of April and November. Much of the trekking route exceeds 4000 metres and is inaccessible, due to snow and freezing temperatures, for the remainder of the year. The busiest part of the season is the two months preceding the monsoon. The coming of the torrential rains in July, causing rock falls and landslides, makes driving conditions extremely hazardous. Despite the fact that over 200 pilgrims a year are killed in motor accidents, people still continue to travel throughout the rainy season and beyond. Post-monsoon, though extremely cold, the mountain scenery is apparently at its most impressive.

The trekking route to the temple, having opened the day before our arrival, was teeming with Hindus flocking from all over India, travelling by foot, coach and jeep to offer *puja*, worship, to their chosen deities. Many had already visited the shrines at Yamunotri and Gangotri while others, like us, were travelling only to Kedarnath. Precarious tracks masquerading as roads, potholed and puddled, twisted up the steep mountainside allowing little room for vehicles to pass. Betrayed by their deep gashes, the strategically placed boulders proved ineffectual in their efforts to prevent heedless drivers from toppling over the edge.

Pilgrims perched on bus roofs, singing, swaying and clutching their luggage. Others hung out the windows with colourful clothes drying and wafting in their faces, unconcerned that their lives were continually at risk. Possibly they subscribed to the common belief that the soul of a pilgrim who dies while participating in the Char Dham will be fast-tracked to moksha. Small stone shrines dotted the route to commemorate those who had perished on the road.

I fully trusted Ramesh at the wheel of our jeep but was scared witless by the reckless antics of the other drivers, especially those from the plains who had clearly never driven in the mountains. Recalling the newspaper reports that I'd read before leaving Dehradun of the several lives already lost in road accidents since the beginning of the pilgrimage season, I was now witnessing the evidence first-hand. The all-too frequent sight of tumbled cars and buses wrapped around trees at the bottom of the ravines did little to calm my nerves.

Only days earlier a coach had tipped over the edge at one particularly precipitous point, taking 26 of its passengers to a cruel and untimely death. On their way to a marriage ceremony, among those killed were the groom, his immediate family and many friends. Was this their karma, I wondered? Pondering how human life appeared so expendable in this fatalistic culture, I distracted myself by focusing on the splendour of the snow-covered peaks.

The trekking base for Kedarnath is the densely compact town of Gaurikund. Words such as "bijou" and "quaint" spring to mind because, in a way, it was. But in most respects, it really wasn't. Grimy guest houses and hotels, stacked one on top of another, evoked the atmosphere of a dilapidated alpine resort, compressed to a quarter of its size but attempting to accommodate many more guests than it ought. Gaurikund was the residential equivalent of a vacuum-packed bag of dehydrated food before boiling water is added; a dense concentration of unpalatably potent flavours. It was a claustrophobic intensity of buildings, people, noise and smells desperately in need of space to expand and breathe.

But what did it matter? Gaurikund was a functional resort serving the needs of the religious tourists wanting to reach Kedarnath. No one stayed more than a day or two.

Arriving at dusk, we were guided by the whistle-blowing traffic police to park on the outskirts of the town. Anticipating a problematic search for accommodation, we decided to split up: Ramesh and I stayed with the jeep while JP, Shailender and Robert trawled the guesthouses for rooms. Mentally exhausted from the perils of the mountain roads, I soon dozed off. An hour or so later the others returned, apparently having managed to secure the last remaining beds in town.

Still half-asleep, I lagged behind as we bumped and pushed our way through the crowded streets and alley ways. Porters, crowned heftily with bags and suitcases, scurried between vehicles and hotels. Chai and tiffin stall owners hurriedly brewed tea and fried samosas to keep up with the roaring demand. Groups of pilgrims huddled together under a collective mass of red, disposable macs as a light drizzle of rain began to fall. Families and friends pitched make-shift camps by the roadside, complete with thermos flasks, blankets, deckchairs, and baskets of curry-filled Tupperware containers.

The pungent blend of wood smoke, buffalo dung, incense and urine choked the air, assaulting my nostrils as only the night-time aroma of a mountain village street can.

We climbed the stairs to the hotel. Knowing that this was the last availability in Gaurikund, I prepared myself for the worst. How surprised was I, then, when the porter opened the door to my room.

Though spartanly furnished, the room was spotlessly clean and contained all I really needed: a large, double bed covered with brand new, bug-free blankets. I discovered later that the room was a recent addition to the hotel and I was its first occupant. Admittedly it was freezing cold and the promise of hot water in the ensuite bathroom was, as usual, a figment of the manager's imagination but, nevertheless, it surpassed all expectation. The thrill of electricity and running water having eluded me for almost two weeks, my impoverished, western constitution jumped with joy at the prospect of such palatial indulgence.

The other guys were also treated royally, sharing a spacious suite of rooms, double beds and a large bathroom.

Famous for its hot springs, Gaurikund has several large, single-sex tanks in which pilgrims bathe en masse to wash away their sins prior to ascending Kedarnath. The women immerse themselves fully clothed in discreetly enclosed chambers while the men strip down to their underwear and bathe publicly, exposed to the chilly elements.

In pursuit of food, we discovered a restaurant opposite one such pool, overcrowded with penitent Hindus cleansing their souls in eighteen inches of murky grey, lukewarm water. Hungry and shivering, I walked past in my five layers of thermal clothing. The idea of a quick dip before supper didn't appeal in the slightest.

The restaurant's crispy dosas, rice and spicy vegetables were among the best that I'd tasted throughout India. It was a sign of good things to come; the following lunchtime we were to enjoy a magnificent array of dishes at the summit of Kedarnath itself, causing me to wonder how such quality produce could be obtained, cooked and priced so reasonably at such a high altitude. As transporting food up the mountain was not an easy task, I had anticipated it would be pre-packaged, dull and expensive, not so tasty, fresh and nutritious.

Replete, we left the restaurant. The soak pit opposite was empty, save a solitary pilgrim. What's more, the few inches of tepid sludge had been replaced by a pool full of invitingly clear, steaming water. Sulphurous emissions hovered, genie-like, over the water, twisting and cavorting into tantalising phrases. 'Come on, jump in - you know you want to,' they hissed seductively.

I shivered and breathed in a gasp of frosty air.

'You only live once,' tempted the words.

JP had already started to take off his clothes.

'It's late at night, my stomach is full and the temperature's sub-zero,' I rationalised.

'Wimp,' the steam cried.

'I'm too tired.'

'Coward.'

'But...'

I was in.

Floating on my back with only my nostrils exposed to the icy air, I imagined my lingering stresses of the day waft upwards, merge with the steam and, poof, dissipate into the nocturnal breeze.

Time for a confession: I'm not a bath person. I find lying in a tub of hot water the most mindless, anti-relaxing activity conceivable. Candles, soothing music, a glass of red wine... forget it. The moment my body is immersed, all the other things I could, and should, be doing race through my mind and I am compelled to climb out. A bath serves one purpose only: to get clean. For that, give me a shower any day.

But wallowing gently in this steaming hot pool of mineral water, the sharp air biting at my nose and toes, gazing at the star-encrusted night sky, the ding-ding of the temple bell tinkling in the distance and Basingstoke a million light years away: that was something else.

Well, up to a point.

Within ten minutes I really had indulged enough and was drying myself as quickly as possible before the beads of sweat on my forehead solidified into ice. You can have too much of a good thing, you know.

Back at the hotel, the conversation turned to whether or not we should attempt an assault on Kedarnath the following morning. To complete the 28 kilometre round trip we would need to start walking soon after dawn. That's not my favourite time of day, but we had come so far to experience this once-in-a-life-time opportunity. Why was I hesitating?

Another confession: I have withheld some vital information.

As we had sat shivering in our rooms earlier in the evening, Ramesh suggested that our bones might be warmed by a shot of rum and hot water. Who was I to disagree? I've also failed to narrate that the day before was my birthday. Due to an abundance of children and an unavailability of alcohol, however, it had been neither appropriate nor possible for my friends to propose a small toast. A post-celebratory libation, therefore, was in order. As if by magic, the sulphur genie of the soak pit materialised, clutching a whisky bottle, or two, and a jug of hot water.

'Janam din mubarak ho, Mark!' (Happy birthday, Mark!)

'Janam din *bahut* mubarak ho, Mark!!' (Very, happy birthday, Mark!!)

'Janam din *bahut bahut* mubarak ho, Mark!!!' (Very, very happy birthday, Mark!!!)

By the time we started to discuss the following day's trek, I was pleasantly drowsy and looking forward to a lie-in.

After further bone-warming deliberation we reached the monumental non-decision to review the situation in the morning. And so to bed.

In the courtyard directly below my bedroom window stood a small temple. Because Hindu houses of worship are amply scattered throughout most Indian towns and villages, I didn't notice it when we arrived the previous evening. But I sure as heck knew it was there at four o'clock the following morning when the pujari started beating his drum, the bell went a-dinging and my head went a-pounding.

A few minutes later, there was a knock on my door: Ramesh, fully dressed, was holding a morning cup of chai. Decision made. We were going up to Kedarnath.

First stop, though, breakfast. We returned to the previous evening's restaurant and ordered dosas and chutney. I also requested three cups of coffee, not out of greed, but because Indian coffee was rarely made the way I like it. It's not unreasonable, I suggest, to expect three things from a morning brew: one, that I can taste it, two, that it contains a modicum of caffeine and, three, that it is served in a vessel larger than a thimble. Most Indian coffee, however, comes in a small metal beaker: two weak mouthfuls and it's gone.

I also like peace and quiet in the morning. Though I'm generally a sociable being, I don't appreciate excessive noise or conversation before seven o'clock.

Shortly after we'd arrived, half a dozen women from the Punjab sat down at the table behind us. I don't know the collective term for a group of Punjabi females, but I suggest a "cackle", "screech", or "yatter" would not be inappropriate. The last seems to capture the mood most effectively.

This yatter of Punjabi prattlers soon started to natter uncontrollably, whipping themselves up into a frenzy within minutes. Gesticulating wildly, chattering hysterically, anyone would have thought they'd just witnessed a murder or won the lottery. Never in my life have I seen such a small group of people communicate with so much vigour. And VOLUME.

Intrigued, I asked JP if he had any idea what they were discussing.

'I don't speak Punjabi, Mark, but I think they're trying to decide what to eat,' he said with a wry smile. Joining me in finding these yattering yatris a huge source of amusement, this was one of those times of convenience when JP distanced himself from his fellow Indians, claiming his Nepali bloodline as his dominant gene pool.

But that was only the first act of the breakfast cabaret. Moments later, a rather corpulent, middle-aged man stood up from the table on my right and removed his coat. Then his pullover. Next his shirt. Standing in his vest, he bent over, untied his laces, took off his shoes, stood upright again and dropped his trousers. I blinked.

Then off came the vest. 'No more, please,' I cried. 'I'm eating my breakfast.'

Dosa in hand, poised between plate and mouth, I couldn't believe my eyes. I looked around and spotted another man in a state of undress. Then one more. Before long we were surrounded by several barefoot, semi-naked Hindu pilgrims, spare tyres wobbling, all arranging their clothes in nice neat piles on their chairs.

What's the collective term for that, I ask?

Adding insult to injury, a large mirror ran the length of the back wall. As one particularly porcine gentleman stood primping and preening himself, a grotesque image of his grooming antics was reflected back into the restaurant. Whichever way I looked, there was no escaping the tawdry performance.

The penny dropped. As they made their way towards the door, I realised that the men were using the place as a changing room. They were preparing to wash away their sins in the outside pool at the expense of my sullied sensibilities and total loss of appetite. I would have been outraged had I not been so bemused by their audacity. Completely oblivious to their audience, they executed the whole routine as if it was quite normal behaviour.

Possessing an inherent Britisher sense of fair play, I suggest that the public removal of clothing at the breakfast table is just not cricket. I half-wished I'd had the foresight to pee in the pool the previous evening as an act of premeditated retribution, if one can have such a thing.

Setting off from the parking area above Gaurikund, I caught intermittent glimpses of the mountain range in which Kedarnath nestled. Knowing that, in a few hours' time, I would be climbing above the snowline of the Himalayas motivated me to persevere through the penetrating chill of the early morning.

As the sun began to creep above the peaks I began to peel off my layers of clothing. I don't recollect ever experiencing so many types of weather as in those hours up and down the trek; freezing air, blazing sunshine, driving rain and an impressive dowsing of snow. The fleece and jacket were in and out of my rucksack every few minutes.

Disappointingly, some of the challenge has been removed from the ascent to Kedarnath. The climb is not so much a trek as a long, steep walk. For most of the way the track is cemented and, for the first few kilometres, shallowly zigzags its route upwards; it rises a hundred metres or so in one direction and then doubles back on itself. I would frequently discover a short cut where a path had been worn away in the scraggy undergrowth by people and goats taking a steeper, but more direct, route between the sections of the main track.

A large number of yatris were attempting the pilgrimage on foot. Others took advantage of alternative modes of transport, the most common being the mule.

While the breakfast cabaret had been in full swing, Robert and Ramesh had disappeared for a few minutes to negotiate a reasonable mule rate, having been informed that it was *impossible* to complete the return journey to Kedarnath on foot:

'You must be taking a mule.'

'Why?'

'It is too far.'

'And what do you do?'

'I hire mules.'

Now there's a surprise.

Great marketing ploy but I didn't buy it. With a quick mental calculation I worked out that we could easily cover the 28 kilometres in seven hours, with time for lunch and several rest-stops thrown in for good measure. But the mule-wallah had obviously worked his persuasive charm and JP, Ramesh, Robert and Shailender insisted that they wouldn't be able to walk all the way. They then tried to persuade me to take one also. After several minutes of persistent nagging, I conceded. Secretly, though, I had no intention of mounting the poor creature unless in an absolute emergency. This trip was the fulfilment of a life-long dream to walk in the Himalayas. I was not going to let anything, man or beast, deprive me of that thrill.

The other reasons for not travelling by mule were far more practical. Firstly, they ambled painstakingly slowly up the paths. It was far quicker to walk. Secondly, and I will try to explain this as delicately as I can, was comfort, or the lack of it. It was clearly evident from the agonized expressions on the riders' faces that leaning backwards at 45 degrees on a worn saddle was an experience to be endured, not enjoyed. This discomfort was compounded, however, on descent, particularly for the men. Tipping forwards, jerked along by the bumpy, rocking motion of the mule produced a level of pain that made me entirely grateful, if not a little smug, that I had decided to walk. Coming down the mountain was a four-legged roller coaster ride on which a certain part of the male anatomy absorbed all the strain of the knocks and jolts. Admittedly, my thighs and calves were a little stiff the next day, but that was nothing in comparison with the pain the others suffered.

The mules trudged up the track at a snail's pace but trotted downwards at a fair old lick, making it necessary to dodge out of the way or risk a nudge sideways by a powerful flick of their head as they passed. Occasionally I was faced with half a dozen rampant creatures careering around the corner at speed, leaving little choice but to dive towards the gutter.

Public toilets strategically lined the route but there were nowhere near enough to service the volume of pilgrims in need of relief. Consequently, many people, no I'll be specific, many men, did their business at the side of the track. The mules were less discerning; they did it anywhere. Whenever the skies opened, a slurry of mule dung, mud and urine gushed down the overflowing gutters and trickled across the path, providing another hurdle to negotiate. If careful, it was usually possible to avoid wading through the squelching excrement but there was no escape from the acrid stench of mule urine.

Some yatris, the frail, rich or lazy, neither walked nor rode a mule. They were transported up the mountain in a *doli*, a simple sedan chair supported by wooden poles and carried by four *doli-wallahs*, young men of considerable strength and stamina. Deserving every rupee they earned, they not only bore the load of the, usually, plump pilgrim but had to carefully synchronise their steps with one another. Intense concentration and pain were painted across their faces. Coming downhill, like the mules, they picked up tremendous speed. Taking a wide corner they would shout 'Side! Side!' and the other pilgrims were wise to part swiftly and let them pass.

Dodging out of the way of the mules, doli-wallahs and streams of excrement, however, didn't prevent me from pausing every so often to savour the view. The greatest exhilaration came the moment I caught sight, for the first time, of the glacial ice fronts rolling down the mountainside.

The Kedarnath path followed the course of the Mandakini River as it flowed out from beneath the icy masses, trickling over the rocky moraine on its journey to the valleys below. Towering above the steep slopes of the river gully rose the austere range of peaks. They suddenly appeared spectacularly close.

The optical games played by mountains have always intrigued me. One moment the range appeared so remote and the next it seemed within touching distance. I felt lost in the distorted perspective of its grandeur.

The land levelled out a few kilometres further up the track, widening into a vast mule-park. Hundreds of animals were tethered together on the plateau, the rich threads of their coloured blankets catching the sunlight and their bells jangling in the slight breeze. In the distance the tapered, grey dome of the temple rose above the sprawling tin-roofed, concrete buildings of Kedarnath, not the most attractive of mountain villages.

The epic *Mahabharata* narrates the story of the temple's origin. The Pandava brothers, fully penitent of the destruction they caused on the battlefields of Kurukshetra, sought forgiveness from Lord Shiva. But the great god was so displeased with their evil acts that he proved deliberately elusive as they chased him through the mountains of the region. To avoid detection he turned himself into a bull and took refuge in the pastures at Kedarnath. Hotly pursued by the Pandavas he plunged headfirst into the ground. One of the brothers, however, managed to catch him by the tail.

Unable to disappear into the mountain entirely, Shiva left his hindquarters jutting out from the earth. Such was the force with which he entered the ground that his body split up. It re-emerged at various places throughout Garhwal: his arms at Tungnath, his face at Rudranath, his hair at Kalpeshwar and his naval at Madhmaheshwar. Known collectively as the *Panch Kedar*, the appearance of these five main shrines ensured that Shiva could be worshiped simultaneously at different temples throughout the region. Impressed by the Pandava brothers' earnest efforts to seek absolution, he eventually forgave them.

To this day, pilgrims congregate around the large rock inside the temple's inner sanctum, believing it to be the protruding rump of Shiva. Worshipping him with gifts of rice, coconuts and flowers, they trust that their endeavours will take them one step closer to achieving moksha and release from the cycle of life and death.

Before entering the surrounding precinct I removed my boots and socks, depositing them with the temple shoe minder in exchange for ten rupees and a promise that he would keep them safe until my return. Sensing the biting stone slabs beneath my feet, I noticed that other people had kept their socks on. I hesitated for a moment before realising I'd done the right thing. As I tentatively moved inside, the light and temperature dropped noticeably and I felt an icy liquid trickle though my toes. Hoping it was water, I looked down but it was too murky to identify. Slightly unnerved, I consoled myself with the though that, whatever it was, at least I would have dry socks to wear later.

Entering the inner chamber, I had to duck down and crawl through a very narrow gap in the rock. Once inside, it was impossible to see anything at all. As my feet sloshed cautiously through several inches of dark, freezing fluid I put my hands out to touch the clammy wall for guidance. Fervent fingers flailed through the air, groping and grappling for the shrine, blindly oblivious to the apprehensive Angrez in their way.

A putrescent whiff shot up my nose. Incomprehensible sounds of zealously chanted mantras snatched the stagnant air, rising and rebounding off the echoing chamber ceiling to produce the most cacophonous din imaginable. Smoke from incense, candles and lamps further stifled the thick, claustrophobic atmosphere, through which I could just discern the large rock in the centre of the sanctum. Devotees were shrieking, wailing, rocking back and forth in a trance-like stupor, adorning the shrine with handfuls of rice, flower petals and coconut. I looked on bewildered, every sense assailed.

The object of worship for these devout pilgrims, the zenith of weeks of travel and their means to salvation appeared to be a lump of rock, Shiva's rump, daubed in a rancid rainbow of rotting vegetables.

I remembered Krishna telling me that many Hindus regard the external world as *maya*, an illusion; it's the internal that counts. But this was a snapshot of Hinduism that, however much I trawled the deepest recesses on my soul, I couldn't fathom. How did this square with the bright lights and joy of the Shiva Temple Festival in Cochin, the exuberance of Holi, or the inner peace I experienced at the Shantivanam Ashram in South India? For me, it was one of two things: the starkest reality or the most disturbing nightmare. Either way, I had to get out.

It may have been the altitude sickness taking hold - we had trekked to a height over 4000 metres - but I suddenly felt weak and nauseous. Gagging and clamouring over the prostrate pilgrims I made a dash for fresh air. Once outside the sanctum gate, I was compelled to retreat further. Tripping down the steps, I retrieved my boots and socks and hurriedly put them on. Convinced I was about to pass out, I had to get away from the temple.

It was only after I found myself beyond the precinct walls that my head started to clear and my pulse calmed. I breathed in a lungful of cold, clean air.

Physically, emotionally and spiritually I had never experienced such an oppressive atmosphere in my life. For the second time in as many days I looked to the mountains for distraction. That's why I was there; I had trekked the fourteen kilometre pilgrimage to savour the sheer magnificence of the Himalayan landscape. And when, a few moments later, the snow began to fall, I was in my own heaven.

Aum Shanti
Let there be peace. Peace, beautiful peace.
Peace within, peace without. Peace in this world,
Peace for all beings.

15
The Certainty of Chance

About 70 million people in India have some form of mental or physical disability

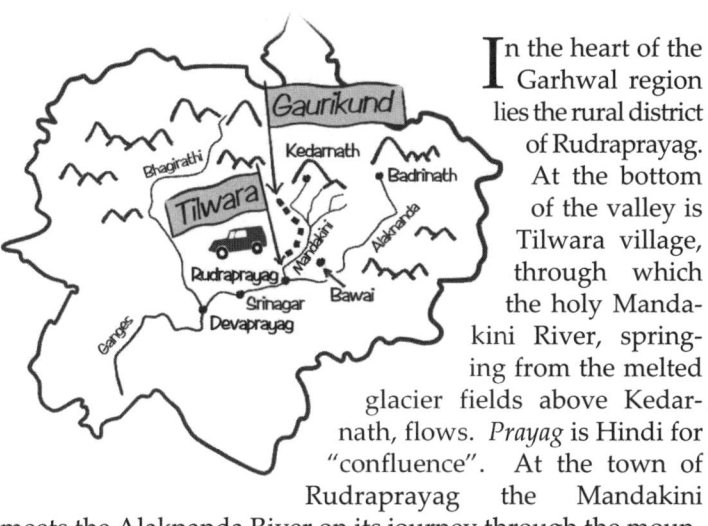

In the heart of the Garhwal region lies the rural district of Rudraprayag. At the bottom of the valley is Tilwara village, through which the holy Mandakini River, springing from the melted glacier fields above Kedarnath, flows. *Prayag* is Hindi for "confluence". At the town of Rudraprayag the Mandakini meets the Alaknanda River on its journey through the mountains from above Badrinath. Both rivers run together until they converge with the holy and legendary Bhagirathi at Devaprayag to form the beginning of the Ganges.

Above the snowline at Kedarnath the weather had been raw and damp. A day later, the sun beat down menacingly as we stood on the parched hillside overlooking the Tilwara valley. The lofty peaks of Kedarnath and Badrinath rose majestically before us, coated with a fresh dusting of snowfall. There was no escaping Shiva's watchful eye.

The physical contour of the land mirrored the hills surrounding SASA Academy but the terraces, dusty and arid, scarcely produced sufficient wheat and rice to feed their inhabitants. As the crow flew, Dhung was only 25 kilometres away but the contrast was pronounced; far fewer trees provided shade in the summer or protection from the harsh winter weather.

Ramesh had driven the jeep up the winding track above Tilwara for a few kilometres but, on reaching the small village of Pali, had pulled over and parked.

'We must continue on foot,' he announced, a decision not made from choice. We had reached the end of the road.

We intended to visit some of the differently-abled children living in the small hamlets Jailli and Kandali who had recently benefited from the medical intervention offered by a pioneering KHW initiative called *Samvedna*.

'There is an unusually high incidence of disability in this part of Garhwal,' said JP.

'Why?' I asked.

'Actually there are many reasons, none of which have been proven. In the first instance, we have committed our resources to help alleviate the problem rather than research the cause. That can happen in time.'

Because the children's homes were so remote, it was only possible for the Samvedna team to visit them every few weeks. Therefore it made sense, as we were in the vicinity, to make a detour on the way back to Dehradun.

'Do you mind, Mark?' JP had asked.

Did I mind? I was relishing every experience.

Joining us was Sujan, a young man who worked as a volunteer on the project. Having lost both his arms in a childhood accident, he had direct experience of the challenges faced by differently-abled children and adults living in the mountains. He had joined our group earlier that morning in Tilwara.

Once we had parked, Sujan approached a nearby house, re-appearing a few minutes later with an athletic lad aged about eleven.

'Our guide,' JP translated.

Climbing up the terraces carved out of unforgiving mountain slopes, I listened as JP and Ramesh explained how Samvedna came into being.

Shankar Thapa, the youngest of three children from Kandoli village near Dehradun, was born with two club feet. Although club foot is the most common birth defect in the world, very little is known about its cause. The genetic malfunction seems to run in families, with incidence rates increasing significantly when several direct family members have the condition.

Due to poor living conditions and his parents' inability to provide for his needs adequately, Shankar suffered constant pain. As the local doctors were unable to help his deteriorating condition, out of desperation, his parents resorted to superstitious remedies. During a solar-eclipse, as his body thrashed about in agony, they buried his twisted feet vertically in mud for several hours.

Shankar started attending Dehradun Public School in 2002. In April of the following year, Mark and Julie Thomas visited the school to see those children, including Shankar, that CHILD's Trust supported.

Observing that he was unable to walk properly, Mark asked if anything could be done to help Shankar. CHILD's Trust agreed to pay for the consultant's advice and the subsequent medical costs. This small, but highly significant, act enabled KHW to facilitate medical assistance.

Although Shankar's parents were initially sceptical, they eventually consented to corrective surgery for their son. Following his operation, they found it difficult to keep his wounds clean. Knowing that any infection would cause greater problems, Dolly Francis, the school's Headteacher, visited his home regularly to dress the wounds. One year later, and after much physiotherapy, Shankar was able to walk and run for the first time in his life. The success of this medical intervention seeded the inspiration to help more children with disabilities.

'Why did you feel it was important that KHW should become involved?' I asked JP.

'Life in India for people affected by physical and mental disabilities is inexplicably tough,' he explained. 'For those living in poor rural communities the difficulties are compounded many times over. Disability is often perceived as a punishment, a curse or bad karma. People accept it as a fact of life. Government policy is weak and most of society takes an apathetic stance, even within the social sector. Historically, those affected by disability have had little voice and no one to advocate on their behalf. The case for urgent steps to facilitate care, treatment and rehabilitation in the mountains was compelling. That's why we're doing this work now.'

Released in August 2004, India's first-ever disability census report states that around 22 million people have some form of mental or physical disability. *Disability and the Law*, a compilation of judgments on disability rights published a year later, claims that the figure is nearer to 70 million. That's more than the entire population of the UK. 75% of those people with disabilities live in rural areas.

Precipitated by a number of campaigns, India slowly woke up to the rights of its disabled citizens during the 1990s. A programme of disability laws passed by central government included the significant 1995 Disability Act which gave people with disabilities equality of opportunity, protection of rights and full participation in society. This ground-breaking legislation, heralding a new dawn for India's disabled minority, represented the end of a long, arduous struggle. But the hard-earned victory of the activists was short-lived. It soon became apparent that the powers-that-be were once again doing what the bureaucratic elite did best: impressive legislation, hopeless implementation. In this regard, little has changed over the past decade.

At policy level, the "in principle" commitment appeared incontrovertible. Translation of intent into action, however, was another matter; the laws were certainly worth the paper on which they were written but that, it seems, is pretty much where they remained.

Despite the passing of the legislation in the mid-nineties, it was clear that society's entrenched attitudes were disinclined to change overnight. The campaigners persevered, however, and the situation improved by degree. Members of the disability rights movement rallied en masse and a number of test cases were tried in the courts. Holes in the law were exposed and the intransigent ignorance of some of the non-disabled population was called to account. A few sound judgements were made and the efforts of the activists were rewarded in part. But they only scratched the surface.

On 10 September, 2004, *OneWorld South Asia* reported that over 100 disabled rights campaigners gathered at a parliamentary convention in Mumbai to present a charter of demands to India's six main political parties. Their four page memorandum focused on issues of basic civil rights, education, employment and access to buildings and public transport. Though it also included a request for appropriate polling facilities ahead of the forthcoming state elections, many people felt unmotivated to exercise their democratic voting rights:

"Why should we vote when none of the political parties are bothered about the disabled?" questioned Ketan Kothari from the National Association for the Blind.

The convenor of the Disabled Rights Group, Javed Abidi, who was instrumental in the passing of the 1995 Disability Act also expressed scepticism: "It has been nine years since the Disability Act was passed but nothing good has been done for the disabled so far."

His claim was supported by Sudha Balchandran, Director of the National Society for Equal Opportunity for Handicap: "There is a constant need to convince the government and general public about the seriousness and sensitivity of the issue," he said. "We had to literally fight with the government of Maharashtra to make a flyover at Ghatkoper in Mumbai disabled-friendly. No one seems to be giving serious thought to implementing the rights of the disabled."

India has a 3% minimum reservation quota in employment and education for people with disabilities. Yet in Maharashtra, India's third largest state, a disabled population of 1.5 million struggled to raise its voice above the parapet of apathy.

The situation is amplified further for those people with disabilities living in the rural interior villages of the Himalayas. There, more than anywhere, the legislation-versus-implementation stumbling block continues to thwart attempts at practical, sustainable action. In theory, for example, the law offers provision for free education, transport and books for young people with disabilities in Uttarakhand. But nowhere in the state is the Act applied, least of all the rural interior.

According to the 2004 disability census report, 2% of the national population is disabled. This figure increases to just under 3% for the districts of Tehri Garhwal and Rudraprayag; that's 50% higher than the national average. Though, to date, no documented evidence has been gathered to prove the causes, these statistics confirm that the *incidence* of disability in the interior villages in Samvedna's target area is unusually high. If the *Disability and the Law* claim that 6% of the population has some form of disability is nearer the truth, the proportional increase it represents for the region is significant.

'Sandeep said you had a fright the other night at SASA!' laughed Shailender.

'What do you mean?'

'The toilet!'

'Ah, that!' We'd been trekking for about 30 minutes by this point. I'd forgotten all about the incident to which Shailender was referring.

'What happened?' asked Robert.

'No!' I was embarrassed. 'Let's carry on walking.'

'Come on!' goaded JP.

Sujan, not understanding why the others were sniggering, asked Ramesh to explain. Then grinning, he joined in the encouragement.

'OK, then,' I said reluctantly, realising that I wasn't going to get away with keeping quiet. 'It's nothing really.'

Shailender coughed.

'The other night I woke up really needing to pee. I tried to get back to sleep but couldn't; it was too cold.'

'So?'

'In the end I got up. Well, you know how far away the toilet is…'

'Yes.'

'… and there are a few trees near the room.'

'Acchha.'

'So what would you do? It was absolutely pitch black and completely silent. Apart from the sound of me, you know…'

'And?'

'Suddenly I heard this noise in the bushes.'

'What kind of noise?' asked Robert.

'Sort of like heavy breathing. A rasping, wheezing sound.'

'A leopard,' said JP, matter-of-factly.

'Yeah right, that's what Sandeep said the next morning.'

'It's the kind of sound they make,' assured Shailender.

'Come on! Don't wind me up.'

'He's right,' said JP.

'I'm serious,' confirmed Shailender. 'Many people around here are terrified of the man-eating leopards.'

'*Man*-eating?'

'They eat animals also. You've seen the dogs owned by many of the families?'

'Yes.' I'd often felt intimidated by the large, ferocious animals, thick, metal-spiked collars around their necks, tethered to the trees outside many houses.

'They keep them for protection. The leopards leap and strike at the throat with their claws. Human or animal.'

'You're joking?'

'No. You've heard of Jim Corbett?'

I had. He was India's most famous hunter and conservationist. Between 1918 and 1926 a leopard stalked and killed 125 people in this area. Corbett eventually tracked it down and wrote about his quest in *The Man-eating Leopard of Rudraprayag*.

'Actually, the beasts prowl the slopes at night as much now as they did in his time,' said Shailender. 'They sometimes carry children off into the forest. It's a real fear for the villagers.'

'I seriously thought that tales of marauding leopards were consigned to the history books,' I said.

'Not so. At least one woman a month is attacked in these parts,' replied Shailender. 'According to the law, though, an animal isn't declared a man-eater until it's killed three humans.'

'Somehow that doesn't surprise me.'

At the same time that Shankar Thapar was receiving his operation in Dehradun, a collective NGO committed to community development called GSVSS had been conducting a comprehensive survey of the 316 villages in the Rudraprayag district to quantify the disability situation. The field visits had been carried out over a period of two years by a small group of dedicated volunteers, many of whom were disabled themselves, including Sujan.

GSVSS had been set up by Ramesh. A Garhwali born and bred, he had relocated his family to a home near Tilwara at considerable personal cost. Driven by a tremendous sense of purpose, he'd made many sacrifices to establish the organisation.

Ramesh was an intense character, occasionally detached. This was partly due, I suspect, to his natural reserve and lack of confidence with the English language. He showed no such reticence, though, when speaking Hindi. JP translated the following conversation as we continued our trek.

'Because I had known JP for many years,' said Ramesh. 'I brought the survey results to his attention hoping that he might support some form of medical intervention.'

'I decided to visit a village in the district to see the work of GSVSS for myself.' said JP, looking at his friend. 'Although I was strongly moved and impressed by Ramesh's commitment, I was also cautious. Engaging with work of this kind would represent a significant venture for KHW. Our resources are continually pulled in many directions.

'So I said to Ramesh: "Bring a group of children down the mountains to Disha Hospital in Dehradun for examination. As an opening gesture we will fund the visit under our medical aid programme".'

'That's what I did,' continued Ramesh. 'In June 2004 we transported twelve children to Dehradun for assessment and treatment. They had already been examined by doctors at the Government Hospital in Srinagar. Although they were helped considerably, the medics decided that only two of them would benefit from further treatment.'

'It then became an issue of resources,' continued JP. 'It crossed my mind that perhaps we could tackle the problem the other way around.'

'How?' I asked.

'Take the professionals from Dehradun *to* the rural communities. Since all the people we were trying to help were very poor, they couldn't afford their travel, food and accommodation in Dehradun. We had to pay for it. When I discovered that only two of that first batch of twelve would have benefited from further intervention, I realised that, cost-wise, it worked out almost the same for us to go to them.'

'As well as having the opportunity to see more people?'

'Right. I sanctioned Ramesh to organise a medical camp. That he did, but with one small flaw! Remember?' JP stopped in the middle of the track and turned to Ramesh, grinning.

'Acchha,' replied Ramesh sheepishly. 'I forgot to invite any medical professionals.'

'Which completely defeated the object of the exercise! So I approached Dr Rajnish Singh, an orthopaedic surgeon at Disha Hospital in Dehradun who had recently returned from working in the UK for eight years. He agreed to visit the next camp. In the meantime Ramesh organised another camp which I decided to attend at the last minute. Once again, no medical professionals were present...'

'...apart from one distinguished gentleman,' said Ramesh.

'Yes, me!' chuckled JP. 'People from the villages had never seen me before and assumed I was a doctor. Not so!'

The visit, however, had a considerable impact on JP. 'Meeting so many children with correctable physical deformities, I decided that something more concrete had to be done, whatever the risk.'

We were now about an hour into our ascent and the land had levelled out slightly. I noticed a healthy green plant thriving in abundance on the otherwise sparse terraces.

'Guess what this is?' our young guide asked teasingly.

'I reckon it's...'

'Yes. Cannabis.' Immediately we all stopped walking and listened with rapt attention. Sujan translated the boy's words from Garhwali to Hindi, JP from Hindi to English.

'A *sadhu* once visited the village over there,' the boy pointed to a group of houses down the slope, 'and asked for food and shelter. The villagers were rude. "Go away!" they shouted. So he cursed this plot of land. Nothing grows there now. Except cannabis!'

'Sounds rather dubious to me,' said JP, ever the sceptic. 'It's more likely to be a tale put into circulation by the ganja mafia to legitimise their growing of the stuff!'

'Entertaining though,' I said, grasping a handful of leaves and rolling them between my palms. The dark green residue smelt sweetly aromatic.

'Kindly put it down, Mark,' ordered JP playfully. 'You'll get us into trouble!'

We climbed onto the next terrace. 'You were telling me about your medical credentials, Dr Singh.'

'Indeed. That trip was two months ago on the 5th March, 2005. Ten days later another medical camp was organised. On that occasion, Dr Rajnish joined us.

'We travelled independently in the morning to Sumari but decided to share a car back to Dehradun later that evening. It was an opportunity meant to be. For six hours, the poor doctor was a captive audience and I made the most of every minute! I talked at great length about the work I wanted to do and the tremendous need among the villages for some form of strategic medical intervention.

'But Dr Rajnish didn't need convincing. Having seen the situation with his own eyes, he had already decided he wanted to become involved in whatever we were about to start. This experience, his first visit to the mountains, had left him profoundly shocked. Encountering so many people living in such a harsh environment who had never seen a doctor, stirred something deep inside. Given the severity of many people's physical disabilities, he was astounded by their sheer determination to reach the medical camp.'

By that point, the track had virtually disappeared and the hillside rose sharply for a few metres. Judging by the scrubby cover of undergrowth, the land must have slipped a few years previously. The others, having gone on ahead, had disappeared from sight. Pausing the conversation, we directed all our concentration on gaining a firm foothold in the crumbling, dry shale. Clutching at the straggly tree roots, we managed to haul ourselves onto flatter ground.

I shared Dr Rajnish's amazement at how people managed to walk, crawl or be carried along tracks like this to reach the nearest motor-able road. Taking stock of our height, we appeared to have walked in an arc, going both around and up the valley sides.

As a result of that first medical camp on 15th March, of the 85 people that attended, fifteen were recommended for further treatment. JP explained that the medical fraternity were astonished by the unusually high number of mentally-challenged children and adults present; over 25% had some form of mental disability. They were also surprised by the number of parents who were caring for their young daughters without any hope of ever being relieved of the burden by marrying them into another family.

'Attempting to deliver such a significant work under KHW's medical aid programme would never adequately address the need.' JP continued, panting, 'So we decided to create a new, independent project. That's how Samvedna was born.'

'What does Samvedna mean?'

'It's a Hindi word, best translated as "empathy". Basically, the project's mission is to address the needs of differently-abled people in the rural communities of the Rudraprayag District and help them lead a life of dignity and purpose.'

Rudraprayag District, I was later to discover, had been carved out from three adjoining districts in 1977, one of which, incorporating the two blocks of Jakholi and Kirtinagar, directly west of the Mandakini and Alaknanda Rivers, was Tehri Garhwal. I found it significant that the exact vicinity in which Ramesh conducted his initial field visits, the same area which presented an unusually high incidence of disability among its inhabitants, was originally part of the old kingdom of Tehri Garhwal with its extraordinary historical record.

'Samvedna is a four-way partnership,' said JP. 'Ramesh, via GSVSS, provides the volunteers. Though without his vision and tenacity, the project would never have been conceived in the first place. Disha Hospital, through the services of Dr Rajnish, supplies the medical intervention and expertise. KHW is the facilitator and risk-taker. We manage the financial resources which are provided mainly by CHILD's Trust.

'Dr Rajnish's commitment, however, extends considerably further than the walls of the operating theatre. His personal involvement and excitement about the work has been contagious. He managed to convince his brother, for example, to donate the first Indian money to the project.

'Initially, Dr Rajnish didn't want any payment for his services. As I insisted on offering some form of remuneration, he has reluctantly agreed to donate his expertise at a fraction of his normal charges. The Medical Director of Disha Hospital, Dr. Maithani, provides a fifty per cent discount from medical costs to the Samvedna candidates of KHW.'

Dr Rajnish dreams that, by 2012, no child in Garhwal will have to live with a correctable disability.

☼

We finally reached our destination, a cluster of stone houses perched high on a ridge that commanded a striking view of the meandering Mandakini River below.

'Please. Can I see?'

I smiled. Our eyes met momentarily. Then his face crumpled and the four-year-old boy ran behind his mother into the house, clutching the small wooden object that I was asking him to show me.

'Actually Mark, you realise you're probably the first white person ever to visit this village?' said JP. 'These children have never seen anyone like you.'

The elder sister stood motionless in the doorway, her hand tightly gripping her mother whose quizzical gaze flickered, then relaxed.

'You're joking?' I considered JP's words for a moment.

For me this was an adventure. But for those living deep in the Garhwal interior, it was another day of monotonous rhythms interrupted by the arrival of a strange white man.

I felt odd, unnerved by the sound of the boy's sobbing from within the house. His sister, still clinging onto her mother's arm, offered a fragile smile. Their older brother, Pintoo, hobbled around the corner. Born with a left club foot, he had recently been transported down to Dehradun for surgery. It was he the team had come to see.

Perched on the low stone wall, I watched the scene unfold. Pintoo was sitting on the doorstep talking to Ramesh, his toes poking out of his grey, plastered foot. While his mother updated JP and Sujan on his progress, Robert and Shailender chatted with two neighbouring boys. It was mid-day and the sun blistered directly overhead. From this exposed vantage point, I could survey the entire rugged valley, its thirsty terraces leading, like a giant stairway, to Shiva's majestic abode.

> *A butterfly flies through the forest rain*
> *And turns the wind into a hurricane*
> *I know that it will happen*
> *'Cause I believe in the certainty of chance.*

JP's words prompted a few of The Divine Comedy's lyrics to enter my head.

First white person. Was it a big deal? It felt like it should be. Surely no place existed on the planet where the Angrez hadn't trod?

I imagined how our little scene might appear to Shiva, gazing down from his Kedarnath kingdom. Would he spot the outsider, seated on the wall purely because, by craving adventure, he had chosen to trust in the certainty of chance? In the same way that the individual mountain springs cascaded down the hillside to become one mighty river, his life now converged with those around him. Like the direction of the rushing waters, there was an inevitability about the course of events.

His life, my life; they, we... were all connected.

No, I wasn't having a Brahman moment. The possibility that the-universe-and-I-were-one continued to elude me. But I *was* beginning to discern a glimmer of purpose, a reason why I was there. Choice? Chance? Dharma?

The white man stuff, I realised, was irrelevant. It's what I did with the experience that mattered.

As with the encounter in Vijayawada, the moment the young boy's tears started to flow, my world spun. Then stopped. The simple desire to meet Lakshme and the SKCV street kids had turned into a quest for adventure. It had now become a labour of love.

In my hands I held a puzzle; a jigsaw of evolving, revolving images. As I began to assemble the pieces, the emerging picture remained unclear. I'm neither a medic nor an anthropologist, but an ordinary person thrown into a remarkable situation. I couldn't accept, however, that "there is an unusually high incidence of disability in this region" without question. I wanted to delve further, to discover why? As disability is a major issue throughout India, what is unique about this particular area that makes the circumstances so severe?

When I was to return to the region a year later, it would become clear that the high incidence of disability is not due to any one single element. It is caused by a number of historical, social, cultural and circumstantial factors, which are prevalent in varying degrees throughout the land but converge in this one, relatively small, area of Garhwal.

Many disabilities in the area, for example, are polio-related. Polio spreads via human-to-human contact, usually entering the body through the mouth due to fecally contaminated water or food. The virus invades the nervous system, often causing an onset of muscular paralysis within a matter of hours that renders the limbs, usually the legs, floppy and lifeless. While polio can strike at any age, over 50% of cases occur in children between the ages of three and five. It's also possible to contract polio without experiencing any significant paralysis at the time, though additional symptoms, such as extreme fatigue and muscle weakness, can arise later in life.

Until 2002, India experienced the highest number of cases in the world per annum. That year's figure of 1,600, however, represented a significant decrease from the 4,791 cases reported in 1994. This number was further reduced to 135 in 2004 as the direct result of a unique public-private partnership, including the World Health Organisation, Rotary International and UNICEF, to eradicate the disease. Alongside Afghanistan and Pakistan, a target was set to eradicate polio completely by the end of 2005.

Although immunisation in the mountains is a challenge, communal awareness, informed by effective government intervention, has now ensured that polio has been almost wiped out in Uttarakhand. This bodes well for the future, but many children and adults are currently affected by a legacy of polio contracted when they were younger. It will be another couple of generations before polio-associated problems are eliminated entirely.

Before Samvedna's intervention, Pintoo had never seen a doctor. Though this was true for most of the villagers, those who had sought medical attention possibly trekked as far as twenty kilometres to reach the nearest trained practitioner.

The form of health treatment on which the Pahari rely is a hybrid of ancient medicine and religious practice. Due to high levels of illiteracy, medical know-how has been communicated orally through the generations. Dependent on communal memory, it is justified by custom and tradition rather than legitimate medical procedures. Consequently, the application of basic health, hygiene, nutrition, prevention and first aid knowledge is often hit and miss. Many illnesses and diseases could be easily prevented.

Rites of passage are integral to Pahari life. The whole future of a child, for example, is directly informed by superstition and primitive practices at birth.

Using dirty rags, an untrained midwife traditionally delivers a baby in a dark, poorly ventilated room, often the lower storey *obara* in which the livestock live. If the child fails to draw breath, she may splash water on his face, slap him profusely, make loud noises or even squeeze an onion in front of his nose to resuscitate him.

The midwife next cuts the umbilical cord with a non-sterile blade and seals the wound with ash, turmeric or cow dung. It's not unusual, then, to roast the child's placenta. Occasionally even part of the baby is burnt to ward off evil spirits.

According to religious custom in this area, a woman, once she has given birth, is ritually unclean. She is locked in the dark, windowless room for a period of five days, called *panchola*, without water or adequate food. The fire burns continuously, filling the cell with thick smoke that has no means of escape. The baby is not breast-fed but given water using a cup and spoon. On the sixth day, the mother is permitted to leave the delivery room, take a bath and eat. As far as the baby is concerned, though, harm may already have been done. If the brain had survived the rigours of birth, it may have become irreparably impaired in the ensuing five days due to oxygen deprivation.

Mother and child are isolated from the rest of the family and village for a further forty days. It is only then that the baby may be breast-fed, though during lactation the mother traditionally avoids certain foods such as pulses, vegetables and some fruit.

Although unproven, the lifestyle of expectant mothers may also have some direct bearing on their child. Even during pregnancy, at the time she needs the most nourishment, the mother is required to consume a restricted diet. She works arduously until almost full-term, labouring in the fields, carrying heavy loads, cutting wood, climbing trees and walking long distances. Many foetuses are prohibited from developing properly in the womb and limbs are frequently contorted due to the physical exertions of the expectant mother.

After forty days of isolation, the traditional religious ceremonies commence. Ironically, prayers for blessing, safety and good health are offered to the devta.

Even though her actions may suggest otherwise, the deep love a mother expresses towards her baby, in most cases, is incontestable. Informed by environmental circumstance, religious custom and often, plain ignorance, she unreservedly believes she is doing the right thing for her child.

Naturally, a baby born with a physical disability demands far more attention than others. Even in more developed environments a child requires a programme of care that includes medicines, support and exercise. As the social and economic system in the interior villages dictates that it's the mother's duty to nurture the child as well as to earn a wage, she is continuously presented with a relentless stream of impossible choices.

The mother of a child with disabilities is caught in a cleft stick. How can she adequately care for her child, look after the needs of everyone else in the family and fulfil her duty as the bread winner? When she walks to the forest to collect wood, who is at home to prevent her young child, disabled or otherwise, from crawling towards the open hearth and getting burned? A mother may leave her child tethered to the leg of the bed for several hours to prevent such accidents from occurring.

In the west this would be regarded as neglect, tantamount to child abuse. In this environment it's a fact of life.

I turned back towards the stone house. The small boy crept into the doorway, a dusty channel of dried tears trickling down each cheek. His top lip quivered as he hesitantly held out the wooden object in his other hand. It was a toy tractor.

'Look, Mark! He wants you to see.'

I knelt down, prised the toy gently from his fingers and pushed it along the ground between us. Slightly, just very slightly, his lips curled up at the ends.

Taking a different path down the hillside, after about thirty minutes we reached a long, single-storey building containing four white-washed houses, each with their own front door. A communal chowk, paved with uneven flagstones, ran along the front. A low wall at the far end marked the boundary of the property.

'Please, sit!' said Ramesh, indicating the wall. 'We go and come.'

He and Sujan walked to the third house and knocked on the frame of the open doorway. A middle-aged woman appeared and smiled at them in recognition. The gap between her tight-fitting orange blouse and green cloth wrapped around her waist revealed a taut midriff. She was clearly no stranger to hard work. After a brief exchange, Ramesh and Sujan returned.

'She was expecting us,' he said. 'She'll bring lunch.'

A girl came over carrying a metal jug and several beakers. Pouring water into each one, she handed them down the line.

She gave two to Ramesh, one of which he placed on the wall next to Sujan who then leant forward, clasped it between his teeth, tipped his head back and drank. Though it was second nature to him, I watched this feat of dexterity in awe.

'I have known this family many years,' Sujan said after he'd put his beaker back on the wall. 'Sometimes, when I have been doing survey work, it has been too late to go back to my village. They have given me a bed for the night.' I noticed that, as he spoke, he naturally gesticulated with his feet in a way that other people would do with their hands.

The woman re-appeared carrying a basket laden with the largest bananas imaginable. Peeling back the thick green skin, I found it impossible to take a bite from the top in the normal way. So I sank my teeth into the side of its soft flesh. It was sweet and chewy.

'Lunch!' chuckled Ramesh, placing a peeled banana on a plate. Sujan bent forward, took a mouthful and sat upright, grinning broadly. As he moved, the two empty short sleeves of his white and blue checked shirt swayed in the breeze.

JP caught me staring in amazement.

'Sujan has an incredible story,' he said.

'Tell me.'

'Why don't you ask him yourself?'

16
Love What You Do

How much more brutal could life be to a seven-year old?

'To understand my story, you need to know about life in the mountains,' Sujan began. 'Of villages ambitiously perched on steep ledges or hidden in violent gorges. Of terraces carved by grit on unforgiving mountain slopes. Of walking hours over treacherous pathways to the nearest school and days to the nearest medical centre. Of women falling out of trees and children being carried off by leopards in the twilight. No electricity, piped water, coloured pencils or candy.

'To understand my story you must know what it is to have no money. No food. No farm land. To be dependent on the fast diminishing charity of family and friends. Of stubborn soil, reluctant to allow even a grain to prosper.

'To understand my story you must have suffered hunger. Pain so severe that mere words cannot express it. Humiliation. Despair. Defeat. To understand my story you must have known the frustration of screaming "I wish I was never born!"

'But I was, on the fourth of January 1977.

'This is my story.'

ॐ

My home village is Bawai, Rudraprayag in Garhwal. We were a poor family of four; my father Gaursingh Chauhan, my mother, Ramdai Devi Chauhan, and my elder brother

Khajansingh Chauhan. Our small stone house, that we shared with my paternal uncle's family, contained two rooms. We lived in one and they had the other. We shared a small kitchen area but there was no running water so we collected it every day from the stream or the *naula*, the well. We went to the fields for the toilet.

Just three months after my birth my father passed away. His death made our precarious existence worse and the condition of my family further deteriorated. My aunt didn't like us and started to make life difficult. She plotted to get rid of us, possibly so that she could take our small piece of land.

After some time my mother, brother and I moved to live with my maternal grandmother in another village. She had met with an accident at a young age and one of her feet was badly burnt. My maternal uncle and his wife had moved to Mumbai and my grandmother was grateful that we went to look after her.

Mother worked very hard to fulfil our basic needs, earning her wages through tough, physical labour. I remember her carrying heavy stones for construction on her head, climbing up and down the steep slopes several times a day. Her daily wage for this work was a meagre ten rupees. There were endless worries for her. She was very keen that we brothers received an education and tried her best to ensure it. This was not easy. For some time we had to stop going to school. Fortunately, we were able to resume our education when my maternal grandmother gave us a cow. We received an income from selling its milk but it was never enough. As a result, my elder brother went to live with my maternal uncle and his wife in Mumbai to work in a private company.

I attended a nearby government primary school which had about 70 pupils. After school each day I took the cow and other animals to graze. Then I would play cricket with my friends, swim in the stream or play a game of leaping from one terrace to another to see who could jump the furthest. One day we tied a rope to a tree to make a swing.

In 1984, while playing with friends, I didn't realise that I was dangerously close to an electrical transformer. My grandmother's village didn't have electricity. I'd never known what it was, its uses or what it did. I accidentally touched one of the live electrical wires. What happened thereafter was my fate. Excruciating pain!

From that day, I started my new life, a journey of torment and suffering, of uncertainty and disillusionment. But finally a journey which has not only given me a sense of purpose and achievement but also, I hope, will also inspire many like me to live a life of self-reliance and dignity.

Despite being poor themselves, my village collected money and rushed me to the nearest hospital in Augustmuni. As my hands were severely burnt the doctors referred me to a bigger hospital in Gopeshwar. I was taken there in an ambulance. I remember it rained very hard that day; I could feel the chill creep up my limbs.

On my way to Gopeshwar, I believed I would be OK and soon able to play again. But to my horror I was told that my left hand would have to be removed. What wrong had I done to deserve such a cruel fate? How much more brutal could life be to a seven-year old? Why me? Why did I have to go through all the pain and loss? My mother believed my accident was a curse from my paternal aunt because she hated us so much. But I'm not so sure.

I couldn't fathom what life would be without a hand. I ached not just physically but also emotionally. I knew I was becoming a burden to my mother. When I saw the anguish on her face, it pained me even more.

I remember the doctor gradually peeling and cutting at my hand and, before I knew it, my left arm was gone. After 13 days in hospital, I was discharged. My maternal uncle arranged for us to go to Delhi for my treatment. I was shown to all the good hospitals but disappointment awaited me. At St Stephen's Hospital, Old Delhi, I was told that gangrene had set in my right hand too and it would have to be amputated.

My world fell apart. There was no will to live. I didn't know how to pick up the pieces and start over again. Everything began to close in on me. I was crippled and I felt there was no way my life could get any worse. I was too distraught to see any reason. My mother and relatives tried to make me understand. Slowly I accepted my condition and realised the futility of wallowing in self-pity and bitterness. I looked around; there were several who were like me or, probably, not even as lucky as I was.

I returned to my village, Bawai. Eyes would look at me and stare at my condition with pity, some wondering what sin I had committed in my previous life to suffer such consequences.

After spending a few months in the village my maternal uncle took me to live with him in Mumbai. He worked in a clerical job and lived with his family in a *chal*, an urban slum, in Saki Naka. Seven people occupied one *kholi*, a room, but we had a separate kitchen. Down the corridor was a public toilet used by everyone in the building. Each morning we stood in line to wait our turn. We had one bed in our kholi on which my aunt and youngest child slept. The rest of us lay on a *chatai*, a mat, covered with a bed sheet.

I was very happy to move to Mumbai. My life was about to change, yet again, and I would learn how to use my legs as I'd never done before. Funded by my uncle, I was admitted to a school for children with similar conditions as mine. There I was taught to be self-sufficient through training in life skills. The institution was based in Haji Ali where they also made customised artificial limbs.

Hope stayed afloat; seeing little boys and girls my age all making efforts to learn, was an inspiration to me. I was determined to become self-sufficient and I knew that I could make my mother proud. More importantly, I needed to convince myself that I could do things on my own. I knew that my self-esteem was at stake.

During my one and a half years in the institution I travelled daily by bus from Saki Naka to Andheri, about fifteen kilometres. I then took another bus for about twenty-five kilometres to Haji Ali. It took a long time through the crawling Mumbai traffic. But I felt confident; travelling was not such a problem, even in a new city. I didn't need a chaperone. On the public bus to Andheri I sat in the special seat at the front reserved for disabled people. I enjoyed the privilege, especially if it was already occupied and someone had to vacate it for me!

Life in Mumbai was completely different but I loved living there. There were so many things that I was seeing for the first time. There was nothing I couldn't do! I was ecstatic about everything I could achieve on my own and it made me swell with pride. Using my feet, I could soon bathe, brush my teeth, comb my hair and sweep the floor. I didn't need anybody's help.

I learnt very quickly; what was expected to take three months I did in three weeks! Putting on clothes was the hardest, particularly putting on a shirt. It would already be buttoned but trying to get inside was difficult and required lots of practice. It took ten days to master the art of getting dressed.

Learning to write I found extremely easy. My teachers strapped a pen to my shoulder with a belt but I soon taught myself to write with my mouth and, eventually, my foot. I preferred writing with my mouth because it meant I didn't have to always carry a belt with me.

After eighteen months of this special training I joined a school for physically-challenged children in Santa Cruz named A.S.D.C. That meant another gruelling routine of Mumbai commuting. Everyday I would travel from Saki Naka to Andheri in the local bus. From there I would take the school bus for seven kilometres to Santa Cruz. But it was worth it.

I was very motivated and taught myself many new skills, sometimes just for fun! I could make tea and learnt to ignite the kerosene stove with my feet. This involved operating the pump with one foot and striking a match with the other. One day my friends challenged me to thread a needle with my toes. I did it – and won twenty rupees! I also received a fifty rupee award for best writing and my art work was commended by the President of India in a painting competition.

This routine continued for almost five years.

In Mumbai there were several young differently-abled girls from well-to-do families. Many marriage proposals were made to me, along with an assured business, income and a life of comfort. Some were more serious than others, particularly one proposal from the family of an Uttar Pradesh girl called Anita, but I was not keen and declined.

Eventually it was time for me to leave the school in Santa Cruz. Since there was no further education facility I could access in Mumbai, I was recommended to an institution in Pratapgarh, Uttar Pradesh. But I would have been on my own, away from my family, and so I opted to return instead to my village, Bawai.

Initially, my experiences in the village weren't very pleasant and I felt acutely conscious of my condition. It had been some time since I had been in the company of normal children so I had to undergo another process of re-learning. I was apprehensive about their attitude and that of the community. I joined the school and over a period of time my classmates became more accepting and helped me. I was sent to the Junior High School of the village and received a lot of support from my friends. I was able to complete Class Eight. My mother's face glowed with pride at my achievements.

After completing Class Eight I had to join the Rajkiya, Government, Inter College which was far away from my village. I moved to my maternal grandmother's house. Even then I had to walk almost two kilometres but I received immense encouragement from my classmates. In their company I never felt disadvantaged by my situation. I passed grade nine and started studying very hard for my board exams.

While I was in Class Ten, my mother fixed my elder brother's marriage with Sarita, daughter of Shri Dhumsingh

Chauhan, resident of village Damar. The wedding went well and, ten days later, my brother left for Mumbai. He corresponded regularly with us.

Six months went by. One fine day, I returned from school to find many people from the village assembled in my house. I began to get a sinking feeling. I saw my uncles had also come. My mother was in bed, crying inconsolably. I didn't want to hear what they had to say.

And then they broke the news to me: my brother had died in an accident.

I was sixteen years old. Yet again my family felt desolate, the ache and pain of another tragedy. We braced ourselves and tried to be strong for Sarita, my sister-in-law, who had been away visiting her parents in Damar. My mother didn't take Khajan's death particularly well and became ill through grief. Sarita also became sick.

My brother had been the bread earner of the family. He was also repaying the money he had borrowed to get married. I now had to bear the yoke of the loan. So many responsibilities and commitments started to weigh me down. It became increasingly difficult to make ends meet and continue my education.

Fortunately that year an organisation, called Centre for Development, came to our village with a women's programme. My sister-in-law enrolled in their course and learnt tailoring. She eventually got a job for 900 rupees per month and worked with them for the next five years. This was a great help to us.

My mother's health didn't improve and she became bedridden. I regularly got medicines for her but she didn't respond very well to any treatment. Her condition deteriorated continuously. Finally she had to be hospitalised at Srinagar, where she passed away after ten days at 7.30 am on 3rd February 1997.

I didn't realise how lonely I would become. My world was now empty; life came to a standstill. Since there was no one to take care of me, my maternal uncle offered to take me back to Mumbai.

Amid all this, I was approached by the *Pradhan*, village head, and *Pramukh*, head of many villages, who were both informed about my situation. They proposed that I married my brother's widow, Sarita. At the time of my brother's death, I had been living with my maternal grandmother in the village to where we'd moved when I was a young child. My sister-in-law and mother were living in a different house and so Sarita and I hardly knew each other. After my mother died, she was living alone.

Marriage between a brother and sister-in-law is highly unusual and I thought the idea weird at first. Sarita also knew the problems involved but, after due consideration, we both agreed.

Our wedding was a big event, attended by many people from the Augustmuni block and other important government officials. It received coverage by the regional Hindi newspaper Dainik Jagran. We married according to Hindu rites and rituals and the expenditure was borne by the *Mahila Jagriti Sansthan*, the Women's Awareness Organisation. The marriage was the union of two unhappy people in the same situation. It was one of the most joyful days of my life.

☼

Now began my newfound life with my wife, Sarita, with everybody's blessings. Living became meaningful again. After a year we were blessed with a son, whom we named Rahul.

We had many responsibilities but there were few ways to fulfil them. I tried very hard to look for work. Sarita was very enterprising and took up a small stitching job in the village to pay our household expenses.

I kept looking for employment so that I could support my family. Sometimes I would go to town and get provisions for the village community and sell them, thereby making a small profit. Since there was a dearth of educated youngsters in the village, I was one of the few people that could help families in need with any kind of documentation work. All the schooled youth had migrated to the big cities in search of jobs or to further their education.

A man marrying a widow receives 11,000 rupees compensation from the government. If he is disabled, he also receives some remuneration. When both the bride and groom are disabled they receive 14,000 rupees. So at our marriage, Sarita and I received some money which all the villagers knew about. My situation brought awareness to others because most people didn't realise they could claim money from the government. The bureaucracy is almost impenetrable but thanks to my education I learnt how to navigate a path through all the red tape and complete the necessary paperwork.

People started approaching me to help them submit claims for disability pensions and certificates. They offered me a proportion of their first payment in exchange for my assistance. That is what they would say. I would travel once a month to the Chief Medical Officer's office in Rudraprayag on their behalf. When they received the money, however, they neither acknowledged my work nor honoured their agreement. I have helped many people to receive benefits, compensation and equipment such as callipers but they rarely paid me. There is one disabled young man in our village whom I have helped on three occasions but I have yet to receive one single rupee for my efforts. Now he avoids me entirely.

If I see someone in trouble I like to help; I cannot say "no" to people in need. At first I didn't mind that people broke their agreements as I was happy to support them in whatever way I could. But now I would rather work voluntarily for honest people than for those who make promises that they do not keep.

One day I chanced upon a new face. A gentleman was conducting research into the number of physically and mentally-challenged orphans and widows living in the village. It was being carried out by an organisation, called GSVSS, of Sumari. I asked if they needed help and Ramesh Prasad Khanduri, its Director, invited me to meet him and talk about its activities.

Six months later, Ramesh offered me some voluntary work. I cannot sit idle in one place. Ideally, I was seeking full-time paid employment. But the work appealed to me as it was in an area in which I was greatly interested. I felt it was my time to give back to my community and to my kind. My training in Mumbai had radically changed my life and, most importantly, restored my self-esteem. I was more than happy to use my education and experience to serve my own people, especially the children who were not as fortunate as I was to receive training in Mumbai. I felt the hand of providence and experienced immense peace of mind. I knew that, in this way, not only the needs of my family would be taken care of, but I would be given an opportunity to work for the disadvantaged.

Later I became involved in an Adult Education programme started by GSVSS but, after some time, gave up my teaching post to a lady from my village that lost her husband in an unfortunate accident. Her need was greater than mine.

As God has always paved the way for me, I was introduced to KHW's Director, JP Singh, a benevolent man dedicated to the cause of child welfare and education. He told me about the Samvedna project for differently-abled people in Rudraprayag district, managed in partnership with GSVSS.

Now I am actively engaged in the process of identification. I travel to Dehradun hospitals and do follow-up work in the villages. This has given a new impetus and meaning to my life.

GSVSS's office is in Tilwara. I go there at least four times a month. It has a room in which I stay. In order to get there, I have to walk from my village down the mountainside through dense forest for about five kilometres. I then pick up a jeep. I plan my work with Ramesh and then trek through the mountains for two or three days at a time visiting several villages. Sometimes I use my own village as a starting point. In many places I am treated like a celebrity. People know of the project's reputation. Rather than go looking for them, people will often seek me out.

When I visit a village I do a number of things. Firstly, I identify children who may need surgery. Some already may have had operations as part of the programme. On behalf of the doctors, I conduct follow-up work such as measuring feet for surgical shoes. Since many parents are entirely ignorant of medical procedures, I help ensure they know how to care for their children. They can be very impatient and rip off the bandages, complaining that the children are in more pain than they were before the operation. They don't realise that there's going to be greater pain at the outset. 'When is my child going to get well again?' they ask.

'Look at me,' I'll say. 'I have no arms, hands and half a foot. But I can eat, drink, walk, write and take care of myself. But it takes time.' I do my best to give them hope.

Although it's not part of my Samvedna work, I also offer support and advice for claiming benefits such as income support and disability certification. I am happy to share this information and help where I am able.

In the past two years I've been very encouraged to see hundreds of differently-abled children and adults examined by doctors in special camps or at Dehradun. Many surgical corrections have been done.

And the future?

I would like the financial resources to care properly for my wife and two sons. A government job is desirable, even a small one, because it provides security. But that is not where my heart is. I wish to continue helping people, get a better education and discover ways in which I can grow.

I have been very encouraged to see the positive impact that my life and work is having on my community and many others. Seeing all this love and concern makes me feel proud to be part of the Samvedna family.

17
If...

*Our intervention should mean
that lives are changed for the better*

'I'm stuffed!' Robert announced. I agreed, amazed that one banana could be so filling.

Fully energised, we were ready to return down the mountain. As Ramesh, Robert and Shailender said goodbye to some of the villagers, JP, Sujan and I went on ahead. It was now mid-afternoon and the sun's rays, fanned by a slight breeze, felt less intense.

'How do the Pahari explain disability?' I asked JP.

'What do you mean?'

'In terms of their belief system - what causes it?'

JP's straightforward explanation surprised me. 'It is a person's karma if they are born with a disability such as a congenital defect,' he replied. 'They have done, or not done, something in a previous life to determine their current state. A child born with a club foot, for example, suffers as a direct result of bad actions in a prior existence.

'If an accident or ill-health befalls someone during their current lifetime, however, this is divine intervention – an infliction from the devta. It could be punishment for a vengeful act or a curse invoked by another person.'

I turned to Sujan. 'You said your mother believed your accident was the result of a curse from your aunt. Is that what you think?

'I don't know,' he replied. 'Belief in the devtas' power is very strong in our village. Occasionally the wrath of a family's devta might be called upon because of a bad relationship between two conflicting households.

'Sometimes, though, if there is a fight or an argument *within* a family, the devta is also brought into the disagreement. It is not uncommon for someone to invoke a curse in retribution for a grievance caused by another family member. I'm not sure whether my aunt did that or not. But I do know that she didn't want us living in the house after my father's death.'

'How did that make you feel?'

JP, who was translating, interjected. 'You need to bear in mind, Mark, that Sujan is the only member of his family now alive. Although he happily talks about the facts, he is less open when expressing his emotions.'

'I understand.' I decided to broaden my questioning. 'In that case, could you ask him how the devtas manifest themselves in daily village life?'

Sujan thought for a moment. 'I'll use an example. A person may make a commitment in front of the devta as part of their *puja*. A young man, say, might promise to sacrifice a small animal if the deity blesses him with a new job. Should he prove successful but fail to honour his agreement, the devta will certainly make its presence known.'

'How?'

'When the devta is annoyed or angry, children fall ill or the cattle stop giving milk. In fact, most troubles, diseases and crop failures come from the household devtas as a result of broken promises or disobedience.'

'Do people always know what is the cause of a particular problem?' I asked.

'No. Sometimes they go to a *baki*, or shaman, for advice. This is someone in the village who falls into a trance and becomes like an oracle. He holds regular sessions, and deals with several clients at a time. That is how he earns a living.

'The spirit of the devta comes over the baki and people ask questions such as "Why is my child ill?" The devta might reply, "You promised to give me a goat if I did this particular work for you. But you didn't, so I am angry." Once he has diagnosed the cause of trouble, the baki then recommends what actions need to be taken. He often advises that puja is performed in honour of the devta. The victim is responsible for ensuring that this is carried out.'

'How often does that happen?' I asked.

'Puja ceremonies of this kind occur every few weeks in the villages,' Sujan replied. 'They are conducted by specialist practitioners called *pujari* who, naturally, require payment for their services. The primary purpose of the puja is to ensure that the devta is appeased and given the opportunity, by possessing the victim's body, to announce any further demands.'

'Is it always the victim or a relative that is possessed?'

'Yes, not the pujari. Their role is to play percussive instruments to accompany the dancing and invoke the spirit of the devta.

'The puja normally happens at night around a fire,' Sujan continued. 'There is a lot of beating drums, shouting and screaming. If a family member has died, especially a young one, their spirit is called to inhabit someone they really loved or really hated. That person will suddenly jump up and start writhing on the floor, making funny noises and speaking in strange tones. People start asking questions.

'Different kinds of instruments are used, depending on who dies; sometimes it is a drum, sometimes a metal plate. The importance of the devta determines how much effort is invested in time and sacrifice. Once or twice a year there are occasions where the devtas require special ceremonies. One annual puja in the region lasts nine days. There is continual reading from the scriptures and a total of seventeen ritual dances.

'Whatever the problem, there is generally a solution. Usually this means something has to be given.'

Sujan's last statement didn't surprise me. Always, it seemed, something had to be given.

Having almost reached the jeep, I lingered behind my colleagues. Captivated by Sujan's story, I wanted a few moments to consider what he'd told me.

It seemed that a Pahari struck with ill-health, even a malnutrition-related ailment, would do his utmost to placate the devta by sacrificing money, rice or other staple foods. If he was too sick, a family member would make an offering on his behalf. Gifts were presented *even if* the worshipper and his family didn't have enough to eat themselves. It was more important to appease the devta.

Sacrifices made at the mandir were received by the pandit, usually the high-caste Brahmin priest who supervised temple activity. By offering his much-needed food, the sick worshipper remained under-nourished, became further ill and was required to produce more gifts. Bound by his conviction, he was trapped in a downward spiral of ill-health.

Such beliefs had been passed down the generations. Poorly educated, the Pahari rarely travelled outside his own village. He didn't know any different.

Of course, the devta, being a spirit, had no need of money or vast quantities of food. Someone else stood to gain from the villager's gifts: the pandit.

Playing on the Pahari's fears and superstitions, he exploited the villager's vulnerability for his own material gain. The pandit lined his pocket with cash and his stomach with goodies.

The worshipper was happy to give, the pandit delighted to receive. Both won.

Driving back towards Tilwara, the track seemed much bumpier than earlier. Or maybe my bones were just more tired and achy; we'd done a lot of walking in the last few days. Sujan remained behind to spend the next few hours with a family in Pali village, where we'd parked the jeep. He would find his own way home later that evening.

IF...

Robert and Shailender sat either side of me, their heads intermittently flopping forward then jerking up as they teetered on the edge of sleep.

'Tired?' I smiled at Robert.

'Mmmm? I'm not used to all this exercise,' he mumbled, his eyes half-shut. Shailender snorted.

'He's off,' said JP, turning from the front seat and grinning.

'JP?' I asked, leaning forward. 'One thing intrigues me.'

'Acchha, my friend. Just one?!'

'Most of the Pahari believe in karma?'

'That's true.'

'Don't they resist the work of Samvedna, then? It's almost like interfering.'

'Actually, no. For simple village folk, they are happy that this work is being done. It fits within their frame of reference; they see the medical intervention as a result of their good merit and ask "What deeds have I done to deserve this help?" They don't question where it comes from. That is irrelevant detail.'

JP went on to explain that, as their traditional beliefs are being challenged, a change of attitude is beginning to emerge: 'People are noticing that children they had seen with deformities and disabilities are now walking around. They are asking questions: "Who has done this?"'

Samvedna, it seems, faces a far greater barrier: a deep-rooted lack of trust from the Pahari.

Elderly women daily carry water on their heads along perilous mountain tracks, paths that are far too demanding for the average government official.

"It's a long climb, the hills are steep, I'm too lazy..." every excuse under the sun prevents the bureaucrat from travelling to the interior villages. The policy-producing politician would rather push paper than medical supplies. NGOs frequently promise support but continually fail to deliver.

The Pahari are disillusioned by platitudinous inactivity. A tremendous cynicism hangs over the mountains like a malevolent brush waiting to daub every good intention with an equal smattering of tar. Representatives from the outside world of officialdom have traded their credibility for apathy. Everyone else is smeared guilty by association.

"Why should we believe that Samvedna is any different?" the Pahari ask. "What makes you so unusual?"

That was certainly the attitude that the Samvedna volunteers encountered when they conducted their first field visits. Establishing credibility was time-consuming and hard work. Slowly, though, people began to understand that the project meant business. By displaying a continual presence in the mountains rather than parachuting workers in and out, the volunteers became accepted. No big promises were made; they simply got on with the job. Each child was frequently visited for care, post-surgery, and a relationship was established with each family. Word spread.

Young people who were sick are now prominent, walking advertisements for Samvedna. People see that a difference has been made.

'Our intervention should mean that the children's lives should change for the better,' JP said. 'If life has not changed, we have failed.' His vision for KHW is 'to do, and be recognised for credible, relevant and meaningful work, regionally and nationally.' This rationale is tempered by an acknowledgement that the organisation can only act with a finite number of people. It is better to have a significant effect on a few, such as Sujan, who can then have an impact on others, than spread limited resources too thinly.

A year after my first visit, Agnes, a rehabilitation psychology student from Germany joined KHW on secondment.

In her final report, she wrote about Urmilla, a young woman who arrived at the GSVSS centre in Tilwara one morning:

> Urmilla came on Sunday. She was young, beautiful and educated. Aged 18, she was suffering from a birth injury called Brachial plexus palsy which had left her with a paralysed left hand. There was tightness between the thumb and index finger, stiffness in the elbow and shoulder and the muscles were

> degenerated. Co-ordination between her right and left hand was not properly developed.
>
> We made a therapy plan for her, concentrating on physiotherapeutic exercises. The target was to increase movement in the left hand, increase visual perception and improve co-ordination between left and right.
>
> For three weeks Urmilla worked very hard. She used to come one hour before school started and continued to do the exercises at home. Daily I could see the advance in the movement capacity. After two and a half weeks she picked up a glass, the first time in her life.

Urmilla's story is a beautiful example of how timely, appropriate intervention can help a young adult. Had she received this simple treatment soon after birth rather than waiting eighteen years, Urmilla's *whole* life may have been significantly different.

This case, sadly, is replicated throughout the region. Though corrective surgery may have helped those Pahari with disabilities when they were younger, they are now too old to benefit from medical aid. If only the intervention could have been sooner.

Providing access to medical care and breaking through the inertia of mountain life has been tough, particularly as the lethargy rolls in from opposing directions. The inept bureaucracies from the "outside" have singularly failed to have much impact in terms of policy implementation. Their main outcome has been the cynicism they've perpetuated.

In the unforgiving "interior" environment, governed by traditional medical practices, superstition and karmic belief, there is a latent tendency not to intervene but to leave things as they are. There's always past justification to maintain the status quo. A villager may attempt to cure her sick daughter by offering a gift to the gods but the deed is more likely to satisfy the carnal urges of a peckish priest than heal her child of a club foot.

A whimsical banner proclaiming "What will be, will be" flutters ineffectually over the Garhwal mountains and valleys. Thankfully, people like Ramesh, JP, Sujan and Dr Rajnish are determined to tear it down, cutting through the culture of apathy that it signifies with positive action.

In many cases, Samvedna has had to work as an uncompromising external force against individual and corporate passivity in order to make things happen: by visiting homes; arranging transport; putting a sick child onto a donkey to transport them to the nearest source of medical help and tactfully, but persistently, banging on the bureaucrats' doors. The medical camps have enabled the project to interact with the local administration, community leaders and medical fraternity, motivating them towards longer term self-sustainability.

Now that Samvedna compassionately acts alongside the differently-abled young people and their families, their hope, dignity and self-worth is slowly being restored.

But we're all human.

☼

'Forty minutes to produce one lousy pot of tea and six cups! And it's cold. Incredible.'

We were sitting outside a government hotel on the banks of the Mandakini River. JP was venting his Nepali outrage at the inept Indian service. The rest of us, though not in disagreement, were too tired to join in his tirade.

I was just happy to relax, contemplate the day and listen to the gurgling river woo the balmy evening towards nightfall.

Robert got up and disappeared in the direction of the jeep. He returned a few minutes later carrying a red cardboard box. Placing it on the table, he removed the lid. Inside was a plum cake.

'We bought this for your birthday, Mark, but forgot all about it! I just remembered it when the tea appeared.' Producing a knife, he cut each of us a slice.

Tea, cake, sunset. Perfect.

IF...

'JP?' I asked between mouthfuls. 'You remember the first house we visited; the one where I made the little boy cry?'

'Yes.' He grinned. 'Such a cruel Angrez!'

'Thanks!' I laughed. 'I'm being serious, though.'

'Sorry.'

'When he came back to show me his toy, you said, "Look! He wants you to see." What did you mean?'

'Well. What *did* you see?'

18
There is a Light that Never Goes Out

Women are very strong, very beautiful. But by the time they are 25, they are already old

What did I see? I saw a tear-stained boy clutching a toy tractor; a symbol of progress carved from the fast-diminishing fruits of the forest.

I saw the Pahari, a poor people living in an area rich in natural resources; skilled and wise, yet denied the right to manage the environment in which they dwelt.

I saw a region facing an idiosyncratic set of circumstances that threatened to place individuals, families and communities in an untenable position.

Though similar challenges are replicated throughout the nation, what characterises Garhwal, is that *so many factors* converge in one place:

1. It is highly susceptible to natural disasters, earthquakes, flooding and landslides
2. It has a history of invasion, tyrannical rule and oppression
3. Education and development have been restrained for decades by an archaic system of raja governance
4. The Pahari youth have raised, but unrealised, aspirations

5 The burden of the workload and family responsibility falls on the women
6 A significant proportion of the men have migrated and/or are "missing"
7 It has a rapidly changing environment ravaged by the effects of deforestation, road-building schemes, large-scale infrastructural development and construction of the second largest dam in South East Asia
8 Some of its districts have an unusually high incidence of physical and mental disability
9 Many medical health and hygiene practices are governed by traditional religious and superstitious belief
10 There's poor communication, a shortage of running water and no sanitation in many homes
11 It has high unemployment, a lack of job prospects and issues of alcoholism

'Another beer?'

Grasping the ice cold Royal Challenge by its neck, I held the amber bottle against my cheek for a moment. Although it was almost ten o'clock, the air hung thick and heavy.

'Did you know that beer is less fattening than milk?' said Robert.

'Cow or buffalo?' asked Shailender.

'Semi-skimmed or full-fat?' I added.

'You Angrez have too much choice!' joked JP.

I fiddled with the bottle, picking off the tiny flakes of gold foil that clung to its mouth.

'Did you also know that if a hippopotamus bit your leg,' continued Robert, 'the hole would be big enough to pass a beer bottle through?'

'When was the last time you saw a hippo in India?' asked JP.

'TK, suppose it was a tiger. If...'

'You wouldn't have a leg left,' Shailender interrupted.

'I'm not sure there're many tigers left either,' I commented.

The levity of our conversation was due less to the effect of alcohol and more to our punch-drunken state from the recent adventures in the mountains. Although we had been back for two days, the exertions of the trip, plus the rising temperature in Dehradun, were taking their toll.

It was Wednesday. Because I was due to leave early Friday morning, Robert had invited JP, Shailender and me around for dinner. Ramesh had returned to Tilwara. Robert had left the KHW office at lunchtime to start preparations.

'That's what he said,' alleged JP. 'I bet he's been asleep most of the afternoon.'

Robert winked at me. He lived with his family in a quiet, residential suburb of Dehradun a few kilometres south of the KHW campus. We were sitting on the flat roof of his two-storey building overlooking the neighbours' properties, surrounded by a healthy scattering of palm trees and wide-leafed pot plants.

'While we're waiting for Robert to finish cooking,' I said to Shailender and JP, 'could you help me with something?'

'Sure,' replied JP, 'as long as it doesn't require movement.'

'I'll be back in a moment.'

I went into the house, picked up the canvas bag that I'd left by the front door, then returned upstairs. I sat down and pulled several strips of exercise paper from an envelope.

'What are they?' asked Shailender.

'When I was at SASA Academy I set a task for the children in Classes Two, Three and Four, asking them to complete the sentence, "If I had one wish..." The only problem is that they responded in Hindi, so I don't know what they said! Could you translate them, please?'

One by one, after I handed JP and Shailender a strip of paper, they did their best to decipher what the children had written. I wrote an English translation under their Hindi script.

'This boy says "If I had one wish, I want to stay alive and be a soldier of my country",' said JP.

'A girl in Class Three would like to study and become a teacher,' translated Shailender.

'This boy just wants a home for his family,' read JP. 'And so does this one,' he said, picking up another strip of paper. 'He was probably sitting next to the first boy!'

' "I would like to be a doctor so I can help poor people",' said Shailender. 'That's good.'

'This one's a poet!' said JP. ' "If I had one wish I would like to make a beautiful house near a waterfall and I would like to grow up to be someone important." '

'Why did you set this task?' Shailender turned to me.

'Their world's so different to mine. I was interested in seeing what they aspired to, what motivated them.'

I was also intrigued to see how their dreams compared with certain views expressed by the older generation. Were the Pahari youth being adequately prepared for the future?

Earlier in the day I had revisited the *Mountain Voices* website.

"The entire educational system needs to be revised," Vijay, a farmer and activist, suggests. "Along with the basics of education, training in our old professions should also be given. Because when a child gets higher education, say up to the degree or intermediate level, he or she is totally ignorant about his traditional profession like farming and cattle rearing."

It seems that many parents and grandparents of today's children, not having attended school themselves, believe that increased access to education is a mixed blessing. Although they acknowledge its merits, they question its perceived benefits for the region; when education becomes too academic and irrelevant, it serves little purpose in preparing children for a future life in the mountains. Young people are often not taught, neither are they interested in acquiring, the traditional skills passed through the generations. Knowledge and expertise, accumulated over many centuries, are in danger of vanishing entirely.

Unrealisable aspirations may inevitably lead to disappointment and frustration. Alternatively, young people are enticed to the plains for further study. The likelihood is that they'll never return to invest their new skills and knowledge in their home communities. Education is synonymous with migration. Mountain villages stand to gain very little from the knowledge of the current generation:

"Today's children are educated, they have started going out, they have seen the world; they have started pointing out shortcomings in our work," states Ramchandri, another elderly farmer from the region. 'We have spent our entire life in the village. We have neither seen anything nor are we well-read. Children have now started working of their own free will."

Once JP and Shailender had translated all the wish-lists, I looked through them. Nine of the children aged between eight and twelve were girls, sixteen were boys. Three of the girls wanted to become doctors or teachers. Four of the boys set their sights on becoming soldiers and three aspired to become engineers. Sixty per cent of the children expressed a desire to pursue some form of professional vocation that required further education and training in the city.

Forty per cent of the children's aspirations, however, were directed at their family and friends, rather than themselves. They wished for a home and clothes. None of them indicated a desire to farm or to continue any of the village traditions.

Although some of the children were possibly too young to know what they wanted to do, their responses were indicative of the choices available to most young Pahari.

Pessimistically, the future for the young men is heading in one of two directions; migration to the plains in search of further education and work, or raised, but unfulfilled, expectations and ultimate discontentment in the villages. They walk a dusty road to nowhere, equipped with scant academic knowledge and little skilled motivation to continue the family and village traditions. They've received sufficient learning to realise that there's no tenable future in mountain life but not enough to be able to do anything about it.

And the young women? As current trends collide with traditional practices, the whole equilibrium of the region could destabilise, setting in motion a potentially catastrophic chain of events.

Due to the persistent migration of the men, the number of women in the region could grow disproportionately high in the short term. Then, with the sustained pressure to produce male offspring combined with a gradual rise in female infanticide rates, the pendulum could swing in the opposite direction; eventually, women could be fighting for their survival. It's hard to envisage, but they could become an endangered species in Garhwal.

Unless society drastically shifts its staunchly patriarchal values, those women who marry will still be compelled to favour a boy-child. But, given the number of men leaving the region, the chances of finding a partner will diminish. An increasing number of women will remain single and the population will go into decline.

Therefore, for different, but entirely inter-connected reasons, both the indigenous male *and* female population are threatened with extinction within the next few decades.

Bhawani Bhai had paused thoughtfully when, sitting in my room at SASA Academy, I'd asked him what he believed was the greatest challenge facing the region.

'Without a doubt it is the erosion of tradition and culture,' he replied after a moment. 'In pursuit of money and material gain, people are becoming more and more capitalistic.'

'And India as a whole?'

Sitting with his palms resting on his knees, he leant forward intently.

'The same. The beauty of India was in its simplicity and non-materialistic aspirations. Now this is being lost to a money-orientated society. People used to be self-reliant.

Everything they needed to do they could do for themselves – water, clothes – but now everything comes from outside. Influenced by the money culture and the vicious circle of borrowing, many people owe money and even the country itself is in great debt.'

Bhawani Bhai wasn't harking back to a halcyon age, rose-tinted by the passing of time. Mountain life has always been undeniably tough. He was lamenting the decline of the traditional values that used to underpin it. As a member of the Sarvodaya movement, his stance was inevitably informed by the Gandhian principles of equality and the fulfilment of everybody's basic needs. These values were increasingly difficult to maintain, however, against the strong tide of financial and material influences that were flowing into the region from the city and across the nation from the West.

'What are the most pressing issues that the hill women face at the moment?' I asked Bhawani.

'Alcoholism still,' he replied without hesitation. 'When the movement first started it was very successful because it tended to be the older people that drank. Now, with more access to television, media and magazines influencing changes in lifestyle, younger people are also drinking. Marriage, for example, used to be a serious religious affair. But now it is totally expected at a wedding party for there to be plenty to drink, otherwise it is considered incomplete.'

'Are there any other concerns that the women's groups are still focusing on?'

'Deforestation remains a major issue. It is having a profound effect on the environment. Some women now have to walk up to fourteen kilometres a day to gather wood for fuel.'

His next statement hit hard.

'Women are very strong, very beautiful. But by the time they are twenty-five they are already old.'

Having gazed into so many weary eyes, I knew that his words expressed nothing but a sad, simple truth.

Change is inevitable for the children and young people that I met through SASA and the Samvedna villages, possibly not for the better. Role models such as Bhawani Bhai and his contemporaries represent a dying generation who fostered only a handful of successors to champion their legacy. Heroes for the current younger generation are the folk they hear about in the cities with decent homes, cars and all the trappings of a 21st century lifestyle. They fail to understand that the grass is not necessarily greener. But they continue to dream.

'What to do, guys?' I threw the question at JP and Shailender. Robert, having excelled himself in the kitchen, had just placed a dish of mango slices on the table to complete the meal. 'It strikes me,' I continued, numbering on my fingers, 'that with such an appalling burden falling on the women, men migrating in their droves, environmental concerns rising to a critical level, increases in alcoholism and unemployment and a steady decline in traditional values and practices, Garhwal's future looked incredibly bleak.'

Although it was getting late, I knew that neither Shailender nor JP would be reluctant to voice their opinions. Both cared too much about their work to remain silent.

'That's quite a list!' said JP. 'But you're not wrong.'

It wasn't the answer I expected to hear.

'Generally, young men living in the cities and plains have a choice once they leave school,' said Shailender.

'*All* young men?' I probed.

'Well, many,' he replied, backtracking slightly. 'My point is that, those living in the mountains, don't. The only way they believe they can earn a living is to do exactly what their brothers, fathers and grandfathers have done. They leave.'

'Isn't it positive, though, that the education system encourages young people to pursue their dreams?'

'Right, but education has a dual responsibility,' continued Shailender. 'It should also nurture their sense of communal identity so that they want to return and re-invest their skills and knowledge back into their families and villages. Perhaps that's where it is failing.'

'The prognosis is that, within a few years, most Garhwalis will be living elsewhere in India in order to earn a living,' said JP.

'Acchha. And a high proportion of the Garhwal population,' added Shailender, 'would come from outside the state, via the tourist industry!'

'The crux of the matter,' JP said, hitting the nail on the head, 'is how do you make the "return" to village life attractive and sustainable?'

'And the answer?' I asked, my mouth full of mango.

'I'm not sure that there is *one* answer,' he replied. 'But it has something to do with what Shailender has just said about a holistic, value-based education. At Dehradun Public School, for example, the children receive traditional and vocational education alongside their formal academic study.

'Actually at SASA, one of our aims is to direct the aspirations of the children towards attainable goals,' said Shailender. 'It is important that they realise they don't have to move out of the area in order to work.'

'What kind of work could they do?'

'They could study agriculture and horticulture, and then develop new farming techniques. There are options available besides the army, engineering and medical training that, as you've discovered, many of the young people say they wish to do.'

'There are other possibilities for employment and stimulating the local economy,' said JP. 'Tourism for example. You've seen the large number of pilgrims and religious tourists that come here every year. Many students and other people with money visit every summer to escape the heat of the cities. Adventure sports, mountaineering, hiking, skiing and rafting, are becoming very popular.'

'Eco-tourism could also be a lucrative source of income for local people,' said Robert, topping up our glasses with beer.

'Acchha. There's certainly the potential to exploit the positive aspects of the Tehri Dam, 'said Shailender. 'The reservoir could provide opportunities for a number of water sports and leisure activities.'

'The danger is, of course, that the big businesses move in and the locals get trampled on as usual,' said JP. 'The ideal scenario is community-based tourism.'

'What do you mean?' I asked.

'An industry that engages the entire community in the provision of hotels, restaurants and other leisure activities,' he replied. 'This includes employing local people at every level, including management. Currently the Pahari are treated as little more than porters and pan scrubbers. Unless we see a shift in attitude, the further development of tourism could bring wide-spread social disaster rather than economic recovery.'

'Shailender, you mentioned that young people could be encouraged to study horticulture?' I asked, passing him the plate of mango.

'Yes, cottage industries, such as medicinal herbs, market gardening and bee keeping, are a viable form of development. They would encourage villagers to develop their expertise and re-kindle the self-sufficient lifestyle that worked so well in the past.'

'Isn't that slightly backward-looking?'

'No. If the hill economy is to thrive once more it must be sustainable at a local level. The coming of better roads and electricity will improve the situation considerably, but trade and communication over any wide distance will always remain problematic. Of course, the idea has many challenges. For cottage industries to succeed, development and infrastructural support would be required on a relatively large scale.'

'A local farmer taking a basket of carrots to the nearest market once a week is not going to sustain his family through the winter!' commented Robert as he began to clear the table.

'You're right,' said JP. 'The biggest stumbling block is marketing and distribution. Farmers need to tap into the existing market and negotiate with wholesalers and retailers on a widespread, consolidated level. This almost certainly requires governmental support and investment at a regional level. There is potential here, but plenty of hard work is required.'

Undeniably, one of Garhwal's greatest assets lies in its natural resources; the conservation of the mountains, forests and water system will ensure a more sustainable future for the region's youth.

'It is our responsibility to protect our environment,' I remembered Bhawani Bhai saying. 'It is a very sensitive region; the more we tinker and tamper with nature the more angry it gets. We now see the evidence.'

The construction of the Tehri Dam seems a spectacular example of gross environmental interference. Whatever the justification for its existence, it only requires one further earthquake to precipitate a disaster of unprecedented proportions. That is a worst case scenario. At best, the damage has already been done, indicative of the escalating pace of change that could ultimately render the region unsustainable.

Perhaps a balanced negotiation between the government, commercial developers and the Pahari is required; one which, while conceding the inevitability of technological advancement, acknowledges the intrinsic role played by the Pahari in safeguarding their own future and halting the effects of deforestation. The hydro-electric project developed by Bihari Lal at Budar Kedar, for example, is a great model for this kind of small-scale project. It is practical, sustainable and successfully run by the local community without any damage to the environment.

'Come, Mark,' said JP, 'it's time we were going. Robert needs his beauty sleep.'

As we drove northwards, the silhouetted Mussoorie Ridge jutted into the horizon. A chain of saffron lights flecked the hillside, draping the neckbone of Nanda Devi, patron goddess of Uttarakhand, with tiny jewels. Rising into the firmament at Gunn Hill, Mussoorie's highest point, they married with the starry pearls that adorned her hair. Glowing with a range of intensity, some lights brightly twinkled alone, others amassed in amber clumps indicating the presence of a village or hamlet. In those homes without electricity, solar lights or firewood to squander, a few flickered faintly, others barely at all.

19
Tonight We Fly

Sir, you are crazy!

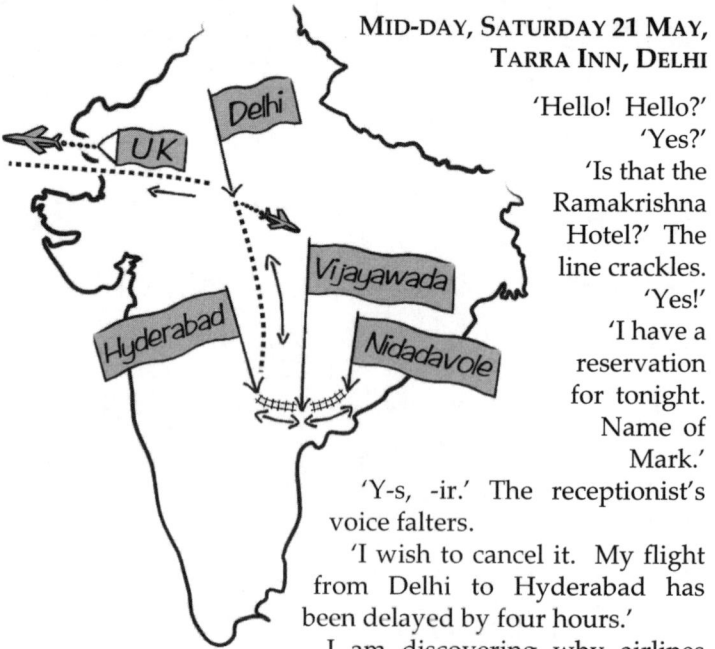

MID-DAY, SATURDAY 21 MAY, TARRA INN, DELHI

'Hello! Hello?'
'Yes?'
'Is that the Ramakrishna Hotel?' The line crackles.
'Yes!'
'I have a reservation for tonight. Name of Mark.'
'Y-s, -ir.' The receptionist's voice falters.
'I wish to cancel it. My flight from Delhi to Hyderabad has been delayed by four hours.'

I am discovering why airlines require passengers to confirm their flights. In a curt conversation with Deccan Airways Customer Services I've just been informed that my plane has been rescheduled to arrive at 3 am. My onward train to Vijayawada is at 6 am. There seems little point in travelling across the city to check into a hotel.

'Ver- g--d, -ir.'

'No, it's not very good,' I bawl, chucking my flight itinerary onto the bed in a fit of pique.

I am holed up in a windowless, airless room on the outskirts of Delhi. The temperature exceeds 45 degrees. The air-conditioning system has just spluttered to a halt. There's a powercut. An itchy rash of insect bites covers my chest. I'm sorely tempted to enquire about available flights back to the UK today. The suffocating heat makes every thought and action a severe effort. I'm struggling.

Saving graces

1. *There's a TV*
   (I'm hopeful the power will return soon)
2. *The manager is accommodating*
   (I can leave my rucksack at the hotel until next week)
3. *The hotel room has a bed and a bathroom*
   (I'm not waiting in a stuffy departure lounge)
4. *The airport is only ten minutes away*
   (when I eventually need to get there)

The prospect of two flights, three train journeys and another long, hot week before I'm back, once more, in the same hotel room fills me with dread. I shake my head in disbelief. Suppose my return flight from Hyderabad to Delhi is also delayed or cancelled? What happens if I'm still in India when my visa expires?

I consider my itinerary for the next week. It's madness. Then I reflect on Jennie's parting words, all those months ago:

'You promise to come back and see us? You must make this the last place you visit before you leave India.'

'I will do my best,' I had replied.

I think of Lakshme and smile. *Go with it, Mark!* Am I mad?

5.45 AM, SUNDAY 22 MAY, PLATFORM 4, SECUNDERABAD STATION, ANDHRA PRADESH

'Sir, you are crazy!'

'I have a ticket for second class AC. Look!'

'Actually you are on the waiting list. You are not having a confirmed reservation,' asserts the TTE.

'Please! I'm number one.' I show him my ticket. 'WL/1.'

'You are not travelling on this train. Buy ticket for tomorrow. Not my problem.'

No. On this occasion the TTE is right. It's my problem. I've been on the waiting list before but my ticket has always moved onto the confirmation list prior to departure. Not on this occasion. The charts have been prepared, the train's about to leave and I have to be on it. Waiting one more day will send my itinerary awry. There would be no point in continuing my journey. I may as well fly back to Delhi.

Even at this unearthly hour the air is heavy with humidity. My brow drips and my bowels make disengaging noises. Confrontation always does that to me.

In reverse order of priority, I need this train and I need a toilet. Now.

A porter wheels a large trunk over my foot. I glare at him. Having been awake all night, my patience is thin.

'Sorry, sir. Sorry. Sorry!' he scuttles away, fear in his eyes. The train judders.

I dash along the platform and locate the unreserved second class compartment. I find a toilet. I find a seat. I collapse.

2.00PM, SUNDAY 22 MAY, VIJAYAWADA, ANDHRA PRADESH

'May I book a room for tonight, please?'

'I'm sorry, sir, we are full.'

'Nothing at all?'

'Sorry, there is a business convention in the city this weekend. Try next door.'

*

'Hi, I'm looking for a room. Cheap. Just for tonight.'
'No, sir. We are fully booked. There is...'
'...a business convention?'
'Yes sir. Try tomorrow.'

*

'Do you have any rooms available for tonight?'
A blank stare.
'Any rooms for tonight?'
'Pardon?'
'Are you having rooms tonight?'
'Sir?'
'Room. Tonight. Please.'
'Sorry, sir. Please be speaking in English.'

*

I'm on the tenth floor. I wade through the shag pile, pick up the telephone and dial 201.
'Room service. Hello.'
'I'd like a beer please. Cold. Thank you.'

I turn the AC dial to maximum. I switch on the TV remote and flick through all 96 channels. I find one that plays music and, by choice, *my* choice, turn up the volume. **LOUD**.

I discard my clothes on the bathroom floor. Hot water steams out of the shower head.

This suite might break the bank but it'll be worth every rupee.

11AM MONDAY 23 MAY, SKCV VILLAGE

'You still don't like buttermilk, brother?'
'I could live in India for the rest of my life and quite happily not let a drop pass my lips.'
Harish laughs. 'What about mango?'
'Now you're talking.'

Bashir gently squeezes my hand. 'You should see my garden *now!*' He has grown an inch or two and is slightly less bouncy.

Although the grounds, gardens and buildings are as immaculately tidy as they were in January, the grass is parched, the earth dry and the trees tired and droopy. Boys lounge in the shade, snooze in their dormitories and relax in front of the TV. An atmosphere of yielding lethargy inhabits the humid air, so thick that you could almost slice off a slab with a knife. The boys' inactivity could be interpreted as laziness. The truth of the matter: it's too darn hot.

*

'We are so needing the rains,' Bhakti, Manihara's wife, tells me. Even she, one of the most calmly industrious people I've ever met, finds the heat exhausting. 'First thing in the morning and after five o'clock is OK outside. Between those times I am staying inside and turning up the AC.'

'How is Manihara?' I ask.

'His hip operation was successful. He is now recuperating in a hotel in Hyderabad. The consultant decided that he would be more comfortable there than in hospital. He would love to see you.'

'I plan to visit on Thursday on my way back to Delhi.'

'You are already booking the tickets?'

'Yes, but you must give me details of the hotel.'

8.30AM, TUESDAY 24 MAY, SKCV VILLAGE

All my thoughts of coming to Andhra Pradesh, the hassle of planes, trains and hotels have been quelled.

The boys grab my arms and hug me. My eyes begin to well up as I put on my sunglasses.

'See you soon, brother,' waves Harish as I walk towards the gate.

I'm sure you might.

2.00PM, WEDNESDAY 25 MAY, HEBRON HOSTEL

'And you can also eat them like this.'

Jennie has bitten a hole in the top of a mango and is sucking out the juice. With a light squeeze, she pushes the oval, flat stone until it emerges, like a bright orange lollipop, from the top of the fruit. When almost all the juice has gone, she neatly folds the skin in half, lengthwise, and flattens it down. She then folds it again and sucks out the remaining drops. She places the green, purse-like, skin on the table. Her fingers and mouth are spotless.

Having watched and copied every detail I also finish. Juice dribbles down my chin, my shirt and onto the table. My fingers are sodden and the mango skin looks as if it's been ravaged by a monkey.

Jennie laughs. 'Another?' she asks. 'We have plenty.'

'I've already had three today!' I reply.

*

Hosanna House is now complete and the girls have moved into their new dormitories. Every building has received a light ochre coat of paint and the courtyard, where the girls eat, is laid with smooth concrete.

The crotons, in all their varieties, are in full bloom. The Christmas tree has grown a few inches and the sweet perfume of jasmine caresses the air. Clumps of bougainvillea tumble from the roof, over the archway and onto the ground.

'Puvvulu,' a little voice says.

'Yes, flower!' I reply, my Telugu flooding back.

'Yes, Uncle!'

The greatest news, though, is that Jennie is up and about on both legs. She can now walk around the compound and to Hermon School.

'It's a miracle!' beams Esther. Although she has moved back with her children to her home in Kakinada, she changed her plans so she could see me here.

A miracle indeed.

'This is my friend JP on a mule and this is a place called Kedarnath in the Himalayas.'

Lakshme giggles at JP. I'm showing her photographs of North India on my camera screen.

'Uncle, who?' She asks, pointing at a picture of Sujan.

'His name is Sujan. Very good man.'

'Sujan,' Lakshme repeats.

I feel completion in the circle of my journey, a link between North and South has been brokered.

'Seeing you, good, Mark.'

Not 'Uncle'. Lakshme says my name for the first time. I wonder if she's aware of its significance to me.

7.00PM, THURSDAY 26 MAY

'Remember you asked me to make Hebron the last place I visit before leaving India?'

'I remember,' Jennie replies.

'I couldn't promise, because I didn't know what would happen.'

'But you came.' She rises from her chair and gives me a hug.

Raju opens the doors and I put my rucksack on the seat of the car.

Beside it is another bag, laden with spices, seeds, nuts and Hebron's unique curry powder, made especially for me.

Raju puts the key in the ignition and we're off. The girls part on either side as we head down the drive.

'To the station, Raju!' I am leaving Nidadavole on the 20.36 Visakha Express. Next stop Secunderabad.

'Yes, sir!' he giggles in his boyish way.

Jennie takes a few steps forward and stands, unaided, waving.

'Next time I want to see you running around the compound,' I call after her.

'Next time?'

'Of course!'

9.00AM, FRIDAY 27 MAY,
URBASI RESIDENCY, SECUNDERABAD

I arrive at 7.30 and check into the hotel that Manihara has recommended. It's bright, clean and yet-to-be completed. Builders are working outside, above and below my room.

I rest for a few hours then decide to find Mani. His room is two floors higher in a quieter part of the hotel.

I am surprised how well he looks despite having only had hip replacement surgery at the beginning of the week.

'The hospital is good,' he tells me. 'The surgeons really know what they're doing.'

'How was your trip?' he asks, as if I've been tootling around the countryside for a few weeks.

I tell him.

'Did you do the Char Dham? I love it up there.' A grimace reveals that he's hiding the pain well.

*

Later in the afternoon I discover a key in my pocket and realise it's from my room at Hebron. I ask at the reception desk for the nearest post office. The assistant hotel manager offers to accompany me there.

Several queues, three counters and one hour later, the key is posted back to Jennie.

'The system is madness,' the hotel manager remarks.

*

Sudhama and Anand, Mani's son, arrive early evening.

'We're going for a pizza,' says Manihara. 'Coming?'

'You're allowed out?' I ask, astonished, as Anand helps him into his wheelchair.

'As long as I'm back in bed by nine!'

After six months, I can't believe I'm about to spend my last evening in Pizza Hut, downtown Secunderabad.

*

I call Deccan Airways to confirm my flight. The phone rings. I hold my breath. I give my details.

'You're absolutely sure?'
'Yes, sir. Your flight *is* on schedule.'
I sleep.
I wake. Drilling on the building site outside my window continues most of the night.

SATURDAY 28 MAY

The flight leaves Hyderabad at 05.40 and arrives in Delhi at 07.40. There are surprisingly few people outside the airport and even fewer taxis. I barely recognise it as the place I arrived at six months ago. No grabbing hands, no staring eyes, no hassle.

Back at Tarra Inn, I retrieve my luggage from the manager, order a coffee and eat masala toast.

The dry Delhi heat scratches my throat like sandpaper. I feel as if I'm being micro-waved from the inside out.

SUNDAY 29 MAY, 2005, FLIGHT BA 142
FROM DELHI TO LONDON HEATHROW

- Buy water ✓
- Go with flow ✓
- ~~No more lists~~

20
Regeneration

Three Years On...

'Mama-ji, look!'

A woman leans forward from her sunbed. As she tilts her head, a light breeze catches her jet-black hair, gently flicking it across her face. Lowering her sunglasses, she glances affectionately at her son and smiles.

Aged about six, he is methodically shaping a pile of sand with his fingers. With his tongue poking through a gap in his bottom teeth, an intense look of purpose is etched across his face.

It is three years since my first trip. I am lounging, beer bottle in hand, in a beach shack in Vagator, North Goa. My toes dabble in the soft sand as the sun begins its descent towards the sea. Golden rays, peeping through the coir-matted roof, produce dappled shadows which dance over the rattan tables and chairs.

This is one of many return trips that I've made to India over the last three years. The simple act of sponsoring a child has changed my life significantly.

Needless to say, I've visited Lakshme, Jennie, Esther and the girls at Hebron on several occasions and been back to see Manihara and the lads at SKCV. I've also returned to some of the projects in the Himalayan foothills.

As I draw my thoughts together, I'm reminded of two simple words: *neti, neti*: "Not this – it is not this alone." Nothing I could say about India is definitive; there's always more to come. Though I could offer my thoughts at this particular time on this particular day, tomorrow I might feel differently. India, undoubtedly, will *be* different.

We were promised a feast of festivities last weekend: Christian Easter, Hindu Holi and Hedonistic full moon parties. But Mother Nature had other plans.

During late Saturday morning, thick brooding clouds squeezed the suffocating air closer to the earth. At mid-day, cracks of lightning ripped open the skies. Throughout the afternoon, rain slashed the beaches, fields and streets. The festivities were a wash-out. Unprecedented freak weather ravaged much of South India for three days, whipping farmers into a frenzy as they surveyed the irreparable damage wrought on this season's crops of fruit and vegetables. The rains, two months early, presage worrying times ahead for 60% or so of the nation who are dependent on agriculture for a living.

Now that the weather has returned to blistering normality, Vagator hums. Buses, displaying banners that read: **JESUS IS THE POWER** and **MOTHER THERESA PRAY FOR US**, spill tourists from neighbouring states onto the beaches. Men, stripped down to their underwear, dive and whoop in the waves. Wives, sisters and aunties giggle gingerly on the water's edge, their sari hems dragging in the wet sand. They gasp and squeal at the exhilaration of their loose abandon, generously sharing their delight with the rest of the beach as the surf tingles their toes.

The bronzed European sun-worshippers don't bat an eyelid. Prostrate in contorted, ray-maximising, positions, they offer unflinching devotion to their god.

Dead on six o'clock, Goan trance music starts to pulsate from Nine Bar, perched on the cliffs behind me. The breeze fuses the techno beat and pounding ocean into a mesmeric contest of the air waves. Beach traders parade up and down the shore, touting sarongs, shirts, CDs, coconuts, fruit, ice cream, pastries, jewellery, leg waxing, hand henna-ing and toenail painting.

A shadow falls across my beer bottle. 'Buy my cheap rubbish, sir!'

I raise my right hand to shield my eyes. 'What the..?'

'Better price than Primark!'

'No, no thank you,' I say to the young woman's silhouetted face.

'Sir, just looking?'

'No!'

'I am selling best trash on beach!'

'I'm sure you are. But I really don't want. Thank you.'

I've come to the conclusion that beach traders possess a sixth sense. After the briefest of exchanges, they're able to detect if someone is interested, even if just slightly, in what they're selling. When that's the case, they hover, hassle and haggle. They also know when, however hard they try, they'll never make a sale. Why bother?

'OK. Bye,' she snorts, sensing correctly that I didn't want her best trash.

☼

The boy continues to shape his construction. Grains of fine sand catch under his nails as he carves small channels in the mounds. The dry surfaces occasionally crumble between his fingers. But he is not perturbed. Before long, the area in front of him features several small buildings linked by a network of tiny paths. He pads down to the shore and searches for shells. Picking up a few strands of seaweed, he returns to make a garden.

🌴🌴🌴

Another young woman saunters assuredly towards me. She is laden with a rucksack on her back and a pile of sarongs and bed sheets under her right arm. A blue-jewelled stud pierces her nose.

'I cut your nails, sir?' she asks, producing a pair of clippers from a small leather pouch. I look at my fingers and hesitate. Proud of my nails, I decide that they could do with a trim. *As long as she does a good job.*

'How much?'

'First I say my price then you say yours.'

'OK.'

'Two hundred and fifty rupees.'

I laugh. 'Forget it. Fifty.'

'I cut verrrry nice, hands and feet. I show.' I let her clip the nail on my left big toe. 'See!'

'I'll give you fifty rupees.'

'Sir? Hands *and* feet? One hundred and fifty.'

Charmed by her delicately attractive features, I eventually agree on one hundred rupees. 'But you do them well!' I instruct.

'Yes, sir. Verrrrry nice.' Her dusky eyes twinkle.

'What's your name?'

'Anita.' Brushing the sand off my toes, she cuts the remaining nails on my feet. I'm not too impressed by her efforts, particularly when she slices far too deeply into my right big toe nail.

'No! Stop!' I exclaim. 'That's too short.'

'Sir?'

'It hurts.'

'Sorry.'

'Don't cut the others like that.'

Anita then clips my left small fingernail. It's fine. But she hacks at the next one.

'Hey, you said you'd do them nicely!' I turn my hand around. 'That's much too short and not straight.'

She takes my middle finger. 'Not too short,' I reiterate. 'Understand?'

'Yes, sir.'

But, when she cuts into my skin, it's clear that she doesn't know what she's doing.

'Enough!' I shout, quickly pulling my hand away. 'You're not doing any more!'

'Why?'

'I'm cross.' I keep my annoyance in check. 'I trusted you. You've done a bad job.'

'Don't worry, sir. Tomorrow they grow back.'

I glance at her contemptuously.

'Maybe next day..?'

'Don't be ridiculous!'

Anita looks crestfallen. Dropping her head, her sad eyes stare into the sand. She says nothing. I turn away dismissively and take a large gulp of beer. It's getting warm. A flock of seagulls, mewling like kittens, circle overhead.

After a few moments Anita looks up. 'Sir. I continue?'

'No,' I respond petulantly, 'I said "no more". You've made me angry. I was in a good mood. Now I'm not.' Picking at the frayed skin around the nail, I feel as if I'm addressing a three-year-old. I dig my feet into the sand and feel the grains shift between my toes.

Anita, sitting motionless, is silent. She seems upset that I'm angry with her.

I fiddle with the label on the beer bottle. Sticky shreds of paper, wet from the condensation, slide down the glass. Anita doesn't move.

'You from Karnataka?' I ask, breaking the impasse. I know that many of the beach traders come from the neighbouring state.

'Yes, sir,' she murmurs. 'Small village.'

'You have brothers and sisters?'

'Yes. One brother, one sister. They are ten.'

'Twins?'

'Ah,' her eyes light up.

'How old are you?'

'Twelve, sir.'

I'm taken aback. Anita looks at least sixteen. Studying her face, I notice a dark brown, round indentation level with her left eye. The size of a small coin, it looks like a burn mark.

'You don't go to school?'

'No. I earn money to take home for my brother and sister to go to school. Fees very expensive.'

'How much?'

'Five thousand rupees a month.'

I calculate that's about £60. 'Would you like to go to school?'

'Yes, to study. But it is too costly.'

'You speak very good English.'

'Thanks. I learn from people on beach.' Shifting her position, she straightens her back.

'What do you want to do when you're older?'

'Same. Work on beach. Then maybe building site.'

'Does that pay well?'

She shrugs. 'Maybe twenty, thirty rupees a day.'

I look at my nails. 'Can I make a suggestion, Anita?'

She looks up at me.

'Cutting nails on the beach is a good idea. You can make quick business and you're not parting with any goods.'

'Yes, sir, I know...'

'But, *please*, ask a friend to show you how to do it properly!'

She grins. I'd rather Anita was in school but that's clearly not going to happen. Many young women come to Goa each season to earn money to send back to their families.

'OK, sir.'

I reach into my pocket and pull out some notes. I hand her thirty rupees.

'Thank you, sir.'

'Not bad business for ten minutes work!'

She smiles wryly. 'No, sir.'

Anita then drops her rucksack to the sand. 'You want to buy jewellery? Shirt?'

'Nice try, but no!' I admire her enterprising spirit.

'Buy just one thing? Bring me good luck.'

'No,' I reply gently. 'I really mean it. I've bought many things already.'

Her eye lashes flicker nervously. 'Is it because of the nails?'

'No, it's not because of the nails. I'm not buying from anyone on the beach today.'

Anita picks up her rucksack, gathers the sarongs under her arm, and stands up.

'OK. See you!' She turns, takes a few paces down the beach, then stoops at another pair of feet.

The boy building the sandcastle takes a break. He has gathered a few admirers. Smiling proudly at his efforts, he points out various features to the onlookers.

Anita typifies why India remains an enigma to me. She is young and bright with a whole future ahead of her. Yet she is uneducated and her aspirations are low. She's also a girl.

According to ASER 2007, the Annual Survey of India Report, the number of children aged six to fourteen not attending school in rural India has dropped from 6.6% in 2006 to 4.2% in 2007. I'm aware that these statistics vary considerably from those cited earlier in the book. As I said then, and still maintain, obtaining verifiable, consistent figures is a challenge. Yet it appears that remarkable progress has been made over the last three years in this respect.

First conducted in 2005, ASER aims to monitor the state of primary education in every rural district throughout India. It is facilitated by Pratham, an NGO working alongside State and Central Governments to achieve the national goal of "universalisation of elementary education" for every child aged six to fourteen by 2010.

The work is impressive. ASER annually involves over 500 organisations and nearly 20,000 volunteers to sample more than 700,000 children living in 16,000 villages. The children, from twenty randomly selected families in each village, are asked to complete a set of simple reading and arithmetic tasks. The compiled results are then aggregated to district, state and national report cards. This kind of information, a core set of annually-collated, meaningful data that offers clear indicators on the state of education, is a scarce commodity in India. Cutting through the bureaucratic mire, the survey appears to demonstrate that focussed planning, goal-setting and consistency produces results.

An encouraging statistic is that school mid-day meal provision has increased by over 20% to 93% in the last two years. India operates the largest, free school lunch programme in the world.

Not all of the report, however, makes positive reading.

Despite clear improvements in facilities, 25% of schools don't have useable water and 40% are without toilets. Though the percentage is down by 2% from 2006, 19% of young people aged fifteen and sixteen are out of school. The figure is higher for young women than men.

Nearly 40% of children in Class Five are unable to read a Class Two-standard text, while around 60% cannot carry out simple arithmetic divisions. Of the children in Class Two, over 90% cannot read the text appropriate to their age and 60% are unable to recognise numbers between 10 and 99. Although more children now attend school than ever before, the ASER report admits that they're not necessarily learning very much.

Resolved to transform this scenario, in July 2007 Pratham launched "Read India", a phased two-year campaign aimed at achieving reading and arithmetic proficiency for all of India's children by 2009. The programme's accelerated teaching technique claims to demonstrate palpable changes in a child's learning levels in three months. Progress so far appears promising: the campaign has reached over 250,000 schools and villages in its first six months. It will be another two years, however, before its impact can be fully measured.

In the meantime, further questions exist. Are those able to read, for example, reading with comprehension? The survey notes that the reading standard of children attending private schools is nearly 12% higher than those in government establishments. With government teacher absenteeism levels remaining at one in four, it is unsurprising that many parents, given the opportunity, prefer either to send their child to a private school or to employ a private coach. By the time they reach Class Eight, 25% of young people receive additional private coaching.

The ASER report emphasises a concern expressed by many commentators. The basic infrastructure within India may have improved in recent years, but the *quality* of education still has a long way to go.

Although criticism of government provision may be justified, the reality is that, unless they attend a government-run school, a considerable proportion of India's youth will not receive an education at all. Many parents simply cannot afford to educate their children privately, unless they're able to enrol them in one of the few charitably-supported establishments such as Dehradun Public School. Or, as in Anita's case, they send the eldest child out to earn money to pay for the education of younger siblings.

Pratham, while acknowledging that the prime responsibility for educating the nation's youth rests with the government, believes that a tripartite partnership between government, NGOs and the private sectors could considerably enhance the scope and quality of provision.

Other organisations have a more forthright approach.

In March 2007, I met Krishan Khanna, founder of the national citizens movement, *iWatch*, when he visited London for a Business-NGO-Government Partnerships conference.

'There are three doors,' he told me, as we sat down to chat in the hotel lobby. 'In recent times, two of them have been opened. Independence in 1947 and the economic reforms in 1991.'

'And the third?' I asked him.

'The third door is the mind. The key for opening that is education.'

'How do you believe that's going to happen?'

'Decontrol all forms of education as business was released in 1991. Involve the local community in the management of primary education and allow private finance and participation in higher and technical education.'

'That sounds radical.'

'We need a change of mindset in India,' said Krishan. 'The government has no money for education. If India is to become a knowledge economy, we need to think and act very differently.'

'Can you give me an example?' I asked.

'Over seventy-two per cent of graduates are *arts* graduates. The remaining twenty-eight per cent are studying science, commerce, engineering and the like. Of those, less than *three* per cent of students are learning a vocational skill or trade. We have plenty of engineers and MBAs in India but where can you find a qualified plumber or carpenter?'

'I've seen plenty on my travels,' I replied.

'*Qualified* and trained to international standards?'

'I see what you mean.'

'We need to encourage at least eighty to ninety per cent of the employable population to pursue some form of vocational education or training,' Krishan said. 'Build their skills and confidence. Actively involve employers and business in leading from the front.'

'What about the role of the NGOs and other umbrella organisations?' I asked.

'We need to see engagement from *all* of the stakeholders. It's only the government that needs to move out of the way.'

'Completely?'

'The government should focus on primary and secondary education only. The rest should be left to the private and third sectors.'

Looking at the current situation, I appreciate Krishan's rationale. India has a large gap in the availability of employable skills. Ten million young people leave school or graduate from higher education each year. However, by 2010, the IT and BPO, Business Process Outsourcing, sector alone will produce fifteen million direct and indirect employment opportunities.

As India improves its healthcare provision, an additional 500,000 nurses and paramedical staff will be required before 2012. Currently, 10% of that number qualify each year.

There are about thirteen million MSMEs (micro, small and medium enterprises) throughout India, accounting for nearly 80% of the nation's GDP. If India sustains its current annual GDP growth rate of over 8%, the sector will require a considerable increase in employees with pharmaceutical, processing, electronics and engineering qualifications within the next five years.

From where is this literate, skilled and confident workforce going to come?

'You want music, boss?' I turn my head in response. A lad in jeans and an imitation Nike T-shirt strolls over. Tucked under his arm is a box of pirate CDs.

'Not really,' I reply.

'Good, good sounds, man.'

'What've you got?'

'The Stoney Roses, Beastie-beastie Boys, Amy Wine...'.

'Any Indian music?'

'Goan trance. You like?'

'That's not what I meant.'

'Where are you from, sir?'

'England.'

'Ah, England! It is very great country. You are so very lucky!'

I never cease to be amazed by the number of people I meet who stand in awe of the English. It's as if two centuries of colonial rule never happened. They like to wear western-branded clothes, copy foreign products and then try to sell them back to us! And it's not just the English; many Indians seem fixated by most things non-Indian. Where's the confidence in their own culture?

"The [Indian] patriot attributes our decline to the ravages of foreign invasion and the benumbing influences of foreign rule," wrote Sri Aurobindo in 1910. I still treasure the book Krishna "gifted" me in Cochin three years ago.

He's probably right. The Moguls, the Portuguese, the British... we all produced systems of governance into which the indigenous population learnt to fit. Under colonial rule, the hierarchy of varna and jati continued to serve the people well. We may have knocked the stuffing out of the nation but they coped, pretty much because they knew where they stood. With the British and the Brahmins occupying the highest positions in government and society, it's little wonder that generations of Indians have been burdened with an innate sense of inferiority and a lack of self-confidence.

I'm in no doubt that the Indian spirit was suppressed by centuries of invasion, domination and foreign rule. Yet I am surprised, as Aurobindo observes, that few societies "have been so eager to preserve themselves in inertia". Everywhere, he says, "there is your 'simple man', that is your average man who will not think and cannot think".

Though it's almost a century since Aurobindo wrote those words and over sixty years since Independence, many of the western systems that India accepted and made its own, remain prolific.

India's "2020 Vision", published by the government in 2002, in calling the nation to awaken an "unswerving confidence in ourselves", emphasises a clear distinction between blind imitation and intelligent emulation. Development which, in practice, is more akin to an assembly line of cloned ideas than a workshop of original thought, does little justice to India's creative potential.

While Sri Aurobindo attributes some of India's ills to the British "hypnosis of a nation", he intimates that society, through its failure to cherish the nation's rich cultural and spiritual heritage, is also culpable. This reminds me of the "cooking pot Hindus" analogy that Krishna from the Shiva Temple had used to illustrate how far the traditional practices of Hindu society have strayed from the original, value-based philosophies. The values of *Sanatana Dharma*, the eternal law, have been supplanted by empty ritual. Idiosyncratic moral codes now sanction behavioural patterns ranging from an inert tolerance of mediocrity to the most tortuously-justified acts of corruption.

This view was echoed by Bhawani Bhai's belief that the greatest threats the nation now faces are the financial and material urges of a money-orientated, Western-influenced, society seeping from the towns and cities into rural India.

The boy walks down to the sea. A wave brushes the bottom of his khaki shorts as he bends to scoop up some water in his cupped hands. Though he treads back attentively, most of the water trickles through his fingers. He sprinkles the remaining drops onto his construction to smooth its craggy edges. He returns to the shoreline, again losing most of the water as he shuffles back up the beach. And again. Though the sun parches his efforts, he perseveres.

On 25 January 2007, Abdul Kalam, India's former president, delivered his final Republic Day address to the nation. "In the eighties," he said, "children always used to ask me questions such as 'When can I sing the Song of India?' Today, the youth are asking me, 'What can I give to India?' This shows that the nation is on a positive growth trajectory. The change in pattern of the questions is indicative of the transformation which has taken place over the years."

Kalam has a passionate vision for the nation, much of which is geared towards empowering and mobilising the country's youth. His aspirations for a prosperous India by 2020 are compelling: a near-zero poverty line, a literacy rate approaching 100%, electrical power supplies to all villages, no shortage of potable water anywhere and good sanitation facilities for every home.

Later in his address, Kalam said that "Our ICT sector is exporting more than U.S. $24 billion and the Indian Pharma Industry is ranked 4th in the world and exports nearly $4 billion of products. Our $44 billion automobile industry is growing at the rate of 17% per annum. Our total exports in the last 8 months has crossed $80 billion."

At the beginning of February 2007, the Tata Group's buy-out of Corus was announced in the press. In 2005 Tata Steel was the world's 56th biggest steel producer. Within two years it had risen to 18th; the latest deal placed it fifth. With interests including Tetley's tea, utilities, car manufacturing, hotels and satellite television as well as steel, the Tata Group is India's largest listed company. Its £6.2 billion takeover is the biggest overseas acquisition ever made by an Indian company.

Here's the paradox. India has the fourth largest economy in the world *but* 150 million families live without electricity.

It has the second largest GDP of any developing country *yet*, in terms of GDP per capita, it's in the bottom 30% of nations.

Ten per cent of the population hold 53% of the nation's wealth. So much remains in the hands of so few.

Before returning to Goa, I re-read an extract from the journal I'd kept on my first trip:

> Every time I talk to young people about their aspirations and share their excitement for the goals they want to achieve, I see the enormous potential waiting to be realised in this country. Then I return to my hotel to wash with cold water from a bucket and ask myself, *will it really happen?*

This polarity is no better typified than in the tensions that I encountered in the Himalayan foothills. Though Garhwal, with its distinct convergence of challenges, stands apart from the rest of India, ironically, it represents a microcosm of the bigger picture; a society in transition, torn between tradition and development, culture and belief.

Is the "Tyranny of the OR" pulling, not just the Garhwal region, but the entire nation in opposing directions? In the spirit of the "Genius of the AND", will India ever find a way to embrace fully all of its contradictory forces to move forward as a unified whole?

Throughout my travels I encountered people floundering in the dust of dead tradition and repetition, trampled by the destructive boot of skewed values, corruption and oppression, bound by the paralysis of inertia and a lack of self-confidence.

I experienced the stark reality of women and their families living a life of extreme hardship in the Garhwal mountains; of people coping with disability in the most unforgiving of environments; of development organisations striving relentlessly to effect change.

History has shown India to be a resilient nation. Its people survive. Only just, though, at times. Despite tremendous advances elsewhere in the economy, about 60% of the population remain dependent on agriculture to earn a living. As India bypasses the industrial revolution and leapfrogs into the service, information and technological age, a significant number of these rural communities could be left behind.

The sun, dipping behind a low bank of cloud, suffuses the sky with coral light, its rich hue absorbed by a few solitary wisps. A distant plane soars above the horizon, trailing a silent streak of lightning in its path. Two minutes later, the sun, dropping through the clouds, begins its rapid descent into the sea.

The boy stands up, wipes his fingers down his T-shirt and beams. 'Mama-ji, look! My city!'

India has a legacy of tremendous visionaries. At the turn of the 19th century, Sri Aurobindo appealed to his countrymen to be proud of their heritage and to strive for the fulfilment of the Indian genius. A century later, Abdul Kalam picked up the baton: "Economic prosperity alone is not sufficient. It has to be complemented with the value systems and our five thousand years old Civilisational heritage which has genetically shaped the Indian people."

The poet Gurudev Rabindranath Tagore, recipient of the Nobel Literature Prize in 1913, described a future India where "the clear stream of reason has not lost its way into the dreary desert sand of dead habit".

India's "2020 Vision", in pursuing this motif, exhorts the nation to discard "outmoded ideas and behaviours that retard future progress" and to re-discover "the well-springs of our own native strength".

In my notebook I carry a copy of a poem composed three years ago by two teenagers, Shubham and Uma, who attended Dehradun Public School. Written in their tiny village in Uttarakhand, the poem encapsulates these national themes with remarkable insight.

The Real Strength

A power of wings,
A shower of springs,
And a heart full of joy begins to sing,
Education is that which gives us everything.
Education is the best policy to know the facts.
It opens the closed door of the mind.
It makes us knowledgeable and confident.
It teaches to face the reality and not to be left behind.

A spring has immense potential. It is a small trickle of water, rising through the ground of the Himalayas, cutting and weaving through the mountains, merging with other streams to forge a potent, holy river. It is a metal coil which, when released, bounces with energy and movement. It is a new season promising growth and hope.

Representing India's youth in all their diversity, it is an unashamedly mixed metaphor that shares a dynamic, common thread: energy liberated from a dormant position; water bubbling up from underground; a metal coil freed from constraint; and a new season following winter.

I saw evidence of this potential reflected in the motivation of the young women at Hebron Hostel; the determination of the young men at SKCV; the aspirations of the students in Kodaikanal; the fortitude of the disabled young people and their families living in the Himalayan foothills and the opportunities offered to the children at Dehradun Public School and SASA Academy.

India is a young nation. Over 40% of the population is under the age of eighteen. Many have tasted opportunity and they want more. They've experienced the lumbering bureaucracies and they're thirsty for change. They can see through the corruption and they've had their fill. A confident generation of young people, hundreds of thousands of engaged, open minds, are keen to play a role in transforming the nation.

Like the springs gushing through the Himalayan hills and valleys, youthful voices are emerging, bursting through the cracks and becoming visible. As the rivers and streams converge to form the mighty Ganges, so India is beginning to experience a torrent of young people surging forward.

Subham and Uma write that education will teach India's youth to face reality and *not* to be left behind. Whether, or not, this vision is realised depends on the way in which their potential is released, nurtured and channelled. That lies in the hands of the relevant stakeholders to deliver a holistic education system that embraces traditional values, academic study AND vocational training.

Many young people, particularly those from rural India, are currently leaving their villages to be educated. But, like Garhwal's "missing men", they are *not* returning to invest their acquired knowledge and skills in their communities. Attracted by the opportunities of modern society, they remain in the cities after completing their studies. An increasing number of graduates now aspire to export their talents abroad.

The prognosis that, within a few years, most Garhwalis could be living in other parts of India, could apply elsewhere. While a sizeable proportion of the nation continues to dwell in the shadow of progress, others are forsaking their roots entirely. The tensions between tradition and development, culture and belief, remain.

Yet I am cautiously optimistic. The great adventurer, Jim Corbett, writing in the Garhwal Mountains prior to India's Independence, expressed a conviction that I long to share:

> A typical son of Garhwal, of that simple and hardy hill-folk; and of that greater India, whose sons only those few who live among them are privileged to know. It is these big-hearted sons of the soil, no matter what their caste or creed, who will one day weld the contending factions into a composite whole, and make of India a great nation.

Therein may lie the secret to India's genius.

Key Players

CHILD'S TRUST
CHILD's Trust aims to make a difference in the lives of underprivileged children. Based in Basingstoke, Hampshire, it has been a registered charity since 1999 and currently supports nine different projects across India. Its founders, Mark and Julie Thomas, five Trustees and Administrator all give of their time voluntarily. The charity has played a significant role in supporting a number of the projects featured in this book.
<http://www.childstrust.org.uk>

KHW - INDIA
Based in Rajpur, just north of Dehradun in the state of Uttarakhand, **KHW - India** is committed to projects which work towards "a poverty free and just world where all children have equal opportunity and access to develop their full potential." It is the Indian affiliate of **Kinderhilfswerk Global Care**, Germany, which currently serves in fourteen developing countries worldwide. Jaywant P. Singh has been Director of the organisation since 1998.
<http://www.kinderhilfswerk.in>

GSVSS
Managed by Ramesh Khanduri, **Grahmin Samudaik Vikas Sewa Sansthan** is a collective NGO committed to disability issues in the Garhwali mountains, Uttarakhand. The name means "Rural Community Organisation for Service and Development".

SASA
Save and Share Association was established in the late 1990s by Shailender David to address educational and community development needs among young people and adults in Tehri Garhwal, Uttarakhand.

Nearly 120 children now attend SASA Academy based just outside the small village of Akori.

SKCV
SKCV is a registered charity situated in Vijayawada, Andhra Pradesh State, South India. Through a wide range of programmes it reaches out to homeless street children who have no other form of support. Presently running seven centres in the city, it offers shelter, accommodation, food, skills training, education, medical aid, recreation and counselling.

Indian website   <http://www.skcv.com>
UK website   <http://www.skcv.org>

Hebron Hostel
Hebron has no acronyms and is exactly what the name suggests: a hostel for almost 300 girls just outside the village of Nidadavole, Andhra Pradesh State, South India.

Jennie Prabhakar has been Superintendent of Hebron Hostel since 1994.

Notes

PAGE

1 IGNORANCE IS BLISS

20 Though Tony Hawks may have done it..: He also attempted to take a piano to the Pyrenees in a white van.

22 *There's not enough lines*...: "Timestretched", from *Regeneration*, by Neil Hannon, The Divine Comedy. Used with permission.

My chapter headings are song titles from The Divine Comedy albums that I loaded onto my mobile phone before leaving the UK.

2 LITTLE ACTS OF KINDNESS

46 I discovered that a *true* Indian veg...: Strict Indian vegetarians do not eat garlic or onions, while Jains do not eat any kind of root vegetable.

49 Tapered at the end...: Drumsticks can now be purchased in many Indian supermarkets and grocery stores in the UK.

59 'I think about four million people...': During 2004 to 2005, a total of 260,000 new leprosy cases were detected, 13.3% of which were children. These figures are according to a UNICEF sponsored study "Resources for Children in the Union Budget 2007-08", produced by The Centre for Child Rights, <http://www.haqcrc.org>

3 FESTIVE ROAD

68 An estimated 22,000 children...: SKCV Annual review 2006, <http://www.skcv.org/newpdfs/skcv-rev.pdf>

73 And why shouldn't there be...: India is a collection of 35 diverse states and union territories. Churchill once observed, in a speech delivered at the Albert Hall on March 18, 1931, that " India is a geographical term. It is no more a united nation than the Equator."

75 The audience erupted wildly...: The Bollywood movie, *Dil Chahta Hai*, was released in 2001. Literally translated as "The Heart Desires", but billed as "Do Your Thing", it won the National Film Award for Best Feature Film in Hindi.

82 'Over eleven million children...': Given their continual mobility from place to place, street children are incredibly difficult to monitor. The figure of eleven million children, based on UNICEF figures from 1994, is considered to be conservative: <http://www.streetchildren.org.uk>. I've not been able to find any figures that are more recent or accurate.

82 'Children contribute to more than...': see <http://www.skcv.com> for further statistics and information about street kids.

4 FREEDOM ROAD

99 'In India, movies are very popular...': In terms of the number of films produced annually, the Indian movie industry is the largest in the world. After Hindi, the predominant language of Bollywood, more movies are produced in Telugu than any other language. Ramoji Film City - "Tollywood" -, based just outside the state capital of Hyderabad, is the world's largest film studio complex. Opened in 1996, it covers 1,666 acres, has 47 sound stages and 500 locations. With permanent sets ranging from railway stations to temples, it has the capacity to produce up to 40 domestic and twenty international movies simultaneously.

105 Sanjeev sat down...: Caste is derived from the Portuguese word, *casta*, meaning "race" or "lineage". Perpetuated by the British, who formalised the system, the term "caste" unhelpfully describes an incredibly complex system of social stratification. Although caste remains in common use, there is no direct equivalent word in any of the Indian languages. The terms *varna*, "colour", and *jati*, "birth", are more accurate. How and why the system actually came into being has been controversially debated for centuries.

106 'Some are calling name Untouchables...': 250 million people, 24% of the population, fall into this category. <http://www.censusindia.gov.in/Census_Data_2001/India_at_Glance/scst.aspx> Traditionally, they are not allowed access to the religious rituals of the other varnas and are referred to by a number of names: Untouchables, Pariahs, Panchamas, Fifth Division, or Backward Class. Mahatma Gandhi gave them the name Harijan, "Children of God". Some, finding the term condescending, preferred Dalit, which means "crushed" or "oppressed", and Adivasis, literally "original inhabitants". The official terms are Scheduled Caste and Scheduled Tribe respectively.

106 'Yes, then there is final group...': There are approximately one million Hijras, the only non-hereditary sub-group, comprising transsexuals, asexuals, transvestites and eunuchs. They often appear uninvited at marriage ceremonies, refusing to leave until they have been given large sums of money.

5 HERE COMES THE FLOOD

121 Unlike in the UK...: Purchasing a train ticket has become very much easier over the last couple of years with the advent of Internet booking.

131 After talking to other villagers...: Subsequent archaeological investigations suggest that Navaj was correct. What he saw may have been the remains of a temple dating back to the 7th Century AD.

6 BAD AMBASSADOR

177 'True. You certainly love...: Although these lads did actually come and talk to me in the park, this small section of dialogue is inspired by the words of James Cameron in *An Indian Summer*, pp. 136-137, in which he

NOTES

recounts one of "the endless discussions in the Club" about the legacy of the British occupation.

7 LOGIC VS EMOTION

185 What was India's secret?..: This chapter is an assimilation of thoughts and opinions informed by numerous conversations and written sources. I owe much to the insights of Nater Singh, JP Singh, Krishan Khanna, John Ponnusamy, Mark and Julie Thomas, Budi Singh Dogra and John Martin Sahajananda. Between them, they helped me to grapple with many of the complex issues that I encountered on my journey. The characters of Krishna and Dilip, who appear later, are composites of several people, one of whom actually was a Brahmin priest called Krishna.

In order to maintain the narrative flow, I've occasionally used dialogue and internal thought, rather than direct quotation, to express those ideas that have been informed by written sources. I've been careful to attribute these accordingly.

185 Referring to the theories...: James Collins, *Built to Last*, pp. 43 - 45.

190 True to Collins'...: Father Bede Griffiths recounts a similar desire in the *The Marriage of East and West*, p. 8, on his he first visit to India.

> I had begun to find there was something lacking not only in the Western world but in the Western Church. We were living from one half of our soul, from the conscious, rational level and we needed to discover the other half, the unconscious, intuitive dimension. I wanted to experience in my life the marriage of these two dimensions of human existence, the rational and the intuitive, the conscious and unconscious, the masculine and feminine.

190 "The venerable city of Cochin...": *The Rough Guide to India*, p. 1183.

197 'I am helping you...': Radhakrishnan, *The Hindu View of Life*, pp. 20 – 21. Bede Griffiths provides a useful insight into an understanding of "neti" in *The Marriage of East and West*, p. 17 and Mark Tully discusses the concept in *India's Unending Journey*, pp. 16 and 45.

199 'The snake is neither...': This metaphor originates from the writings of Samkara, a Vedantist Brahmin, widely regarded as one of the most authoritative Hindu philosophers of all time. It is understood that he consolidated the teachings of the Upanishads to reform Hinduism in the eighth century AD, around the time that the popularity of Buddhism, then the dominant religion in India, was beginning to decline.

200 '"There are two Hinduisms..."': Sri Aurobindo, *India's Rebirth*, p. 82.

200 '"In practice this resolves..."': ibid. p 69.

201 'Haan. I am explaining...': About 3,000 years BC, an urban culture developed along the banks of the River Indus, known as the Indus River Civilisation. Although, according to the archaeological sites, they were a highly advanced and literate civilisation, no one has ever been able to

decipher their writing system. Little is known about their religious beliefs. The only information that scholars have gleaned is that they seem to have worshipped both male and female deities which may have influenced later Hindu beliefs.

In the middle of the second millennium BC the civilisation went into decline. The many possible reasons for its disappearance are widely contested. Some scholars claim that it was destroyed by floods. Others suggest that climate change caused the river valleys to dry out. There is another theory that the inhabitants were driven away by Aryan invaders from the west.

This, the Aryan Invasion theory, is a deeply controversial hypothesis first suggested by Friedrich Max Muller in the mid 19th century. It has been widely disputed in more recent times by those who do not accept that there was any migration from the west to India. They believe quite the reverse, in fact; the Aryans originated in India and then migrated to Central Asia and into Europe. Krishna subscribed to this latter theory. Regardless of their origin, the Aryans started to colonise the northern plains around 1,500 BC bringing with them Vedism, a polytheistic religion. This is the Vedic civilisation to which Krishna was referring. Many of their gods and goddesses represented natural forces that shared similarities with other mythologies; the sun, moon, fire, wind and rain. Because the Aryans were illiterate, their priests relied on memorising and orally recounting the Vedas.

Although the precise details are unclear, it seems that the Aryan and non-Aryan beliefs integrated over time and a common mythology emerged. Polytheism gradually gave way to Monotheism and, by about 800 BC, the doctrine of Brahman appeared in the texts of the Upanishads, also referred to as Vedanta.

202 'Actually, there are three main paths...': Bhakti, the school of devotion, possibly originates from the Dravidian races of South India which predate the Indus Valley Civilisation of the north by some considerable time. This movement emphasises the relationship between humans and a compassionate Supreme Person, usually the deities Shiva or Vishnu. Believing that the human soul and the deity are separate, yet connected, entities, devotees approach God through devotion at home, or in the temple, rather than pure knowledge. They are less bothered by the cerebral theological doctrine and more concerned with ritual acts of adoration from the heart.

205 'Of course not...': In *India's Unending Journey*, p. 259, Mark Tully quotes from Julius Lipner's book, *Hindus*:

> The pursuit of artha and kama were set in an ethical context very early on. They were never recommended as goals to be sought for their own sake irrespective of an ethical code of practice.

206 'He should be accepting...': The *Bhagavad Gita* presents a classic dharma dilemma. Although the action is located on a battlefield, its central

NOTES

theme focuses on the internal war with which Arjuna, the main character, struggles. Facing an opposing army that includes some members of his family, as a warrior, he knows that it is his duty to fight. But, in his heart, he cannot bring himself to kill them. The pivotal dialogue of the story is his discussion with Lord Krishna, disguised as his charioteer, about what he should do. Krishna advises him to perform his duty and leave the consequences to God.

212 Recalling the events...: I wish to credit Pavan Varma, in *Being Indian*, pp. 79 and 80, for his insights in helping me to analyse the possible motivation of the women I encountered in Mamallapuram.

214 Although dharma embodies...: ibid., p. 130.

214 *India's Rebirth*...: Sri Aurobindo, *India's Rebirth*, p. 15.

214 Maybe those that describe...: Varma writes about the tolerance of mediocrity in *Being Indian*, pp. 134-135.

214 Sri Aurobindo depicts...: Sri Aurobindo, *India's Rebirth*, p. 183.

215 Generalisation, though, is..: Varma, *Being Indian*, pp. 82 and 91.

217 'Three per cent of the population...': Patwant Singh, *The Sikhs*, p. 11.

217 'India became a democracy...: I discussed the impact of democracy post-Independence with several people. These views were corroborated by Varma, who writes about the "opportunities for upward mobility" in *Being Indian*, p. 54 and 117.

224 'Correct behaviour...: ibid., p. 76.

8 OUR MUTUAL FRIENDS

229 Before you are...: <http://www.wr.indianrail.gov.in/india_by_rail.htm>

229 I was waiting patiently...: Dehra means "camp". *Dun*, or *Doon*, refers to the river valley in which the city is located Although, traditionally, the name comprises two words, Dehra Dun, nowadays it is more commonly spelt Dehradun.

230 As we chatted...: At a height of 2,000 metres, Mussoorie is the closest hill station to Delhi. Like Kodaikanal in the South, it attracts those folk wishing, and able, to retreat from the summer heat of the plains. Known as "The Queen of the Hills", its history dates back to 1823 when Captain Young, a British military officer, spotted its potential as a holiday resort. During the summer months nowadays, Mussoorie also proves a popular base for trekkers and foreign students wishing to learn Hindi. Numerous language schools scatter the hillside.

The hillstation's main thoroughfare is the Mall, a pedestrianised walkway that accommodates numerous Kashmiri souvenir shops selling silk and goat's wool pashminas, wood carvings and walking sticks. Behind the bustling centre, a stroll along Camel's Back Road offers, on a clear day, an arresting panorama of the snow-capped Himalayan peaks.

The night-time view across the villages of the Doon Valley is particularly special, the largest mass of light radiating from the state's interim capital, Dehradun, six hours and 250 kilometres north of Delhi.

431

Rising from the Dust

232 Weaving their way...: *Mai* means "mother".
232 Rolling down the valley...: The sal tree is a slow-growing hardwood, often attaining heights of over 30 metres. Very common in the Himalayan foothills, its resin is often burned at Hindu ceremonies. Sal seeds and fruit are used to make lamp oil.
234 Between 1947 and 2000...: Uttar means "north", while Khand is best translated as "territory".
235 'But in so doing...': The Bharatiya Janata Party (BJP: "Indian People's Party") is one of the largest political parties in India. It is dedicated to a redefinition of Indian nationhood guided by the philosophies of Integral Humanism and Hindutva, "Hindu-ness".
236 It has little impact...: Ironically, in October 2006, with the power having shifted from the BJP to the Congress Party, the Uttaranchal Assembly passed a bill approving the change of the state's name from Uttaranchal to Uttarakhand. BJP members staged a walkout in protest. The Parliamentary Minister, Indira Hridayesh, claimed that a long standing demand from the indigenous population influenced the decision. She said that the name Uttarakhand was synonymous with statehood agitation; the change represented a true tribute to the activists who laid down their lives for the cause. Rediff News, 13 October 2006, <http://www.rediff.com/news/2006/oct/13uttar.htm>

In December, the Indian Parliament passed the Uttaranchal (Alteration of Name) Bill, 2006. From 1 January 2007 the state officially became known as Uttarakhand. I refer to the state as Uttarakhand from this point forward.

9 THE BOOKLOVERS

238 40% of...: These figures are cited in the 2004 KHW Annual Report. The source is CRY (Child Relief and You), extracted from the 7th All India Education Survey, 2002, conducted by the National Council of Educational Research and Training under the Ministry of Human Resource Development, Government of India. <http://www.cry.org> Refer to the Chapter 20 for an update and different perspective on these statistics.
243 Gathered over several years...: These quotation have been used with permission of The Panos Institute, an organisation that promotes the participation of poor and marginalised people in national and international development debates through media and communication projects: <http://www.panos.org.uk> The website for the Mountain Voices programme is <http://www.mountainvoices.org>.

Information about the Himalaya Trust can be found at <http://uttarakhand.prayaga.org/HT/ht-network.html>
252 The 2001 Census. Claims that 54%..: Census of India, Office of the Registrar General and Census Commissioner, India, <http://www.censusindia.gov.in>

NOTES

252 By contrast...: "Human Development Report", The Human Development Index: India, <http://hdrstats.undp.org/countries/country_fact_sheets/cty_fs_IND.html>

252 A research paper...: Kothari, Pandey and Chudgar "Reading out of the 'Idiot Box': Same-Language Subtitling on Television in India", p. 25.

252 On a subsequent visit...: Chaudhuri, Malay and Arindam Chaudhuri, *The Great Indian Dream*, pp. 49 and 50.

252 According to the first post-Independence...: Kingdom, "The Progress of School Education in India", p. 5.

253 Article 45...: <http://indiacode.nic.in/coiweb/welcome.html> This information is downloaded from the website of Ministry of Law and Justice (Legislative Department).

253 Thirty-six years later...: National Policy on Education, 1986, <http://education.nic.in/cd50years/r/2R/I3/2RI30101.htm>

253 In November 2000...: Sarva Shiksha Abhiyan (SSA) Mission Statement, <http://ssa.nic.in/ssamissionstat.asp>

253 Two years into the millennium...: see note for page 238 above

253 The organisation iWatch...: iWatch, *Transforming India* - "The India You May Not Know".

254 Translating policy into practice...: Kingdom, "The Progress of School Education in India", p. 2. Kingdom writes about the weak base of India's "education pyramid" and, on p. 6, suggests that the goals of the Constitution have proved "elusive" over the last 55 years.

254 nearly 50 million degree graduates...: According to the "India Science Report", p. 7, the number of degree graduates in India has increased from 20.5 million in 1991 to 48.7 million in 2004.

254 Over the last fifty years...: In *Being Indian*, Varma states that the budget allocation for technical education, as a proportion of the nation's total education budget, rose from 14% (1956-61) to 25% (1966-69). It was consistently higher than that allocated to secondary education, p. 115. However, although the original 1950 target of "free and compulsory education for all children until they complete the age of fourteen years" has yet to be realised, there have been encouraging moves in the last three years. Please refer to pp. 413-415.

255 The MHRD...: iWatch, Transforming India - "Education 1st".

10 DON'T LOOK DOWN

259 In its earliest days...: Kedar means "Mountain Lord" and Nath, "Protector" or "Refuge". Hindu scriptures refer to a number of tribes that inhabited the region, among them the Sakas, Nagas and Khasas. The Sakas were possibly the earliest ruling race of the Kumaon hills, establishing hill colonies between the second and first centuries BC.

263 The dawn of Independence...: Although British Garhwal became part of the Indian Union in 1947, it was not until two years later that Tehri Garhwal joined independent India as a district of Uttar Pradesh.

265 India is one of...: IRN (International Rivers Network) Fact Sheet, October 2002, "Tehri Dam", <http://www.irn.org/programs/india>
267 The Himalayas are one...: Himalaya originates from Sanskrit and means "abode of snow and ice": *hima*, "snow", *alaya*, "abode".
268 With diminishing vegetation...: A catastrophe of this scale is not unprecedented. Jim Corbett, the famous conservationist and hunter of man-eating tigers and leopards, recounts that Srinagar, the ancient capital of Garhwal, was swept away by the bursting of the Gohna Lake dam in 1894. *Omnibus* p. 430.

11 NOTE TO SELF

276 SASA, Save and Share Association...: As well as building the school, SASA, alongside other partners such as Seva Bharat, undertook a large scale literacy programme to train 450 illiterate women in the area to read and write. Incorporated into this work were a number of other self-help projects focusing on social awareness, health and financial management, all of which generated several opportunities for the villagers.
277 Although the people...: Pahari often refers to hill people living all along the North Indian Himalayan ridge. Throughout this section of the book, however, I use the name specifically to refer to people living in the interior villages of Tehri Garhwal and Rudraprayag. Similarly, the term Garhwali refers to people who live in both the mountains and plains of Garhwal. In this context, a person living in the hills is both a Garhwali and a Pahari.
280 Throughout India...: iWatch, *Transforming India* - "Making India a Knowledge Economy".
281 Teacher absenteeism...: Michael Kremer, "Teacher Absence in India: A Shapshot", p. 666.
285 Lord Macaulay's argument...: Lord Macaulay's Minute on Education, 2nd February 1835. Macaulay was Secretary to the Board on Control from 1832 to 1833 and first went to India in 1834.
286 Hindi, the official language...: *Manorama Yearbook 2007*, p. 511
287 As I discovered...: Two interesting discussions on language can be found in *Being Indian*, Varma, pp. 121 - 127 and *India Unbound*, Das, pp. 368 - 372.

12 GOING DOWNHILL FAST

293 Gender discrimination...: CRY, <http://www.cry.org>
293 Of the twelve million girls...: ibid.
293 Analysis of the 20001...: "The Rise of Sex Selection in India" by Dr Meeta Singh and Vasu Mohan. The authors are members of IFES' (International Foundation for Electoral Systems) team in India that is implementing a Dignity of the Girl-Child programme that addresses female foeticide and adverse sex ratio, <http://www.ifes.org/india>

NOTES

293 The most recently available..: These figures are cited in the report, "Disappearing Daughters", produced by Action Aid and the IRDC in June 2008. <http://www.actionaid.org.uk>. With reference to the note above, the report updates the figure relating to the number of "missing" women to 35 million.

294 As scientific procedures...: see above, "The Rise of Sex Selection in India".

295 The chai ritual...: Definitions of the Poverty Line vary enormously, depending on the purpose of the statistics. The simplest I have encountered defines it as the threshold between being able to afford two meals a day or not.

Assessing poverty worldwide, the World Bank uses the same reference point as a common unit across all nations, defining extreme poverty as living on less than $1 a day and moderate poverty as less than $2 a day. Using this definition, based on 2004 figures, iWatch estimates that 450 million people in India are below the extreme poverty line and 700 million are below the moderate poverty line.

Since the seventies, the Indian government has based its definition of the poverty line on a calorific value: "a norm of 2,400 calories per capita per day for rural areas and 2100 per capita per day for urban areas", source: Government of India Ministry of Statistics and Programme Implementation, <http://www.mospi.nic.in>

The most recent iWatch report, <http://www.wakeupcall.org> suggests that the cost of food to sustain these nutritional levels is eleven rupees (rural) and fourteen rupees (urban) per day, an average of 380 rupees per person a month. Using the government's definition, only 260 million people are below the official poverty line. This low threshold, based on the assumption that a person's entire income is spent on food, does not take into account other essentials such as shelter, clean water, sanitation, healthcare, clothing and transport.

The Centre for Policy Alternatives in New Delhi produced a report in February 2006 proposing a redefinition of the poverty line that should include all basic needs at 840 rupees per month. At this level, almost 70% of Indians live in poverty.

295 I didn't relish such decisions...: Health warning! Always take the guide books' advice on food and drink. Don't do as I did.

298 Today, though the hills...: According to the Himalaya Trust, over 140 types of food are produced in the mountains including 24 forest fruits and 32 types of vegetables. The Himalaya Trust is an environmental organisation working in the western Himalayan region, <www.uttarakhand.prayaga.org/HT>

300 At the time...: see pp. 390-391 for an explanation of how the seemingly conflicting scenarios of a widening male-to-female margin and an increase in female foeticide and infanticide may be reconciled.

305 The parents also...: There are various Hindi translations of *kanya*: "daughter", "female", "girl" or "virgin". *Daan* means "gift" or "given away".

306 The practice was legally...: The way a woman is treated in the home is often relative to the value of her dowry. When it is considered insufficient or demands of the groom's family are not met, she is often abused and her life made unbearable. In extreme, but all too common, cases she may meet with a "cooking" mishap, her death reported as a kitchen accident or suicide. The reality is that her husband or, frequently, her mother-in-law, has doused her in kerosene and tossed in a match to set fire to her clothes. Official records of such incidents are low but the number of dowry murders is rising. Reports of alleged dowry deaths continually appear in the media and a number of groups are campaigning for the issues to be faced head on. UNICEF estimates that around 5,000 Indian women are killed in dowry-related incidents each year. <http://www.unicef.org/newsline/00pr17.htm>

13 THE WRECK OF THE BEAUTIFUL

310 'Actually, nowadays it is worse...': I found it fascinating that, in view of other conversations earlier in my trip, Bhawani Bhai talked directly about *caste* rather than the system of *jati* and *varna*. This serves as a good example of the bewildering differences in thinking, terminology and expression that I encountered throughout my travels.

312 There is no doubt...: Sri Aurobindo, *India's Rebirth*, p. 28.

314 'The women's development and empowerment...': It is interesting to note that there are "more elected women representatives in India than in the rest of the world put together. It is a degree of political and social empowerment of a much discriminated-against gender that it is quite remarkable for a country that is as hidebound in its traditions as India is." Speech of Honourable Minister Mani Shnkar Aiyer, at the Champions of Democracy and Participaiton Workshop in Lewes, UK, June 2007. <http://www.pria.org/manishankar.php>

328 We have harvest...: <http://www.mountainvoices.org>

330 Devotion to one particular...: Confusingly, I occasionally heard isht devta and kul devta used interchangeably; sometimes a family god was adopted as the village god and vice versa.

15 THE CERTAINTY OF CHANCE

347 About 70 million people...: *Disability and the Law*, preface, p. vi

348 We intended to visit...: The term "differently-abled" was coined in the early 1980s by the US Democratic National Committee as an attempt to view people with disabilities in a more positive light. Political correctness undoubtedly had an influence. Many projects in North India appear to favour the term over any other.

350 Released in August 2002...: This report is based on data gathered from the 2001 Census of India. <http://www.censusindia.gov.in>

Notes

350 *Disability and the Law...*: Shruti Pandey, Priyanka Chirimar, Deepika D'Souza, *Disability and the Law*, Human Rights Law Network, India, 2005, preface page vi.
351 On 10 September...: OneWorld South Asia, 10 September 2004, reporter Payal Singhal <http://southasia.oneworld.net>
352 The situation is amplified...: "Ek Prayas 2005", KHW Annual Report p. 21.
352 This figure increases...: I have made these calculations based on the 2001 Census of India results. Figures for the districts of Tehri Garhwal and Rudraprayag may be found at <http://www.indianngos.com>
354 At the same time...: GSVSS is an acronym for *Grahmin Samudaik Vikas Sewa Sansthan*, translated as "Rural Community Organisation for Service and Development".
358 'Attempting to deliver...': Samvedna has developed five key objectives:
   i   to encourage the process of quantification of the disability situation in selected districts of Uttarakhand;
   ii to facilitate the identification, evaluation, treatment and rehabilitation of young children whose disability can be cured or arrested by appropriate interventions;
   iii to encourage educated individuals with disability through appropriate training and employment;
   iv to network with other organisations and individuals working in the area of disability;
   v   to advocate on behalf of the differently-abled.
360 *A butterfly* flies...: "The Certainty of Chance" from *Fin de Siecle*, by Neil Hannon, The Divine Comedy. Used with permission.
361 Although immunisation...: In 2006 a new polio outbreak caused concern with a total of 676 reported cases, 90% of which were in Uttar Pradesh. This represented a tenfold jump from the 66 cases registered with the health ministry in 2005, one third of the world's total.
According to The Hindu, 3 August 2007, the disease is once again in decline, with 124 reported cases in the first seven months of the year (three in Uttarakhand). Of those, about 39 belong to the most virulent P1 strain which spreads fast and paralyses one out of every 200 children infected. The Type 3 strain is weaker and easier to control.
<http://www.hindu.com/thehindu/holnus/001200708031560.htm>

16 Love What You Do

366 'This is my story...': Sujan told me his story over several days, painstakingly translated by JP Singh and Anubha Williams (KHW's Communications Manager).
373 Marriage between a brother...: Although Sujan may not have been aware, *tekwa*, the marriage between a younger brother and the widow of his elder brother and his younger brother is a known practice within

the region. Bisht, *Guide to Garhwal and Kumaon Hills* p. 9; Thapliyal, *Uttaranchal, Historical and Cultural Perspectives*, p. 136.

18 THERE IS A LIGHT THAT NEVER GOES OUT
389 Earlier in the day...: <http://www.mountainvoices.org/india.asp>

20 REGENERATION
408 The rains, two months...: CIA Factbook: India, <https://www.cia.gov>
'The government should focus...': As a result of pressure from all stakeholders, the Government's has increased the budget for education in the present five year 11th Plan (2007 to 2012) by an uplift of 500% on the last Plan (2002 to 2007). Fifty thousand new public-private-partnership vocational institutions are planned for the next four years. India currently has 6,000 similar institutions.
416 India has a large gap...: Dr. A. P. J. Abdul Kalam, "Employment and Education", 2 August 2007, <http://www.abdulkalam.com>. The figure of ten million comprises seven million students leaving education in Years 10 and 12 and three million graduates and post-graduates .
417 "The [Indian] patriot...": Sri Aurobindo, *India's Rebirth*, p. 85.
418 I'm in no doubt...: ibid.
418 India's "2020...: "India Vision 2020", Summary and Overview, p. 1.
418 While Sri Aurobindo...: To address the balance, I subsequently learnt from Krishan Khanna that, during the time of Lord Macaulay, a number of significant changes were made to the education system, including the closing of nearly 250,000 *Gurukuls*. A Gurukul is a place where a Guru, or Master, trains and educates students in subjects that include culture, history, mathematics, sports and traditional skills. The imported British education system, dropping Indian history, culture and tradition from the curriculum, focused on training civil servants to run the Empire.
419 On 25 January 2007...: Kalam, DR. A. P. J. Abdul, "What Can I Give My Nation", Republic Day Address 2007.
420 At the beginning...: <http://news.bbc.co.uk/go/pr/fr/-/2/hi/business/6058746.stm>
420 Ten per cent...: <http://www.newsvote.bbc.co.uk> 8 August 2007
421 At the turn...: Sri Aurobindo, *India's Rebirth*, p. 30.
421 A century later...: Dr A. P. J Abdul Kalam, "Challenges of the 21st Century", Anna University, Chennai, July 2007, <http://www.abdulkalam.com>
422 The poet...: Gurudev Rabindranath Tagore, "Gitanjali" verse XXXV.
422 India's "2020...: "India Vision 2020", Conclusion, p. 97; ibid., Summary and Overview, p. 14.
424 A typical son...: Jim Corbett: Epilogue to *The Man-eating Leopard of Rudraprayag*, p. 604.

Glossary

aarti	ceremonial circling of a lamp in front of a god during *puja*
accha	good; a-ha; whatever; all right; really?
Adivasi	official term for tribal people, literally "the ones who were already here"
aloo	potato
Angrez	foreigner, usually English
artha	the acquisition of wealth, one of the four *purusharthas*
ashram	centre for spiritual learning and practice
atman	soul
aum / om	symbol denoting the origin of all things and the ultimate divine essence, used in meditation by Hindus and Buddhists
auto rickshaw	three-wheeled taxi transport found throughout India. Also called an auto, rickshaw, tuk-tuk or three-wheeler
avtaar	incarnation
ayurveda	traditional form of herbal medicine. *Ayus* mean life and *veda* means knowledge. *Ayurveda* literally is "the knowledge of life"
babu	bureaucrat or clerk, literally meaning "educated gentleman"; petty bureaucrat
baki	shaman, someone who divines a problem and suggests its solution
betel	leaf popularly chewed by men and spat out in the street
bhai	brother
Bharat	India in Hindi and Sanskrit
bhavan	building
Bhotiya	Tibeto-Burmese speaking people of the higher Himalayas
Bhot	Tibet
bigha	area of land varying in size in different regions but measuring approximately 90 x 90 feet in Garhwal: 8,100 square feet
bindi	form of *tilak*, it is a dot on the forehead, frequently on married women
block	next administration level above a village
Brahman	the Ultimate Reality, the supreme essence of the Universe
Brahmin	highest-ranking of the four *varnas*: priests and academics
brinjal	eggplant / aubergine
burans	rhododendron
catai	sleeping mat
chaan	cowshed and seasonal thatched shelter

chai	tea
chal	from the Hindi verb "walk", it is similar to OK as in "Chal, I must get going." A *chal* is also a slum
channa	chickpeas
chapati	unleavened wholewheat bread
chappals	slippers, sandals or flipflops
Char Dham	*char* meaning four and *dham*, bode or seat, the phrase specifically refers to the four pilgrimage centres of Yamunotri, Gangotri, Kedarnath and Badrinath in the Himalayas
charpoy	wooden-framed bed strung with thin rope
Chipko	literally meaning "to stick together" or "to embrace", Chipko refers to the spontaneous village-level movement to protect forests that became nationally influential
chowk	stone-slabbed courtyard, a crossroads and a bazaar
crore	ten million, or one hundred *lakh*
croton	multi-coloured, evergreen shrub
dal	generic term for lentils
Dalit	"the oppressed", formerly known as Untouchables
darshan	to be in the presence of a deity
deodar	Himalayan cedar
devi	goddess
devta	god / deity
dhanyavad	"thank you" in Hindi
Dharamsala	rest house for pilgrims
dharma	obedience to the cosmic law; one of the four *purusharthas*
dhobi	washerman
dholi	sedan chair carried by four men
dhoti	literally meaning "unstitched cloth", it is a white cotton cloth worn by men, tied around the waist. Men in South India often hitch it up through their legs
dosa	South Indian thin pancake made from a batter of ground rice and lentils
dowry	payment in cash or kind by the bride's family to the groom's family
drumsticks	called *Munagakaya* in Andhra Pradesh
expire	euphemism for "death"
gangajal	water from the Ganges
ghats	steps leading to a bathing place or river; also mountains
ghee	clarified butter
gobi	cauliflower
Gurkhas	ethnic group from Nepal
haan	"yes" in Hindi
Harijan	term coined by Gandhi for the Untouchables, literally translated as "child of God"

GLOSSARY

Hijras	social group of about one million people comprising transsexuals, asexuals, transvestites and eunuchs
idli	South Indian rice cake made from a batter of ground rice and lentils often eaten with *sambar* and chutneys
isht devta	village deity
jati	community or clan whose members are of the same *varna*
jeera	cumin
-ji	suffix denoting respect
jungle	forest
kama	pursuit of desire, one of the four *purursharthas*.
Kanyadaan	the parents' gift of their daughter to the groom's family.
karma	literally meaning "something that is done". Often translated as "action", it is the driving force behind rebirth
kheer	condensed milk and rice pudding
khichari	dish of boiled rice and lentils
kholi	room
kolam	see *muggulu*
Kshatriya	second-ranking of the four *varnas*: rulers and warriors
kul devta	family or household deity
kumkum	red powder symbolic of the sexual power of goddesses, often used to make a bindi on a married woman's forehead
kurta	loose-fitting collarless shirt
laddu	a popular sweet made from flour and other ingredients formed into balls and dipped in sugar syrup
lakh	one hundred thousand
lassi	buttermilk
lingam	phallic emblem representing Shiva
lok	people
lunghi	length of cloth wrapped around a man's waist which drops to the ankles and then is hitched up above the knees, not dissimilar to a dhoti but usually made from coloured fabric
machaa	"mate" or "dude" in Tamil, literally "brother-in-law"
mandir	temple
mantra	sacred formula or chant
masala bun	bread roll stuffed with lightly spiced potatoes and onions
masala dosa	thin rice and lentils pancake stuffed with lightly spiced potatoes and onions
masjid	mosque
moksha	liberation from the cycle of death and rebirth, one of the four *purusharthas*
muggulu	Telugu name for *Kolam*, ornate pavement paintings made with rice flower
munagakaya	green vegetable that looks like a drumstick and tastes rather like asparagus
naan	flat bread cooked in a *tandoor*

nahi	"no" in Hindi
Namaskaram	Telugu greeting translated literally as "I bow to you"
Namaste	Hindi greeting, translated literally as "I bow to you"
nath	nose ring
naula	traditional water spring or well in Garhwal
obara	the lower storey of a Garhwali house in which the livestock live
paan	*betel* leaf and areca nut mixed with lime chewed as a digestive
Pahari	meaning "of the hills", it is a generic term referring to the people of the sub-Himalayan hills from western Kashmir to eastern Nepal
paisa	there are 100 *paisas* in one rupee
pakoda	fried savoury snack, also called a pakora
palanquin	covered litter for one person, consisting of a large box supported on two poles and carried by four bearers
panchayat	council
Pandavas	the five warrior Princes of the Mahabharata
pandit	priest or learned person, sometimes used to refer to a Brahmin
papad	thin, crispy wafer typically made from lentil, chickpea, blackgram or rice flour. More commonly called a poppadom in the west
paratha	wholewheat bread fried on a griddle, often stuffed with vegetables
pilau	rice cooked with vegetables or meat
pitr devta	a deceased family member worshipped as a god
pradhan	head of the *Panchayat* or Head of the village
pramukh	head of many villages
prasad	blessed food distributed after worship
prayag	confluence of two or more rivers
pucca /pukka	good, proper, permanent
puja	worship
pujari	Hindu priest who performs ritual worship
puri	type of fried bread
Purusharthas	the four fundamental goals in life
pyjama	pair of loose trousers tied by a drawstring around the waist, worn by both sexes in India. The origin is early 19th century from Urdu and Persian. *pay* "leg" + *jama* "clothing"
raj	literally "king's rule", it often refers to the British colonial period, 1857 to 1947. More generically, it means "state"
Rajputs	originally warriors, part of the *Kshatriya* group ranked second in the varna system
Rama	legendary Hindu figure, epitome of all that is good, whose story is told in the Ramayana

GLOSSARY

roti	unleavened bread
rupee	Indian unit of currency. At the time of publication there were about 80 rupees to the sterling £1.00
Sadhu	Hindu ascetic or holy man
sambar	South Indian sweet and sour dal soup made with mixed vegetables
samosa	fried triangular snack
sari	garment worn by women made of unstitched fabric wound around the waist and draped over one shoulder
Sarvodaya	literally meaning "compassion for everyone", it is a particularly powerful movement in the Garhwali hill areas
sati	illegal practice of widow-burning and self-sacrifice
seviya	sweet, toasted vermicelli milk pudding
Shiva	major Hindu god
Sri	Hindu title of respect
streedham	gift traditionally given by parents to their daughter at the time of her marriage that evolved into the dowry
Su Prabhat	Good morning!
Sudhra	lowest ranking of the four *varnas*: labourers, peasants and servants
tabla	pair of small hand drums used in Hindu music
tandoor	clay oven
tava	griddle
Telugu	the state language of Andhra Pradesh
Theek hai	literally translated as "fine is", it is the equivalent of the western "OK"
tiffin tin	three-tiered metal food container
tilak	sacred mark on a Hindu's forehead or other parts of the body. Married women often wear a tilak between the parting of their hair.
tuk-tuk	see auto rickshaw
udipi	South Indian canteen serving cheap meals and snacks
ukhal	stone vessel designed for pounding and dehusking rice
Upanishads	part of the Vedas. Focussing on the doctrine of *Brahman* and *Atman*, they form the core spiritual philosophy of Vedantic Hinduism. Upanishads means, literally, "to sit at the feet of the master".
urad	variety of pulse
Vaishya	third-ranking of the four *varnas*: farmers, landlords and merchants
varna	Sanskrit name for the four social hierarchies defined in the Rig Veda, more commonly referred to as castes
Vedas	the Hindu sacred texts. Veda means "knowledge"
yatra	pilgrimage, procession or journey
yatri	pilgrim

Further Reading

Books

Aitken, Bill, *The Nanda Devi Affair*, Penguin Books India, 1994

Alter, Robert C., *Water for Pabole: Stories about People and Development in the Himalayas*, Orient Longman, 2002

Alter, Stephen, *Sacred Waters: A Pilgrimage to the Many Sources of the Ganga*, Penguin Books India, 2001

Baker, Sophie, *Caste*, Jonathan Cape, 1990

Berreman, Gerald D., *Hindus of the Himalayas*, Oxford University Press, 1999

Bisht, Khila, ed., *Uttarakhand: Children in the Himalaya*, Shri Bhuvaneshwari Mahila Ashram, 2000

Bisht, Major D. S., *Guide to Garhwal and Kumaon Hills*, Trishul Publications, 2001

Bond, Ruskin, *The Best of Ruskin Bond*, Penguin Books India, 1994

Bose, Sugata and Ayesha Jalal, *Modern South Asia: History, Culture, Political Economy*, Routledge, 1998

Cameron, James, *An Indian Summer*, Penguin Books, 1987

Cameron, James, *Point of Departure*, Oriel Press Ltd, 1978

Chaudhuri, Malay and Arindam Chaudhuri, *The Great Indian Dream*, Macmillan India Ltd, 2003

Chaudhuri, Nirad C., *Hinduism: A Religion To Live By*, Chatto & Windus, 1979

Collingham Lizzie, *Curry*, Vintage, 2006

Corbett, Jim, *The Jim Corbett Omnibus: The Man-eaters of Kumaon; The Temple Tiger and More Man-eaters of Kumaon; The Man-eating Leopard of Rudraprayag*, Oxford University Press, 2006

Dalrymple, William, *City of Djinns*, Harper Perennial, 2005

Dalrymple, William, *The Age of Kali*, Flamingo, 1999

Das, Gurcharan, *India Unbound: From Independence to the Global Information Age*, Penguin Books India, 2007

Deliege, Robert, *The Untouchables of India*, Berg, 1999

Dubois, Abbe J. A., *Hindu Manners, Customs and Ceremonies*, Rupa & Co, 2002

Easwaran, Eknath, tr., *The Bhagavad Gita*, Penguin, 1996

Eden, Emily, *Up the Country: Letters from India*, Virago Press Ltd, 1984

Ellinger, Herbert, *The Basics 4: Hinduism*, SCM Press Ltd, 1995

Flood, Gavin, *An Introduction to Hinduism*, Cambridge University Press, 1996

Forster, E. M., *A Passage to India*, Penguin Books Ltd, 1998

Gandhi, M. K., *An Autobiography or The Story of My Experiments with Truth*, Navajivan Publishing House, 2003

Griffiths, Bede, *The Marriage of East and West*, Fount Paperbacks, London, 1985

Grihault, Nicki, *Culture Smart: India*, Kuperard, 2004

Guha, Ramachandra, *The Unquiet Woods: Ecological Change and Peasant Resistance in the Himalaya*, Oxford India Paperbacks, 2001

FURTHER READING

Handa, O. C., *History of Uttaranchal*, Indus Publishing Company, 2002
Hiro, Dilip, *The Rough Guide Chronicle: India*, Penguin, 2002
India 2007, Publications Division, Ministry of Information & Broadcasting, Government of India
James C. Collins & Jerry I. Porras, *Built to Last: Successful Habits of Visionary Companies*, Random House, 2000
Jung, C. G., "The Dreamlike World of India" & "What India Can Teach Us" in *Collected Works of C. G. Jung, Volume 10: Civilisation in Transition*, translated by Gerhard Adler and R. F. C. Hull, Routledge & Kegan Paul Ltd, 1964
Kalam, A. P. J. Abdul, *Ignited Minds*, Penguin, 2003
Kandari, O. P. and O.P. Gusain, *Garhwal Himalaya: Nature, Culture & Society*, Transmedia 2001
Keay, John, *India: A History*, Harper Collins, 2000
Keay, John, *Into India*, John Murray, 1999
Khilnani Sunil, *The Idea of India*, Penguin 1997
Klostermaier, Klaus K., *Hinduism: A Short Introduction*, Oneworld Publications, 2000
Lipner, Julius, *Hindus: Their Religious Beliefs and Practices*, Routledge, 1994
Luce, Edward, *In Spite of the Gods*, Abacus, 2007
Manorama Yearbook 2007, Malayala Manorama Press
McDonald, Sarah, *Holy Cow*, Bantam Books, 2004
Mehta, Gita, *Karma Cola*, Peguin Books India, 1993
Mitra, Rathin, *Temples of Garhwal*, Garhwal Mandal Vikas Nigam Ltd, 1994
Moorhouse, Geoffrey, *India Britannica*, William Collins, 1983
Morris, Jan, *Destinations*, Oxford Paperbacks, 1982
Murphy, Dervla, *On a Shoestring to Coorg*, Century Hutchinson, 1985
Naipul, V. S., *India: A Million Mutinies Now*, Minerva, 1991
Naipul, V. S., *India: A Wounded Civilization*, Penguin, 1977
O'Brien, Derek, ed., *The Penguin India Reference Yearbook 2006*, Penguin 2006
Pandey, Shruti and Priyanka Chirimar, Deepika D'Souza, *Disability and the Law*, Human Rights Law Network, India, 2005
Radhakrishnan, *Eastern Religions and Western Thought*, Oxford University Press, 1940
Radhakrishnan, *The Hindu View of Life*, Unwin Books, London, 1963
Rough Guide to India, The, Rough Guides, November 2003
Sachs, Jeffrey, *The End of Poverty*, Penguin, 2005
Saili, Ganesh, ed., *Glorious Garhwal*, Roli Books 1995
Sarpal, Kewal, *Reflections on Hinduism*, Sarpal, 1999
Sen, Amartya, *The Argumentative Indian: Writings on Indian Culture, History and Identity*, Penguin, 2005
Sen, K. M., *Hinduism*, Penguin Books, 2005
Shattuck, Cybelle, *Hinduism*, Routledge, 1999
Singh, Patwant, *The Sikhs*, John Murray, London, 1999
Sri Aurobindo, *India's Rebirth*, Institut de Recherches Evolutives, Paris, 2003
Swami Krishnananda, *The Mandukya Upanishad*, The Divine Life Society, 1996

Tammita-Delgoda, SinhaRaja, *India: A Travellers History*, Cassell & Co, 2002
Thapar, Romila, ed., *India: Another Millennium?* Penguin Books India, 2000
Thapliyal, Uma Prasad, *Uttaranchal, Historical and Cultural Perspectives*, B. R. Publishing Corporation, Delhi, 2005
Tully, Mark, *India in Slow Motion*, Penguin, 2003
Tully, Mark, *India's Unending Journey*, Rider, 2007
Tully, Mark, *No Full Stops in India*, Penguin, 1992
Tully, Mark, *The Heart of India*, Penguin, 1996
Twain, Mark, *More Tramps Abroad*, Chatto and Windus, 1898
Varma, Pavan K., *Being Indian*, Penguin, 2005
Wolpert, Stanley, *A New History of India*, Oxford University Press, 2000
Woodham, Carl E., tr., *The Bhagavad Gita*, Pilgrims Publishing, 2003

Articles and Reports

Aide Memoire, SARVA SHIKSHA ABHIYAN (SSA), 6th Review Mission of Sarva Shiksha Abhiyan, Government of India, July 2007

HAQ: Centre for Child Rights, "Budget 2007-08 and Children, A First Glance" and "Budget 2008-09 and Children, A First Glance", HAQ, New Delhi

Huttenlocher, Agnes, "Report on Samvedna", 2006

"India Vision 2020", Planning Commission, Government of India, New Delhi, December 2002

International Rivers Network (IRN) Fact Sheet, October 2002, "Tehri Dam"

Kalam, DR. A. P. J. Abdul, "What Can I Give My Nation", Republic Day Address 2007, <www.abdulkalam.com>

Kelly, Annie, "Disappearing Daughters", Action Aid and the International Development Research Centre (IRDC), 2008, <http://www.actionaid.org.uk>

Khanna, Krishan, ed., *Transforming India*, iWatch, Mumbai, January 2007

KHW, "Annual Report", 2004, 2005 and 2006.

Kingdom, Geeta Gandhi, "The Progress of School Education in India", ESRC Global Poverty Research Group, <http://www.gprg.org> 2007

Kothari, Kothari, "Reading out of the 'Idiot Box': Same-Language Subtitling on Television in India", Information Technologies and International Development, The Massachusetts Institute of Technology, Vol. 2, No. 1, 2004, 23-44

Kremer, Michael, "Teacher Absence in India: A Shapshot", *Journal of the Economic European Association*, Vol 3, April-May 2005, 658-667

Mullins, Julie, "Gender Discrimination", <http://www.childreninneed.com/magazine/gender.html>

Pratham, "ASER 2006 – Annual Status of Education Report (Rural)" and "ASER 2007 – Annual Status of Education Report (Rural)", Pratham, New Delhi

Shukla, Rajesh, "India Science Report", NCAER, 2005, <http://www.ncaer.org>

Singh, Dr. Meeta and Vasu Mohan, "The Rise of Sex Selection in India", IFES, <http://www.ifes.org/india>

UNICEF, "The State of the World's Children, 2006", <http://www.unicef.org>

About the Author

Mark Helyar was born in 1966 in Kent. He has a degree in English and Music from Birmingham University and a postgraduate diploma in Theatre and Education from Central School of Speech and Drama.

He has worked extensively as a freelance director and musical director and composed the scores for nine shows.

In the early nineties Mark founded West 28th Street, company in residence at Fairfield, Croydon. He was subsequently appointed Artistic Director of Proteus, one of the south's leading touring companies, where he remained until the end of 2004. For reasons explained in this book, he then travelled to India for six months. He has returned on several occasions.